Perfect Places to Stay in Italy

 Lifestyle Guides

Italian Touring Club

President: *Giancarlo Lunati*

Editorial Department

General Executive Managing Director: *Armando Peres*

Director: *Marco Ausenda*

Editorial director: *Michele D'Innella*

Publishing and illustration coordinator, Indexing and special effects: *Alberto Dragone*
Responsible for workforce: *Ornella Pavone*
Cartography: *Servizio Cartografico del Touring Club Italiano*
Chief Editor: *Giovanna Rosselli*
Editor's secretary: *Agostina Pizzocri*
Technical coordinator: *Vittorio Sironi*
Establishments selected by: *Luigi & Teresa Cremona*
Text for regional introductions: *Luca Selmi*
Graphic design: *Ariberto srl, Milano*
Thanks to: *Cecilia Bombieri, Giovanna Lanciano, Elisa Smaniotto*

Cover image: *Villa Ducale, Taormina, Sicily*
Photo credits: *Valle d'Aosta, p. 25: L.A.Scatola/Realy Easy Star; T. Spagone/Realy Easy Star. Piemonte, p. 32: T. Spagone/Realy Easy Star. Lombardia, p. 49: R.Valterza/Realy Easy Star. Trentino-Alto Adige, p. 79: G. Rodante/Realy Easy Star. Veneto, p. 101: F. Soletti; F. Mairani. Friuli-Venezia Giulia, p. 128: M. La Tona/Realy Easy Star. Liguria, p. 136: F. Mairani. Emilia-Romagna, p. 150: S. Benini/Realy Easy Star. Toscana, p. 183: F. Mairani; Photo Press/Realy Easy Star. Marche, p. 224: Cresci/TCI. Umbria, p. 239: C. Concina/Realy Easy Star. Lazio, p. 264: F. Mairani; L. Pranovi/Realy Easy Star. Abruzzo, p. 282: V. Rossato/Realy Easy Star. Campania, p. 296: F. Mairani. Molise, p. 290: T. Spagone/Realy Easy Star; F. Mairani. Puglia, p. 309: T. Spagone/ Realy Easy Star. Basilicata, p. 321: F. Mairani; T. Spagone/Realy Easy Star. Calabria, p. 330: F. Mairani. Sicilia, p. 340: P. Ongaro/Laura Ronchi. Sardegna, p. 357: T. Spagone/Realy Easy Star; G. Iacono/Realy Easy Star.*

Thanks to the proprietors of the hotels, agrituristical companies, apartments, and bed & breakfasts for their help in supplying information and photographic material for inclusion and reproduction in this guide.

Great care and attention has been taken in compiling this guide and in checking the accuracy of the information contained within it. The publishers cannot however assume responsibility for any changes that may occur to opening times, telephone numbers, addresses, conditions of access or other amendments, or to any inconvenience or problems experienced as a consequence of the use of this guide and the information provided within it.

Head of Advertising: *Luca Roccatagliata*

Advertising Agency: *Progetto*
Milano, piazza Fidia 1, tel. 02 69007848, fax 02 69009334
Trento, via Grazioli 67, tel. 0461 231056, fax 0461 231984

Typesetting: *Emmegi Multimedia, Milano*
Printed and bound by: *Grafiche Mazzucchelli,SpA Milan*

Touring Club Italiano - corso Italia 10, 20122 Milano
www.touringclub.it

© 2000 Touring Editore, Milano
Codice DBY
ISBN 0749523271

Translated into English by G and W Advertising and Publishing, Chinnor; English language version published by AA Publishing which is a trading name of Automobile Association Developments Limited, whose registered office is Norfolk House, Priestly Road, Basingstoke, Hanmpshire RG24 9NY, Registered Number 1878835
English language version © AA Developments Ltd 2000

CONTENTS

*H*ow to use the guide

How to find a REGION

The Guide is divided into 20 regions, as follows

Valle d'Aosta, Piemonte, Lombardia, Trentino-Alto Adige, Veneto, Friuli-Venezia Giulia, Liguria, Emilia-Romagna, Toscana, Marche, Umbria, Lazio, Abruzzo, Molise, Campania, Puglia, Basilicata, Calabria, Sicilia,Sardegna.

The name of the region appears at the top right and left hand side of each page.

How to find a TOWN

If you are looking for a specific town location it may help to refer to the atlas (pages 9 to 24). Map references appear in the entries.

Town names can be found in the heading box of each entry. An alphabetical index of locations can be found on pages 378 to 383. All the townslisted have their region in brackets, and the page(s) of the guide on which the entries for that town may be found.

Towns are listed alphabetically within each region.

Agriturismo Il Covone, Perugia.

How to find an ESTABLISHMENT

Within each town, establishments are listed in alphabetical order. The town name appears in capital letters after the postal address in each entry.

Map References

The map reference for each establishment shows the atlas page number first, followed by the co-ordinates of the location on the map.

Fax, e-mail addresses and web sites

Fax numbers, e-mail and web site addresses are given where appropriate.

Villa San Michele, at Ravello, in Campania.

Tenuta Le Dune, at Arbus, in Sardinia.

Telephone

The telephone number of each establishment is given. The telephone area codes given are for use within Italy. The international dialling code for Italy is 39. To telephone Italy from abroad, dial the international network access code (00 from Europe, 001 from the US and Canada), followed by 39, then the number, excluding the initial zero.

Address and directions

The full postal address of the establishment is given, followed by brief directions.

Rooms

The number of rooms available is indicated in the heading box after the directions. Further details are given in the main description. Check when booking that the facilities you require are available.

Right, *Villa Revedin, in Gorgo al Monticano, Veneto.* Below, *Agriturismo Masseria Salamina, in Fasano, Puglia.*

Prices

The price band is shown in the heading box. The symbol (£) indicates the average price per night for a double room. The price may vary depending on the style of the room or the length of the stay, and the price band is intended only as an indication. Please check prices and what is included in that price when booking.

£ = less than 100.000 lire

££ = from 100.000 to 200.000 lire

£££ = over 200.000 lire

Credit Cards

The major credit cards accepted are shown.

Description

The description for each entry includes information about the type of establishment (farms, apartments, lodgings, B&Bs etc), architecture and history of the building, as well as the style and facilities, and whether breakfast is available. This information may be subject to change during the currency of the guide, so please check details when booking.

Recommended In the Area

A selection of restaurants, places to visit and regional specialites, chosen by the Italian Touring Club, and within a short distance of the establishment.

Guest Accommodation in Italy

The establishments in this Guide have been chosen and inspected by the Italian Touring Club (TCI).

Selected for their character and charm, these establishments all have that certain indefinable 'something', which makes them memorable - a combination of atmosphere, character, good taste, friendliness and an authentically warm welcome that can't be given a simple monetary value. It is a concept implying quality, comfort (though not

Villa Belfiore, at Ostellato, in Emilia-Romagna.

necessarily luxury), and which may vary from one region to another. The welcome may be particularly Tuscan, or typically Umbrian, and this is why the guide includes such different types of accommodation, from hotels to agriturismi (farm businesses with accommodation) bed and breakfasts, and holiday homes/apartments.

information about establishments in this guide, contact the establishment direct - if you write to them, remember to enclose an international reply coupon.

Italy is a diverse country, offering a wide range of landscapes and cities. Some regions have a long tradition of hospitality, and tourist accommodation is rich and varied. Other regions have beautiful art and scenery, or excellent food, but there are fewer establishments to choose from. Inevitably, this affects the choice available, but it is the concept of charm which is important, and you can be sure that all the establishments have been chosen with this in mind.

How the choice was made

As well as character and charm, the establishments selected are reasonably priced relative to their standard of service, warmth of welcome and overall quality. A few exceptions have been made in the larger cities and a few very special places (although out of season, or at weekends, these, too, may cost less than you might expect). If you require any further

Hotel Madonnina, at Cantello, in Lombardy.

Travelling in Italy

Documents

Always carry a current passport; keep a photocopy somewhere safe for extra security. If you will be driving you should carry your full valid national driving licence or International Driving Permit (IDP) as well as the vehicle registration document and certificate of motor insurance. Your vehicle should display the approved standard design International Distinguishing Sign (IDS), for example GB for UK residents. Cycle racks should not obscure your registration plate or IDS; ski tips should point to the rear.

Lights

Full-beam headlights can be used only outside cities and towns. Dipped headlights are compulsory when passing through tunnels, even if they are well-lit.

Roads

Italy has more than 4,000 miles of motorway (autostrada) with tolls payable on most sections. Emergency telephones are located every 2km on most motorways; there are two call buttons, one to call for technical assistance and one to alert the Red

Cross services. Main and secondary roads are generally good and mountain roads are usually well engineered.

Speed Limits

The speed limit in built-up areas is 50kph (31mph), outside built-up areas, 90kph (55mph), 110kph (68mph) on main roads and 130kph (80mph) on motorways. Motorcycles under 150cc are not allowed on motorways.

Warning Triangle

The use of a warning triangle is compulsory outside built-up areas in the event of accident or breakdown. The triangle must be placed 50 metres (55yds) behind the vehicle on ordinary roads and 100 metres (109yds) on motorways. Motorists who fail to do this are liable to an administrative fine.

Emergency Services Telephone Numbers

Police 113, Ambulance 113 or 118, Fire 115 Carabinieri (military police) 112

Tourist Information:

Italian State Tourist Office (ENIT)
UK 1 Princes Street, London W1R 8AY
Tel 020 7408 1254
USA 630 Fifth Avenue, Suite 1565, New York, NY 10111
Tel (212) 245 5618

Money

Establishments may not accept traveller's cheques or credit cards so ask about payment methods when you book. Make sure you have currency for your everyday needs, particularly in rural areas, as there may be little opportunity to exchange currency.

Medical treatment and health insurance

Before travelling to Italy make sure you are covered by insurance for emergency medical and dental treatment as a minimum. Check whether your homeowner or health insurance policy covers you for travel abroad. Many European countries have reciprocal agreements for medical treatment and will require EU citizens to obtain a validated E111 certificate of entitlement before travel.

Electrical appliances

These may require an adaptor for the plug, as well as an electrical voltage converter that will allow, for example, a normal 110-volt American appliance to take 220-240-volt British current. Two-in-one adaptor/convertors are available from some hardware stores.

Locanda dei Mai Intees, Azzate, in Lombardia.

*F*urther

information

AA Publishing also produce English language versions of the following TCI guides which may be useful:
Italy; Florence; Italian Riviera; Marche; Milan & Turin; Rome & The Vatican; Sicily; Umbria; and Venice.

AA Road Maps are also available: Italy; North and Central Italy; Southern Italy and Sardinia; Tuscany; and Umbria.
Visit the AA bookshop at www.TheAA.com

Hotel Margherita, at the Golfo Aranci, in Sardinia.

The following brief glossary of Italian words may also be of use

agriturismo	a farm business that offers accommodation to visitors
autopista (A)	motorway
bocce	type of Italian bowls played on beaten earth
centro	centre
circonvallazione	ring road/beltway
enoteca	a wine cellar where wines can be tasted and bought
est	east
località	zone (of a town/city)
ovest	west
piazza	(town) square
stazione	station
strada provinciale (S.P.)	local road
strada statale (S.S.)	trunk road
superstrada	dual carriageway/main highway
tangenziale	by-pass
trattoria	simple restaurant
uscita	exit
vaporetto	water bus (Venice)
via	street

Hints for Booking Your Stay

When travelling it is always a good idea to bear the following in mind:

1. Contact the establishment you intend to visit beforehand - mentioning this guide - to check prices and terms, and whether credit cards or cheques are accepted.

2. Give details of any requirements or particular travel arrangements (e.g. small children, pets, arrival on public transport etc.)

3. Pay any deposit required beforehand and ask for confirmation of the booking.

4. Arrive at an agreed time

5. On arrival, inform the management immediately of any problems , and ask for these to be rectified.

6. In the case of serious disputes, get in touch with the appropriate authorities (e.g. 'Comune' - town council, APT - transport organization, police, carabinieri (military police).

7. Remember that it is not reasonable to expect the same service from an 'agriturismo' as from a hotel, just as it is clear that a bed and breakfast will offer different services from a rented apartment. The regions have different standards for different types of establishment.

8. If you have to cancel a booking, you should do so as soon as possible. If a room cannot be re-let, you will lose any deposit you may have paid.

Villa De Pertis, at Dragoni, in Campania.

Atlas

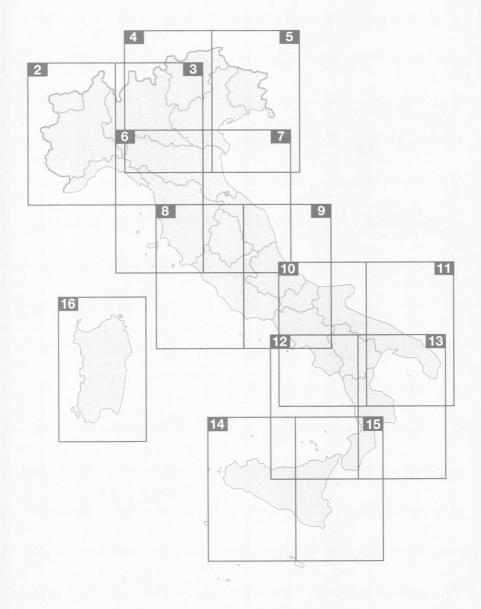

Scale 1 : 1 500 000 (1 cm = 15 km) 0 15 30km

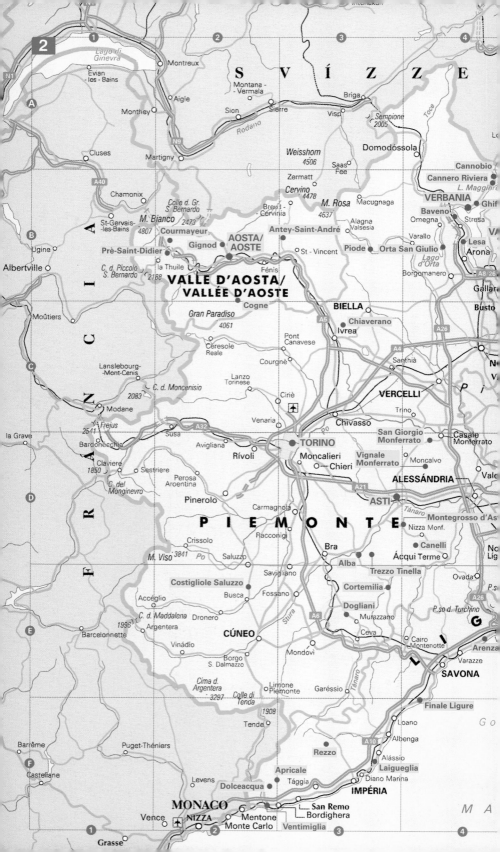

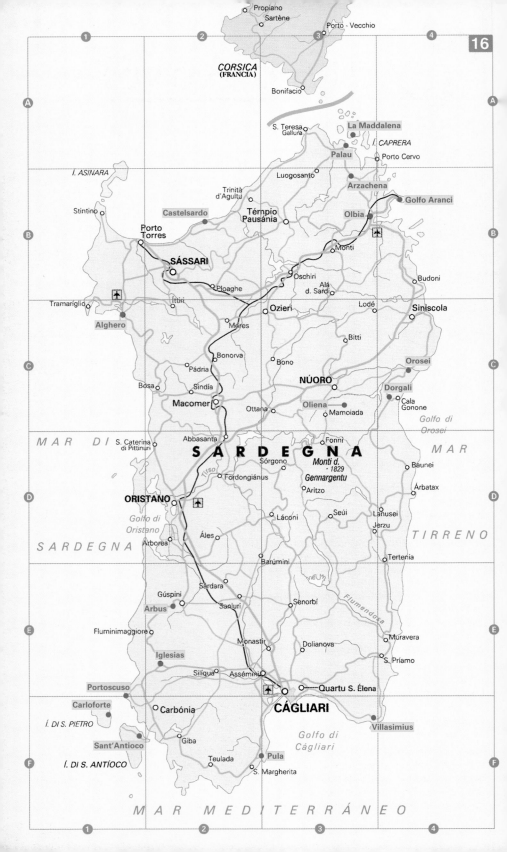

Valle d'Aosta

A paradise for tourists keen on mountains and natural beauty, the Valle d'Aosta is the smallest and the least populated Italian region. It is part of the arc of the Alps in the north-west of the country and consists of the valley of the Dora Baltea River and the valleys of its tributaries, enclosed within a spectacular circle of ridges and great mountains. It is still entered through ancient Alpine passes which are now part of a system integrated with the Monte Bianco (Mont Blanc) and Gran San Bernardo (Grand St Bernard) tunnels. The roads from these passes and tunnels converge into the road and motorway from Piedmont at a narrow point north of Pont-Saint-Martin.

The peaks include the Matterhorn and are the highest in Europe and amongst the most beautiful in the world. Mountaineering, skiing and tourism – in long-famous places like Courmayeur, Breuil-Cervinia and Cogne – have been enjoyed for centuries.

The vertical landscape reaches an impressive 4,000 metres. It starts from the fields and rural settlements of the plain and rises up slopes that are sometimes terraced to villages and castles, and to shady green

Above: the Magdeleine, 1664 metres high, in Valtournenche. Right: Castel Savoia at Gressoney-Saint-Jean

forests and Alpine meadows. The land continues upwards to rocks and waterfalls that freeze in winter, and finally reaches peaks of sparkling ice. The marks of history and of a remote but strong culture are evident in important Roman remains, medieval monuments (the most outstanding of these being the Sant' Orso complex at Aosta), and atmospheric late-Gothic castles. But there are also rustic stone and wood buildings, Alpine huts and chalets, which often give a cordial welcome to tourists.

The region offers traditional, warm and friendly hospitality: comfort and charm have their own authentic and original flavour – as do the local wines, cheeses and honey produced laboriously from the difficult terrain.

$\mathcal{D}$es Roses

$\mathcal{T}$his is a pretty little hotel built in the classic chalet style with a sloping tiled roof and constructed out of the traditional materials of wood and stone used in mountain villages.

It is situated not far from the road which leads to Cervinia (17 km away), in the middle of green fields.

The neat, simple rooms are furnished with pine and all have satellite television. Bathrooms are reasonable. The sitting room, with its fireplace and wooden ceiling, leads on to the hotel's private garden.

The bar and dining room are very pleasant and furnished in the typical Valle d'Aosta style. The hotel is run by the owners and they make their guests feel most welcome. The delightful garden and a pitch for *bocce* (a kind of bowls) add to the attraction.

A chalet-style inn, near Cervinia

☎ 0166 548527 📠 0166 548248
località Poutaz 5
11020 ANTEY ST. ANDRÉ (Aosta)
Ref map 2, B3
A5, Saint Vincent-Chatillon exit, follow the signs for Valtournenche-Cervinia
21 rooms; £
Credit card: 💳, bancomat

RECOMMENDED IN THE AREA

RESTAURANTS:
Pierre, *Verrès;* Brean, *Col di Joux di Saint Vincent*

LOCAL SPECIALITIES:
Items in wood, stone and lace

VISIT:
Cervinia and Plateau Rosà; Sant' Orso Fair (January 30 and 31)

$\mathcal{M}$iravalle

A guest-house atmosphere

☎ 0165 236130 📠 0165 35705
località Porossan 87, 11100 AOSTA
Ref map 2, B2
A5, Aosta Est/Ovest exit, towards Aosta Centro, then towards Porossan
24 rooms; £
Credit card: 💳

$\mathcal{I}$n a peaceful setting with panoramic views, the hotel has comfortably large rooms with stylish interior decoration.

The hotel is run efficiently and with attention to detail. The size of its rooms and the unusual mix of furnishings call to mind certain English guest houses. Grouped together harmoniously are all sorts of artefacts from different places and periods, giving the hotel a particular character.

Other attractions include a garden and solarium, a children's playroom and a garage.

RECOMMENDED IN THE AREA

RESTAURANTS:
Vecchia Aosta, *Piazza Porte Pretoriane 4;* La Bagatelle, *Corso Ivrea 69*

LOCAL SPECIALITY:
Wooden goblets (grolle), said to be named after the cup of the Holy Grail

VISIT:
Roman and medieval Aosta; the collegiate church of Sant'Orso; art exhibitions at the Tour Fromage, the Torre del Lebbroso and the Centro Saint-Benin

Milleluci

*F*rom its origins as an old family farmhouse made of wood and stone, the building has been completely renovated. Now it combines both the traditional rural style of the area and modern comfort.

The hotel retains the pleasing proportions of another era which managed to construct buildings that blended with their natural surroundings and were at the same time very practical. It stands out on a hill with a wonderful view of the collegiate church of Sant'Orso, and is very close to the historic centre of Aosta. This hotel might well be a good choice for people making a tour of the art and architecture of the area, or for those wanting simply to relax in rural surroundings. Some of the rooms are up on the attic floor with its sloping roof and exposed wooden beams, and all rooms are very romantic in style and furnished tastefully. Ten are reserved for non-smokers. Two suites have satellite television, mini-bar, modem sockets and safes. The bathrooms are good.

The communal rooms are furnished with many items which recall the antique past of this lovely building: cow bells, period furniture of the Valle d'Aosta, massive doors which give a special character to the interiors. A huge fireplace in the hall is especially warming.

A building from another era

☎ 0165 235278 📠 0165 235284
✉ hotel.milleluci@galactica.it
località Porossan-Roppoz 15
11100 AOSTA
Ref map 2, B2
A5, Aosta Est/Ovest exit, towards Aosta Centro, then head for Porossan
33 rooms; ££
Credit card: AE VISA SI , bancomat

RECOMMENDED IN THE AREA

RESTAURANT:
Vecchio Ristoro, *via Tourneuve 4*

LOCAL SPECIALITIES:
Fontina *cheese, fondue and* valpellinenze *soup; wooden goblets, wooden sculpture and hand carvings*

VISIT:
Gran Paradiso National Park; Mont Avic Nature Park; excursions and Alpine sports in the valleys on either side

Notre Maison

Recommended in the area

Restaurants:
Brasserie du bon bec *and*
Les Trempeurs

Visit:
Lace museum; Museo Mineraio;
Paradisia Botanical Gardens
at Valmontey

A chalet in the natural haven of the Gran Paradiso National Park

☎ 0165 74104
🖷 0165 749186
✉ notremaison@netvallee.it
località Cretaz 8
11012 COGNE (Aosta)
Ref map 2, B2

A5, Aosta Ovest exit, 1.5 km before centre of Cogne on the local road between Aosta and Cogne
23 rooms; ££
Credit card: 𝖵𝖨𝖲𝖠 SI ⓪, bancomat

*T*his is a mountain chalet built in stone and wood, with typical undulating tiled roofs and little attic windows. The hotel is situated in the middle of a well-tended garden at the edge of the wooded slopes of the park. The rooms and two suites are furnished in a style that blends with the natural surroundings: they have modern facilities and the pine furniture gives them a welcoming feel. In the hotel lounge the huge fireplace gives the room great character.

The communal rooms are furnished rustically but stylishly. The restaurant, open to non-residents, serves speciality dishes from the Cogne region. Guests can take advantage of a swimming pool, hydro-massage, sauna, Turkish bath and fitness centre. There is also a garage and ski storage facilities.

$\mathcal{L}$a Barme

An unparalleled setting to appreciate the natural beauty of the area

☎ 0165 749177 🖷 0165 749213
📧 labarme@netvallee.it
Valnontey
11012 COGNE (Aosta)
Ref map 2, B2

A5, Aosta Ovest exit towards Cogne, follow the signs for Valnontey

15 rooms; £

Credit card: AE VISA SI ⓄⒹ, bancomat

*I*n 1856 Vittorio Emanuele di Savoia preserved the last ibex in the Alps by creating a reserve which, in 1922, became the Gran Paradiso National Park.

An Alpine hut was recently renovated and rebuilt to make the present hotel which is located in the heart of the park in the village of Valnontey, a jewel in the Cogne valley. The hotel is a refuge for those who love the natural world and also a starting point for summer walks, cross-country and mountain skiing and for trips beyond the snow-line. It has comfortable rooms (all non-smoking) with satellite television. The restaurant serves fine cuisine including many typical dishes of the region.

Also available to guests are a ski-waxing room, sauna, children's playroom, garden, solarium and bicycles for hire.

RECOMMENDED IN THE AREA

RESTAURANT:
Lou Ressignon, *Valmontey*

LOCAL SPECIALITY:
Cogne lace

VISIT:
Gran Paradiso National Park

$\mathcal{D}$olonne

A new look at the cooking of the region

☎ 0165 846674
🖷 0165 846671
📧 hdolonne@courmayeur.valdigne.com
Strada della Vittoria
11013 COURMAYEUR (Aosta)
Ref map 2, B2

30 rooms; ££

Credit card: AE VISA SI ⓄⒹ

*R*ebuilt in 1995 within a 16th-century fortified house, the hotel has small but welcoming rooms. Situated where the ski slopes finish, the hotel is surrounded by green fields and is in a peaceful position about a kilometre from the church square of Courmayeur. The rooms are comfortable with period furniture and nearly all the simple but adequate bathrooms have showers. In the communal rooms there are open fires and the atmosphere encourages guests to linger, socialise or read in quiet corners. The restaurant interprets traditional regional cooking with style. The owners of the hotel run it in way that is both courteous and thoughtful.

RECOMMENDED IN THE AREA

RESTAURANT:
La maison de Filippo, *Entrèves*

La Clusaz

Once upon a time it was a pilgrim's hospice, then a local inn, now it's a charming hotel

☎ 0165 56075
📠 0165 54426
località La Clusaz 1
11010 GIGNOD (Aosta)
Ref map 2, B2
A5, Aosta Est exit, S.S. 87, towards Gran San Bernardo (St. Bernard's Pass)
14 rooms; **££**
Credit card: AE VISA SI ⓪, bancomat

RECOMMENDED IN THE AREA

RESTAURANT:
Suisse, *Saint-Rhémy-en-Bosse*

LOCAL SPECIALITIES:
Local woodland fruits can be bought direct from producers at Etroubles

VISIT:
Archaeological Park of L'Arco Augusto, 12 km away at Aosta; many local castles

*T*his delightful small hotel is in a lovely position in the valley going up towards the Gran San Bernardo pass and not far from Aosta. With its few rooms it gives a warm welcome to guests.

The particular charm of the hotel derives from the fact that it dates back to the beginning of the 20th century and is still run with great attentiveness by the same family. A pleasant stay will be enriched by the high standard of the cuisine. The interior decoration is in the local valley style with pretty rooms and pleasing colour schemes.

The restaurant is the jewel of this little treasure of a hotel: the ingredients are home-grown by the family farm business, and the person in charge is both a passionately interested cook and also skilful. The dishes are regional in style and the wine list is extensive.

This would be a good stopping place in the course of a gastronomic tour.

$\mathcal{B}$eau Séjour

*I*n its peaceful and verdant location surrounded by green and with panoramic views, the hotel is managed with great care under family ownership. The rooms are pleasingly spacious, nearly all with a balcony. The bathrooms are good with towel heaters and hair-dryers, some with hydro-massage. The lounge is welcoming with an open fire in the hearth. The large dining room, where a buffet breakfast is also served, offers home-made dishes based on the traditional cooking of the region.

Guests can make use of a bar, cellar bar, table tennis room, children's playroom and a veranda with a view of the whole Mont Blanc range. There is a well-tended garden which in summer is full of flowers. The hotel also has a garage.

Amidst natural surroundings at the foot of Mont Blanc
☎ 0165 87801
🖷 0165 87961
Au Dent du Géant 18
località Pallesieux
11010 PRÈ-SAINT-DIDIER (Aosta)
Ref map 2, B2
A5, Morgex exit
33 rooms; £
Credit card: AE VISA SI

RECOMMENDED IN THE AREA

RESTAURANT: Golf

Piedmont

Piedmont offers every kind of landscape except the sea. In fact mountains make up more than 40 per cent of the region, the most westerly and extensive after Sicily. The Alps enclose the plain of the River Po on three sides, forming a sharp, majestic background.

In the central and south-east provinces of Novara and Vercelli as well as Alessandria, neatly geometric fields of rice and other crops are bordered with poplars. A good third of Piedmont is composed of the hills of the Langhe, Monferrato, Canavese, Turin and Ivrea areas. Continuous rolling hills and varied lines of vineyards are dotted with farmhouses and little villages, green meadows and woods. Sometimes they are sharpened by ridges and harsh river valleys, sometimes they are gentle, curved and open into poetic horizons of silhouettes of towers and castles in the distance. Between the mountains and the plain are the lakes – Orta, Maggiore and Verbano.

This geographical variety is unified by historical events that here more than elsewhere are linked to a royal house – that of Savoy, first lords of the region and then kings of Italy. This aristocratic self-confidence may explain many aspects of the Piedmont region.

Attractions – of nature, culture, art and atmosphere – are all around. Very good food supported by remarkable wines completes an ancient, elegant tradition of welcoming visitors. Guests will discover this, whether they are staying in lovely rural homes amidst green countryside, in historic hotels in the heart of Turin, or in rustically elegant farmhouses between the dense vineyards of the Langhe or Monferrato area. They will find it too in late 19th-century villas overlooking gardens and enchanting views of a lake, in old family residences and religious houses converted into inns, or in chalets at the foot of the rocks and snow of Monte Rosa.

*L*a Meridiana

Country tranquillity on a hillside

☎ & ✆ 0173 440112
località Altavilla 9
12051 ALBA (Cuneo)
Ref map 2, D3
A21, Asti Est exit, then S.S. 231
6 rooms; **££**
Credit cards not accepted

*T*he town of Alba is both near and distant: the town is only a kilometre away, but here we are on a hill in the midst of the green countryside. The main family house is an elegant villa in Art Nouveau style, with a sundial painted on the upper part of the façade – hence the name. Attached is the annexe given over to accommodation, with its rustic outlines covered by beautiful creepers. From the windows of the rooms and through the trees can be seen the Alps, the towers of Alba and the ancient city. The pleasantly spacious rooms have period furniture that has been handed down through the family. Open to guests are are the reading room, the breakfast room, gym and billiards room. Outside is a lovely garden with a portico, a leisure area and a barbeque. Sports lovers will find table tennis, *bocce* (bowls), and archery. Parking is outside, but within the owners' private courtyard.

RECOMMENDED IN THE AREA

RESTAURANTS:
L'Osteria dell'Arco *and* Il vicoletto*;*
La Luna nel Pozzo, *Neive*

VISIT:
Truffle fair at Alba, October; Palio horse race at Asti, September

---

*R*eale

*S*ituated in the historic centre of Asti, this was already a hotel in 1793. The entrance is under the porticoes of the Piazza Alfieri, a few steps away from the pedestrian zone. The rooms still have character and charm, with vaulted ceilings and large dimensions. A staircase with an antique balustrade in wrought iron is lit from above by a big skylight. The bedrooms are very big, and all are personalised and furnished with care. Every bathroom has a window, double washbasins and a little lobby. There are a few pieces of antique furniture together with large comfortable sofas in the corridors. The breakfast room on the mezzanine floor is lovely. Management is kind and thoughtful.

A great tradition of hospitality in surroundings of character and charm

☎ 0141 530240 ✆ 0141 34357
piazza V. Alfieri 6
14100 ASTI
Ref map 2, D3
A21, Asti exit, follow the signs for Poste
23 rooms; **££**
Credit card: AE VISA SI ⓪

RECOMMENDED IN THE AREA

RESTAURANTS:
Gener Neuv *and* Angolo del Beato

Lido Palace Hotel Baveno

Set in the gracious surroundings of a centuries-old park, the hotel has the most beautiful view of the Borromee islands

☎ 0323 924444 🖷 0323 924744
S.S. Sempione 30
28042 BAVENO (Novara)

Ref map 2, B4
A26, Baveno exit
102 rooms; **££**
Credit card: ᴀᴇ 🆅🆂🄰 🆂🄸 ⓪

*T*his is an elegant white *fin de siècle* building overlooking the lake with a wonderful view of the Borromee islands and surrounded by a large old park. Like the exterior of the building, the rooms inside are suitably gracious. There is a harmonious blend of crystal lamps, high vaulted ceilings embellished with stucco, carved picture frames, mirrors decorating the beautiful doors, and antique furniture.

Most of the rooms look out on to the lake and all are delightful and well furnished. The dining room has large windows on three sides so that in winter the panoramic view is uninterrupted; in summer meals are served outside on the terrace. In addition there is a tennis court, swimming pool, private beach, canoeing and a golf course nearby.

RECOMMENDED IN THE AREA

RESTAURANT:
Ascot

VISIT:
Borromee islands

La Casa in Collina

*T*his lovely Piedmontese farmhouse has been elegantly and carefully reconstructed and stands on the side of a hill. Its architecture is typical of the area and it is a pleasure to see how it has been renovated in its new capacity as a hotel. From Canelli the eye takes in an infinite number of vineyards where the Moscato grape is cultivated.

The simple yet beautiful materials used in rebuilding – stone, brick, terracotta and wrought iron – are complemented by the interior of the house with its antique Piedmontese furniture. In the bedrooms are canopied beds trimmed in white, and on the ground floor there are private corners in the lounge for reading or conversation as well as an airy breakfast room.

The hotel's surroundings are quiet and peaceful and there are delightful views of natural countryside and of cultivated land.

RECOMMENDED IN THE AREA

RESTAURANT:
San Marco, *Canelli*

LOCAL SPECIALITY:
The hotel's own DOC Moscato wine,
Cà del Giaj

VISIT:
Palazzo Gancia (Scarampi-Crivelli), an old castle; traditional market (on the third Sunday of each month), barrel race (the third Sunday in April) and the truffle show (beginning of November), all at Nizza Monferrato

Amidst rows of vines, with the atmosphere of a private house

☎ 0141 822827 ✆ 0141 823543
✉ g.amerio@areacom.it
località Sant'Antonio 30
14053 CANELLI (Asti)

Ref map 2, D3
A21, Asti Est exit, S.S. 431 as far as Piano, then turn left in the direction of Costigliole d'Asti, Boglietto, Canelli
6 rooms; **££**
Credit card: AE VISA SI ⓪, bancomat

*L*a Luna e i Falò

A rustic building set among vineyards

☎ & 🖷 0141 831643
regione Aie 37
14053 CANELLI (Asti)
Ref map 2, D3
A21, Asti Est exit, S.S. 431 as far as Piano,
then turn left in the direction of Costigliole
d'Asti, Boglietto, Canelli
9 rooms; ££
Credit cards not accepted

*T*he view is wonderful. Below is Canelli, around are hills criss-crossed with vine trellises, and overlooking them is this charming building which has been renovated and rebuilt by its owners who are also wine-producers. We are in the midst of the Cortese, Dolcetto and Moscato vineyards, between the Langhe hills and Monferrato. The hotel is in a rustic style with broad arches.

Inside, the antique period furniture, paintings, carpets and objects which have belonged to the owner's family for generations all contribute to the welcoming atmosphere of a private house.

RECOMMENDED IN THE AREA

RESTAURANT:
San Marco

LOCAL SPECIALITIES:
Wine, grapes, hazelnuts, truffles, cakes and local pastries

VISIT:
11th-century cathedral at Acqui Terme; thermal baths at Agliano

*C*annero

Graceful and stylish surroundings

☎ 0323 788046 🖷 0323 788048
📧 hcannero@tin.it
via Lungo Lago 2
28821 CANNERO RIVIERA (Verbania)
Ref map 2, B4
A26, Gravellona Toce exit, then S.S. 34
towards Locarno
40 rooms, 14 apartments; ££
Credit card: AE VISA SI ⓄⒹ

*S*tanding out on the north-eastern shore of lake Maggiore, at the foot of the mountains, was a monastery built in the 12th-century. The family that now own it transformed it into an elegant hotel and for four generations has treated its visitors attentively and warmly. The graceful building, which is situated very near the little port beloved of tourists, is adorned with large windows and spacious balconies.

Inside the hotel is airy and well furnished, with floral decorations on the glass doors and the walls. All the simple but tastefully furnished rooms enjoy a view of the lake. The hotel's bar, Il Caffè Le Vele, is particularly romantic in the late afternoon and evening. A heated swimming pool and tennis court may well tempt even the most relaxed guest.

RECOMMENDED IN THE AREA

RESTAURANTS:
Il Monastero, *Verbania;* Grotto Sant'Anna, *Cannobio*

LOCAL SPECIALITY:
Honey from Cannero flowers

VISIT:
The castles of Cannero; Roman road, Carmine; ancient press, Donego

$\mathcal{L}$a Rondinella

A villa in the Art Nouveau style

☎ 0323 788098 🖶 0323 788365
✉ hrondine@tin.it
via Sacchetti 50
28821 CANNERO RIVIERA (Verbania)
Ref map 2, B4
A26, Gravellona Toce exit, then S.S. 34
towards Locarno
13 rooms, 3 apartments; £/££
Credit card: AE VISA SI ◉

$\mathcal{A}$t sunset the lake's own particular light is reflected on the façade of the Art Nouveau-style villa which houses the hotel: the colours are astonishing, and the effect very atmospheric. The morning sunshine, on the other hand, can be enjoyed at breakfast on the veranda or else under the trees. Inside the hotel is a harmonious blend of modern and traditional furniture. The rooms are decorated in period style with wrought iron bedsteads and large windows. And as a constant background there is the lake which is visible from any point in the hotel.

RECOMMENDED IN THE AREA

RESTAURANTS:
Milano *and* Torchio, *Verbania*

VISIT:
Villa Taranto; guided tours of the lake

$\mathcal{D}$el Lago

A delightful hotel which uses the lake to add to its charms

☎ & 🖶 0323 70595
✉ lago@cannobio.net
via Nazionale 2, località Carmine
28821 CANNOBIO (Verbania)
Ref map 2, B4
A26, Gravellona Toce exit, then S.S. 34
towards Locarno
10 rooms; ££
Credit card: AE VISA SI ◉

RECOMMENDED IN THE AREA

RESTAURANT:
Lo Scalo

VISIT:
The 16th-century Pietà Sanctuary

$\mathcal{F}$acing the lake and surrounded by greenery, this charming hotel has every requirement of elegance and good taste. The delightful private beach provides a sense of exclusivity. In keeping with the lakeside scenery, the hotel is constructed on several levels.

The rooms inside are well lit, decorated in light colours and furnished in original style. The bedrooms have pastel-coloured walls, carpets and either classical-style armchairs or else modern functional furniture painted in white. The restaurant is large with big windows on either side giving a view of the lake and there is a terrace overlooking the water for meals in the open. A specialised wine annexe provides a vast selection of vintage wines.

Castello San Giuseppe

With a past life as a monastery and a fortress, this is a place rich in history

☎ 0125 424370 📠 0125 641278
località Castello San Giuseppe
10010 CHIAVERANO (Torino)
Ref map 2, C3

A5, Ivrea exit, follow the signs for the city centre, next take the lago Sirio direction and once past the lake go to Chiaverano
16 rooms, 3 suites; **££/£££**
Credit card: AE VISA SI ⓓ

*H*igh on the hillside, the hotel is surrounded by an 11-hectare park with tall trees and every now and then a little lake amid the green. This is a 17th-century building which was originally a monastery for the Telesian order and then for the Carmelites. At the time of Napoleon it was transformed into a military fortress. Then, at the beginning of the 20th century, it became a meeting place for famous people where artists and writers used to stay.

Now it is a romantic hotel with rooms decorated in period style in keeping with the building, the ceilings and the frescoes. The rooms are named after famous visitors of the past: the Eleanora Duse room has a canopied bed, the Giuseppe Giacosa and Arrigo Boito rooms have charmingly austere antique furnishings. The restaurant is dedicated to Joséphine de Beauharnais, the wife of Napoleon Bonaparte.

In summertime meals are served in the open air. The former chapel has been changed into a meeting room specially equipped for small conferences.

RECOMMENDED IN THE AREA

RESTAURANT:
Il Convento, *Ivrea*

LOCAL SPECIALITIES:
Revel Chion grappa and Chiaverano tomini; vintage wines, Carena

VISIT:
Canavese castles; panoramic walks on the morainic Serra hills; Graglia and Oropa sanctuaries; mementoes of Guido Gozzano at Agliè Canavese

San Carlo

*T*his modern villa was built in 1981 and its sloping roofs with eaves contrast pleasantly with the green of the countryside around. It is in upper Langa, a region noted for its gastronomy and fine wines. The rooms are carefully appointed with modern furnishings, satellite television, mini-bars and good bathrooms. Much attention is paid to the cooking: the restaurant is in a romantic little room and the dishes served are typically Piedmontese with individual touches. More than 600 vintage wines from all over the world are kept in the stone cellar. The hotel organises courses on cooking and on Piedmontese wines.

A cellar with more that 600 wines and very distinctive cuisine

☎ 0173 81435 ⊕ 0173 8125
📧 sancarlo@langhe.monferrato.roero.it
corso Divisioni Alpine 41
12074 CORTEMILIA (Cuneo)
Ref map 2, E3
A26, Alessandria Est exit,
S.S. 30 towards Acqui Terme,
Bubbio, Cortemilia
19 rooms; ££
Credit card: ⒜Ⓔ ⓥⒾⓈⒶ Ⓢ Ⓘ ⓄⒹ

RECOMMENDED IN THE AREA

RESTAURANT:
Carlo Parisio, *Aqui Terme*

LOCAL SPECIALITIES:
Wine, salami and cheeses

VISIT:
Hazelnut Festival (August); Madonna della Pieve church

Castello Rosso

Modern comfort in a 16th-century residence

☎ 0175 230030
📠 0175 239315
via Ammiraglio Reynaudi 5
12024 COSTIGLIOLE SALUZZO (Cuneo)
Ref map 2, E2
A6, Marene exit, S.S. 662 as far as Saluzzo, then left for Costigliole Saluzzo
16 rooms, 3 suites; **£££**
Credit card: 💳 💳 💳 💳

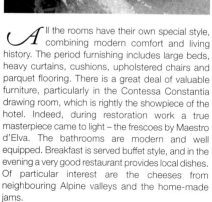

*A*ll the rooms have their own special style, combining modern comfort and living history. The period furnishing includes large beds, heavy curtains, cushions, upholstered chairs and parquet flooring. There is a great deal of valuable furniture, particularly in the Contessa Constantia drawing room, which is rightly the showpiece of the hotel. Indeed, during restoration work a true masterpiece came to light – the frescoes by Maestro d'Elva. The bathrooms are modern and well equipped. Breakfast is served buffet style, and in the evening a very good restaurant provides local dishes. Of particular interest are the cheeses from neighbouring Alpine valleys and the home-made jams.

Hotel guests have the use of a health centre on the lower floor with modern equipment and a heated swimming pool.

RECOMMENDED IN THE AREA

RESTAURANTS:
Gargotta del Pellico *and* Ostù dij Baloss

VISIT:
Source of the River Po at Monviso, Varaita valley and Varaita and Costigliole rivers; Castello di Racconigi e di Castellar and other castles in the Saluzzo area; Palazzo Giriodi di Monastero and Palazzo La Tour

Foresteria Poderi Einaudi

Eighteenth-century charm in the historic home of the Einaudi family

☎ 0173 70414 📠 0173 742017
📧 poderi.einaudi@areacom.it
borgata Gombe 31
12063 DOGLIANI (Cuneo)
Ref map 2, E3
A6, Carrù exit, towards Farigliano, then right before reaching Dogliano, towards Belvedere and immediately right again for Podere
4 rooms, 1 suite; **££/£££**
Credit card: 💳 🆂

*T*his is a charming residence in the midst of the Teucc vineyards on the Einaudi estates. The building dates back to the 18th century and the Einaudi family has been here since the beginning of the 20th century. The main house was used as the winter residence of Luigi Einaudi, the first president of the Italian republic. Over the course of time it assumed importance by providing the cellars for the wine business, especially following the recent introduction of modern techniques. The large airy rooms are on the first floor and are furnished entirely in 1900s-style. The bathrooms are simple but spacious. Breakfast is prepared with great care and served in the homely environment of a parlour next to the small kitchen. Specialist wine magazines can found in the drawing room, and a visit to the hotel's cellar is a must.

RECOMMENDED IN THE AREA

RESTAURANT:
L'Albero Fiorita, *Dogliani*

VISIT:
Archaeological Museum, Gabetti; the parish church, Dogliano

Ghiffa

*T*his is a first-class hotel facing the lake and only a few metres away from the landing stage for tourist boats. The elegant building is in Art Nouveau style. There is a delightful private beach, a swimming pool and solarium, and a flower garden in the midst of lush vegetation which is the ideal place for quiet reading or relaxation. The hotel rooms are bathed in light streaming through the large windows. The attractive dining room has period furniture and parquet flooring, and at sunset affords a splendid

A hotel which blends perfectly with the countryside around

☎ 0323 59285 📠 0323 59585
corso Belvedere
28823 GHIFFA (Verbania)
Ref map 2, B4
A26, Gravellona Toce exit, then S.S. 34 towards Locarno
39 rooms, 1 suite; **££/£££**
Credit card: 🆎 💳 🆂 🅾

view of the sailing boats slowly crossing the lake. The comfortable bedrooms in more modern style all have balconies overlooking the water.

RECOMMENDED IN THE AREA

RESTAURANT:
Milano, *Verbania*

LOCAL SPECIALITIES:
Local wines, hand-crafted products in wood and granite

VISIT:
Holy Trinity Sanctuary, Ronco

Villa Lidia

1930s villa in wooded parkland on the shores of Lake Maggiore

☎ 0322 7095/02 58103076
🖷 02 34973214
✉ lanfranconiconsulta@interbusiness.it
via Giuseppe Ferrari 9
28040 LESA (Novara)
Ref map 2, B4
A26, towards Meina, Solcio, Lesa
3 rooms; **££**
Credit cards not accepted

*B*ed and breakfast accommodation is provided in this villa built in the typical Lake Maggiore style of the 1930s and with original period furnishings. Recently renovated, it has large welcoming rooms, each with a bathroom and a terrace looking out over the park. Two hundred metres from the shore of the lake, the villa is quiet and peaceful and is surrounded by parkland with tall trees.

Breakfast is served in the ground-floor dining room with its large windows that face the garden. A short distance away from the hotel are local facilities for sailing, tennis, canoeing and swimming, while the rural location is ideal for walks and outings.

There is a minimum stay of two nights.

RECOMMENDED IN THE AREA

RESTAURANTS:
Rapanello, Hostaria la Speranza *and* Lago Maggiore
VISIT:
Stresa; Ascona; Brissago islands; Monte Verità

Locanda del Boscogrande

On the green hills of Monferrato

☎ 0141 956390 📠 0141 956800
via Boscogrande 47
14048 MONTEGROSSO D'ASTI (Asti)
Ref map 2, D3
A21, Asti Est exit, towards Isola d'Asti,
Montegrosso d'Asti
8 rooms; **££**
Credit card: AE VISA SI ⓪, bancomat

RECOMMENDED IN THE AREA

RESTAURANTS:
La Grotta *and* Convivio
VISIT:
14th-century church of La Madonna di Viatosto, Asti

A late-19th-century farmhouse in the peaceful surroundings of the hills of upper Monferrato was renovated to make this inn. Only a 10-minute drive away from Asti, in an area of great wines and gastronomic tradition, the inn has airy, well-furnished rooms with parquet floors. The restaurant is elegant and welcoming, and there are little rooms with vaulted brick ceilings for business or private dinners.

The garden is large and well tended, with terraces for relaxing and enjoying the view. There is also an open-air swimming pool.

Leon d'Oro

The hotel overlooks the charming Lake Orta

☎ 0322 911991
📠 0322 90303
✉ leondoro@lycosmail.com
piazza Motta 43
28016 ORTA SAN GIULIO (Novara)
Ref map 2, B4
A26, Arona exit, then S.P.142 for
Borgomanero-Gozzano-Lago d'Orta
36 rooms, 3 suites; **££**
Credit card: AE VISA SI ⓪

RECOMMENDED IN THE AREA

RESTAURANTS:
Villa Crespi *and* Sacro Monte
VISIT:
The island of San Giulio on the lake, with its 12th-century basilica

*T*o the west of Lake Maggiore and surrounded by green hills is Lake Orta, an historic site full of monuments and interesting places. One of the most attractive spots is Orta San Giulio, where the hotel is situated in a wonderful position. It was recently renovated and has modern furnishings. There is a large solarium terrace, with tables where guests may take refreshments outside under the decorated ceiling and graceful columns. The restaurant specialises in local dishes and during the summer season also serves meals outside. The hotel is managed with attention to detail and there is a private landing-stage for mooring motor boats.

43

Giardini

Thoughtful and attentive hospitality

☎ 0163 71135 📠 0163 71988
via Umberto I 9
13020 PIODE (Vercelli)
Ref map 2, B2
A4 for Gravellona Toce, Romagnano-
Ghemme exit, then S.S. 299 in the
direction of Alagna Sesia
17 apartments; £
Credit card: AE VISA SI Ⓞ, bancomat

RECOMMENDED IN THE AREA

RESTAURANT:
Delzanino, *Varallo*

LOCAL SPECIALITIES:
Local toma *cheese; intricate* puncetto *embroidery; wooden country artefacts*

VISIT:
Folklore and palaeontological museums at Borgosesia; Sacromonte, Varallo; Altoa Valsesia Park and Weber Museum, Alagna; sports, excursions on Monte Rosa

*T*he hotel is in a charming early-19th-century building with the characteristic tiled roof of the Alpine region. It is in the centre of the village facing the River Sesia. Accommodation is in neat single and double apartments that are practical and well decorated with dark wood rustic furniture. Some apartments have terraces with a panoramic view over the valley, and all of them have satellite television, linen and crockery and may be hired for a week or a weekend. The bar and restaurant are particularly welcoming. Diners may use the well-appointed solarium terrace, with its wonderful view. Antonella runs the kitchen and her husband, Mauro, takes care of the restaurant and the wine service.

Castello di San Giorgio

The air of an aristocratic country residence

☎ 0142 806203 📠 0142 806505
via Cavalli d'Olivola 3,
**15020 SAN GIORGIO
MONFERRATO (Alessandria)**
Ref map 2, D4
A26, Casale Sud exit, then S.S. Casale-Asti
11 rooms; £££
Credit card: AE VISA SI Ⓞ

*W*ith its beautiful and severe architecture softened by pale pink and stone colours, this looks like a noble country house. Indeed it probably was once such a house but nowadays it serves as both a hotel and a restaurant. Surrounding it are a large park and the delightful countryside of Monferrato. Maurizio and Luisella Grossi manage both the accommodation and the delicious traditional cooking with great attention to detail. The bedrooms are large with high ceilings and period furniture, and all have air-conditioning, mini-bar and satellite television.

The dining room and drawing rooms are elegant and welcoming. There is also a banqueting room for parties and ceremonies.

RECOMMENDED IN THE AREA

RESTAURANT:
La Torre, *Casale Monferrato*

LOCAL SPECIALITY:
Wine from La Puledra *cellar*

La Traversina

*T*his pretty house is typical of the countryside, covered with creepers and surrounded by a wonderful garden which has been lovingly cultivated for years and is full of flowers, especially roses (of which there are more than 400). Nearby are woods of oak

and chestnut trees, and in the summer thousands of fireflies illuminate the night. The house is in the middle of a farm that has belonged to the Varese family for 300 years, and specialises in the cultivation of perennial herbaceous plants. The furnishings of the attractive rooms, all with private bathroom, recall the history and interests of the family. Guests are welcomed like friends here. The hotel accommodation also includes a little apartment that is ideal for families with children, as well as a single apartment. The living room and kitchen are communal.

The hotel offers its guests peace and quiet, a warm welcome, attractive rooms, an indoor swimming pool, and a bowls (*bocce*) pitch.

A charming place, away from noise and pollution

☎ and 🖷 0143 61377
cascina Traversina 109
15060 STAZZANO (Alessandria)
Ref map 2, D4
A7, Serravalle Scrivia exit, take the road for Stazzano and follow the signs for the farm
3 rooms, 3 apartments; **££**
Credit cards not accepted

RECOMMENDED IN THE AREA

RESTAURANT:
Forlino, *Montacuto*

LOCAL SPECIALITY:
Pastries at the pasticceria Carrea, Serravalle Scrivia

VISIT:
Roman city, Libarna; the Borbera valley; castles in upper Monferrato; art gallery in Capuchin Monastery, Voltaggio

45

Liberty

You feel as if you're in fin de siècle Paris or Vienna

☎ 011 5628801
📠 011 5628163
✉ liberty@fileita.it
via Pietro Micca 15
10121 TORINO (TURIN)
Ref map 2, D3
A4, Turino Centro exit
35 rooms; ££
Credit card: AE VISA SI ⓌD, bancomat

This period villa in the style of 1890s Paris or Vienna is situated in the historic centre of the city in the beautiful Via Pietro Micca which runs from Piazza Castello to Piazza Solferino. The villa is a residential building and the hotel on its third floor is reached by a lift. It was already famous at the end of the 19th century and has accommodated noted members of the aristocracy, sometimes for long periods. There is antique furniture in nearly all the very large bedrooms, making them seem like bedrooms of a past era. The bathrooms are practical

RECOMMENDED IN THE AREA

RESTAURANT:
Vintage 1997, *piazza Solferino 16/H*

LOCAL SPECIALITIES:
Fiorio ice creams and Piedmontese gianduiotto *chocolate by Stratta*

VISIT:
Egyptian Museum, Turin; hunting reserve of the Savoy family at Venaria Reale

and the communal drawing rooms are very elegant.

Guest are received like family, warmly and attentively. Buffet breakfast includes hot dishes. The restaurant offers homely regional cooking, and there is 24-hour bar service.

Luxor

Turin city style, in comfortable and relaxing surroundings

☎ 011 5620777 📠 011 5628324
✉ hotel.luxor@hotelves.it
corso Stati Uniti 7
10128 TORINO (TURIN)
Ref map 2, D3
A4, corso G. Cesare
70 rooms, 4 suites; ££/£££
Credit card: AE VISA SI ⓌD

Set in Turin's business centre, near the Lingotto and Turin exhibition centres, this modern hotel was completely refurbished in 1990 and has many rooms, some with terraces overlooking the whole city. The medium-sized rooms are furnished in modern style with attractive wallpaper, fitted carpets, mini-bars, air conditioning and satellite television. The practical bathrooms all have hair-dryers. The communal rooms have been furnished for the convenience of business visitors. An American bar is open in the evening, and the hotel also provides a well-equipped conference room.

RECOMMENDED IN THE AREA

RESTAURANTS:
Neuv Caval 'd Bronz, *piazza San Carlo 151;*
Savoia, *via Corte d'Appello 13*

$\mathcal{A}$ntico Borgo del Riondino

In the heart of the Langhe hills

☎ and 🖷 0173 630313
via dei Fiori 13
12050 TREZZO TINELLA (Cuneo)
Ref map 2, D-E3
A21 Piacenza-Torino, Ast Est exit, towards
Alba. After 17km turn left for Castagnole
Lanze-Neive, then from Neive follow the sign
for Tresso Tinella
8 rooms; ££
Credit card: VISA SI

RECOMMENDED IN THE AREA

RESTAURANT:
DEL CASTELLO, *Mango*

LOCAL SPECIALITIES:
Piedmontese wines; white truffles from Alba; local cheeses; traditional hazelnut confectionary

$\mathcal{T}$his elegant hotel in the Langhe hills region stands on site of a medieval village. It looks out over ancient little streets between which every now and then is a panoramic view of the countryside around. The modest houses here were built as poor rural dwellings, but their proportions and use of materials never jars with the landscape.

The pleasantly welcoming interior of the hotel has been renovated and restructured. Traditional materials, stone walls, beamed ceilings, brick and stone are cleverly combined with modern furniture to elegant effect. The rooms have names remiscent of agricultural processes: 'the olive press', 'the drying room' and 'the apple store'. These names were inspired by some of the antique furnishings in the rooms or else by the reputed use to which they were put during their past village life.

$\mathcal{P}$iccolo Lago

Sought-after cuisine and an excellent wine cellar

☎ 0323 586792 🖷 0323 586791
🄴 h.piccololago@stresa.net
via Filippo Turati 87
località Fondotoce
28924 VERBANIA
Ref map 2, B4
A26, Gravellona Toce exit, then S.S. 34
towards Locarno
12 rooms; ££
Credit card: VISA SI AE, bancomat

RECOMMENDED IN THE AREA

RESTAURANT:
Le Oche di Bracchio, *Bracchio*

VISIT:
Lake Mergozzo offers a peaceful lakeside stay and is just as convenient to get to as the more famous Lake Maggiore, but more relaxing as it is more secluded

$\mathcal{T}$his has always been a family-run hotel, but now that the new generation has taken over it has found a new lease of life. The 1960s building has been modernised in successive years. The rooms, on two floors of the hotel, are simple but comfortable and all have a view of the lake. Parking is convenient.

On the other side of the road, by the lake shore, is the hotel restaurant with a garden and private beach. Guests may make use of the bathing facilities and can take a canoe trip round the lake. The Verbania golf course is also nearby. There is a well-equipped gym underneath the restaurant, which may be reached directly from the beach.

The restaurant, with its regional cooking, is noteworthy. The owners are passionate about the ingredients they choose, and find wonderful cheeses and sausages from the valley. This local but refined cuisine is accompanied by a superb selection of wines.

*D*ré Castè

RECOMMENDED IN THE AREA

RESTAURANTS:
Natalina-L'albergotto, *Grazzano-Badoglio; I tre re,
Montcalvo;* La Fermata, *Alessandria*

---

*An 18th-century mansion between the
Mongferrato Casalese hills*

☎ and 🖷 0142 933442
📧 mongetto@italnet.it
via Piave 2
**15049 VIGNALE MONFERRATO
(Alessandria)**
Ref map 2, D4

A21, Alessandria ovest exit, S.S. 10 as far as
Solerpo, then follow the signs for Fubine and
Vignole on the local road going north
5 rooms, 2 apartments; **£/££**
Credit card: 💳

---

*A*n elegantly grand mansion, which dates
from the end of the 18th century. Its name
Dré Castè means 'behind the castle'. In fact the
mansion is beneath what was Cardinal Callori's castle,
and looks out over the hills of Montferrato Casalese.
On clear days you can see Mont Blanc and Monte Rosa
on the horizon. The guest house belongs to the
Mongetto farm and comprises two small apartments
and two double rooms with shared bathrooms, plus a
further double room.

The lovely rooms of the guest house have painted ceilings
and antique furnishings. They are named after the farm's
vineyards: Ridifà, Baldea, Solin Palareto and Guera.
Meals are served in a 'house party' style, in two rooms
on the ground floor which have fireplaces, comfortable
sofas and lots of attractive details. Equal care is shown in
the preparation of the food, much of which includes
ingredients grown on the farm.

Lombardy

'The territory of Lombardy on which I gazed from all around this tower, full as it was of such inexpressible variety of things of every kind, … made it seem to me as if I were really looking at the Elysian Fields…' The 'tower' is the *Duomo* (cathedral) of Milan described by one of the 17th-century English pioneers of the Grand Tour. This judgement is still fit to describe the extraordinary number of reasons to visit the region.

These range from the Alpine scenery of the Stelvio national park and of Bernina and Adamello – great forests and grasslands dominated by peaks and glaciers – to the delightfully varied scenery around Lakes Maggiore and Garda (on its Lombard shore), Lugano, Como, Varese and Iseo. These offer classical pictures of water, villas and gardens, with mountains looming above the banks, and the surprise of lemons and olives. Then there is the 'low' plain with rivers and canals, the red farmhouses, lines of poplars and the green hills. There is an established tradition of taking holidays here.

Places like Valtellina, Valcamonica and the

Lake scenery is almost a symbol of the region; the photograph shows the garden of villa Melzi at Bellagio on Lake Como

Prealpi of Bergamo retain a strong identity through their countryside and culture. The many centres of art include Bergamo, Brescia, the Mantua of the Gonzaga family, the Milan of the Visconti, Sforza and the Borromeo families, and Pavia, Sabbioneta and Vigevano.

The Lombardian imprint on history and art has its own special, solid dimension. The colour of brick is very evident: in the farmhouses and the medieval towns, in Romanesque churches, charterhouses and abbeys. Certain landscapes remind one of Leonardo Da Vinci.

Nowadays visitors can choose between delightful hotels right in the centre of Milan, enchanting rustic dwellings amongst vineyards, peaceful, stylish historic mansions, or the comfort and warmth of mountain chalets before or after skiing. Good food and robust wines contribute to the enjoyment of the visit.

Cornaleto

Among the green hills of the Franciacorta wine-growing area

☎ 030 7450554/030 7450507
📠 030 7450552
via Cornaletto 2
25030 ADRO (Brescia)
Ref map 3, B6
A4, Palazzolo sull'Oglio, towards
Capriolo-Adro
7 rooms, 6 apartments; £/££
Credit cards:

RECOMMENDED IN THE AREA

RESTAURANTS:
Le due Colombe, *Rovato;* Al Desco, *Sarnico;*
Osteria il volto, *Iseo*

LOCAL SPECIALITIES:
Wrought ironwork; local crafts; antiques and bric-à-brac

WINE CELLARS:
Cantine di Franciacorta, *Erbusco*

VISIT:
Lake Iseo; villas, palaces, castles and monasteries in the Franciacorte area

*T*he name of this particular spot, Adro, may come from *Adresco* which refers to a village with many vineyards or else from *Atrusca* which describes the quality of grapes already prized at the time of the Etruscans. Indeed this is an area with a very ancient tradition of vineyards. Whatever the derivation of the name, the municipal coat of arms is embellished with succulent grapes. The building that accommodates visitors stands high among the vineyards, affording a good view of the surroundings. It is modern but built in traditional style. The rooms and two-roomed apartments are well furnished with rustic details such as terracotta floors and wooden ceilings. The restaurant is modern and serves dishes that complement the farm's wine cellar. There is also a small conference room, and

$\mathcal{L}$ocanda dei Mai Intees

A handful of buildings make up the ancient centre of the village. However, these are no ordinary houses but mansions or castles of considerable architectural interest. The romantic inn is situated in an aristocratic 16th-century residence and one look at it is enough to captivate visitors. Locando dei Mai Intees means 'those who could never agree', but a guest here immediately feels in harmony with surroundings which are not only beautiful in their own right, but are furnished delightfully with period pieces. Parts of the interior look out on to a lovely garden, others on to porticoes.

The few bedrooms, again charmingly decorated, are reached by means of secret corridors and staircases, and the views from them give the visitor glimpses of the past. The multicoloured marble bathrooms are very practical and well-equipped. The owner of the inn takes care of every detail of the accommodation and the restaurant as if this were her own house.

An attentive and elegant welcome in a 16th-century villa

☎ 0332 457223
📠 0332 459339
📧 maintees@tin.it
via Nobile Claudio Riva 2
21022 AZZATE (Varese)
Ref map 2, B4
A8, Buguggiate, towards Varese
6 rooms, 1 suite; £££
Credit cards: AE VISA SI ◉, bancomat

RECOMMENDED IN THE AREA

RESTAURANTS:
Al Vecchio Convento, *Varese;*
Ma. Ri. Na., *Olgate Olona*

VISIT:
The historic centre of Azzate;
Palazzo Estense and il Sacro Monte, Varese

$\mathcal{F}$lorence

This romantic building on the shore of Lake Como has long attracted intellectuals and artists

☎ 031 950342
📠 031 951722
✉ hotflore@tin.it
piazza Mazzini 46
22010 BELLAGIO (Como)
Ref map 3, B5
A9, Como Sud exit, then S.S. 583
going north and follow the signs for Bellagio
32 rooms, 4 suites; **££/£££**
Credit cards: AE VISA SI

RECOMMENDED IN THE AREA

RESTAURANTS:
La Barcherra *and* Silvio

VISIT:
*Lake Como's lovely villas:
Melzi and Sebelloni at Bellagio;
Carlotta at Tremezzo;
Cipressi and Monastero at Varenna;
church of Madonna del
Ghisallo, Magreglio*

HOTEL FLORENCE
BELLAGIO

*T*he charm of the hotel lies not only in the building itself but in its tradition. This delightful old lakeside house stands by the shore. It has been a hotel for more than 150 years and in that time Mark Twain, Puccini, Toscanini, Sartre, Simone de Beauvoir and many male and female intellectuals have stayed here. The bedrooms are large, decorated with antique furniture, and have parquet flooring and floral wallpaper. The bathrooms are not modern but they are practical. The communal rooms have great character and the hall has a lovely fireplace while the restaurant is beautifully light and airy. The restaurant-bar on the ground floor, which is reached through the hotel's lakeside porticoes, is charmingly informal.

Cascina Caremma

Deep in the countryside of the Cistercian monks

☎ 02 9050020
📠 02 9050020
✉ caremma@demosdata.it
via Cascina Caremma
20080 BESATE (Milano)
Ref map 3, C4-5
Coming from the north: A7, Binasco exit, towards Casorate Primo, then road for Besate
Coming from the south: A7, Bereguardo exit, towards Motta Visconti, the road for Besate
10 rooms; **£**
Credit cards: SI

*T*ypical of Lombardian architecture, this very old farm with its rectangular courtyard has been transformed into an innovatory type of farm/guest house, an *agriturismo*. With its own livestock and 36 hectares of cultivated land, it is organised according to the most modern principles of organic farming. It is therefore the perfect place to escape to, ideal especially for anyone interested in environmental issues.

This unspoilt farmhouse fits perfectly into its surroundings. The peaceful rooms are rustic, spacious and welcoming. All the rooms have air conditioning.

RECOMMENDED IN THE AREA

RESTAURANTS:
Vecchio Mulino, *Certosa di Pavia;* I castagni, *Vigevano*

LOCAL SPECIALITIES:
Cured meats, salami and cereal products direct from the farm shop, Besate; organic products from Abbiategrasso

VISIT:
Morimondo Abbey; Certosa di Pavia Monastery; Vigevano; Pavia; Ticino Park

*L*arice Bianco

Comfortable and welcoming surroundings

📞 and 📠 0342 904614
📧 larice@valtline.it
via Funivie 10
23032 BORMIO (Sondrio)
Ref map 3, A7
From Milan, S.S. 36 as far as Cloico, then
S.S. 38 towards Sondrio, Tirano, Bormio
45 rooms; **££**
Credit cards: AE VISA SI ⓪, bancomat

*I*n the heart of the upper Valtellina valley, the hotel stands only a few minutes from the ski lifts and is near the historic centre of Bormio. This is an ideal hotel, either for a winter or summer holiday, for it is very welcoming and comfortable. Its stylish building overlooks the valley and enjoys an exclusive view of both the city and the mountain.

The rooms are all well furnished and reflect the lively warmth of this area. The hall, with its fireplace and armchairs, is very inviting to guests after skiing or long walks. The bedrooms have traditional wooden walls and their large windows make them light and airy.

RECOMMENDED IN THE AREA

RESTAURANTS:
Kuerc *and* Sassella; Delle Alpi, *Sóndalo*

VISIT:
Alpine sports; Stelvio National Park; 16th-century church, Tirano; Palazzo Salis and other historic buildings, Bormio

*M*iramonti

Enjoy a mountain holiday in either winter or summer

📞 0342 903312 📠 0342 905222
📧 mirapark@valtline.it
via Milano 50
23032 BORMIO (Sondrio)
Ref map 3, A7
From Milan, S.S. 36 as far as Colico, then
S.S. 38 towards Sondrio, Tirano, Bormio
43 rooms; **££**
Credit cards: AE VISA SI ⓪, bancomat

*I*n a large private park situated in a secluded peaceful area near the historic centre, this hotel is ideally placed for those who wish to enjoy a mountain holiday whether

in winter or summer. The ski lifts are only 500 metres away from it and so can be reached on foot. The hotel building is modern but in harmony with the countryside, and its interior is welcoming and attractively furnished.

The spacious modern rooms all have balconies designed for sunbathing. Guests may also use the sauna and Turkish bath to enjoy an even more relaxing stay. The restaurant serves delicious local dishes.

RECOMMENDED IN THE AREA

RESTAURANTS:
Taulà; Baira de Mario, *Ciuk*

VISIT:
Livigno, Santa Caterina; L'Engadina painted by Segantini

Madonnina

In a romantic 1900s house

☎ 0332 417731 🖷 0332 418403
largo Lanfranco 1
21050 CANTELLO (Varese)
Ref map 2, B4

A8, Gazzada exit, take the *superstrada* (dual carriageway) 27 as far as Lozza, the Varese Est *tangenziale* (ring road) towards Gaggiolo, then left for Cantello

15 rooms; ££
Credit cards: AE SI ⓓ

*T*he façade of the beautifully designed 18th-century building is a fitting introduction to the gracious interior. This historic residence is situated on a hillside, with a view of wide open spaces, in the midst of the lush green and the colourful flowers of a park which has its own winter garden.

Inside the house is indeed welcoming and furnished with great taste to give the look of a private house. Period furniture and objects with the charm and patina of age enhance delightful quiet corners where every attention has been paid to detail and nothing left to chance.

The beautiful large windows are a feature, bringing the outside world into the building. The 15 bedrooms are classically pretty and all are furnished elegantly. Each one, however, is different and has its own personality. All have large practical bathrooms.

This is an exquisite and historic setting for the restaurant, that focal and creative aspect of hospitality. The standard of the cooking here is the boast of the area.

RECOMMENDED IN THE AREA

RESTAURANTS:
Da Vittorio, *pazza Beccaria 1, Varese;*
Da Annetta, *Capalago*

VISIT:
Villa Medici, Induno Olona

Ricci Curbastro & Figli

The sign of traditional and spontaneous hospitality

☎ 030 736094
📠 030 74600558
✉ agrit.riccicur@imp.it
via Adro 37
25031 CAPRIOLO (Brescia)
Ref map 3, B6

A14, Palazzolo exit, go as far as Capriolo, then turn right towards Adro; the farm is 500 metres away
7 apartments; £/££
Credit cards: AE VISA SI

This is the Franciacorte hills area which is famous not only for its wines but for its gastronomy and for countryside. Visitors can also go on enjoyable rambles to see various renowned works of art in the area. Farm apartments have been made in a late 19th-century rural building on the edge of the agricultural village of Capriolo in the countryside stretching between the Oglio River and Monte Alto. These apartments, with names like 'butterfly' or 'cherry', are all different but all equally well renovated, comfortable and practical.

The restoration work has conserved a number of original features, and the apartments are furnished in an old-fashioned homely style. Visits can be made to the farm's wine cellar as well as to the agricultural museum and to the Vino Ricci Curbastro. A short distance away is a golf course, and there are 300 km of tracks in the area for mountain bikes.

RECOMMENDED IN THE AREA

RESTAURANTS:
Villa Giuseppina *and* Punta-Da Dino

VISIT:
Lake Iseo; Torbiere di Iseo Park and San Pietro in Lamosa Monastery; church of San Paolo, Sarnico; San Pietro Lamosa Monastery, Provaglio d'Iseo

*A*urora

An ideal place to stay in close contact with nature

☎ 0346 60004 📠 0346 60246
✉ hotel.aurora@cooraltur.it
via Sant'Antonio 19
**24020 CASTIONE
DELLA PRESOLANA (Bergamo)**
Ref map 3, B6
A4, Bergamo exit, towards Clusone,
Rovetta, then Castione
28 rooms; ££
Credit cards: AE VISA SI ◉

The hotel stands just outside the village in a quiet position with a wonderful view. The building is modern but built on traditional lines, with sloping roofs and lots of wood which is both decorative and warm. The pretty little bedrooms have attractive wallpaper and furniture in the country style of the mountain region, and some of the bathrooms have been completely refurbished recently. The communal rooms are furnished in modern style, and a fireplace makes the television room cosy. The terrace outside is well appointed, and there is a tennis court and facilities for games of *bocce* (bowls) and table tennis. Inside the hotel is a small gym.

The family who own the hotel are not intrusive, but very attentive and keen to make their guests' stay enjoyable. The home cooking is typical of the region, and breakfast includes pastries made on the premises.

RECOMMENDED IN THE AREA

RESTAURANTS:
Caminone *and* Cascina delle noci, *Bratto Dorga*

VISIT:
*Bergamo town; Lakes Iseo and Endine;
Presolana pass; the milk-producing area called
Via del Latte; Oratorio dei Discipli, Clusone;
Iron-Age settlement, Parre*

Parco Borromeo

Visit this hotel in its parkland and step back into the past

☎ 0362 551796
🖷 0362 550182
✉ info@hotelparcoborromeo.it
via Borromeo 29
20031 CESANO MADERNO (Milano)
Ref map 3, B5
Milano-Meda *superstrada* (dual carriageway), towards Como
40 rooms; **££/£££**
Credit cards: AE VISA SI ⑩, bancomat

$\mathscr{A}$ Lombardic palace dating from the 17th century which has, under the direction of the Beni Ambientali (the official body which protects historic buildings), been restored to its former splendour. Now belonging to the Cesano Maderno council, it stands just outside Milan, and is surrounded by a park and a garden in the Italian style.

The 'humble' parts of the palace provide the hotel's accommodation: the old stables have become the entrance hall where old and new are cleverly combined. The rooms and the corridors owe their particular character to the original ceilings, whether these are of the wooden beamed type or painted plaster. The rooms have been furnished with great care to suit their architecture: the wood floors suit this less grand part of the building. The windows open on to green countryside and in every room there is a sense of the natural world outside.

RECOMMENDED IN THE AREA

RESTAURANTS:
Green Pepper, *Seregno;* La Rimessa, *Mariano Comense*

LOCAL SPECIALITIES:
Hand-woven articles at the Bottega de Gegia Bronzini, Cesano Maderno

VISIT:
The gardens of Lombardy's horticultural school, Minoprio; Santo Stefano Oratory, Lentate sul Seveso

Crimea

Where history and tradition meet on Alpine roads

☎ 0343 34343
🖨 0343 35935
viale Pratogiano 116
**23022 CHIAVENNA
(Sondrio)**
Ref map 3, A5
S.S. 36, Colico exit, towards the border, then in the city centre go in the direction of the railway station
36 rooms; £
Credit cards: ☐ ☐ ☐ ☐, bancomat

RECOMMENDED IN THE AREA

RESTAURANTS:
Cenacolo *and* Passerini

LOCAL SPECIALITY:
Crafts using ollare *stone*

VISIT:
Palazzo Vertemate Franchi, Cortinaccio di Pietro; the unpolluted Codera valley; the Maloja pass towards Engandina; Marmitte dei Giganti Park along the River Mera

*C*hiavenna is an ancient Roman town, full of history and tradition, with palaces and highly considered works of art. What is more, the city is in the San Giacomo valley, surrounded by mountains and in a wonderful position of natural beauty. The hotel's elegant building is in a very peaceful area. Rooms are furnished in a happy combination of styles. The bedrooms are attractive, with wooden panelling and ceilings that make them very welcoming and cosy. The restaurant serves local and international specialities, with great care taken in their preparation.

Palù

Charm and tranquillity for those who love mountains

☎ 0342 451142 🖨 0342 451595
✉ hotelpalu@novanet.it
via Roma 22
**23023 CHIESA IN VALMALENCO
(Sondrio)**
Ref map 3, A6
S.S. 36, Sondrio exit, towards Valmalenco
32 rooms; £
Credit cards: ☐ ☐ ☐ ☐, bancomat

RECOMMENDED IN THE AREA

RESTAURANT:
Malenco

LOCAL SPECIALITIES:
Type of patchwork carpet called pezzotti; *wooden objects, and the famous craftsmanship in slate and* ollare *stone;* bitto *and* casera *cheese*

VISIT:
Many different mountain excursions for both beginners and for experts, especially the trip up to Bernina Peak at the top of the mountain

*S*ituated in the middle of the village, in a peaceful area used mainly by skiers and lovers of mountaineering, guests at this hotel can enjoy the charm and peacefulness of the beautiful view, but can also dedicate themselves to sport and physical activity. Various sports facilities include a squash court, gym and sauna. The rooms are simple and furnished in a style which is modern but in keeping with tradition. The large sitting room, with a fire always burning in the hearth, is quiet and well lit while the dining room has a rustic atmosphere. The bedrooms are comfortable and attractive, furnished in the mountain style and all with balcony and large windows.

$\mathcal{T}$re Re

A quiet spot in the centre of Como

☎ 031 265374 📠 031 241349
✉ trere@tin.it
via Boldoni 20
22100 COMO
Ref map 3, B5
A9, Como Sud exit, towards the centre
41 rooms; **££**
Credit cards: 💳 SÌ

The hotel stands in the centre of the city in the vicinity of the Duomo (cathedral), but in a quiet street with very little traffic. The building was long ago a religious house, but over the course of time the historic architecture has made way for more functional design.

The bedrooms have been recently refurbished. They are large and airy, with practical modern furniture made of attractive light cherry wood, parquet flooring, queen-size beds and every modern comfort. The spacious communal rooms still have traces of their historic past and the high vaulted ceilings are decorated with paintings.

The hotel has its own garage.

RECOMMENDED IN THE AREA

RESTAURANTS:
Imbarcadero, Crotto del Lupo *and* Osteria l'angolo
VISIT:
Museum and display dedicated to silk production; tourist trips on Lake Como; the express cable railway to the Brunate slopes

---

$\mathcal{P}$iroscafo

Facing the old port

☎ 030 9141128 📠 030 9912586
✉ piroscaf@tin.it
via Porto Vecchio 11
25015 DESENZANO DEL GARDA
(Brescia)
Ref map 3, C7
A4, Desenzano del Garda exit
32 rooms; **££**
Credit cards: AE 💳 SÌ ⑩, bancomat

RECOMMENDED IN

RESTAURANTS:
Cavallino *and* Il Molino
LOCAL SPECIALITIES:
Trout and other fish from the lake
VISIT:
Caves of Catullo, castle and famous thermal baths, Sirmione; Gardaland Amusement Park, Peschiera; Mincio riviera

$\mathcal{D}$esenzano, on the southern shore of Lake Garda, is not only a busy little tourist town with lots of shops and quite a good night life, it is also full of history and tradition. The hotel is right in the centre of the town, facing the old port and very close to the lake. The building is embellished with an ancient portico, and guests can take their breakfast under the arches there. The entrance hall has a vaulted ceiling made of small rough bricks and the floors are terracotta. The dining room, which is very light because of its large windows, is well furnished in modern style combined with more rustic details, and its rough stone walls make it particularly attractive. The bedrooms, where the white of the walls and furnishings is the predominant colour, are practical and comfortable and have good modern furniture. The restaurant prepares its dishes with great care and enthusiasm.

Piccola Vela

This is a hotel which seems like a home. It owes its particular character to the fact that its dimensions are small and the architecture reminds one of a private house. It is right in the centre of Desenzano, yet almost magically out of normal time because it is off the beaten tourist track. Surrounded by a large park full of olive trees, it is in the midst of greenery and tranquillity.

The interior design makes use of many elegant Art Nouveau details among essentially modern furnishings. All the bedrooms are very well appointed and there is a graceful mix of period furniture and functional modern design. Every now and then a winged armchair, a console table or a little chest of drawers is a charming addition to the scene and, again, adds a homely touch.

There are many peaceful open spaces to be enjoyed with other guests: under the olive trees and around the swimming pool. There are also pleasant communal areas indoors: conversational corners, dining room, bar and meeting rooms.

A hotel that feels like a home, in the traditional style

☎ and ❋ 030 9914666
via Dal Molin 36
25015 DESENZANO DEL GARDA (Brescia)
Ref map 3, C7
A4, Desenzano del Garda exit
43 rooms; **££/£££**
Credit cards: 🇦🇪 💳 🆂 ⓪

RECOMMENDED IN THE AREA

RESTAURANTS:
Esplanade; Al Porto, *Moniga del Garda*

LOCAL SPECIALITY:
Lake Garda extra virgin olive oil

VISIT:
The castle, Roman villa, archaeological museum and cathedral, Desenzano del Garda; the fortified hilltop, Lonato; San Martino Tower in San Martino della Battaglia

Du Lac

In a romantic 1900s house

☎ 0365 71107
🖷 0365 71055
✉ info@hotel-dulac.it
via Colletta 21, località Villa
25084 GARGNANO (Brescia)
Ref map 3, B7
A4, Brescia Est exit, S.S. 45 and
follow the signs for the Porto di Villa
11 rooms; **££**
Credit cards: VISA

A small early 20th-century mansion which is perfectly placed at the foot of the mountain, right by the side of the lake in a charming little village. It is a peaceful spot in the midst of lush green.

The hotel is delightful and has great style. Its interior is adorned with antique furniture, paintings and prints, and everywhere there are examples of elegant taste. The bedrooms are all different sizes and styles but all have antique furniture and wooden beds. Six overlook the lake with balconies or terraces. The bathrooms are very practical.

The hotel has large windows, verandas and a little courtyard garden. There is a parlour with a piano and a bright, pretty dining room that in high season extends on to a balcony overlooking the lake. In summer it is also possible to dine on the large terrace with its panoramic view. The young staff are very welcoming.

RECOMMENDED IN THE AREA

RESTAURANT:
Barrabel

LOCAL SPECIALITIES:
Extra virgin olive oil from the press; lemons grown by the lake; wines from the Brescia area; fish from the lake; craft products using olive wood and ceramics

La Corte

Where everything is deliciously home-made

☎ 031 699690
📠 031 982069-9755990
via Mazzini 20
22040 LURAGO D'ERBA (Como)
Ref map 3, B5
A4, Cinisello Balsamo-Sesto San Giovanni
exit, carry straight on as far as Erba
8 rooms; ££
Credit cards: ⒶⒺ 🆅🅸🆂🅰 🆂🅸 ⑩, bancomat

*T*his charming hotel, which is managed attentively and with great enthusiasm, is in an 18th-century farmhouse with its enclosed courtyard typical of the architecture of the Brianza region. Recent renovation has treated period details with care and has left unaltered the harmonious outlines of the building which blends perfectly with the countryside around. The farmhouse stands in a panoramic position on a hill, overlooking the peaks surrounding Erba and Lecco. Inside the hotel is elegantly rustic, bright and attractive with wooden furniture. The bedrooms are practical and comfortable. The restaurant serves a wide variety of dishes of the Como region together with original recipes, accompanied by a vast selection of vintage wines from the attached *enoteca* cellar. Altogether this is a peaceful corner of the world where there is a happy mix of natural beauty, hospitality and good food and drink.

RECOMMENDED IN THE AREA

RESTAURANTS:
Barchetta, *Como;* Il Cantuccio, *Albavilla*

LOCAL SPECIALITY:
Hand-produced wickerwork

VISIT:
Lakes Alserio, Pusiano and Annone

Villa Schindler

A calm and intimate atmosphere in an old country residence

☎ and 🖷 0365 554877
✉ villaschindler@tin.it
via Bresciani 68
25080 MANERBA DEL GARDA (Brescia)
Ref map 3, C7
A4, Desenzano exit, towards Salò-Riva,
then follow signs for San Felice
8 rooms; **££**
Credit cards not accepted

RECOMMENDED IN THE AREA

RESTAURANTS:
Piccolo Grill *and* Capriccio

LOCAL SPECIALITIES:
Extra virgin olive oil

VISIT:
Sigurtà Park at Valeggio sul Mincio.

*C*amouflaged in thick foliage amidst beautiful countryside and looking out over the gulf of Manerba, the hotel is in an old private villa. Recent restoration work has enriched the building and grounds with many works of art: sundials and sculptures outside, valuable frescoes inside. Bedrooms are practical and attractive, and all have parquet flooring and dark wood furniture. The interior is comfortable and welcoming, with wooden ceilings and panelling, and is furnished in a rustic but elegant style. A splendid terrace overlooks the lake and the mountains around. Guests can relax and also take breakfast here. The large shady garden is ideal for walks and has a swimming pool and a little pond. The restaurant serves local and classic dishes. Olive oil and wine are produced by the owners.

Antica Locanda dei Mercanti

An atmosphere of warmth and attention to detail which gives you the sense of being 'at home'

☎ 02 8054080 🖷 02 8054090
via San Tomaso 6
20123 MILANO (MILAN)
Ref map 3, C5
From the *tangenziale* (by-pass) towards the centre, then follow the signs for the Cairoli/
Castello Sforzesco zone
10 rooms; **£££**
Credit cards: 💳 💳, bancomat

RECOMMENDED IN THE AREA

RESTAURANTS:
Joia, *via Panfilo Castaldi 18;* L'Ulmet, *via Olmetto 21*

VISIT:
Sforzeso Castle, the Duomo *(cathedral), La Scala Opera House and the elegant shops of via della Spiga and Montenapoleone are all within easy walking distance*

*T*here is no special sign, simply the name by the bell, but all the same everyone should know about this charming little hotel. It is in the city centre, in an old 18th-century palace, and it combines tradition and modernity in a perfect way. There are only a few bedrooms, but all of them are well furnished and distinctive. The welcoming atmosphere with such attention paid to detail ensures that the atmosphere is that of an elegant private house. The furnishing of each room, both classical and modern, is always well chosen and blends with that of the rest of the hotel. The bathrooms are practical. The one meal served is an ample breakfast which is served in the bedroom.

$\mathcal{A}$ntica Locanda Leonardo

*T*his hotel is ideal for cultural or commercial visits to Milan. The hotel is in an early 19th-century building near the refectory of the church of Santa Maria delle Grazie. This is the city of Bramante and Leonardo da Vinci, Renaissance Milan with its cobbled streets and charming stone buildings.

The bedrooms of the hotel, or rather inn, are all individual and have stylish antiques. Many of them look on to a little private garden and reflect the colours of the seasons, contributing to the delightful atmosphere of the hotel. The windows give a view of the flowering wisteria during spring and of golden leaves in autumn.

A little haven of peace, just steps from Leonardo's Last Supper

☎ 02 463317 📠 02 48019012
✉ desk@leoloc.com
corso Magenta 78
20123 MILANO (MILAN)
Ref map 3, C5

From the *tangenziale* (by-pass) towards the centre, piazza Cordusio district
14 rooms; **££/£££**
Credit cards: AE VISA SI ①, bancomat

There is a comfortable sitting room and guests receive a courteous welcome.

RECOMMENDED IN THE AREA

RESTAURANTS:
Al Porto, *piazza Cantoren and* La Terrazza di via Palestro, *via Palestro 2*

VISIT:
Leonardo da Vinci Museum of Science and Technology in the former Olivetani Monastery

$\mathcal{A}$ntica Locanda Solferino

*T*his old inn has only a few rooms that must be booked a long time in advance as they are always in demand. It stands in the historic centre of Milan, with its old houses and streets frequented by artists.

Set in the Brera district, a short distance from the Pinacoteca in the same road as the *Corriere della Sera* newspaper, the hotel has tastefully furnished bedrooms that are made particularly attractive by the attention to detail.. The bathrooms are very practical.

The service is good, with newspapers provided each morning with breakfast which is served in the bedrooms .

In the historic and cultural centre of Milan

☎ 02 6570129 📠 02 6571361
via Castelfidardo 2
20121 MILANO (MILAN)
Ref map 3, C5

From the *tangenziale* (by-pass), go towards the centre, Brera district
11 rooms; **£££**
Credit cards: AE VISA SI

RECOMMENDED IN THE AREA

RESTAURANTS:
Torre di Pisa, *via Fiori Chiari 21*, Rigolo, *via Solferino 11, and* Osteria del Cinima, *via Solferino*

$\mathcal{A}$riosto

A refined tradition of hospitality in an elegant residential district

☎ 02 4817844
🖷 02 4980516
via Ariosto 22
20145 MILANO (MILAN)
Ref map 3, C5
From the *tangenziale* (by-pass), go towards the centre, parco Sempione district
53 rooms; **££/£££**
Credit cards: AE VISA SI Ⓞ

This hotel is situated in a residential district, a short distance from the *Fiera* (exhibition centre) and not far from the historic centre of Milan. It is in a building that dates from 1910 with an elegant façade marked out with windows and lovely railings. The decorations, vaults and balustrades are all executed in Art Nouveau style. They have been emphasised by recent refurbishment that has cleverly maintained the original features while adding convenient, practical services to make this a comfortable place to stay.

The reasonable-sized bedrooms have high ceilings and are furnished with elegant modern pieces. The sitting rooms are simple and well furnished, and the communal areas have a striking marble staircase that goes up to the upper floors. The rails of the staircase are elegant wrought-iron with decorative flower and scroll designs.

The old wine cellars have been transformed into a small additional meetings room, with original vaulted ceilings.

RECOMMENDED IN THE AREA

RESTAURANTS:
Altra Pharmacia, *via Rosmini 3, and* Boccondivino, *via Carducci 17*

$\mathcal{A}$riston

A pioneer ecologically-friendly hotel

☎ 02 72000556
🖷 02 72000914
largo Carrobbio 2
20123 MILANO (MILAN)
Ref map 3, C5
From the *tangenziale* (by-pass), go towards the centre, behind via Torino
48 rooms; **££/£££**
Credit cards: AE VISA SI Ⓞ, bancomat

RECOMMENDED IN THE AREA

RESTAURANTS:
All Collina Pistoiese, *via Amedei 1, and* L'Infinito, *via Leopardi 25*

VISIT:
Church of Santa Maria presso San Satiro

This hotel is an unusual combination, for it embodies respect for the environment and yet is right in the centre of Milan. The little mansion that houses it was restructured a few years ago in accordance with the criteria of 'bio-architecture'. The building materials used have given the building an elegant, simple appearance. Care has been taken over every tiny detail, not only to maintain the environmental theme but also to give the guests a comfortable and welcoming stay.

The furnishings, fabrics, paint and glue used are all made of natural non-toxic materials. All the attractive bedrooms are equipped with air purifiers that constantly freshen the air. There are also complimentary bicycles available.

Gala

*T*he 19th-century style mansion that houses this hotel is surrounded by trees and plants and has flowers at all the windows, yet it is only five minutes from the centre of the city. Its location makes it an ideal hotel for those who want to be close to the *Fiera* (exhibition centre), the city centre and all the major motorway junctions.

A big private car park enables guests to leave their cars and travel round the centre unencumbered. The bedrooms are large and elegantly furnished with wrought-iron beds and light-coloured curtains. The dining room is small but attractive and has an elegant style in keeping with the rest of the hotel.

A few minutes from the centre of Milan and the Fiera *(exhibition centre)*

☎ 02 66800891
🖷 02 66800463
viale Zara 89/91
20159 MILANO (MILAN)
Ref map 3, C5
From the *tangenziale* (by-pass), go towards the centre, piazzale Lagosta area
23 rooms; **££**
Credit cards: AE VISA SI ①

RECOMMENDED IN THE AREA

RESTAURANTS:
A'Riccione, *via Taramelli 70, and* Tre Pini, *via T. Morgagni 19*

VISIT:
Villa Simonetta, via Stilicone 36, which houses the Civic School of Music

---

Florence

In a small Art Nouveau mansion

☎ 02 2361125 🖷 02 26680911
📧 mabula@tin.it
piazza Aspromonte 22
20131 MILANO (MILAN)
Ref map 3, C5
From the *tangenziale* (by-pass) towards the centre, piazzale Loreto area
30 rooms; **£/££**
Credit cards: AE VISA SI ①

*T*he large piazza is flanked by trees and small gracious buildings dating from the beginning of the 20th century. These miraculously escaped destruction during World War II.

The hotel is in two small Art Nouveau style mansions that have been made into one building as the result of recent restructuring work. They were residential houses and still preserve some original details that give character to the accommodation.

The bedrooms are quite big, the furniture is of light wood and is uninspiring but very new. The bathrooms are practical and some have been refurbished. There is a small reception hall and a simple, bright breakfast room. The hotel management is very much in the family style.

RECOMMENDED IN THE AREA

RESTAURANTS:
Trattoria del Nuovo Macello, *via Lombroso 20, and* Capanna, *via Donatello 9*

VISIT:
Aristocratic mansions on corso di porta Venezia, including Silvestri House and Sebelloni Palace

$\mathcal{L}$iberty

An elegant hotel a few steps away from the University of Bocconi

☎ 02 58318562 🖷 02 58319061
viale Bligny 56
20136 MILANO (MILAN)
Ref map 3, C5
From the *tangenziale* (by-pass), go towards the centre, porto Romana area
52 rooms, 3 suite; ££/£££
Credit cards: AE VISA SI

$\mathcal{T}$his hotel is situated in the centre of Milan, within the old ring of Spanish walls, near to the University of Bocconi. It is in a typical 19th-century mansion. The lovely building has the harmonious proportions of period constructions and, following recent refurbishment, can offer practical and high-quality accommodation.

The furnishing is elegant and careful. The bedrooms have modern furniture with fitted carpets and matching upholstery. They are comfortable and have a relaxing atmosphere. In the sitting rooms the light filters through the Art Nouveau windows and enhances the colours of the marble and carpets. Everywhere there are peaceful corners in which to relax, with well-designed furniture and English-style armchairs. A small garden adds grace and colour. The hotel also has a private garage.

RECOMMENDED IN THE AREA

RESTAURANT:
Sadler, *via Conchetta*

VISIT:
Basilica of San Lorenzo Maggiore; the Portinari chapel within the basilica of Sant' Eustorgio

$\mathcal{R}$egency

$\mathcal{T}$his is one of the most charming hotels in Milan with its perfect combination of style and good taste. The refined old mansion is a splendid building in the *Coppedè* style from the early years of the 20th century, and is located in a lovely residential area a few minutes away from the *Fiera* (exhibition centre) and access to the motorways.

The bedrooms have decorative floral wallpaper and are furnished in a pleasing original manner. The interior of the hotel is very elegant, welcoming and full of atmosphere. The reception is spacious and very comfortable, and the light of the table lamps mingles perfectly with that from the skylights set in the panelled wooden ceiling. The restaurant is tastefully furnished.

Peace, charm and atmosphere even in the middle of a major city

☎ 02 39216021 🖷 02 39217734
📧 regency@virtualia.it
via G. Arimondi 12
20155 MILANO (MILAN)
Ref map 3, C5
A1, west *tangenziale* (by-pass), Milano Certosa exit
59 rooms; ££
Credit cards: AE SI ⓄⒹ

RECOMMENDED IN THE AREA

RESTAURANTS:
Innocenti evasioni, *via della Bindellina, and* Bistro Duomo, *via san Raffaele 2*

*S*an Francisco

An elegant mansion and an unusual, luxuriant garden

☎ 02 2360302 📠 02 26680377
📧 h.s.francisco@hotel-sanfrancisco.it
viale Lombardia 55
20131 MILANO (MILAN)
Ref map 3, C5
From the *tangenziale* (by-pass), go towards the centre, piazzale Piola area
31 rooms; £/££
Credit cards: AE VISA SI ⑩

*S*et in a lovely tree-lined avenue, the elegant mansion housing this hotel is ten minutes from the centre, the station and from the main motorway junctions.

The hotel is attractive and welcoming. All the rooms are simply furnished. A spacious garden full of lush foliage, a true rarity amongst Milanese hotels, is the ideal place for taking breakfast during the summer and for spending free time relaxing. The bedrooms are comfortable with basic furnishing of simple modern wood. Of particular prominence are the large windows which have a view of the really lovely garden and add an airy coolness to the pale-coloured walls.

RECOMMENDED IN THE AREA

RESTAURANTS:
La Fattoria del Seiperseo, *via A. Maffei 12,* and Peppino, *via Durini 7*

---

*S*anpi

*T*he initials of the proprietors' names have been joined together to make an unusual and original name for this hotel, playfully implying the tasteful and well-designed nature of the place.

The hotel is situated between the station and the centre and is in a pleasing, well-presented building built around an old construction. The bedrooms have modern, elegant furniture in olive green. The sitting rooms are very welcoming and full of comfortable sofas arranged in secluded corners.

The bar has a large window giving a view of the garden. In the garden itself there is unexpected evidence of former times, for there is a small building that once was a gatekeeper's lodge. It is a reminder of when, at the beginning of the 20th century, a now forgotten railway passed by here. This lodge has been transformed into an annexe retaining the character of the original and containing a few elegant bedrooms. It is painted in bright colours and has cheerful green blinds.

RECOMMENDED IN THE AREA

RESTAURANTS:
Corso Como Caffè, *corso Como 10*

A secluded, comfortable atmosphere

☎ 02 29513341
📠 02 29402451
📧 hotelsanpimilano@traveleurope.it
via Lazzaro Palazzi 18
20124 MILANO
Ref map 3, C5
From the *tangenziale* (by-pass) towards the centre, piazza della Repubblica area
63 rooms; ££/£££
Credit cards: AE VISA SI ⑩, bancomat

Stube

Character and tranquillity in the most traditional Alpine countryside

☎ 036 4590100
via Fane 12
25050 PIAN CAMUNO (Brescia)
Ref map 3, B8
A4, Brescia Ovest, towards Boario Terme
9 rooms; £/££
Credit cards: AE VISA SI, bancomat

RECOMMENDED IN THE AREA

RESTAURANTS:
Landò, *Boario;*
Sant' Antonio, *Lovere*

VISIT:
*Valcamonica Archaeological Museum,
Cividate Camuno; Santa Maria in
Valvendra Basilica, Lovere*

The first impression of this chalet house is one of welcoming charm and typical mountain architecture. There are few bedrooms, all simple and hospitable, and a restaurant that is just as inviting.

Outside the wood, which covers nearly every part of the building, is particularly finely worked. Inside the hotel wood is also much used in the decoration and this gives it a charmingly restful appearance.

On the ground floor the restaurant is both heated and adorned by a big majolica stove: the cooking is of the region and includes mushrooms, game and home-made pasta.

Il Leone

A 16th-century palace in Gonzaga territory

☎ 0375 86077/0375 86145
🖷 0375 86770
piazza IV Martiri 2
46030 POMPONESCO (Mantova)
Ref map 3, A7
A1, Parma exit, approaching from the
circonvallazione (ring road) take the
S.S. 62 towards Brescello-Viadana
8 rooms; **££**
Credit cards: AE VISA SI ①, bancomat

RECOMMENDED IN THE AREA

RESTAURANT:
Nizzoli, *Dosolo*

LOCAL SPECIALITIES:
Viadanese salami; ciccioli *(a boiled pork dish);* Gran
Padano *cheese of the Parmesan type; Viadanese pickle*

VISIT:
The little town of Sabbioneta; Parma and Mantua;
trips along the banks of the River Po

History and tradition are both the foundations and the fabric of this lovely 16th-century building which is situated close to the banks of the River Po and the historic centre of Pomponesco. The real heart of the building is the dining room. This has a wonderful panelled ceiling and walls decorated with very precious frescoes. The tables and chairs are in the traditional elegant style, and valuable paintings and prints contribute to the refined atmosphere. The quiet, comfortable bedrooms are furnished stylishly and practically. For relaxation there is the large walled courtyard with herb gardens and a swimming pool. The restaurant has used 19th-century recipes to reproduce the traditional cooking of the Po region. There is a very good and extensive wine list.

Al Duca

RECOMMENDED IN THE AREA

RESTAURANT:
Parco Cappuccini

VISIT:
Bibbiena church at Villa Pasquali; town walls
at Bozzolo

Sabbioneta, on the Mantuan plain, is one of the most interesting examples of urban layout of the Renaissance period. Right in the centre of the typical road grid, within the octagonal walls, is the hotel. The splendid 16th-century façade of this little mansion is perfectly complemented by the attractive and relaxing interior. Thoughtful family management gives a sense of local tradition in a fairly informal way. The hotel is run admirably and offers ideal space for anyone who is looking for relaxation and quiet. The bedrooms, all of which are large and very comfortable, are furnished in a practical and simple style. The hotel's restaurant is also run in a friendly and homely manner, and serves specialities of Mantuan cooking, most noteworthy of which are *tortelli di zucca* (pasta with a pumpkin and almond filling).

In a noble Renaissance palace at Sabbioneta

☎ 0375 52474 🖷 0375 220021
via della Stamperia 18
46018 SABBIONETA (Mantova)
Ref map 3, A7
A1, Parma exit, then S.S. 343
towards Colomo-Casalmaggiore
10 rooms; **£**
Credit cards: AE VISA SI

Villa Kinzika

*With a large garden,
opposite the lake*

☎ 030 9820975
📠 030 9820990
✉ snerett@tin.it
via Provinciale 1
25057 SALE MARASINO (Brescia)
Ref map 3, B6

A4, Rovato exit, go on in the direction of
Lake Iseo , then follow the signs for val
Camonica
18 rooms; ££
Credit cards: AE VISA SI OO, bancomat

Surrounded by the luxuriant green of a large
garden full of olive trees, the hotel is situated in a
very quiet spot on the shore of the lake in one of the
most charming corners of the Franciacorte region. The
drawing room with its fireplace and the reading room
are both welcoming and tastefully decorated with
elegant furniture, paintings and decorations on the
walls, valuable carpets and large windows. There are
lake views from every bedroom and from nearly
everywhere else in the hotel. The breakfast room and
the American bar are both attractive and welcoming
places to linger and relax.

RECOMMENDED IN THE AREA

RESTAURANTS:
Le Palafitte; Punta-Da Dino, *Iseo*

LOCAL SPECIALITIES:
Wines from the Franciacorte region; tinca al forno *and*
casoncelli, *goat's meat prepared in the style of Brescia*

VISIT:
Rodengo Saiano Abbey and the Piramidi *Zone*

Il Bagnolo

*The taste of simple, mouth-watering
food*

☎ and 📠 0365 20290
☎ 0365 21877
✉ jafpa@tin.it
località Bagnolo di Serniga
25087 SALÒ (Brescia)
Ref map 3, C7

A4C, Brescia Est exit, towards Salò,
S.S. Gardesana and follow the signs for
agriturismo Il Bagnolo
9 rooms; ££
Credit cards: AE VISA SI, bancomat

This hotel is set in 25 hectares of fields and woods,
in an area known for its natural beauty.
Accommodation is in an elegant modern building with
sloping roofs, large windows, many architectural
features in wood and a panoramic view of the lake. The
bedrooms are carefully furnished with floral fabric for
the upholstery and hangings and canopied iron beds.
The public rooms have a characteristic country feel with
their use of wood, checked tablecloths, antique
furniture and a welcoming atmosphere. In the hotel
grounds there is a little church, dating from 1600, which
has been completely renovated. Bicycles are available,
and there is also a riding school. Maps are provided for
the many walks in the area.

RECOMMENDED IN THE AREA

RESTAURANTS:
Alla Campagnola, *Salò;* Oscar, *Lonato*

WINE CELLARS:
Enoteca Berealto, *viale Europa 2, Salò;*
Cantina Santa Giustina, *Cunettone*

VISIT:
Hruska Botanic Garden, Villa Alba and the Duomo
(cathedral) at Salò

Dogana

18th-century origin. The building is indeed historic and was built in the first decades of that century.

First it was used as a barracks at the time of the Austro-Hungarian Empire. Then it was transformed into a customs house. Recent renovation has respected its original association and has also enhanced the elegant harmony of the building. It stands in a secluded position very close to a luxuriant park, and the hospitality offered is ideal for anyone looking for a relaxing holiday or brief stay, or else as a starting point for outings and gastronomic trips in the surrounding region.

The hotel is family run, tried and tested by 30 years of experience, and manages to create an atmosphere that is informal, friendly and welcoming. The rooms are spacious, well lit and tastefully decorated. Bedrooms are simple and elegant and nearly all of them look out on to the lake. The restaurant serves typical dishes of the Lombary/Veneto region and great care is taken over their preparation.

*T*his little town, which is dominated by a large fortress, is famous as a health resort with waters springing up from the bottom of the lake 18 metres down and also as the home of the Roman poet, Catullus. The hotel's façade, with elegant windows at regular intervals, is overhung by a tympanum in light colours which reveal its

---

An informal and welcoming atmosphere in an old barracks

☎ 030 919026 📠 030 9196066
✉ dogana@gardanet.it
Ref map 3, C7
via Verona 149, località Lugana
25019 SIRMIONE (Brescia)
A4, Peschiera exit, then S.S. 11, Sirmione
29 rooms; ££
Credit cards: AE VISA SI ⓞ

RECOMMENDED IN THE AREA

RESTAURANTS:
Trattoiral Antica Contrada; Vecchia Lugana, *Lugana;* Veliero, *Desenzano*

LOCAL SPECIALITIES:
Local Lugano and Bardolino wines; olive oil . It is possible to visit wine cellars and oil producers and sample their products

VISIT:
Grotte di Catullo, where the archaeological zone includes the ruins of a Roman villa; San Martino della Battaglia tower; Il Vittoriale and Gabriele D'Annuncio's house, Gardone Riviera

La Paül

The enchantment of the lake in a little city praised by Catullus

☎ 030 916077 📠 030 9905505 ✉ hotellapaul@numerica.it
via XXV Aprile 26
25019 SIRMIONE (Brescia)
Ref map 3, C7
A4, Sirmione exit
Rooms 42 (La Paül), 20 (Smeraldo); **£/££**
Credit cards: AE VISA SI OD, bancomat

*T*his was where patrician Romans came to spend their holidays, here lived Catullus who loved the gentle climate and the delightful countryside, and this was the strategic position of the Scaligera fleet of which the 200-year-old fortress is a reminder. Tourists can benefit from much history and many archaeological finds which can still be seen today and which enhance the beauty of the countryside and the interest of the places around. It is a good idea to plan for a reasonable length of stay in order to appreciate everything fully.

On the lake, along the road closed to traffic leading to the Scaliger castle, stand the hotels La Paul and Smeraldo. These two buildings are separate but near each other and have been run by the same family for generations with great care to make guests feel welcome.

The hotels are by the lake but only a short walk from the historic centre. They are modern, constructed in the 1950s, and have been renovated a number of times. The last refurbishment in 1995 involved the hotel La Paül which has large, modern, well-furnished rooms with balconies. Here there is also a private beach complete with a landing stage.

Guests can hire boats, oars and bicycles.

Smeraldo

Hotel Smeraldo offers the same quality of service as La Paül. In addition to the private beach there is a covered swimming pool and an area reserved for children with games and activities especially for them.

The hotel has welcoming lounges with big windows that allow visitors to continue enjoying the panoramic view from inside.

The cooking is very good, and many of the ingredients used come from the local countryside. The family that owns the hotels offers guests an attentive and friendly welcome.

RECOMMENDED IN THE AREA

RESTAURANTS:
La Rucola *and* Vecchia Lugana*;*
Hostaria Viola*, Castiglione delle Stiviere*

WINE CELLARS:
Provenza, *Desenzano*

VISIT:
Church of San Pancrazio, Montichiari; museum of history, Solferino; Battaglia Museum, San Martino

*A*griturismo
Le Sorgive & Le Volpi

*F*irst class *agriturismo* (farm with accommodation) complex within an elegant 19th-century farmhouse, with porticoes and pigeon-lofts, which has recently been refurbished. It is not unusual to see horses grazing freely in the open spaces of the delightful hilly countryside around. The rooms are rich in rural atmosphere, with fires always burning in the hearths during the winter and rustic furnishing which makes them attractive and welcoming. The dining room is light thanks to the large windows on three sides and it has a wooden ceiling and terracotta floor. The bedrooms are spacious and tastefully decorated, with wrought iron beds and rustic furniture. The restaurant offers regional dishes, especially the famous Mantuan sausages and local salami. The wine produced locally is also of very good quality.

Encounter the land of Mantua in unspoilt countryside

☎ 0376 854252/0376 54028
📠 0376 855256
✉ sorgive@gvnet.it
via Piridello 6
46040 SOLFERINO (Mantova)
Ref map A3, C7
A4, Desenzano exit, towards Castiglione-Solferino
8 rooms, 2 apartments; **££**
Credit cards: AE VISA SI ⓪

RECOMMENDED IN THE AREA

RESTAURANT:
Tomasi, *Castiglione delle stiviere*

LOCAL SPECIALITIES:
Organic products of the agriturismo *complex: wine, salami, honey, jam and cheese*

VISIT:
The medieval villages of the Morainal hills; Valtenese castles

Della Torre

The hotel abuts one of the most important monuments of Trescore, an old 14th-century tower made of rough stone which once housed the market for products from the entire valley. The hotel building is attractive, with large windows and balconies, and is situated in the animated centre of the little spa town. Inside it is furnished elegantly and the atmosphere is both lively and relaxing. Guests can happily devote themselves to reading or to conversation as they wait for dinner in the drawing room where a fire is always burning in the hearth during the winter. In summertime they can have breakfast under the pergola or in the garden. The bedrooms are modern and comfortable, with simple furniture and fitted carpets. The restaurant is managed with great skill and offers local gastronomic specialities combined with some international touches.

A centuries-old tradition of hospitality

☎ and 🖷 035 941365
📧 info@albergotorre.it
piazza Cavour 26-28
24069 TRESCORE BALNEARIO (Bergamo)
Ref map 3, B6
A4, Bergamo exit, take the new *tangenziale sud* (southern by-pass) or else the S.S. 42 towards Lovere
29 rooms; **££**
Credit cards: AE VISA SI ⓄⒹ, bancomat

RECOMMENDED IN THE AREA

RESTAURANT:
Antica Trattoria Balicco

VISIT:
Church of Santa Barbara; Villa Terzi, Cantore suburb; Cavallina valley and Lake Endine

Stella d'Italia

An 'historic little world' on the shores of Lake Lugano

☎ 0344 68139 🖷 0344 68729
📧 stelladitalia@mclink.it
piazza Roma 1, località San Mamete
22010 VALSOLDA (Como)
Ref map 3, B5
A9, Como exit, follow the signs for Menaggio, Porlezza, Valsolda
35 rooms; **££/£££**
Credit cards: AE VISA SI

This area owes its charm to the beauty of the lake, the tranquil view, and the garland of mountains around, together with small villages, groups of houses, little hamlets of charming old houses that climb up the slopes from the shores of the lake. There is nothing to spoil the magic here.

In a typical example of such a hamlet, right on the lake, is an old 18th-century villa which has been well refurbished and offers accommodation in lovely rooms, some with a balcony and superb views. Across the garden surrounding the villa is a private beach where the rowing boats bobbing on the water are for the use of guests.

In high season the hotel's restaurant serves romantic meals outside (also to non-residents) on a terrace overlooking the lake and underneath a pergola.

RECOMMENDED IN THE AREA

RESTAURANTS:
Chez Mario, *Menaggio;* Mella, *Bellagio;* Al Veluu, *Tremezzo*

VISIT:
Lake Como (Bellagio, Varenna, Villa Carlotta); Lugano and the Ticino River; Valsolda churches

$\mathcal{D}$u Lac

An historic and romantic villa which rises up out of the water

☎ 0341 830238
🖷 0341 831081
via del Prestino 4
23829 VARENNA (Lecco)
Ref map 3, B5
Coming from Milan, S.S. 36, Varenna exit
18 rooms; **££/£££**
Credit cards: AE VISA SI, bancomat

*T*his historic and romantic villa preserves the architectural form typical of medieval Varenna and is still called 'Teodolinda house' because, according to legend, the Lombard queen used to come here and rest during the summer. In 1823 a house was built on the old foundations and at the beginning of the 20th century this became the property of an English family. Transformed into a hotel in 1950, the bedrooms open out on to the lake with terraces and balconies. They are large and bright with modern furnishings. The drawing rooms are attractive and welcoming. The restaurant is on the side of the hotel which looks on to the Piazza della Chiesa, also accessible from the lake by means of a private landing stage. In the summer meals are served on the terrace facing the lake.

RECOMMENDED IN THE AREA

RESTAURANTS:
Locanda dell'Isola comacina, *Varenna;* Il Griso, *Malgrate*

LOCAL SPECIALITIES:
Valtellina dishes: bresaola *(a kind of dried salted beef);* pizzoccheri *fish from the lake; rice and perch cooked Como style; whitefish with sage; carpe with shad fish*

VISIT:
Villa Monastero gardens and Villa Cipresi, Varenna; Villa Sebelloni and Villa Melzi, Bellagio; Villa Carlotta, Cadenabbia

$\mathcal{V}$ecchia Riva

On the banks of a romantic lake

☎ 0332 329335 🖷 0332 329300
via Giovanni Macchi 146
località Schiranna
21100 VARESE
Ref map 2, B4
A8, Buguggiate-Azzate exit,
the follow the signs for Schiranna
11 rooms; **£**
Credit cards: AE VISA SI ⓪

*T*he shore of Varese lake where the hotel is situated is a charmingly romantic place, which enjoys beautiful sunsets. The scenery around almost seems to be part of the old country house hotel that is enclosed by trees and gardens.

Recent refurbishment has left the outside unchanged, but has given a modern appearance to the interior. The reception hall and the restaurant are spacious and light thanks to large windows. The bedrooms all have very modern bathrooms and are simple in style with pale walls and fitted carpets. The restaurant is particularly noted for its *antipasti* (appetisers), of which it has about 50 different kinds every evening, and for the good quality of its meat.

RECOMMENDED IN THE AREA

RESTAURANTS:
Lago Maggiore *and* Da Vittorio

LOCAL SPECIALITIES:
Peaches in syrup from Monate; cheese from Val Cuvia

VISIT:
Campo dei Fiori astronomical observatory; San Vittore Basilica; San Giovani Baptistery, Varese

Trentino-Alto Adige

Here there are hillsides of green meadows, little villages on the slopes of each valley, with pointed spires or the 'onions' of baroque bell towers, castles, vineyards, orchards and vast fir woods. And there are pools, grassland plateaux, peaks that turn rose and purple at sunset. This is one of the most welcoming and well-organised regions for those who love the countryside, the open air and sport. It boasts a spectacular system of ski lifts and ski slopes, a constellation of nature reserves and parks (Stelvio, Brenta and Admello), and a tradition of hospitality.

Trentino is crossed by numerous valleys. These start from the Adige valley – from Ala through the Venosta valley as far as the springs in the area of the Resia pass. To the west there is the Noce valley, to the east the Isarco valley with Rienza (Pusteria, Aurina, Badia and Gardena valleys) and Avisio (Fassa, Gemme and Cembra valleys). Then there is Valsugana, the high Brenta valley to the east and the Sarca valley to the west.

Mountains, plateaux and holiday resorts have names that are immediately evocative. History, culture, art and atmosphere are intimately connected with the multilingual and multi-ethnic (Italian, Tyrolean and Ladin) nature of this frontier area between the Italian and the Germanic worlds, between Habsburg middle Europe and the 'South'. The cities of art are Trent, Merano and Bressanone, where early medieval, Romanesque, Gothic and baroque treasures are scattered in churches and castles. Hospitality has an Alpine flavour and charm: old post stations and inns with wooden exteriors, sloping roofs, fretworked balconies, flowers, painted walls, furnishings in the warm mountain style and stove rooms. And all is surrounded by enchanting countryside.

The village of Corte Chiesa in the Marebbe valley

$\mathcal{S}$erena

*Silence and greenery with the Dolomite
mountains the background*

☎ 0461 585727 📠 0461 585702
📧 hotel.serena@interline.it
via Crosare 15
38010 ANDALO (Trento)
Ref map 4, C3
A22, Trento Centro exit, S.S. 12 to San Michele
all'Adige, S.S. 43 to Mezzolombardo, then left
for Andalo
39 rooms; £
Credit card: AE VISA SI ⓄⒹ, bancomat

*T*he modern but traditional-style building stands in a wide-open sunny space a short distance from the ski lifts and from the centre of Andalo. It is surrounded by a panorama of woods dominated by the Paganella massif. The hotel is run pleasantly by a family with a strong sense of hospitality. The bedrooms are all carefully decorated in the rustic style with light wood furniture chosen to fit the dimensions of each. The bathrooms are very practical and all have a window.

There are many communal areas, beginning with the dining room. This is heated by a large majolica stove and adorned with large wooden beams and with windows which open on to the countryside. The sitting rooms are light and airy, and there is a spacious and welcoming children's play area with lots of games. For adults there is a room for dancing and socializing. Putting the finishing touch to the facilities are a garden and a solarium terrace that allow guests to enjoy the natural world around.

RECOMMENDED IN THE AREA

RESTAURANTS:
Caminetto, *Molveno;* Cacciatora,
Mezzocorona; Sole, *Mezzolombardo*

VISIT:
*Adamello-Brenta Nature Park, brown
bear reserve and Castel Belfort,
Spormaggiore*

*G*ran Ander

Deep in the countryside with particularly fine cooking

☎ 0471 839741 📠 0471 839741
✉ granander@altabadia.it
via Runcac 29, località Pedraces
39036 BADIA (Bolzano)
Ref map 4, B4

A22, Chiusa (Val Gardena) exit, S.S. 242d as far as Selva di Val Gardena, then S.S. 243 as far as Corvara and S.S. 244
29 rooms; £/£££
Credit card: VISA SI

RECOMMENDED IN THE AREA

RESTAURANTS:
L'Fanà, *La Villa;* La Siriola, *San Cassiano*

LOCAL SPECIALITIES:
Fabrics, ceramics and sculpture in wood

VISIT:
Púez-Odle and Fânes-Sénnes-Bráies nature parks

A large modern chalet hotel adorned with lots of wood, the building has been recently refurbished. The bedrooms are large and light with bright cotton fabrics and light wood furniture, mouldings which brings to mind the 1900s era.

The sitting rooms are decorated with some period furniture and open on to a well-equipped terrace where breakfast is served and where barbecues are prepared. The hotel is family run, and the man of the house is personally responsible for the kitchen. The Tyrolean *Stube* (stove) room is characteristically welcoming and serves typical dishes of the region. Table tennis and bicycling add to the diversions available. Gran Ander was a finalist in the 'Hotel of the Year' award in 1996.

*T*aela

A relaxing stay between emerald green fields and impressive mountains

☎ 0471 849301 📠 0471 849340
✉ taela@interpromotion.com
via Costadedoi 69, località San Cassiano
39030 BADIA (Bolzano)
Ref map 4, B4

A22, Chiusa (Val Gardena) exit, S.S. 242d as far as Selva di Val Gardena, then S.S. 243 towards San Cassiano
4 apartments; £/£££
Credit cards not accepted

RECOMMENDED IN THE AREA

RESTAURANT:
St. Hubertus

LOCAL SPECIALITY:
Wooden sculpture

VISIT:
The old Santa Croce Sanctuary, 2,000 metres up, and the nearby inn with the same name under the Ciaval still higher up the mountain

*T*his is a pleasing modern building in the traditional style surrounded by verdant countryside and fields.

Accommodation consists of apartments to suit from two to six people. These are tastefully furnished and provide every comfort. The location is quiet and sunny, with a panoramic view over Villa and San Cassiano. Around the building are large green spaces where guests can take the sun, and safe and well-equipped places for children to play. During the summer guests can go on cycling or walking excursions in the vicinity of the hotel, accompanied by expert guides. In the winter, besides cross-country and Alpine skiing, again accompanied by guides, there are trips to make using snow-shoes.

The minimum length of stay is a week.

Due Spade

A hotel with a centuries-old tradition and renowned cuisine

☎ and 🖷 0461 723113
piazza Municipio 2
38052 CALDONAZZO (Trento)
Ref map 4, C3-4
A22, Trento Centro exit, then go on in a southerly direction on the S.S. 349
24 rooms; £
Credit card: VISA SÌ

A pleasingly small and simple building, this hotel with a very long tradition of hospitality stands in the centre of Caldonazzo. Guests are received on the flower-filled terrace of the hotel. Each bedroom is different: those in the attic have beamed wooden ceilings and rustic furniture; others are furnished in modern style and are different but always elegant, welcoming and with colourful bedspreads. Bathrooms are large and practical.

The sitting rooms, bar, restaurant and breakfast room are all furnished simply but, again, with details such as flower arrangements, period furniture and pastel colours which make them comfortable and attractive. The little reception hall gives on to a well-equipped veranda, and from there to the garden with swimming pool. The lake and its sporting activities are one kilometre away and can be reached by bus from a stop very close to the hotel.

RECOMMENDED IN THE AREA

RESTAURANT:
T. Boivin, *Levico*

VISIT:
The lakes of Caldonazzo and Lévico; the Dolomites at Brenta

Romantik Hotel Stafler

☎ 0472 771136
📠 0472 771094
✉ stafler@acs.it

Mules 10, località Mules

39040 CAMPO DI TRENS (Bolzano)

Ref map 4, A4

A22, Bressanone exit, then S.S. 12 towards Vipiteno, before Campo di Trens turn right for Mules

38 rooms, 2 apartments; **££/£££**

Credit card: 💳 VISA SI, bancomat

*T*his hotel was originally built around 1270 as a posthouse, then in 1738 it was transformed into the *All'Unicorno* inn and has provided travellers with hospitality ever since. Over the course of time the type of accommodation and the standards of comfort have changed, but affection for tradition has meant that the nature of the building has never altered. For this reason, even today, architectural details bear witness to its historic origins.

Rustically beautiful on the outside, the building inside lives up to all expectations. This is true for the well appointed, attractive rooms just as it is for the sitting rooms adorned with antique Tyrolean furniture, with lovely chests and painted 19th-century cupboards or with humbler objects from the wool-winder to the cradle. All these things have their own long history. Particularly charming is the *Stube* (stove room) where decorations and precious furnishings create a very intimate atmosphere.

RECOMMENDED IN THE AREA

RESTAURANTS:
Pichler, *Rio de Pusteria*; Kleine Flamme, *Vipiteno*

VISIT:
Pusteria valley with the towns of Brunico, Dobbiaco, San Candido and Sesto

Cavallino d'Oro

Six hundred years of tradition at the sign of hospitality

☎ 0471 706337 📠 0471 707172
✉ cavallino@cavallino.it
piazza Kraus 1
39040 CASTELROTTO
(Bolzano)
Ref map 4, B4
A22, Bolzano Nord exit,
towards Prato Isarco
20 rooms; **£/££/£££**
Credit card: AE VISA SI ⓪,
bancomat

An ancient inn that even today continues to be a meeting point for visitors and locals. The period building, with its decorative paintings on the façade, stands on the historic piazza Castelrotto. The hotel has been restored with great care and the interior has been enriched with Tyrolean ornaments and antique objects. Inside it is full of atmosphere. There are romantic bedrooms with canopied beds and pretty painted furniture, corridors and communal rooms with antique chests and decorated doors. A *carte* restaurant and two intimate *Stube* (stove rooms) add the finishing touches. The physical wellbeing of the guests is also catered for with a Finnish sauna, Turkish bath and a solarium. The hotel has its own private ski school.

RECOMMENDED IN THE AREA

RESTAURANT:
Waldruhe, *Laion*

VISIT:
The Siusi Alp; historic centre of Bressanone; Novacella Abbey

Villa Kassewalder

A family-run chalet in the delightful valley of Pusteria

☎ 0474 972211 ✉ apcracco@welt.it
via Alemagna 8
località Dobbiaco Nuovo
39034 DOBBIACO (Bolzano)
Ref map 5, B5
A22, Bressanone exit, S.S. 49, before
Dobbiaco turn right towards Cortina
4 rooms; **£/££**
Credit cards not accepted

This is a very pretty house dating from the beginning of the 20th century and surrounded by trees. It has been completely refurbished and is extremely attractive inside, with period furniture, country-style fabrics in bright colours and the welcoming warmth of fireplaces and big majolica stoves. Each bedroom is named after a flower – rhododendron, arnica, gentian and forget-me-not – and the colours of the furnishings and linen match these, being red, yellow, dark blue and pale blue.

All the bedrooms are tastefully furnished and some have attic-style ceilings, creating a lovely contrast between the white plaster and the warm tones of the wood and the furnishings. Guests have the use of the welcoming *taverna* bar and a large, well-kept garden. There is a minimum stay of three nights.

RECOMMENDED IN THE AREA

RESTAURANT:
Gratschwirt

LOCAL SPECIALITIES:
Hand-woven carpets, hand-carved wooden items, speck *(smoked, cured ham) and various salamis*

VISIT:
Baroque church at Dobbiaco; Romanesque church at Candido; the lakes of Dobbiaco and Bráies

$\mathcal{D}$er Punthof

A place full of tradition with a touch of romance in the air

📞 0473 448553
📠 0473 449919
via Steinach 25
39022 LAGUNDO (Bolzano)
Ref map 4, B3

A22, Bolzano Sud exit, then *superstrada* (dual carriageway) Merano-Bolzano, Merano exit, S.S. 38 then right for Lagundo
14 rooms, 6 apartments; **££/£££**
Credit card: AE VISA SI Ⓞ

$\mathcal{F}$ramed by vineyards and orchards, Der Punthof is only three kilometres from Merano on the track of what was the old Claudia Augusta Roman road running northwards. The building, a farmstead dedicated to agriculture and rural life dating back to medieval times, still has a façade decorated with paintings together with architectural details which reveal its ancient origins.

Inside it is very welcoming, with antique furniture, parquet flooring, family photographs, hunting trophies, cosy rooms, the Tyrolean *Stube* (stove room) and an elegant restaurant. The bedrooms are big with comfortable period furniture. In addition there is a garden outside amidst the greenery, an open-air swimming pool, tennis court and sauna. The hotel can also offer four apartments for family use.

RECOMMENDED IN THE AREA

RESTAURANTS:
Ruster; Steghof *and* Wiedenplatzer-Keller, *Naturno*

WINE CELLARS:
Cooperative wine-growers' association where wines can be sampled, Merano

---

$\mathcal{M}$onte Sella

A hotel with unmistakable charm where guests can absorb history and tradition

📞 0474 501034 📠 0474 501714
✉ info@monte-sella.com
via Catarina Lanz 7,
località San Vigilio di Marebbe
39030 MAREBBE (Bolzano)
Ref map 4, B5

A22, Bressanone, S.S. 49 as far as Brunico, then left for Marebbe
30 rooms; **££**
Credit card: VISA SI

RECOMMENDED IN THE AREA

RESTAURANTS:
Tabarel *and* Fana Ladina

LOCAL SPECIALITIES:
Canederli *(salami and bread dumplings); goulash*

VISIT:
Teodone Agricultural Museum; Fánes-Sénnes-Bráies Nature Park with Lake Bráies

$\mathcal{T}$his hotel, located in the countryside dominated by the peaks of the Fánes-Sénnes-Bráies Nature Park, was built in 1901 and has belonged to the same family since 1909. Its elegant and unusual exterior immediately catches the eye, for it is in the style of the mountain region enriched with the spires and the affectations of Art Nouveau. Inside, many of the architectural features bestow a particular atmosphere. These include painted decorations on the walls representing romantic countryside or very decorative borders showing garlands of inter-twined nymphs. Halls and drawing rooms are well

proportioned and light streams through antique windows. In the delightful bed-rooms modern and antique furniture blend harmoniously. The hotel also offers a health centre, sauna, bicycle hire and, during the summer, welcoming aperitifs and open-air barbecues in the garden. But whatever the season, the service is very attentive.

Castel Fragsburg

A romantic situation ideal for lovers of peace and quiet and for those who appreciate the pleasures of the palate

☎ 0473 244071 📠 0473 244493
✉ info@fragsburg.com
via Fragsburg 3, località Labers
39012 MERANO (Bolzano)
Ref map 4, B3
A22, Bolzano Sud exit, Bolzano-Merano *superstrada* (dual carriageway), Merano Sud exit, follow the signs for Merano 2000
18 rooms; **££/£££**
Credit card: bancomat

RECOMMENDED IN THE AREA

RESTAURANTS:
Grillstube schloss Maur *and* Artemis

*F*raming this hotel is the wide-open and sunny countryside of the beautiful Pusteria valley, with its gentle slopes and the great Dolomites in the background. The little chalet was built according to Tyrolean traditions with its steep roofs, fretworked balconies, floral decorations at the windows and, during the summer, masses of cheerful geraniums. The bedrooms are all golden in colour with wood for the furniture, the floors and, in the attic, also for the ceilings. The dining room and the living room are in the same style and, of course, there is a pretty *Stube* (stove room). The hotel is family run and service is friendly and attentive. Cooking is simple with traditional dishes of the region and local milk, butter and cheeses are used. In front of the hotel is a lovely lawn with a swimming pool and terrace for sun bathing. Woodland walks are just a few minutes away.

Eremita

Set amongst wonderful green meadows

☎ 0473 232191 📠 0473 211575
✉ einsiedeler@initalia.it
via Val di Nova 29
località Maia Alta
39012 MERANO (Bolzano)
Ref map 4, B3
A22, Bolzano Sud exit, then Bolzano-Merano *superstrada* (dual carriageway), Merano Sud exit
37 rooms; **£/££**
Credit card: AE VISA SI ⓪, bancomat

*S*ituated 400 metres away from the Merano 2000 funicular station amidst beautiful countryside where green fields alternate with apple orchards, the hotel is in a pretty Tyrolean building. The bedrooms and living rooms are welcoming, and the cooking is homely but with careful attention to detail. There are many facilities available to guests: a heated indoor swimming pool, sauna and solarium with UVA rays, plus hydro-massage. The hotel is surrounded by 10,000 square metres of parkland with tennis court, indoor swimming pool and table tennis, a large garden and a well-equipped terrace. During the summer there are organised tours along the paths of the Merano basin and organised children's activities every Thursday. The bus stop is a very short distance away, and the hotel is only three kilometres from the centre of town.

RECOMMENDED IN THE AREA

RESTAURANT:
Sissi

LOCAL SPECIALITIES:
Craft in wood; speck *(smoked, cured ham),* canederli *(salami and bread dumplings), cured loin, goulash, apple strudel, Lagrein Dunkel wine*

VISIT:
Thermal baths, botanic garden and racecourse, Merano; Örzi Museum and Similaun mummy, Bolzano

$\mathcal{P}$osta Cavallino Bianco

$\mathcal{A}$ charming old photograph shows Alois Wiedenhofer, farmer and postmaster under the Austro-Hungarian Empire, together with his wife. In 1875 they were the founders of this hotel, and their descendants run it still. There is no better guarantee than family management over generations.

The renowned old posthouse has been able to maintain the atmosphere of the past whilst still being equipped with every modern comfort. All the rooms are delightfully welcoming with an Alpine feel but in an elegant style. Just as pleasing are the bedrooms which are well furnished and bright. The hotel has a Turkish bath, sauna, open-air swimming pool and tennis court, outside playground as well as play areas for children inside, cycles for hire and terraces with a lovely view.

RECOMMENDED IN THE AREA

RESTAURANTS:
Zur Rose, *Appiano;* Moritzingerho, *Bolzano;* Ristorantino, *Terlano*

VISIT:
Lake Carezza; the Dolomite and the Marmolada mountain passes

Tradition of the southern Tyrol in a fairy-tale atmosphere

☎ 0471 613113
📠 0471 613390
✉ posthotel@postcavallino.com
via Carezza 30
39056 NOVA LEVANTE (Bolzano)
Ref map 4, B4
A22, Bolzano Nord exit, S.S. 241
64 rooms; **£/££/£££**
Credit card: AE VISA SI ⑪, bancomat

$\mathcal{G}$rien

In the wonderful setting of the Gardena valley

☎ 0471 796340 📠 0471 796303
✉ grien@val-gardena.com
via Mureda 178
39046 ORTISEI (Bolzano)
Ref map 4, B4
A22, Chiusa (Val Gardena), S.S. 242d
25 rooms, 3 apartments; **£/££**
Credit card: bancomat

$\mathcal{I}$nspired by typical mountain architecture, this modern building is situated in a sunny peaceful location. The rooms, with balconies or private gardens, are well furnished and some have a little sitting room. The communal rooms are divided into a number of areas and are practical both for adults and for children. They include a bar, television lounge, games room and billiard room, and in the garden there is a children's play area. In winter a shuttle service is provided taking guests straight up to the ski slopes. During the summer there are trips to the private hut on the Siusi Alp. The food is typical of the region and is prepared by the owner herself. There are Tyrolean evenings, and tastings of cheeses and local specialities. Hotel facilities include a gym, sauna, use of a local swimming pool and tennis court, and bicycles for hire.

RECOMMENDED IN THE AREA

RESTAURANTS:
Concordia; La Stua de Michl, *Corvana*

LOCAL SPECIALITIES:
Cured loin of pork with sauerkraut, saddle of deer and chamois with bilberry jam

VISIT:
Odle and Sciliar nature parks; San Giacomo village

*K*ristiania

Stylishly elegant and in keeping with the natural world around

☎ 0463 746510 📠 0463 746510
via Sant'Antonio 18, località Cogolo
38024 PEJO (Trento)
Ref map 4, B3
A22, San Michele all'Adige exit, then S.S. 43, towards the Tonale pass
51 rooms; **£/££/£££**
Credit card: 💳 SI ⓪

*T*he hotel stands in a wide valley on the edge of the wood, surrounded by a silent panorama. It is near the cross-country slopes and the ski lifts, and close also to the ski school. The building is on the traditional lines of Alpine architecture with wood predominating and providing an attractive decorative effect.

Bagno Romano

RECOMMENDED IN THE AREA

RESTAURANT:
Mezzosoldo, *Spiazzo*

LOCAL SPECIALITY:
Home-made salami from Cooperativa la Famiglia,
Saone di Tione (Spiazzo)

VISIT:
Little church of San Giorgio; Stelvio National Park at
the foot of the Ortles-Cevedale group of mountainss;
Le Terme (baths) with the famous ferruginous mineral
water; Civiltà Solandra Museum at Malè

Rooms for families too

The bedrooms are large and well furnished, some with delightfully moulded panelling of light wood. The bathrooms are good and some are very new. Also available are adjoining rooms with shared bathrooms that are ideal for families.

One suite on two levels has wooden beams, windows with a wonderful view and a ceramic stove. The sitting rooms are comfortable, large and welcoming. Then there are the many facilities: a very good fitness centre with hydro-massage, beauty salon, Turkish bath, sauna, solariums and a lovely swimming pool are all within the hotel. There is also a disco, video games room, mini-club and games outside for children, a park, gardens and solarium terrace. The hotel is family run, and the service is very polite and attentive to all the guests' requirements.

Chalet dei Pini

All the warmth of family hospitality

☎ 0465 441489
📠 0465 441658
✉ jalla@tin.it
via Campanile Basco 24
località Madonna di Campiglio
38084 PINZOLO (Trento)
Ref map 4, C3
A4, Brescia Centro exit, S.S. 237
11 rooms; ££/£££
Credit card: VISA SI, bancomat

RECOMMENDED IN THE AREA

RESTAURANTS:
Artinini, Crozzon *and* Alfiero

VISIT:
The church of Santa Maria, Pinzolo; the Bocchette
iron-paved way up the Dolomites of Brenta;
Adamello-Presanella Nature Park;
the abbey of San Romedio; Folgarida and
Campo Carlo Magno ski stations

*T*his little chalet in the midst of pine trees is almost completely clad in wood. It is in a very quiet secluded spot, but is also very close to the town centre and just a few steps away from the ski lifts and the numerous paths which in summer make lovely walks. On the scale of a private home, it has few rooms and is run by an exceptionally kind lady. The interior is furnished in wood and is simple and welcoming. Here too the owner has been responsible for the little details and touches that make the rooms so delightfully personal. The bathrooms have showers and are small but new. The sitting room seems like a tree house, with enormous windows and wicker furniture – an interior that could be confused with the outside. Then there is the secluded little stove room, the *Stube*, a period room where the atmosphere is really cosy.

Bagni di Salomone

A relaxing holiday in natural surroundings

📞 0474 492199 📠 0474 492378
✉ bagnidisalomone@dnet.it
località Anterselva di Sotto
**39030 RASUN ANTERSELVA
(Bolzano)**
Ref map 5, A5
A22, Bressanone exit, then S.S. 49,
towards Dobbiaco
24 rooms; £
Credit card: AE VISA SI ◑, bancomat

O n the borders of the Riese Glacier National Park and in an incomparably beautiful valley, this hotel is a kilometre outside Rasun Anterselva in the heart of magnificent scenery. With its Tyrolean architecture, it charms the visitor at first sight.

The rooms and their furnishings together evoke the tradition of the area and the story of the family who own this hotel. There are antiques, rustic fabrics, wood boarded floors, and rooms which open on to the green of the garden. In the garden itself guests can sit under trees that are hundreds of years old and admire the painting that decorates the exterior of the house, blending in with the geraniums in flower and with the greenery. The dining room is elegant and well furnished, and guests can enjoy traditionally-inspired cuisine which also takes account of modern dietary requirements.

The winter garden, the *thermarium* (covered and heated veranda) and the well-equipped terraces are the finishing touches of this gracious hotel , which is a member of the *Charme and Relax* chain of establishments. It also has its own fishing reserve.

RECOMMENDED IN THE AREA

RESTAURANTS:
Schönec, *Falzes;* Ansitz Heufler, *Rasun di Sopra*

LOCAL SPECIALITIES:
The famous strudel; wooden sculpture; loden *cloth; table-cloths*

$\mathcal{L}$ichtenstern

*Unspoilt nature and ancient treasures
amassed over the course of 2000 years*

☎ 0471 345147 🖷 0471 345635
✉ hotel_lichtenstern@dnet.it
Lichtestern 8, località Soprabolzano
39059 RENON (Bolzano)
Ref map 4, B4
A22, Bolzano Nord exit,
then road for Renòn
27 rooms; £/££/£££
Credit card: 🆅🆂🅰 🆂🅸

RECOMMENDED IN THE AREA

RESTAURANT:
Belle Epoque, *via Laurin 4, Bolzano*

WINE CELLAR:
Cantina Sociale Gries *(wine-growers' cooperative)
renowned for wines from the Lagrein grapes*

VISIT:
*Earth-pyramids at Longomoso and Soprabolzano;
Archaeological Museum, Bolzano*

$\mathcal{T}$he hotel is located on the high plateau of Renòn,
in the heart of Alro Adige. It is surrounded by
green and looks over the beautiful panorama of the
Dolomites. It is a typical Alpine-style building, with
wooden balconies and flowers that add colour
to the exterior. It is on a small scale and is
dedicated to providing friendly, personal
hospitality. The interior is attractive and
welcoming and makes guests feel as though they
are staying in a friend's home. There are
comfortable corners with the warmth of wood, small
parlours, and the welcoming but more elegant dining
room with its veranda looking on to the wonderful view
and flooded by light from its huge windows. Cooking
is done with great care, and there are home-made ice
creams, breakfast including local specialities, and
lunches with characteristic dishes. Finally, there is a
Turkish bath and an open-air swimming pool.

$\mathcal{B}$runnerhof

*Breathe in the fragrant woodland air
during this unforgettable stay*

☎ and 🖷 0472 849591
località Spinga 5
39037 RIO DI PUSTERIA (Bolzano)
Ref map 4, A4
A22, Bressanone, S.S. 49,
turn left for Spinga
9 rooms; £
Credit cards not accepted

RECOMMENDED IN THE AREA

RESTAURANT:
Pichler

LOCAL SPECIALITIES:
Pasticceria Kersbaumer, Vandoies *(pastries from the Alto
Adige region and an infinite variety of traditional breads)*

$\mathcal{F}$raming this hotel is the wide-open and sunny
countryside of the beautiful Pusteria valley, with
its gentle slopes and the great Dolomites in the
background. The little chalet was built according to
Tyrolean traditions with its steep roofs, fretworked
balconies, floral decorations at the windows and, during
the summer, masses of cheerful geraniums.

The bedrooms are all golden in colour with wood for
the furniture, the floors and, in the attic, also for the
ceilings. The dining room and the living room are in the
same style and, of course, there is a pretty *Stube* (stove
room). The hotel is family run and service is friendly and
attentive. Cooking is simple with traditional dishes of
the region and local milk, butter and cheeses are used.

In front of the hotel is a lovely lawn with a swimming
pool and terrace for sun bathing. Woodland walks are
just a few minutes away.

$\mathcal{L}$ouise

*Courtesy, smiles and good humour
in a welcoming atmosphere*

☎ 0464 552796
📠 0464 554250
✉ luise@rivadelgarda.com
viale Rovereto 9
38066 RIVA DEL GARDA (Trento)
Ref map 4, C3
A22, Rovereto Sud exit, then S.S. 240
69 rooms; **££/£££**
Credit card: AE VISA SI ◑

*T*his modern hotel, with the latest kind of glass-walled lift giving a view all round, is situated on the road which leads into Riva only a short distance away from the historic centre. Its various rooms, of different grades, are all spacious. Those in the standard category are furnished in pastel tones and have a welcoming atmosphere, plus good bathrooms.

The reception area is large and bright with some antique furniture. The bar, which looks over the swimming pool, is furnished like a winter garden with fresh-coloured hangings and wicker furniture. There are large windows and a *trompe-l'oeil* in the breakfast room. Guests may sample wines from the Garda and Trentino regions and taste various salamis and cheeses at the Pernbacco *enoteca* (wine cellar). The restaurant serves regional and vegetarian dishes. In the garden are a children's play area, large well-equipped spaces for adult relaxation, an open-air swimming pool with hydromassage and a tennis court. There is a garage for motorbikes and bicycles.

RECOMMENDED IN THE AREA

RESTAURANTS:
Al Volt *and* La Casa della Trota

VISIT:
Medieval city and fortress, Riva del Garda; medieval city and Art Nouveau buildings, Arco de Trento

Rovereto

An attentive welcome in a warm family atmosphere

☎ 0464 435222
🖷 0464 439644
✉ rovereto@rovhotels.com
corso Rosmini 82/D
38068 ROVERETO (Trento)
Ref map 4, C3
A4, Rovereto Nord exit
49 rooms; **£/££**
Credit card: AE VISA SI Ⓞ

*D*ating back to the first years of the 20th century, this elegant hotel stands on a lovely tree-lined avenue near the station and not far from the historic centre, a short distance from the museum dedicated to Depero. Everywhere is easily accessible on foot. The hotel has only recently been completely refurbished and has soundproof rooms that are well equipped and furnished elegantly. Many of the bedrooms have balconies looking out on to the mountains. The reception hall is almost an art gallery with original paintings exhibited on its walls, and from there guests have access to various sitting rooms and to the *Novecento* restaurant which is renowned in the area for the quality of its cooking. During the summer restaurant service is on the delightful veranda at the front of the hotel.

RECOMMENDED IN THE AREA

RESTAURANTS:
Mozart *and* San Colombano, *just outside Rovereto*

WINE CELLAR:
Il Castello de Noarna, *neighbourhood of Villa Lagarina, where wine can be tasted and bought*

VISIT:
Historic centre of Rovereto, the famous campana dei caduti *(a large bell made from the iron of disused guns) and the futuristic museum of Fortunato Depero; Avio and Beseno castles, towards Trento*

Parkhotel Sole Paradiso

An old farmstead amidst a conifer forest in the heart of the Pusteria valley

☎ 0474 913120 📠 0474 913193
✉ parkhotel@sole-paradiso.com
via Sesto 13
39038 SAN CANDIDO (Bolzano)
Ref map 5, C5

A22, Bressanone exit, S.S. 49
43 rooms, 1 apartment; **££/£££**
Credit card: A̅E̅ V̅I̅S̅A̅ S̅I̅ , bancomat

indoor swimming pool, sauna, tennis court, gym, bicycles for hire, *bocce* (bowls), billiards and Turkish bath. There are huge green spaces outside, cross-country skiing from the front of the hotel and ski lifts 300 metres away.

This fairy-tale chalet was built as a farmstead in 1876 and became a hotel a few years later. It has romantic rooms with original period furniture and delightful four-poster beds, or else modern furnishings which are nevertheless pretty because of attention to detail and charming touches.

The living rooms and the Tyrolean *Stube* (stove room) evoke the pleasure of coming indoors with friends after a long outing in the countryside, of being together in the warmth when it's cold outside. The homely patina of history on the furniture in these rooms reveals their use in this way over many years.

Here tradition is combined with modern comfort:

RECOMMENDED IN THE AREA

RESTAURANTS:
Friederlerhof, *Villabassa;* Beppe Sello, *Cortina*

LOCAL SPECIALITIES:
Milk, butter, cheeses from the Pusteria valley at Latteria di San Candido; traditionally produced speck *(smoked, cured ham); felt hats from Zacher*

VISIT:
Ruined Art Nouveau thermal hotel, Bagni di San Candido; San Candido Collegiate Church and the museum; Dolomiti di Sesto Nature Park; the town of Cortina d'Ampezzo, the jewel of the Dolomites

Berghotel Tirol

An ideal holiday in the heart of the Sesto Dolomites

☎ 0474 710386 📠 0474 710455
✉ info@berghotel.com
via Monte Elmo 10
località Moso
39030 SESTO (Bolzano)
Ref map 5, B5
A22, Bressanone exit, towards Brunico,
San Candido, Sesto, Moso
59 rooms; **£/££/£££**
Credit card: ⓓ, bancomat

RECOMMENDED IN THE AREA

RESTAURANT:
Maso Froneben

VISIT:
*Fiscalina valley; San Candido in the Pusteria valley;
Lienz, Austria*

*T*he Fiscalina valley is crowned by an amphitheatre of mountains. This is a wide rolling valley with the scattered houses of little picturesque villages. Surrounded by a large green lawn, the hotel and apartment block are in the most beautiful sunny position a few steps away from the village and 50 metres from the Alpine and cross-country ski slopes. In the summer, this is a starting point for lovely walks. Accommodation consists of pleasing and well-furnished rooms, nearly all with a balcony, and single and double apartments for up to four people. The interiors are in particularly attractive Tyrolean style using lots of wood and giving careful attention to detail. The apartment block is linked to the main hotel by an underground passage. Guests may also take advantage of a health centre with sauna, gym, whirlpool and – for the pleasures of the mind – a little library and a sitting room with fireplace. There is also a children's playroom and bicycles can be hired. Great care is taken over the cooking, which uses products from the valley, especially milk and butter.

$\mathcal{R}$io Stava

Sports lovers rule here

☎ 0462 814446 ☻ 0462 813785
via Mulini 20
38038 TESERO (Trento)
Ref map 4, C4
A22, Egna-Ora, S.S. 48
46 rooms; **£/££/£££**
Credit card: AE VISA SI ⑩, bancomat

RECOMMENDED IN THE AREA

RESTAURANTS:
Malga Panna *and* Tyrol, *Moena*

LOCAL SPECIALITIES:
Wooden sculpture; strudel; Späzle (*type of pasta*)

VISIT:
Fiemme valley; Panevéggio Park

$\mathcal{T}$he clear waters of the Stava brook run close by, on the horizon is the majestic chain of the Lagorai mountains and all around is a wonderful park. This is the beautiful healthy environment of the hotel. The building is modern, but its architecture and decoration are inspired by the traditional mountain style. There are wooden balconies outside, and more wood is used for the walls, furniture and decorative details inside, giving a sense of homely warmth and tradition.

The bedrooms are large, with balconies overlooking the magnificent view, and are furnished in modern but classically elegant style with spotless walls bordered in wood and cosy fitted carpets that match the curtains. There is a *taverna* bar for sociable moments, and a lovely terrace with panoramamic views where guests can sunbathe and also take a Finnish sauna, steam sauna and hydromassage. Less than two kilometres away there are facilities for riding and tennis.

*A*merica

A friendly welcome from the early 20th century

☎ 0461 983010 📠 0461 230603
✉ hotel_america@iol.it
via Torre Verde 50
38100 TRENTO
Ref map 4, C3
A22, Trento Centro exit, cross the bridge over the River Adige
65 rooms, 15 apartments; ££/£££
Credit card: 🆎 🈯 🆋 ⓄⒹ, bancomat

*T*he name 'America' has its origins in the history of the hotel. A certain Sior Minico built the hotel is 1923 when he returned home from America. During the Second World War the building was destroyed then rebuilt and it is still run by the same family.

Accommodation consists of bedrooms and little apartments. Everything is welcoming. The rooms are bright, the floors covered with lovely parquet or soft fitted carpet. Charming curtains match the bedspreads, and the pretty wallpaper has decorative borders. Double rooms have queen-size bed. The tasteful modern furniture blends well with the rooms. Guests are given a friendly welcome.

RECOMMENDED IN THE AREA

RESTAURANTS:
Cantinota, *via San Marco 22/24, and* Osteria a le due spade, *via Don Rizzi 11*

LOCAL SPECIALITIES:
Crafts in wood; dried flowers

VISIT:
All Trento's artistic treasures and the monuments to the two cultures of Italy and of Central Europe; good starting point for visiting the Dolomite mountains

*V*illa Madruzzo

A 19th-century villa in a splendid old park

☎ 0461 986220 📠 0461 986361
✉ info@villamadruzzo.it
località Ponte Alto 26, frazione Cognola
38050 TRENTO
Ref map 4, C3
A4, Trento Centro/Nord,
towards Padova
50 rooms; ££
Credit card: AE VISA SI ⑩, bancomat

*T*he 19th-century villa standing in a dominant position amidst the old trees of a large park welcomes visitors with a terrace of tables and chairs outside the entrance. Once inside there is a reception hall which serves also as a bar, where newspapers are always available.

The charming dining room is on a small scale but has large windows looking out on to the lawn. A cool terrace is the delightful setting for meals during the summer.

The old chapel has been turned into a reception and meeting room. The bedrooms are of various types. In the old part of the hotel they are large with high ceilings, period furniture and some have a fireplace. In the new wing, the rooms are smaller but comfortable, well furnished, bright and practical. Service is always good and efficient. There are bicycles for hire and a tennis court.

RECOMMENDED IN THE AREA

RESTAURANTS:
Accademia, *vicolo Colico 6-8, and* Cantinota, *via San Marco 22-24*

VISIT:
The cathedral (Duomo) square; the city centre and its monuments; Buonconsiglio Castle

$\mathcal{A}$i Pini

★ ★ ★

The charm of the Dolomites

☎ 0462 764501
📠 0462 764109
✉ aipini@tin.it
via Nuova 19
38039 VIGO DI FASSA (Trento)
Ref map 4, B4
A22, Bolzano Nord exit, S.S. 241
30 rooms; £/££
Credit card: AE VISA SI ⓪

RECOMMENDED IN THE AREA

RESTAURANTS:
Malga Panna, *Moena;* La Bolp, *Canazei;* Rifugio Fuchiade, *Soraga*

WINE CELLAR:
Claudio Valentini, *Campitello di Fassa*

LOCAL SPECIALITY:
Puzzone *cheese from the Fassa valley at Caseificio Sociale, Predazzo*

VISIT:
Dolomite passes: Costalunga, San Pellegrino, Pordoi, Sella, Valles, Lavazè; groups of the Dolomite mountains: Catinaccio, Sella, Sassolungo, Roda di Vael, Latemar; Marmolada glacier

*C*ome here in summer and you are greeted by balconies covered with geraniums that almost hide the carved wooden balustrades so typical of this mountain region. In the winter, however, the decorations on the façade and the graceful architecture of the chalet stand out well against the snow.

The hotel is in a quiet position near to the funicular and not far from the village. It is surrounded by fields and has a wide panoramic view over the mountains. The bedrooms have all been refurbished and nearly all of them have a balcony and are furnished with modern furniture in light wood. The sitting rooms are large with separate corners for more private conversations. From the dining and breakfast rooms big windows give a view of the valley. Additional facilities are a pizzeria, a games room with evening activities, French billiards and a health centre with sauna, Turkish bath, hydromassage and gym. Outside there is a well-equipped garden and a solarium terrace.

Veneto

Veneto occupies an extensive part of the north-eastern Po valley, defined to the west by Lake Garda and by the River Mincio, to the south by the Po and to the east by the Adriatic sea. In the north it includes the massifs and plateaux of meadows and woods in the Pre-Alps, then the Cadore and the wonderful Dolomite peaks in the heart of the Alps. On the plain between Padua and Vicenza begin the green rolling Colli Berici and Euganei hills.

An ideal itinerary starts, inevitably, with Venice: a unique city of water and changing reflections, of palaces fretworked with porticoes and loggias, of art both inside and outside the churches and museums. In the labyrinth of little canals, streets and bridges, with sudden glimpses of squares and water, there is also the practical daily life to discover, the Venice of markets and taverns.

Beyond the lagoon, along the shores of the Brenta river, extends the Veneto of canal systems and villas, the old 'dry-land' part of the city state. Palladian buildings stand out in the countryside that was once the setting for aristocratic holidays. Nowadays the classical or rustic villas and the delightful places of accommodation among the vineyards and

Above: view of the Ducal palace, Venice
Top: 'La Rotonda' Palladian villa, Vicenza

orchards are ideal bases for visiting cities full of artistic treasures. Padua has the Saints' Basilica, the Church of the Hermits, frescos by Giotto in the Scrovegni Chapel and the nearby pleasures of the Euganean thermal baths. Treviso, with its famous monuments and medieval layout, is furrowed by canals. The Montello mountain and little town of Asolo are also very interesting. Palladio's Vicenza has graceful hills, woods, vineyards and noble residences (and restaurants) in the Berici hills. There is beautiful Verona with its Arena and castle, and trips to the wine-growing valleys of Lessinia.

Lake Garda is a Mediterranean enclave of olives and cypresses, palms and lemons on the banks, old villages and Venetian colours. At the two extremes of the region are Rovigo and Belluno, the lowlands of the River Po and the valleys on the way to the Dolomites.

The natural beauty waiting to be explored consists of the moving, silent landscapes of the Delta coupled with the amazing Dolomite scenery of Cortina d'Ampezzo.

$\mathcal{D}$ue Torri

A charming atmosphere of times past

☎ 049 8669277
🖷 049 8669927
via Pietro d'Abano 18
35031 ABANO TERME (Padova)
Ref map 4, D-E4

A4, Padova Ovest exit, then follow the *circonvallazione* (ring road) for Albano Terme
80 rooms; **££**
Credit cards: AE VISA SI ⓪, bancomat

$\mathcal{T}$he hotel is in the very centre of town, with direct access to the pedestrian precinct. Surrounded by a large park and garden, it is silent and peaceful and very green. This is a hotel with a long tradition and much experience. Many of the bedrooms have a terrace and they are large and well furnished with period furniture. The drawing rooms have classically elegant furnishings, chandeliers made of Murano crystal and velvet upholstery. There are drawing rooms for conversation, a lovely terrace with bar service overlooking the swimming pool and a games room. The dining room is very attractively furnished and there is attention to detail both in the cooking and in the service. The hotel guests can make use of the modern thermal cure centre, a beauty salon and connecting indoor and outdoor swimming pools using thermal water.

RECOMMENDED IN THE AREA

RESTAURANTS:
Antica Trattoria Ballotta, *Torreglia;*
Casa Vecia, *Monterosso*

VISIT:
Monteortone Sanctuary; Praglia Abbey, 14.5 km from Abano

$\mathcal{S}$weet Home

$\mathcal{O}$nly 15 kilometres from the centre of Padua (Padova), this former religious house is surrounded by a big garden. The rooms inside are attractive and there is a romantic atmosphere. The lady of the house receives guests warmly.

The bedrooms, with television on request, have flowered curtains and light furnishings inspired by the garden outside. There is a drawing room with a fireplace for spending pleasant winter evenings. There are many facilities in the vicinity: riding schools, swimming pool and tennis courts, health centres and cures in the thermal baths of Abano and Montegrotto. The hotel is within a series of cycle paths and guests may hire bicycles.

*In an old religious house
with a big garden*

☎ 049 711715
via V. Bellini 7, località Lion
55020 ALBIGNASEGO (Padova)
Ref map 4, D-E4

A4, Padova Ovest exit, towards Abano Terme, Montegrotto, Monselice as far as Albignasego
2 rooms; **£/££**
Credit cards not accepted

RECOMMENDED IN THE AREA

RESTAURANTS:
Cà Dottom *and* La Siesta*;*
In bloom, *Maserà di Padova*

VISIT:
Scrovegni chapel, cathedral, baptistery and botanical garden, Padua

Genziana

A warm atmosphere and particularly fine cooking

☎ 0444 572398 📠 0444 574310
via Mazzini 75/77
36077 ALTAVILLA VICENTINA (Vicenza)
Ref map 4, D4
A4, Montecchio exit, turn right in the direction of Altavilla
27 rooms; ££
Credit cards: AE VISA SI OD, bancomat

Situated at the foot of the Berici hills, the hotel is in a rustic building of the Tyrolean style. Inside the atmosphere is warm and friendly: the furniture is elegant, the decorations and soft furnishings are chosen with care, and there are good original paintings adorning the walls.

There is also a welcoming atmosphere in the cosy parlour with stove that can accommodate up to 20 people. Other facilities are a tennis court and an open-air swimming pool.

RECOMMENDED IN THE AREA

RESTAURANT:
Leoncino

LOCAL SPECIALITIES:
Local wines including Recioto, Durello and Pinot; Asiago cheese; ceramics

VISIT:
Piazza dei Signori and the city centre monuments, Vicenza; Scaligeri castles of Viella and Bella Guardia, Montecchio

---

Le Clementine

Lush greenery, the river and places steeped in history and art

☎ 0425 597029
📠 0425 589273
📧 clementine@netbusiness.it
via Colombano 1239/B
45021 BADIA POLESINE (Rovigo)
Ref map 4, E4
A13, Rovigo exit, towards Badia Polesine
Credit cards not accepted

There are bicycles for guests to go on exploratory rides. Lush greenery and the waters of the River Adige are nearby, and not far away there is Golene dell'Adige with its Palladian villas, abbeys and churches full of works of art and the big cities with their artistic treasures. Using this *agriturismo* (farm accommodation) as a starting point, various excursions can be made. The house is a delightful pink colour and dates back to the early years of the 20th century. It has preserved all the graceful elegance of the Art Nouveau style: there are painted ceilings, period flooring, glass doors and antique furniture. It is family run, and the lady of the house welcomes guests with friendly kindness. This *agriturismo* won the *Cuoco d'oro internazionale* for its cooking in 1999/2000.

RECOMMENDED IN THE AREA

RESTAURANTS:
Belvedere da Romano *and* Cauccio, *Rovigo;*
La Colombara, *Legnago*

LOCAL SPECIALITIES:
Montagnana prosciutto (similar to Parma ham)

VISIT:
Museuo Nazionale Atestino with important archaeological finds from northern Italy; 14th-century city walls and Palladian Pisani Palace, Montagnana

Locanda Greco

In the green countryside around Vicenza

☎ 0444 350588 ✆ 0444 350695
✉ grego@mail.protec.it
via Roma 24
36050 BOLZANO VICENTINO
(Vicenza)
Ref map 4, D4

A4, Vicnenza Nord exit, towards Treviso, turn left immediately for Bolzano Vicentino
19 rooms; £/££
Credit cards: [AE] [VISA] [SI] [⑩]

This is a classic inn of the Vicenza region with its roots deep in tradition. Once upon a time there was a post house here, then it was the place for public weighing, paying duties and taxes. So it has always been a meeting point for local people, but not only for them. The inn is in a simple but attractive building, pleasingly small in scale, and stands in the middle of the town. The family who run it are very experienced, having been here for four generations, and do so in a very friendly way.

The restaurant is noted for its refined cooking: the dishes are a mix of traditional and original, using local ingredients in season. The bedrooms are comfortable and welcoming. There is a garden, and an arrangement whereby guests at the inn may use the neighbouring sports centres.

RECOMMENDED IN THE AREA

RESTAURANT:
Giardinetto, *Monticello Conte Otto*

LOCAL SPECIALITIES:
Baccalà *(dried cod)*, *white asparagus*, Grana Padano *(similar to Parmesan) and* Asiago *cheeses*

VISIT:
Historic centre of Vicenza; Villa Monza, Dueville

Locanda Perinella

A charming and original place with a combination of the antique and modern

☎ 0445 947688
✆ 0445 947688
via Bregonza 34
36070 BROGLIANO (Vicenza)
Ref map 4, D4

A4, Vicenza Nord exit, then S.S. 53 towards Treviso
28 rooms; £/££/£££
Credit cards: [AE] [VISA] [SI] [⑩], bancomat

RECOMMENDED IN THE

RESTAURANT:
Principe, *Arzignano*

VISIT:
Trissino-Marzotto Villa, Trissino; gorge at Montagna Spaccata

The inn is situated 20 kilometres from Vicenza in a small town halfway up a hillside. It is an old agricultural building that has been transformed into a hotel. The inn and attached restaurant are a little family-run entity, and the fact that three generations have now been responsible for them means that the management is both kind and experienced.

Accommodation is in attractive bedrooms and suites that are well furnished with every facility. In fact the hotel was a finalist in the 'Premio hotel of the Year 1997' award. One of the inn's strongest points is its restaurant where simplicity is the rule and cooking is inspired by traditional food of the Veneto region.

Ca' Rustica

The flavour of the country between Venice and Padua

☎ 041 5200562
🖷 041 5209061
✉ saccoman@unive.it
via Ca' de Luca, località Ca' Lino
30015 CHIOGGIA (Venezia)
Ref map 5, E5
A4, Marghera exit, S.S. 309 (Romea),
towards Ravenna; after Brenta turn right for
about 1 km in the direction of Ca' Lino
1 apartment; ££
Credit cards not accepted

Surrounded by a large garden that is equipped for outdoor relaxation and meals in the open, the farmhouse is part of a mainly market-gardening business and stands in the hinterland of the lagoon near Venice. You can get directly to that city of artistic treasures by ferry from Chioggia. Padua (Padova) too is very near by, and can be reached by going along the riviera of the Brenta canal.

Accommodation is in one apartment composed of three rooms: sitting room with fireplace, two bedrooms, large bathroom and fully equipped kitchen with washing machine. It is furnished with care and embellished with some antique furniture. A rustic wooden staircase leading up to the bedrooms adds further character. There are bicycles for hire and table tennis. A minimum of three days' stay is requested.

RECOMMENDED IN THE AREA

RESTAURANT:
El Gato

VISIT:
Museo Civico della Laguna Sud, Chioggia; traditional peach festival

$\mathcal{F}$ilanda

Nobility, elegance and every comfort

☎ 049 9400000
📠 049 9402111
✉ filanda@tin.it
via Palladio 34
35013 CITTADELLA (Padova)
Ref map 4, D4
A4, Vicenza Nord exit, then S.S. 53
towards Treviso
71 rooms; ££/£££
Credit cards: AE VISA SI ⓪, bancomat

RECOMMENDED IN THE AREA

RESTAURANTS:
San Bassiano *and* Alle Mura, *Castelfranco Veneto*

VISIT:
City walls, neoclassical parish church, Cittadella; castle and cathedral, Castelfranco Veneto; last day of carnevale *in February/March, with procession of floats*

$\mathcal{N}$ineteenth-century mills and a former bottle depository have been rejuvenated. Two hundred metres from the city walls of Cittadella an industrial building of archaeological interest has been transformed into a comfortable hotel. The bedrooms are light, well furnished and those on the top floor are attic style. The bathrooms are very practical and nearly all of them have a window. The sitting rooms, which have been only recently refurbished, are large, modern, decorated with care and have well-designed furniture. Other facilities include a gym, small indoor swimming pool with hydromassage, and adjacent terrace and a gazebo for summer restaurant service. A courtesy bus links guests with the Fiera di Padova exhibition centre. The family-style management of the hotel ensures that every attention is paid to visitors' needs.

$\mathcal{A}$ncora

$\mathcal{D}$ating back to 1842, this is a hotel with a well-established tradition that offers hospitality of the highest quality. It is situated in Cortina's  historic centre, in the heart of the pedestrian zone. Its very elegant rooms with their valuable antiques are full of atmosphere. The rooms include the delightful Viennese *Terrazza* which is furnished in the Biedermeier style and, like the reception hall, is embellished by a splendid panelled ceiling and an 18th-century majolica stove which is still in perfect working order. All the sitting rooms, the restaurant and the parlour with stove have great character – both in the architecture and in the furnishing. The bedrooms are in the delightful local style and some of them have a bath with hydromassage.

An atmosphere rich in history and cuisine of the highest quality

☎ 0436 3261 📠 0436 3265
✉ hancora@sunrise.it
corso Italia 62
32043 CORTINA D'AMPEZZO (Belluno)
Ref map 5, B5
A4, as far as the end of the motorway, then S.S. 51
64 rooms; ££/£££
Credit cards: AE VISA SI, bancomat

RECOMMENDED IN THE AREA

RESTAURANTS:
Tivoli *and* Leone & Anna

VISIT:
The Pusteria valley; Brunico; San Candido; Dobbiaco

Villa Ducale

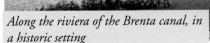

Along the riviera of the Brenta canal, in a historic setting

☎ 041 5608020
📠 041 5608004
✉ info@viladucale.it
riviera Martiri della Libertà 75
località Cesare Musatti
30031 DOLO (Venezia)
Ref map 5, D5
A4, Dolo-Mirano exit, towards S.S. 11
11 rooms, 1 apartment; **££/£££**
Credit cards: AE VISA SI ⓪

RECOMMENDED IN THE AREA

RESTAURANTS:
Locanda alla Posta; Al Paradiso, *Mirano*

LOCAL SPECIALITIES:
Footwear; Murano glass

VISIT:
The villas along the riviera of the Brenta Canal

*T*his is a villa in the Palladian style, surrounded by an age-old park. In 1884 Count Giulio Rocca ordered its construction on the site of the ruins of an 18th-century building. Lately refurbishments have brought it up to modern standards of accommodation and comfort. There is a lovely façade with arches.

The rooms inside still have period frescoes, antique furniture, stucco-work, marble fireplaces and original Venetian floors. The bedrooms and the small apartment available to guests are large with high ceilings and are well furnished with attractive curtains, Murano lamps and furniture inspired by the architecture. The restaurant looks on to the garden. Bicycles can be hired.

107

Villa Abbazia

The atmosphere of an elegant private house

☎ 0438 971277
🖷 0438 970001
✉ info@hotelabbazia.it
piazza IV Novembre
31051 FOLLINA (Treviso)
Ref map 5, C5

A4 as far as the junction with the A27, Vittorio Veneto Nord exit, then left towards Valdobbiadene
24 rooms; **££/£££**
Credit cards: AE VISA SI ⓪, bancomat

*H*ere is a graceful combination of a 17th-century palace with an annexe of the Art Nouveau era. Their architectural style is different, but their atmosphere, welcome and service are identical.

The furnishing is very refined: suffused lights and the glow of candles, tables with beautiful tablecloths, and antique furniture, curtains and tasteful ornaments. The bedrooms are lovely, the sitting rooms delightful for relaxation and conversation. Every detail is taken care of, for there is family-style management with a personal touch.

The hotel has many facilities for recreation and sport. These include free or reduced fees at the nearby Asolo golf course (18 and 9 holes) and delightful cycle rides in the district (cycles are available for hire at the hotel). Also for the use of guests is an open-air swimming pool in the garden. There are noteworthy places of artistic and gastronomic interest in the vicinity.

RECOMMENDED IN THE AREA

RESTAURANTS:
Castelletto *and* Trattoria a la Becasse

LOCAL SPECIALITIES:
Prosecco *wine,* mushrooms, chestnuts, radicchio *salad,* asparagus *and* polenta *(cornmeal); wickerwork; wool, silk and cashmere; wrought ironwork; ceramics*

VISIT:
The 7th-century Santa Maria Abbey; Barberis-Rusca Palace

$\mathcal{V}$illa Revedin

Modern comforts and a respect for tradition

☎ 0422 800033 ✆ 0422 800272
✉ info@villarevedin.it
via Palazzi 4
31040 GORGO AL MONTICANO (Treviso)
Ref map 5, D5-6
A4, Cessalto exit, then towards Chiarano Fossalta Maggiore-Cavalier-Gorgo al Monticano
32 rooms; **££/£££**
Credit cards: AE VISA SI ⑩, bancomat

$\mathcal{B}$ etween 1400 and 1500 the villa and barns were built by a Venetian noble family, the Morosini. At the end of the 18th century the building became the summer residence ot the Foscari family and was later bought by the Revedin counts. Finally, in 1976, it was transformed into a hotel. It provides modern comforts and an historic atmosphere. In the bedrooms there is air conditioning, satellite television, a mini-bar, safe and, in the suites, baths with hydromassage or Turkish bath. The rooms are of different sizes and pleasing architecture, with period furniture and windows facing the peaceful park. The drawing rooms are large and decorative and well suited to conferences or ceremonies. The restaurant rooms are different in style and in the summer meals are also served on the terrace. Food is prepared with great care, and fish is a speciality. Surrounding the villa is a large park with ancient and rare trees, and a well-tended garden on the banks of the Monticano river.

RECOMMENDED IN THE AREA

RESTAURANT:
Antica Osteria Zanatta, *Maserada sul Piave*

LOCAL SPECIALITIES:
Radicchio rosso *(salad) from Treviso; white asparagus*

VISIT:
The cathedral, Oderzo

Casa Mia

A warm welcome amongst vineyards and the olive groves

☎ 045 6470244 🖷 045 7580554
✉ casamia@lazise.com
località Risare 1
37017 LAZISE (Verona)
Ref map 4, D3
A4, Peschiera del Garda exit, S.S. 249 north
39 rooms; ££
Credit cards: AE VISA SI, bancomat

This is a modern building, but both its architecture and its name denote it as a warm and hospitable place, for its classic design is both traditional and on a small scale. It has balconies of flowers and sloping roofs, and is surrounded by a large garden in the midst of a panorama of olive groves and vineyards. The location is very peaceful, but it is only six kilometres from the Gardaland Amusement Park and is near beautiful Lake Garda. The hotel has light and practical bedrooms that have recently been refurbished. The public areas are large and there are attractive terraces with bar and breakfast service. In the garden is a small lake with a little bridge in the Japanese style, and a pavilion on an island. The hotel is well equipped for comfort and sport: there are a swimming pool, tennis, table tennis and bicycles. The restaurant is noted for the quality of its cooking and serves meals outside during the summer.

RECOMMENDED IN THE AREA

RESTAURANT:
La Forgia

LOCAL SPECIALITIES:
Wine and olive oil from the Lake Garda area

VISIT:
Thermal baths of Villa dei Cedri; Gardaland Amusement Park; San Vigilio point

$\mathcal{L}$e Vescovane

Between green fields and dense woods

☎ 0444 273570

🖷 0444 273265

via San Rocco 19
località San Rocco
36023 LONGARE (Vicenza)
Ref map 4, D4

A4, Vecenza Est exit, after 50 metres turn left towards Riviera Berica
9 rooms; ££
Credit cards: AE VISA SI ①①

*T*ne farmhouse complex dates back to the 15th century and was successively enlarged over the following centuries. The building has been recently restored with great care, and has a lovely architectural style with stone walls and characteristic arches. The farm is in the Berici hills between the fields and woodlands of unspoilt countryside that is ideal for walks and trips on mountain bikes. It is in the area of Costozza, an old medieval town that is considered to be a rare example of the former splendour of the province of Vicenza. Accommodation is in bedrooms with bath, air conditioning and satellite television. They are spacious and architectural details form an integral part of their character: the ceilings have wooden beams and the rooms are decorated with delightful furniture from the early 1900s. Outside there is a large garden with a solarium and a summerhouse. Guests of the *agriturismo* (farm accommodation) are given discounts at the tennis courts and riding stables.

RECOMMENDED IN THE AREA

RESTAURANT:
Taverna Aeolia

VISIT:
The ancient town of Costozza

$\mathcal{C}$ampocroce

This little rural dwelling, with its white plaster and red tiled roof, blends with the green countryside and is surrounded by a lovely garden with a pergola where breakfast is served. A terrace at ground level enables guests to pass pleasant hours in the garden. Nearby is the countryside and the riviera of the Brenta canal, a beautiful area with historic Venetian villas. Venice is a short distance away and can be reached by parking at Fusina and taking the ferry that goes directly to the city centre. Accommodation at Campocroce consists of two double bedrooms with private bathroom and their own entrance. The furnishing make guests feel as though they are staying with friends. A minimum stay of two days is requested.

A historic setting in the Veneto countryside

☎ 041 5728694

🖷 041 5702199

via Caorliega 69/c
località Campocroce
30035 MIRANO (Venezia)
Ref map 5, D5

A4, Dolo-Mirano exit; from Mirano follow the signs for Santa Maria di Sala, after 3 kms turn left towards Pianiga in via Fratte, then left into via Caorliega
2 rooms; ££
Credit cards not accepted

RECOMMENDED IN THE AREA

RESTAURANTS:
Al Paradiso; Margherita, *Mira*

VISIT:
The many historic villas in the scattered districts of Mira: Mira Vecchia, Mira Taglio, Mira Porte and Mira Ponte

La Casa Di Bacco

Comfort and sporting activities in the heart of the countryside

☎ 0422 768488
🖷 0422 765091
✉ contact@casadibacco.it
via Callalta 52
31045 MOTTA DI LIVENZA (Treviso)
Ref map 5, D5-6

A4, San Stino di Livenza, towards Lorenzaga, then S.S. 53 towards Annone Veneto
11 rooms; £/££
Credit cards: VISA, bancomat

*T*his *agriturismo* (farm with accommodation) is in an early 19th-century farmhouse with 40 hectares of land. The house has been well refurbished and is very pretty with a tiled sloping roof and a façade decorated in brick with the outline of wide arches.

The bedrooms are air-conditioned and the communal rooms have a welcoming atmosphere with lots of wood decoration, fires always burning in the hearths during the winter, floors in warm stone, shining copper pans and many bottles adorning the walls of the cellar dedicated to wine tasting. Throughout their stay guests can use the library, piano and the *taverna* bar.

Outside there are green spaces and a play area for children, bicycles for hire, picnics and barbecues during the spring. Not far from the farm are indoor and outdoor swimming pools, tennis courts and riding stables.

RECOMMENDED IN THE AREA

RESTAURANTS:
Bertacco

VISIT:
16th-century preserved village of Portobuffolè; every second Sunday of the month, antiques and bric-à-brac market at Portobuffolè

Da Lino

Many paintings and flowers give a particular character and warmth to the restaurant where excellent food is served. The guests' bedrooms too, are simple, charming and carefully prepared. During the summer restaurant service is transferred into the garden under a lovely pergola.

RECOMMENDED IN THE AREA

RESTAURANTS:
Al Ringraziamento *and* Antica Trattoria Marinelli

VISIT:
Follina Abbey; medieval village of Asolo; the historic centres of Vittorio Veneto and Conegliano

S ituated on the Prosecco road in an old farmhouse is this well-restored inn. From the outside it is delightful, and the atmosphere inside is just as warm and stylish. Guests are welcomed in a number of rooms that have been furnished with antique collectors' items. These are not only decorative, but are also evidence of the loving care shown by the owners. A collection of more than 2,000 copper pans and cauldrons adorn the ceilings and the walls.

Excellent cuisine in a period atmosphere

☎ 0438 82150 3261
🖷 0438 980577 3265 ✉ dalino@tmn.it
via Brandolini 31
località Solighetto
31050 PIEVE DI SOLIGO (Treviso)
Ref map 5, C5

A27, Conegliano exit, follow the signs for Pieve di Soligo and then for Solighetto

17 rooms and 7 suites; **££**

Credit cards: AE VISA SI ⓪, bancomat

Locanda San Lorenzo

The little inn dating from the early 1900s is just outside the residential area, in a lovely situation. This was the work of the owners' paternal grandparents and was built as a simple tavern, but the next generation added accommodation in a few rooms and also the restaurant. Now the brothers and sisters of the new generation, Farra, Osvaldo, Renzo and Sandra, run the inn which has improved still further under their management.

At the entrance is the bar with its *larin* – a characteristic fireplace of this region. Being welcomed into a room heated by a real fire warms the heart and makes guests ready to appreciate the cooking of the restaurant that is amongst the best in the area. All the bedrooms are different and personalised with little details and a charming atmosphere. The bathrooms are new and spacious with bath or shower and hydromassage. Simplicity, courtesy and friendliness on the part of the owners add to the hospitality in this delightful place. The hotel was a finalist for the 'Premio Hotel of the Year 1997' award.

The fragrance of traditional cooking and the flavours of new dishes

☎ 0437 454048
📠 0437 454049
📧 loslor@tin.it
via IV Novembre 79
32015 PUOS D'ALPAGO (Belluno)
Ref map 5, C5

A27, Santa Croce exit and for 7 kms follow the signs for Puos d'Alpago
12 rooms and 2 suites; **£/££**
Credit cards: AE VISA SI ⓪, bancomat

RECOMMENDED IN THE AREA

RESTAURANT:
Al Borgo

$\mathcal{L}$ocanda Due Mori

A welcoming atmosphere in a small 18th-century mansion

☎ 0445 671635 ✆ 0445 511611
via Rigobello 39
36030 SAN VITO DI LEGUZZANO (Vicenza)
Ref map 4, D4
A4, Vicenza Ovest exit, *tangenziale* (by-pass) towards the north, then S.S. 46 towards Isola Vicentina, Malo, San Vito di Leguzzano
10 rooms; **£**
Credit cards: AE VISA SI ⓪, bancomat

RECOMMENDED IN THE AREA

RESTAURANTS:
Principe, *Arzignano;* Nuovo Cinzia e Valerio, *Vicenza*

LOCAL SPECIALITIES:
Soppressa *salami from the Pasubio valley;* Asiago cheese; *ceramics from Bassano del Grappa and Nove*

VISIT:
Villa Godi-Valmarana, Thiene

*I*n a typical street in the historic centre of the town there is a little 18th-century mansion with wooden shutters and flowers at the windows. It has been completely refurbished. Everything is very refined: real lace curtains at the windows, fresh flowers and a courteous reception. The bedrooms are simple but neat, and the communal rooms have a period feel with carefully chosen decoration and elegantly rustic wooden furniture. Each bedroom has a mini-bar and television, and the bathrooms are spotlessly clean. There is a welcoming restaurant, serving local dishes, with a fire burning in the big hearth and wooden beams. An elegantly furnished room is available for ceremonies and formal meals.

$\mathcal{V}$illa Soranzo Conestabile

An exclusive setting in wonderful countryside

☎ 041 445027 ✆ 041 5840088
📧 vsoranzo@tin.it
via Roma 1
30037 SCORZÈ (Venezia)
Ref map 5, D5
A4, Marghera exit, then S.S. Castellana, towards Castelfranco
17 rooms, 3 suites; **££/£££**
Credit cards: AE VISA SI ⓪

*T*he frescoes on the first floor, attributed to the school of Veronese, depict the former building which stood where this elegant 17th-century palace was constructed. The palace was transformed from a private residence into a hotel in 1960. Accommodation consists of bedrooms and suites, and modern facilities have been introduced into this antique setting. Each room has air conditioning and furniture, curtains and carpets to suit the lovely architecture. The bathrooms are satisfactory. In the dining room, sitting rooms and parlours there are beautiful doors and period wainscotting: pink for the countess, yellow for the count, green for the dining room with Sansovino beams and a fireplace bearing the Mocenigo Soranzo coat of arms. Breakfast is served by a roaring fire during the winter; in the summer it is on the terrace, surrounded by the park that was designed by Giuseppe Jappelli.

RECOMMENDED IN THE AREA

RESTAURANT:
La Ragnatela, *Mirano*

VISIT:
The villas of the Veneto region; Noale with its 13th-century walls; antiques markets every weekend, Scorzè

La Torre

An elegant little castle in the Art Nouveau style, situated amidst the Euganean hills

☎ 049 9930111 ✆ 049 9930033
piazza Capitello 27
35038 TORREGLIA (Padova)
Ref map 4, E4
A4, Padova Ovest exit, then take the road for Abano Terme, Montegrotto
13 rooms, 3 junior suites; **££**

Credit cards: A͞E V͞I͞S͞A S͞I̅ ⑩

*T*his was built as a private residence at the end of the 19th century but after only a short time was transformed, in 1912, into a hotel.

Since 1993 it has been under the protection of the ministry in charge of buildings of cultural and historic interest, and recently it was very carefully restored. Architectural characteristics have been preserved and modern comforts have been added. Nowadays

the hotel offers accommodation in rooms with elegant period furnishings, decorative details, lovely carpets and the welcoming atmosphere of a private house. The bathrooms are very practical and have showers, Turkish baths or hydromassage. The

communal rooms are attractive, and there is a cosy atmosphere in the three little dining rooms where the chef prepares dishes inspired by the cooking of the region. The wine cellar has over 200 labels and the attentive and expert members of staff will suggest suitable wines to accompany the meal.

A short distance away there are three 18-hole golf courses, the thermal baths of Abano and Montegrotto, bicycle or walking excursions and cities famed for their artistic treasures.

Also available at the hotel is a meeting room with modern audiovisual facilities for conferences.

RECOMMENDED IN THE AREA

RESTAURANT:
Le Calandre, *Rubano*

VISIT:
The regional park of the Euganean hills;
geo-palentologico museum and the geological excursion
on Cinto mountain, Cinto Euganeo; castle, road to the
sanctuary and old cathedral, Montselice;
Atestino National Museum and the city walls, Este

Gardesana

Age-old tradition in a lakeside palace with 500 years of history

☎ 045 7225411 📠 045 7225771
✉ gardesana@easynet.it
piazza Calderini
37010 TORRI DEL BENACO (Verona)
Ref map 4, D3
A4, Peschiera del Garda exit, S.S. 209
34 rooms; ££/£££
Credit cards: AE VISA SI ⓪

RECOMMENDED IN THE AREA

RESTAURANTS:
Al Caval; Il Porticciolo, *Lazise*

LOCAL SPECIALITIES:
Wines, olive oil, cheeses and truffles from Monte Baldo

VISIT:
The eastern shore of Lake Garda

*I*n 1452 the Venetian republic built this palace for the meetings of the council of the ten municipalities of the Gardesana dell'Acqua, the Veronese shore of Lake Garda. Then, 110 years ago, it was transformed into a hotel that immediately became a place beloved of important people in the fields of art and culture. Right on the little square in front of the old port, the elegant and historic building offers recently refurbished rooms with 19th-century Venetian furniture. The sitting rooms are all lovely, and the restaurant is in the former council room. During the summer meals are served on the romantic terrace overlooking the lake with boats bobbing on the water, the sound of gently rustling leaves and the Scaliger ramparts in the background.

Al Fogher

Modern comfort and elegant hospitality

☎ 0422 432950
🖷 0422 430391
viale della Repubblica
31100 TREVISO
Ref map 5, D5
A4, S.S. 14 exit; A12 as far as Treviso
54 rooms and 1 suite; **££/£££**
Credit cards: AE VISA SI ⓪, bancomat

J ust outside the historic centre of Treviso is this small-scale modern building. A furnished terrace leads into the reception hall. This is small but neat and contemporary in style, with carpets, plants and decorations in classically elegant taste.

The bedrooms are well soundproofed, and have functional modern furniture in charming pastel colours. There are fitted carpets and large windows giving light to the interior. The bathrooms are very practical. The dining room is attractive and welcoming, with a fire always lit during the winter. The restaurant is also open to non-residents, and has a separate entrance.

Bicycles are available for guests and the hotel service is very professional. Al Fogher belongs to the Best Western chain of hotels.

RECOMMENDED IN THE AREA

RESTAURANTS:
Le Beccheri *and* I Due mori

LOCAL SPECIALITIES:
Trevsio radicchio *salad (in winter); asparagus and herbs (spring/summer);* Montello *mushrooms (autumn);* baccalà *(dried cod)*

VISIT:
The historic centre, Duomo *(cathedral), church of San Nicolò, piazza dei Signori and the Civico Luigi Bailo Museum, Treviso*

*I*ris

The hotel is in San Polo, an area which is easy to reach from the San Tomà stop of the number 10 water bus (*vaporetto*) which goes along the Grand Canal. The small reception hall is well decorated. Most of the furniture is modern and some rooms still preserve their decorated ceilings. The lovely bedrooms are furnished in period style, and the beds have padded headboards in keeping with the very old hotel building. The little breakfast rooms still have wood-beamed ceilings, but the furniture here is modern. The hotel has no restaurant, but the nearby Giardinetto restaurant, which is under the same ownership, has a 16th-century dining room with a fireplace and specialises in fish. During the summer meals are served in the garden, and there is also a piano bar.

Exquisite hospitality only a few steps away from the Grand Canal

☎ and 🖷 041 5222882 ✉ htliris@tin.it
San Polo 2910/A
30125 VENEZIA (VENICE)
Ref map 5, D5

A4, Venezia exit, towards ponte della Libertà, then take *vaporetto* 10 (water bus), San Tomà
30 rooms; **££/£££**
Credit cards: 🝙 🝙 🝙 🝙

RECOMMENDED IN THE AREA

RESTAURANT:
Gondolieri, *Dorsoduro, San Vio 366*

VISIT:
Santa Maria dei Frari Basilica, the San Rocco School, Campo San Polo, the Corner Mocenigo, ca' Rezzonico Palace with the museum of 17th-century Venice, the San Giovanni Evangelista School

*W*ildner

The romantic atmosphere of the centre of Venice

☎ 041 5227463 📠 041 5265615
📧 wildner@veneziahotels.com
riva degli Schiavoni 4161
30122 VENEZIA (VENICE)
Ref map 5, D5
A4, Venezia exit, towards ponte della Libertà,
then take *vaporetto* 1 or 51 (water buses),
San Zaccaria stop
16 rooms; **£££**
Credit cards: AE VISA SI ⑩, bancomat

*R*iva degli Schiavoni is a wide promenade built during the 19th century; its name recalls the sailors from Schiavonia in Slavonia, present-day Dalmatia, who worked here. By the end of the 19th century, this part of the city was already primarily residential and for tourists. The bedrooms in the hotel have an elegant atmosphere and are furnished in period style. They also have air conditioning and satellite television, and some of them look out on to the lagoon. Those on the top floor have a good view of the cloister of the adjacent church of San Zaccaria.

The reception hall is small and simple. On the top floor there is a lovely terrace-veranda which acts as a restaurant and bar and has a breathtaking view of the basin of St Mark's. Here too buffets are prepared and breakfast is served. Hotel guests are welcomed in a kind and friendly way.

RECOMMENDED IN THE AREA

RESTAURANTS:
Gondolieri *and*
Giardinetto da Severino
VISIT:
Church of San Zaccaria

$\mathcal{F}$irenze

Art Nouveau style, with a view of the city

☎ 041 5222858
🖷 041 5202668
📧 hotel.firenze@flashnet.it
San Marco – San Moisé 1490
30124 VENEZIA (VENICE)
Ref map 5, D5

A4, Venezia exit, towards ponte della Libertà, then take *vaporetti* 1 or 82 (water buses), San Marco stop
25 rooms; **££/£££**
Credit cards: A̲E̲ V̲I̲S̲A̲ S̲I̲ ⊙

$\mathcal{W}$hen someone says 'a few steps' it usually means a short distance, but in this case the hotel really is a few steps (30 metres) from St Mark's Square and from the water-bus (*vaporetto*) stop. The hotel is in a building which, having been refurbished at the beginning of the 20th century, has maintained a façade with the detail, marble decorations and wrought ironwork of the Art Nouveau style. The bedrooms are comfortable and furnished in pale colours and in a classically elegant style of antique Venetian furniture. They have air conditioning, satellite television and mini-bar. The bathrooms are satisfactory. There is a pretty room for breakfast and a lovely terrace on the top floor, where there is bar service and breakfast in the summer, and a superb view of the city.

RECOMMENDED IN THE AREA

RESTAURANTS:
Le Bistrot de Venise, *calle dei Fabbri;* Nico, *Frezzeria;* Ivo, *caler dei Fuseri*

$\mathcal{A}$ccademia

RECOMMENDED IN THE AREA

RESTAURANTS:
Dona Onesta, ponte de la Dona Onesta; Trattoria alla Madonna, San Polo, calle della Madonna

In the gardens of a 17th-century villa

☎ 041 5210188 🖷 041 5239152
📧 pensioneaccademia@flashnet.it
Dorsoduro 1058
30123 VENEZIA (VENICE)
Ref map 5, D5

A4, Venezia exit, towards ponte della Libertà, then take *vaporetti* 1 or 82 (water buses), Accademia stop
27 rooms; **££/£££**
Credit cards not accepted.

$\mathcal{T}$his delightful hotel is in a little mansion painted deep-pink with pretty windows scalloped with circles and pillars. Situated near the Grand Canal and the galleries of the Accademia, the hotel has an unusual feature for Venice in that it opens on to a lovely garden full of flowers and greenery. Here, during high season, guests can take breakfast overlooking the canal. Inside, the hotel's bedrooms have period furniture and are comfortable and welcoming with satellite television and air conditioning. Many of them have parquet floors and some have beds with light canopies. The bathrooms are reasonable. The sitting, reading and breakfast rooms have Venetian floors, gilt-framed mirrors and chandeliers. The hotel staff provide very attentive service.

*A*la

*T*he little square on to which the hotel looks out is a few steps away from St Mark's Square, but slightly removed from the stream of tourists. At the beginning of the 18th century the palace which is now the Ala hotel was a family residence depicted in some of Canaletto's paintings. Afterwards it was divided into a number of apartments, and at the beginning of the 20th century was the scene of the fatal passions that inspired the writer Annie Vivanti to write her novel *Circe*.

A large and austere reception hall with high ceilings and antique armour welcomes guests into the hotel. The bedrooms are divided into two separate blocks and are furnished differently: some maintain the antique atmosphere, others are more modern. Some have painted ceilings and Venetian floors while others have parquet flooring or fitted carpets. Nearly all are soundproofed. The sitting area is large and divided into several rooms.

An 18th-century residence in the heart of Venice

☎ 041 5208333   📠 041 5206390
✉ alahtlve@gpnet.it
San Marco 2494, Campo Santa Maria del Giglio
30124 VENEZIA (VENICE)
Ref map 5, D5
A4, Venezia exit, towards ponte della Libertà, then take *vaporetto* 1 (water bus), Santa Maria del Giglio stop
85 rooms, 1 suite; **££/£££**
Credit cards: ᴀᴇ ᴠɪsᴀ ꜱɪ ⑩, bancomat

RECOMMENDED IN THE AREA

RESTAURANTS:
Osteria da Fiore, *San Polo 2202/A, calle del Scaleter;*
La Zucca, *Santa Croce 1762, ramo del Megio*

VISIT:
The church of Santa Maria del Giglio;
the antique market in Campo San Maurizio

$\mathscr{A}$merican

Centrally placed, but quiet
☎ 041 5204733 📠 041 5204048
📧 hotameri@tin.it
San Vio 628
30123 VENEZIA (VENICE)
Ref map 5, D5
A4, Venezia exit, towards ponte della Libertà,
then take *vaporetti* 82 or 1 (water buses),
Accademia stop
28 rooms; **££/£££**
Credit cards: AE VISA SI

*T*his small pretty building is in a central but quiet position. The furnishing of the bedrooms is Venetian inspired, and they also have a mini bar, satellite television, safe and air conditioning. Restoration work has preserved some of the features of the former building with details that add charm to the interior. The bathrooms are fairly good. The communal rooms are furnished in period style, and there is a charming terrace under a pergola where breakfast is served during the spring and summer. The hotel has a private landing stage for gondolas and motor launches.

RECOMMENDED IN THE AREA

RESTAURANTS:
Antica Besseta, *Santa Croce 1395, salizada de ca' Zusto;*
Do Forni, *San Marco 457, calle dei Specchieri*
VISIT:
The Accademia galleries and the Guggenheim Collection

$\mathscr{G}$iorgione

At the heart of Venetian life
☎ 041 5225810 📠 041 5239092
📧 giorgione@hotelgiorgione.com
Cannaregio 4613
30121 VENEZIA (VENICE)
Ref map 5, D5
A4, Venezia exit, *vaporetti* 1 or 51 or 82 (water buses), San Zaccaria stop
68 rooms, 13 suites; **££/£££**
Credit cards: AE VISA SI Ⓞ, bancomat

RECOMMENDED IN THE AREA

RESTAURANT:
Vini da Gigio, *fondamenta San Felice*

*T*his little 15th-century palace that has been a hotel for the past 100 years, and was refurbished in 1995, is situated in a central position a short distance away from St Mark's. It is very convenient and tastefully furnished. The interior has conserved some antique features that have been cleverly blended in with comfortable modern surroundings. The bedrooms all have air conditioning, mini-bar, satellite television and are elegant furniture in pastel colours. Bathrooms are practical. Some of the suites have a private covered roof-terrace with a view over the rooftops of Venice.

Both the sitting room and breakfast room are attractive, and there is a games room with computer facilities and Internet connection. In the high season the American-style buffet

breakfast is served outside in a small courtyard with a little pond, recalling the characteristic Venetian *campielli* (small squares).

*P*ausania

The charm of a 14th-century noble palace with its own garden

☎ and 🖷 041 5222083
Dorsoduro 2824
30123 VENEZIA (VENICE)
Ref map 5, D5

A4, Venezia exit, towards piazzale Roma, *vaporetto* 1 (water bus), ca' Rezzonico stop
26 rooms; **£/££/£££**
Credit cards: AE VISA SI

RECOMMENDED IN THE AREA

RESTAURANTS:
Antico Martini *and* Antica Locanda Montin
VISIT:
Ca' Rezzonico; sestiere *(quarter) of Dorsoduro*

*A*n ancient palace in the Venetian gothic style standing in the Dorsoduro *sestiere* (quarter). This area of the city has a dense proportion of originally Gothic buildings and this was the old residential quarter of the Venetian nobles. It is made up of a fascinating arrangement of *calli* (narrow lanes), octagonal courtyards and *rii* (canals).

The hotel is on the San Barnaba canal, between the ca' Rezzonico museum and the Accademia, in a central but peaceful position. The old palace preserves architectural details of the era in which it was a private residence: Gothic windows, a little courtyard with an original 14th-century well and a marble staircase with graceful pillars and a lovely baluster.

The bedrooms, with air conditioning, satellite television and mini-bar, are furnished in period style. Communal rooms combine period features with modern furniture. Breakfast is served in a room that, in the high season, opens on to the garden. There is a friendly welcome for guests here.

Santo Stefano

*A special atmosphere in a
15th-century watch-tower*

☎ 041 5200166 ✆ 041 5224460
Campo Santo Stefano, San Marco 2957
30124 VENEZIA (VENICE)
Ref map 5, D5
A4, Venezia exit, then from piazzale Roma or
the railway station with *vaporetto* 82 (water
bus), San Samuele stop; with *vaporetto* 1,
Accademia stop
11 rooms, 3 junior suites; £££
Credit cards: AE VISA SI, bancomat

*H*oused in the 15th-century watch-tower of the
adjacent religious house, the hotel is a Gothic-
style building a few steps away from St Mark's
Square. The main façade looks out on to the campo
San Stefano which, for many reasons, resembles a
drawing room more than a square.

The little entrance hall has been recently renovated
and furnished in modern style, but it has retained its
period ceiling decorated with panels. The hotel
has pretty bedrooms with Venetian style furniture
hand-painted in cream by craftsmen, tables with

decorative cloths and
Murano lamps. They also
have air conditioning,
mini-bar and satellite
television. The breakfast
room is small and
carefully furnished, and
equally small is the
outside courtyard where
there is an antique well in
perfect condition. Space
is reserved on the square
in front of the hotel for
breakfast during the high
season.

RECOMMENDED IN THE AREA

RESTAURANTS:
Le café *(ice-cream parlour) and* Ai morosi

LOCAL SPECIALITIES:
Antique shops; art galleries; antique restorers

VISIT:
The church of Santo Stefano; Loredan Palace

Cà del Borgo

A charming 15th-century building with every modern comfort

☎ 041 770749 ☒ 041 770744
✉ info@villamabapa.com
piazza delle Erbe 8, località Malamocco
30126 VENEZIA (VENICE)
Ref map 5, D5

A4, Venezia exit, towards ponte della Libertà, in the direction of Tronchetto, ferry-boat 17 for the Lido
7 rooms; £££
Credit cards: AE VISA SI ◐

Cà del Borgo is a house with a rural air which looks on to the calm waters of the lagoon. This pretty, elegant building has private mooring for boats and gondolas. Next to it is the typical Borgo a Malamocco bridge and a few metres away is the Murazzi sea. This historic 16th-century mansion provides charming accommodation. The bedrooms with period furniture create an unusually romantic atmosphere. The entrance hall, sitting rooms and parlours have fireplaces, antique furnishings, blown-glass lamps, beamed ceilings and original floors. There is also a garden terrace.

The hotel has a motorboat for taking guests across the lagoon and bicycles for hire. Guests may also use the facilities of a nearby tennis club. The hotel is in the *Charme & Relax* chain.

RECOMMENDED IN THE AREA

RESTAURANTS:
Osteria alle Testiere, *castello 5801, calle del Mondo Novo*; Al Vecio Cantier, *on the Lido*

La Fenice et des Artistes

A bohemian atmosphere

☎ 041 5232333
☒ 041 5203721
✉ fenice@fenicehotels.it
San Marco – Campiello della Fenice 1936
30124 VENEZIA (VENICE)
Ref map 5, D5

A4, Venezia exit, from Piazzale Roma or Tronchetto, *vaporetto* 82 (water bus), San Marco stop, towards La Fenice theatre.
69 rooms; ££/£££
Credit cards: AE VISA SI ◐, bancomat

This hotel is in a charming mansion in the Venetian style which stands in a romantic piazza next to La Fenice Theatre. The hotel has traditionally been used by actors and singers and has a delightful bohemian atmosphere.

It has bedrooms with traditional furnishings, satellite television and safes. A few bedrooms and some bathrooms have been recently renovated and the bathrooms are practical. The communal rooms are charming and full of atmosphere and have period furniture. The hall opens on to a little garden and a pretty green internal courtyard. Guests receive a warm welcome.

RECOMMENDED IN THE AREA

RESTAURANTS:
Taverna La Fenice *and* Covo
VISIT:
The church of San Fantin

127

Friuli-Venezia Giulia

This is a border region, the extreme west tip of Italy, and an important European cultural crossroads: Latin, Slav and Germanic. Trieste is its symbol, for it is both suburban and cosmopolitan. 'A little compendium of the universe, Alpine, plain and lake in 60 miles from the north to south', is the description by the writer Ippolito Nievo who came from Trieste. As for the double name of the region, the Tagliamento and Livenza rivers on the one hand and the Isonzo on the other define Friuli. More easterly is Venezia-Giulia – the Collio and Carso rivers, the cities of Gorizia and Trieste – a small part of an historic area that nowadays is mainly Slovenian.

From the coast, composed of lagoons as far as the Gulf of Trieste, one reaches a low plain furrowed by rivers, a place of wide horizons. From Udine's castle, Italy's borders can be seen to the north and east, marked by an immense amphitheatre of green and bluish mountains. Beyond the meagre grasslands (the *magredi*) and the area of the morainic hills of the River Tagliamento, the Carnic Pre-Alps, Cansiglio forest and Cavallo mountain, stand the sheer walls of the Carnic Alps.

Tourists can choose between seaside resorts like Grado and Lignano, the Tarvisio forests and the Fusine lakes in Valcellina or the Natisone valley, and mountain and sporting holidays in the Carnia valleys. Important examples of art include: Roman civilisation (Aquileia), the early Christian (Grado), Lombard (Cividale del Friuli) and Romanesque (Aquileia again) civilisations, and graceful Venetian (Pordenone, Palmanova and Udine) or Habsburg (Trieste). The character of the hospitality is linked with the quality of the regional culture: simple, reserved, and based on a traditional sense of solidarity, with the idea of the *fogolàr* (fireplace) symbolising a warm welcome.

The Miramare castle, a few kilometres from Trieste

Patriarchi

Fine cuisine and a wide choice of quality wines

☎ 0431 919595
📠 0431 919596
✉ patriarchi@hotelpatriarchi.it
via Giulia Augusta 12
33051 AQUILEIA (Udine)
Ref map 5, D7

A4, Palmova exit, then S.S. 352 which goes to Grado from Udine

23 rooms; £/££
Credit cards: AE VISA SI ⓄⒹ, bancomat

*A*s soon as you enter Aquileia you will see the pillars of the forum, part of the settlement of Aquileia, which was in a strategic position between the *pianura padana* (plain of the Po valley) and central and eastern Europe. The town was founded by the Romans in 181 BC. It rapidly became one of the 10 richest and most important cities of the Empire. In AD 452 it was destroyed by Attila the Hun and completely lost its power when the Lombards chose Cividale as the capital of their duchy. Nevertheless, though it had lost its power it retained its prestige. As the seat of patriarchs, the dukes of Friuli, for the whole medieval period it was the most important diocese in Europe.

The hotel is very close to the famous basilica. It has large bedrooms with modern furniture, air conditioning, television and mini bar. The spacious bathrooms are practical and spotless; the characteristic wood panelling gives the communal rooms a welcoming but simple appearance. Guests are received with attentive friendliness. The restaurant serves fine food. The garden is large and in summer meals are served here. The price of the room includes large sun-umbrellas which guests may borrow to use on the beach.

RECOMMENDED IN THE AREA

RESTAURANTS:
La Colombara; Hosteria al Posta and Osteria all'Armoniche, Ontagnano

LOCAL SPECIALITIES:
Young white wine, Cervignano; quality 'DOC' wines Friuli-Grave

VISIT:
Basilica and Archaeological Museum, Aquileia

Locanda al Pomo d'Oro

*Charming old-style hospitality
in a medieval inn*

☎ and 🖷 0432 731489
piazza San Giovanni 20
33043 CIVIDALE DEL FRIULI (Udine)
Ref map 5, C7
A23, Udine Nord or Sud exit, then S.S. 54
for Cividale del Friuli
17 rooms; £
Credit cards: AE VISA SI ◑

*T*his pretty little hotel painted in pink looks over a square in the historic centre of Cividale where there is also the 18th-century façade of the church of San Giovanni. The square is lovely and the hotel building is typical of the area. It is situated in the heart of Cividale, the old Lombard capital and later the seat of the rulers of Aquileia. In distant times the hotel building was already an inn: here in the Middle Ages stood the *Xenodochio*, an inn of the 11th and 12th centuries.

The hotel has been carefully restored and has practical rooms with simple modern furnishings and good bathrooms with hair-dryers and showers. Some bedrooms overlook the old walls of the city. The communal rooms have preserved their stone walls and wooden beams, brick arches dating back to 1300, and details which all create a warm atmosphere. The attractive and rustic-style restaurant serves typical dishes of the Friuli area. The proprietors give their guests a warm welcome.

RECOMMENDED IN THE AREA

RESTAURANTS:
Il Forino *and* Il Castello

LOCAL SPECIALITIES:
Collio wine, San Daniele cured ham

VISIT:
*Cervignano Cathedral; Archaeological Museum;
Feast Day on 6 January (*Mittlefest *and* Spadone *mass)
in Cividale Cathedral*

Locanda al Castello

Inspired by the architecture of a palace in the Holy Land

☎ 0432 733242 📠 0432 700901
✉ castello@ud.nettuno.it
via del Castello 20
33043 CIVIDALE DEL FRIULI (Udine)
Ref map 5, C7
A23, Udine Nord or Sud exit,
then S.S. 54 for Cividale del Friuli
17 rooms; **££**
Credit cards: AE VISA SI ⓓ, bancomat

RECOMMENDED IN THE AREA

RESTAURANTS:
L'Elefante, La Taverna di Bacco, La Taverna
Longobarda *and* Zorutti

LOCAL SPECIALITIES:
Gubana vogrig *(typical cake of the Friuli region),
white grappa*

VISIT:
Castelmonte Sanctuary, San Giovanni d'Antro Grotto

S tanding in a lofty position on a hill near the
historic centre, this hotel is in an early 19th-
century castle. Monsignor Costantini of Civedale
had been inspired by a palace in the Holy Land, and
it was to serve as a place of spiritual retreat for the
Jesuit fathers. In 1960 the building was transformed
into an inn serving food. Now it is a hotel with large
bedrooms, furniture in period style and a panoramic
view. There are two restaurants: one, with a big
fogolàr (fireplace), preserves the intimate character
of the Friuli style; the other, which is large with pillars,
is for banquets. In the summer meals are served on
the terrace. The kitchen prepares typical Friuli dishes
using local ingredients. The hotel has a sitting room,
bar, solarium and garden.

La Subida

T his hotel is on the hillside amongst some of the
most famous vineyards of Collio. Its two-
roomed apartments, equipped with every comfort,
are restored farm workers' houses at the edge of a
luxuriant wood where there are lovely walks. The
buildings preserve their antique exterior and there is
careful attention to architectural detail. The
apartments are pleasingly decorated with period
country furniture. In the garden is a swimming pool,
tennis court, playground and a stable that provides
horses for guests. The hotel has its own welcoming
trattoria restaurant, 'Il cacciatore', with an open
portico for dining outside in summer and a *fogolàr*
hearth inside for the winter. Cooking is in the traditional
style, and there is a large wine cellar.

RECOMMENDED IN THE AREA

RESTAURANT:
Sale e Pepe, *Stregna*

LOCAL SPECIALITIES:
Osvaldo cured ham; crafts using ollare *stone*

VISIT:
*Regional park of the Bosco de Plessiva; Lombard
city of Civedale; Italian and Slovenian quarters of
Collio; Borgo Castello at Gorizia*

*A place in the heart of Collio
where you can still dream*

☎ 0481 60531 📠 0481 61616
località Monte 22, fraz. Subida
34071 CORMÒNS (Gorizia)
Ref map 5, C7
A4, Villesse Gradiscoa exit,
then S.S. Udine-Gorizia
13 apartments; **££**
Credit cards: VISA SI

L'ultimo Mulino

A 17th-century mill built of stone and still working – one of the last in the Friuli region. It is peacefully situated by the clear waters of the River Sile in a large park with a private lake, surrounded by greenery. Eight bedrooms have been constructed inside and these welcome guests into an elegant and romantic atmosphere with panelled ceilings, period furniture and decorations using tastefully chosen ornaments to add charm to the place. On the ground floor is a bar and little corners for quiet conversation. On the first floor is a large sitting room. The same atmosphere and attention to detail is found in the restaurant which is reserved for hotel guests only.

A very old building with a romantic atmosphere

☏ 0434 957911
🖷 0434 958483
🖂 fllonder@tin.it

Molino 45, località Bannia
33080 FIUME VENETO (Pordenone)
Ref map 5, C6

A28, Azzano Decimo exit, northwards as far as Bannia, then left for Fiume Veneto
8 rooms; ££
Credit cards: AE VISA SÌ ⓄⒹ

RECOMMENDED IN THE AREA

RESTAURANT:
Novecento, *Casarsa della Delizia*
VISIT:
Cathedral and town hall, Pordenone

*I*l Borgo Soleschiano

Simple but stylish surroundings

☎ 0432 754119
🖷 0432 755417
via Principale 24
33044 MANZANO (Udine)
Ref map 5, C6-7
A4, Udine Sud exit, follow the signs for
Buttrio, Manzano and San Giovanni
al Natisone; then turn right for
Soleschiano di Manzano
10 rooms; £
Credit cards: VISA SI AE ◑, bancomat

A couple of kilometres separate this
tranquil corner of the world from the
industrial area of Monzano, which is famous for its
manufacture of chairs. The road goes through fertile
cultivated countryside, and just beyond the splendid
Villa Magnaghi is the hotel. It is surrounded by a
large garden, and a little further on is a riding school
which guests may use. The bedrooms have
furnishings suited to an old country house: wooden
floors, antique bedside tables, period tables
covered with decorative cloths, big wooden beds
with soft duvets. The staircase to the bedrooms is
rather steep (note that there is no lift), similar to the
staircases of old country homes. The bathrooms
with shower are average-sized. The very attractive
restaurant is furnished in the same country style: in
one of the little rooms is an antique *fogolàr*
(fireplace). Equally welcoming are the sitting room
and the small bar. Guests may take breakfast under
the lovely pergola outside.

RECOMMENDED IN THE AREA

RESTAURANT:
Il Campiello, *San Giovanni al Natisone*
VISIT:
*Many cellars in this area for well-known wines;
craft and industrial producers of chairs*

---

*A*l Vescovo

*A friendly welcome in
delightful countryside*

☎ and 🖷 0432 726375/726376
via Capoluogo 67
33046 PULFERO (Udine)
Ref map 5, C7
Venezia-Udine *autostrada* (motorway),
Udine Sud (*Centro*) exit, then S.S. 54,
follow signs from Cividale towards
the border with Slovenia; Pulfero is 10 kms
from Cividale
18 rooms; £
Credit cards: AE VISA SI ◑

RECOMMENDED IN THE AREA

RESTAURANTS:
Taverna Di Bacco *and* Taverna Longobarda, *Cividale*

LOCAL SPECIALITIES:
Cheese, ricotta *cheese and butter from Montefosca
(Pulfero); organic seasonal products (e.g. raspberries
and strawberries in spring, chestnuts in autumn),
San Pietro al Natisone*

VISIT:
*San Giovanni d'Antro Grotto, Caporetto;
Natisone valleys*

T he Natisone valleys are formed from the river of
the same name and from the valleys of the rivers
Alberone, Erbezzo and Cosizza. The hotel stands on
the banks of the River Natisone. It has a good
restaurant and is in a modern building where the wood
and stone materials used reflect traditional architecture.
The bedrooms are spacious and have modern
furniture in classically elegant design. The communal
areas are decorated with the same attention to detail,
and bright arrangements of wild flowers are a reminder
of the close links between art, cooking and the natural
world. The restaurant is heated by a lovely hearth and
offers typical dishes of the area. The hotel has a
garden, solarium terrace and bicycles for hire.

Valcalda

Cuisine allied to the flavours of the region in the shadow of the Avernis massif

☎ 0433 66120
🖷 0433 66420
✉ hotelvalcalda@ud.nettuno.it
via Edelweiss 8/10
33020 RAVASCLETTO (Udine)
Ref map 5, B6

A23, Carnia-Tolmezzo exit, go on towards Tolmezzo, Arta Terme, Ravascietto
13 rooms; £/££
Credit cards: ◪ ◪ ◪ ◪, bancomat

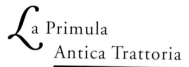

RECOMMENDED IN THE AREA

RESTAURANT:
La Perla

VISIT:
*The ancient centre of Ravascletto;
Carnic folk Art Museum, Tolmezzo*

*T*hrough the tall trees of the woods in a valley dominated by the Avernis massif, you climb up towards Ravascletto in the so-called 'Valcalda' which is anything but hot. In fact it gets its name not from the Italian *caldo* (hot) but from the German *kalt* meaning cold. You pass through little villages with very old centres, places that were already documented in the 13th century, with their typical houses built in the architecture of this Carnic Alpine region. The hotel is in a pretty modern building using wood in a way that recalls traditional mountain houses. It has light, airy bedrooms with lovely views over the valley and modern light-wood furniture. The bathrooms are well appointed. Communal rooms are large and spacious. The restaurant, offering local dishes with a seasonal flavour, is furnished in an attractive modern style and has large panoramic windows. There is a free garage, but no lift.

La Primula Antica Trattoria

For more than 100 years it has made an art out of refreshment

☎ 0434 91005
🖷 0434 919280
via San Rocco 47
33080 SAN QUIRINO (Pordenone)
Ref map 5, C6

A28, Portogruaro-Pordenone junction, towards Cordenons and Aviano
7 rooms; ££
Credit cards: ◪ ◪ ◪ ◪

*I*n the beginning, at the time of the family's great-grandfather, it was the grocer's shop. Then in 1875, according to the sign outside, it became the *Alle Nanzoni* tavern and was a local meeting place where people took refreshment, relaxed, exchanged news and even did business. Since then it has been a place of refreshment, and for years the Canton family has dedicated iitself with great energy and enthusiasm to providing it. The restaurant was opened in 1951 and,

with the family's continued professionalism, it is one of the best in the area. Access to the restaurant is from the courtyard, or else you can go from inside to the tavern. Both places, though very different, operate side by side and are complemented by the hotel accommodation of a few simple bedrooms on the floor above. These are furnished in the modern style but are comfortable and very welcoming.

RECOMMENDED IN THE AREA

RESTAURANT:
Casetta, *Porcia*

LOCAL SPECIALITIES:
Montasio *and salted cheese;
San Daniele cured ham; trout*

VISIT:
Pordenone; Sacile; Tramontina and Cellina valleys

$\mathcal{R}$iglarhaus

Simplicity and comfort on the road of the little mountain huts

☎ 0433 86013 📠 0433 86049
fraz. Lateis 3
33020 SAURIS (Udine)
Ref map 5, B6
A23, Carnia exit, go on through
Tolmezzo-Villa Santina-Ampezzo, at
Ampezzo turn right for Sauris,
at the lake follow the sign
on the right for Lateis
14 rooms; **£/££**
Credit cards: AE VISA SI ⓪, bancomat

$\mathcal{R}$ecently refurbished, this hotel has architecture typical of the Sauris area: the lower floor is in stone and the space once occupied by barns is surrounded by a wooden gallery. The lower part is whitewashed and the windows are beautifully finished in grey stone. Lots of flowers on the balconies add further charm. The hotel is on the *via delle Malghe* (road of the little mountain huts), a charming country route. It has 14 bedrooms with terraces (six of which are reserved for non-smokers), furnished in a simple comfortable style. Fireplaces add warmth to the communal rooms. Fine recipes of the Carnic region using local ingredients are served by the kitchen.

RECOMMENDED IN THE AREA

RESTAURANTS:
Antica Trattoria Cooperativa, *Tolmezzo;*
Osteria Monta, *Socchieve*

LOCAL SPECIALITIES:
Weaving at the Sauris mill; wooden carvings

VISIT:
Carnival season (February/March) where typical wooden masks are worn; fossil walks and museum at Ampezzo and Preone; nature park of the Carnic Alps; museums dedicated to history and war at Timau

Clocchiati

Romance in a 19th-century atmosphere

☎ and 📠 0432 505047
via Cividale 29
33100 UDINE
Ref map 5, C6-7
A23, Udine Sud exit: go on for Udine Centro, *stazione ferroviaria* (train station), continue straight for about 1.5 kms following the signs for Cividale (second traffic light on the right)
13 rooms; **£/££**
Credit cards: VISA SI AE ⓪, bancomat

The bedrooms are spacious and those in the attic have wooden ceilings. They have recently been renewed, both structurally and decoratively, and have fitted carpets, television and safe. Nearly all have air conditioning. The bathrooms are small but practical. The car park is reserved for hotel guests and there is a little garden. Guests receive a warm welcome from the family who run the hotel with great care.

$\mathcal{T}$his romantic hotel has been created out of an elegant late-19th-century villa which is a few steps away from the heart of the city and 500 metres from the new 'Giovanni da Udine' theatre. The communal areas are very attractive because they still have the stamp of a private house and the original structure of the villa. Thus there is a large handsome staircase to the first floor and on the ground floor are a number of charming small parlours, decorated with great care.

RECOMMENDED IN THE AREA

RESTAURANTS:
Agli Amici, *Gódia;* la Taverna, *Colloredo di Monte Albano*

LOCAL SPECIALITIES:
Cheeses from Friuli; Friuli wine tasting

VISIT:
Scenic route from Udine towards the lagoon via Aquileia and Palmanova

Liguria

Liguria is small in area, an arching strip of coast that stretches between sea and mountains, but it has great charm and a tradition of tourism. Holidays and hospitality seem at one with the landscape. The architecture ranges from mannerist villas built in the 16th century for Genoan nobles, to the homes of the rich 19th-century middle classes, to big villas of varied or Art Nouveau style surrounded by green perfumed gardens with bright bougainvilleas, palms and pine trees. Everywhere, however, even where the exclusive character of the past has been lost, the old seafaring villages are brought to life again in the picturesque house-fronts facing the ports and beach. They are tall, narrow and sometimes have painted decoration. Here and there a tower, a castle or a church is a reminder of medieval origins. The contrast between sea and mountain pervades the whole region, its gastronomy and culture.

Beyond the waterfronts shaded by pine, palm and tamarisk trees, you find villages which

Vernazza, one of the Cinque Terre (Five Lands), on the Levante coast

are old both in layout and appearance; they huddle on the ridges of hills, with back-to-back houses, lanes and flights of steps. From the beaches and cliffs you can look up to olives and vines climbing the terraces. The two aspects seem to unite from above, between the blue of the sky and the blue of the sea. Liguria's coastal arc is divided by Genoa's two celebrated Rivieras, di Ponente and di Levante. Famous places include Lerici, Portovenere and the Cinque Terre (Five Lands), Comogli, Portofino and Alassio.

Genoa itself is a Mediterranean metropolis full of history and art, with multiple charms, compact and with an intensely Ligurian character. It has the salty atmosphere and fascination of an old seaport which, in a sense, affects the whole region. Hospitality here has a flavour of the sunny Mediterranean but is civilised to the point of refinement, with traces of old cultures, and rare wines.

Locanda Delle Tamerici

So romantic and by the sea

☎ 0187 64262

📠 0187 64627

via Litoranea 106
località Fiumoretta
19031 AMEGLIA (La Spezia)
Ref map 3, F6

A12, Sarzana exit, S.S. 432 as far as
Ameglia, then towards Fiumaretta
7 rooms; **££/£££**
Credit cards: AE VISA SI, bancomat

*O*nce the little building which houses the hotel was a farmstead. Now it offers guests charming sitting rooms and a restaurant that is special both for the quality of its food and for its atmosphere. The hotel is by the sea and has a private beach with facilities for bathers, and in the summer there is bar service and a restaurant serving hot and cold dishes.

Accommodation is in bedrooms with old furniture, not items from an antique shop but charming pieces that have been in constant use, with matching curtains and furnishings. Together these create a romantic and delightful atmosphere. Outside there is a garden with a pergola for aperitifs and breakfast when the weather permits.

RECOMMENDED IN THE AREA

RESTAURANT:
Pironcelli, *Montemarcello*

LOCAL SPECIALITIES:
Pesto *sauce for pasta dishes;* anchovies; spongata *(Sarzana desert)*

VISIT:
Panoramic trips to Montemarcello and to Corvo Point

Locanda dell'Angelo

*H*ere you will find the cooking of an inspired chef, also the owner, who organises cooking seminars each year for enthusiasts.

The inn is of a modern, practical construction, built on very pure lines. The furnishings are also practical, without superfluous decoration. The rooms for conversation, meetings and receptions are bright with few but well-placed pieces of modern furniture, pale curtains and light from low lamps.

The comfortable bedrooms are large and furnished in a similar way, with fitted carpets, and features of 1970s design. There is a newly built swimming pool in the garden. Guests are welcomed in a very professional manner.

In the Lunigiana area, a region with a very old civilisation

☎ 0187 64391 📠 0187 64393

viale XXV aprile 60
località Ca' di Scabero
19031 AMEGLIA (La Spezia)
Ref map 3, F6

A12, Sarzana exit, S.S. 432 as far as
Ameglia
37 rooms; **£/££/£££**
Credit cards: AE VISA SI ⓓ, bancomat

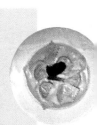

RECOMMENDED IN THE AREA

RESTAURANT:
Capannina-da Ciccio

LOCAL SPECIALITIES:
Spongata (Sarzana desert); local Vermentino and other quality wines

VISIT:
Archaeological site of the ancient town of Luni; Roman villa at Bocca di Magra

La Favorita

Simplicity and peace in the Ligurian hinterland

☎ 0184 208186 📠 0184 208247
Strada San Pietro 1
18030 APRICALE (Imperia)
Ref map 2, F2-3
A10, Ventimiglia exit, towards Dolceacqua, Apricale
7 rooms; £
Credit cards: AE VISA SI ⓄⒹ

*I*n the town everything is a succession of rooftops. Houses squeeze together around the church and bell tower, then straddle the ridge, and seeming to be almost part of the rock underneath, descend the hill in a lovely green undulating landscape typical of the region.

La Favorita was built in 1972 in the rustic style on uncluttered lines with a sloping tiled roof. Accommodation is in simple bedrooms that are neat and quiet.

On the ground floor is the restaurant where delicious local and regional cooking is served. At the heart of the room is the large grill that heats the interior and tempts the appetite of diners.

RECOMMENDED IN THE AREA

RESTAURANT:
Conchiglia, *Arma di Taggia*
VISIT:
The ancient village of Cerianoa; Armea valley

𝒱illa Ducci

An unforgettable stay, halfway between Liguria and Tuscany

☎ and 🖷 0187 982918
✉ villaducci@yahoo.it
via Nosedro 2
località Monti
19021 ARCOLA (La Spezia)
Ref map 3, F6
A12, Sarzana exit, S.S. 1 towards La Spezia
3 rooms; ££
Credit cards not accepted

The surrounding area is waiting to be explored, and guests can choose between the sea on the Ligurian coast or the Verilia beaches, the castles and medieval villages of Lunigiana, the churches and fortresses, museums and cities of artistic treasures.

The hotel is in a villa built between the 17th and 18th centuries on the hills that separate the gulf of Spezia from the valley of the River Magra. It overlooks a large estate with olive trees and woods of chestnut and oak. The building is white, with grey stone emphasising details, and is inspired by the architecture of neighbouring Tuscany. The bedrooms are charming and have frescoes on the walls, light stucco-work with pastel colours, and period furniture. The communal rooms have the atmosphere of a large well-furnished family house. The big garden is shaded and romantic.

RECOMMENDED IN THE AREA

RESTAURANTS:
Locanda dell' Angelo, *Ameglia;* I pescatori, *Lerici;* Il setaccio *and* Trattoria delle Sette Lune, *Sarzana*

LOCAL SPECIALITIES:
Monterosso anchovies; mussels from the gulf

VISIT:
San Giorgio Castle; Tecnico Navale Museum, Spezia

ℰna

The quiet charm of a house amidst the greenery

☎ 010 9127379
🖷 010 9123139
✉ luxehotels@upbase.net
via G. Matteotti 12
16011 ARENZANO (Genova)
Ref map 2, E4
A10, Arenzano exit, towards Arenzano Centro
24 rooms; ££
Credit cards: AE VISA SI ⓓ

RECOMMENDED IN THE AREA

RESTAURANTS:
Parodi; Antico Genoese, *Varazze*

LOCAL SPECIALITIES:
Pesto *sauce;* focaccia *bread;* Pasqualina *cake;* Genoese panettone *cake*

VISIT:
Sanctuary at Arenzano; aquarium and Città dei Bambini (children's city), Genoa; sandy beaches of Cogoleto

This is a graceful villa with harmonious proportions in the Art Nouveau style. It stands on the Arenzano seafront in a lovely avenue of palm trees in a very central area. Recently refurbished, it has very light and comfortable bedrooms with period-style furniture made of light wood, and a variety of delightful curtains and bedspreads. The bathrooms are new, all have a little window in addition to the ventilator and nearly all have showers. The breakfast room has a large period window and is furnished with a number of antiques. On the ground floor there are a very small bar, a small, well-furnished sitting room and a terrace equipped for relaxing and watching the sea. The *Osteria degli Archi* restaurant is in the former wine cellar. The reception staff are kind and helpful.

Carlo e Marina dell'Amico

On a hillside amidst olive groves and orchards

☎ 0187 674043
✉ lillo@luna.it
via Montefrancio 70
località Montecchio
**19030 CASTELNUOVO MAGRA
(La Spezia)**
Ref map 3, F6

A12, Sarzana exit, S.S. 1 towards Massa, turn left after San Lazzaro for Castelnuovo Magra
2 rooms; **£/££**
Credit cards not accepted

There are only two bedrooms, where the accommodation is simple but attractive, with charming period furniture, terracotta floors and a warm family atmosphere in the sitting rooms.

A pink-plastered country house shaded by a lovely pergola and standing on a hillside in the middle of a big olive grove. Guests are able to taste fruit and vegetables from the farm in season. Those who wish may have half board, and the old threshing-floor in front of the house is ideal for lunches or breakfast in the open, with panoramic views from the blue sea to the green Magra valley.

RECOMMENDED IN THE AREA

RESTAURANTS:
Armanda *and* Mulino del Cibus

VISIT:
Cathedral at Sarzana

Clelia

Surroundings that are simple, bright and welcoming

☎ 0187 815827
🖷 0187 816234
✉ hotel@clelia.it
corso Italia 23
19013 DEIVA MARINA (La Spezia)
Ref map 3, E 5-6

A12, Deiva Marina exit
24 rooms; **£/££**
Credit cards: AE VISA SI ⓓ, bancomat

accommodation, except in August), play areas and special facilities for children. The hotel is in the *0–6 International* chain.

In the centre of Deiva, 50 metres from the sea, is a pink Genoese house built in the early 1900s and surrounded by a lush green garden. Here a brand new swimming pool with hydromassage has just been built. The bedrooms, some with terrace, have pale blue furniture trimmed with *canneté* and terracotta floors. The whole effect is simple, but bright and welcoming. The restaurant has rustic furniture with a few period pieces to add character. The family who own it welcomes guests very warmly. There are many extras provided: bicycles, private beach facilities (included in the price of

RECOMMENDED IN THE AREA

RESTAURANT:
Armia, *Chiavari*

LOCAL SPECIALITIES:
Slate; marble; macramé lace; ceramics

VISIT:
Ancient village of Moneglia, remains of two castles

 Altavia

Among the hills in the most westerly part of Liguria

☎ 0184 206754
strada militare la Colla Gouta
18035 DOLCEACQUA (Imperia)
Ref map 2, F2-3
A10, Bordighera exit, S.S. 1 towards Ventimiglia, then right after Vallecrosia in the direction of Dolceacqua, then Rocchetta, left at the Colla-Gonta-Rifugio-Altavia junction
4 rooms; £
Credit cards not accepted

Situated 500 metres above sea level, this hotel is among the hills in the most westerly part of Liguria, with Sanremo and the Costa Azzurra nearby and the sea 18 kilometres away. Far from more public and crowded places, there is peace to enjoy and countryside to explore on foot or on mountain bikes. This mountain retreat is reached along what was once a military road. Built in stone, it has characteristically charming architecture with thick walls, windows framed in light stone and a little iron staircase with a gallery on the upper floors. The bedrooms are simple and welcoming, with windows overlooking panoramic views. The sitting rooms are warm and pleasant: wood, stone and terracotta together with rustic furniture and Provençal stoves. Horse-riding is available for guests.

RECOMMENDED IN THE AREA

RESTAURANTS:
La Veccchia, Gastone *and* Trattoria Re

VISIT:
Hanbury Gardens, Mòrtola Inferiore

Terre Bianche

Among vineyards, in a medieval village

☎ 0184 31426
📠 0184 31230
✉ terrebianche@terrebianche.com
località Arcagna
18035 DOLCEACQUA (Imperia)
Ref map 2, F2-3
A10, Bordighera exit, S.S. 1 in the Ventimiglia direction, towards Val Nervia–Dolceacqua
8 rooms; ££
Credit cards: AE VISA SI ⊕, bancomat

This *agritourismo* (farm accommodation) is set in the Arcagna vineyards, in a property of 18 hectares dating back to 1870, amongst cultivated land, Vino Rossesse vineyards and olive groves of the *taggiasca* type. The hotel is in a lovely old tower. We are 400 metres away from the sea in the most westerly part of Liguria, above the medieval town of Dolceacqua. The bedrooms are pretty and have 19th-century furniture, with windows overlooking panoramic views including that of Dolceacqua and Doria castle. Nearly every bedroom has a little terrace or a small garden designed for relaxing outside. The restaurant is in a characterful area of the hotel, and serves specialities of Liguria with ingredients from the farm itself or from others nearby, and Arcagna wines. Table tennis, *bocce* (bowls), riding and mountain bikes are available to guests, whilst the area is ideal for exploring.

RECOMMENDED IN THE AREA

RESTAURANTS:
La via romana, *Bordighera;* La Favorita, *Apricale*

LOCAL SPECIALITIES:
Quality Riviera Ligure de Ponente wine; locally produced vegetables, jams and extra virgin olive oil

VISIT:
Dolceacqua; Apricale; the Balzi Rossi headland

$\mathcal{A}$rabesque

In the ancient Moorish countryside of Varigotti

☎ 019 698262, 019 698263
piazza Cappello da Prete
località Varigotti
17024 FINALE LIGURE (Savona)
Ref map 2, E-F4

A10, Spotorno exit, S.S. 1 towards Ventimiglia
32 rooms, 6 suites; **££/£££**
Credit cards not accepted

RECOMMENDED IN THE AREA

RESTAURANTS:
Muraglia-Conchilglia d'Oro *and* Osteria del Castel Gavone

VISIT:
Ruins of Govone Castle, Finale Ligure; church of Nostra Signora di Loreto, Perti

$\mathcal{D}$uring the 18th century privateer ships docked in the little cove called *porto dei Saraceni* (Saracens' port). At the west and the east of the cove were watchtowers, signalling the warning of 'the black peril which comes from the sea'. The privateers left their traces in both customs and architecture. The typical small village with sailors' houses on the beach is quite oriental in style. The hotel has shaded patios, courtyards with luxuriant palm trees, rooms where archways are ornately curved, and arabesque shapes decorating the pale blue and white bedrooms. In the bright and relaxing communal rooms the furniture is made from wicker and bamboo.

$\mathcal{A}$gnello d'oro

On a steep Genoese lane in the heart of the old city

☎ 010 2462084
📠 010 2462327
via delle Monachette 6
16126 GONOVA (GENOA)
Ref map 3, E5

A7, Genova Ovest exit, follow the signs for stazione Porta Principe
35 rooms; **££**
Credit cards: AE VISA SI ⓪, bancomat

$\mathcal{T}$his hotel is in a mansion that recalls the inns of times past, situated in the historic centre at the heart of old Genoa (Genova). It is in a typical steep and narrow *carrugio* (a characteristic Genoese lane). The hotel has small rooms with modern furniture. The building is old; the rooms have been refurbished and preserve only a little of their past character, but they are neat, bright and clean.

The windows of the attic bedrooms on the top floor open on to a panorama of tiled roofs as far as the sea. The bathrooms are very practical. The furnishing and decoration of the communal areas are simple. The street, the location and the building all give the hotel a charming and unusual air.

RECOMMENDED IN THE AREA

RESTAURANT:
Al Veliero, *via Ponte Calvi 10/r*

VISIT:
Palazzo Reale *(Royal Palace)*

$\mathcal{S}$plendid

A hotel with very old origins

☎ 0182 690325 📠 0182 690894
📧 splendid@ags.sv.it
piazza Badaro 3
17053 LAIGUEGLIA (Savona)
Ref map 2, F3
A10, Laigueglia exit
48 rooms; **£/£££**
Credit cards: ☰ ☰ ☰ ⓪

$\mathcal{T}$he hotel building is typical of Liguria, and full of history. In fact it was a monastery constructed between 1300 and 1400, and inside – in the architecture, the corridors, windows and many details – its original charm remains. It is situated in a pedestrian zone just a few metres from the sea. It has light bedrooms, some with a terrace overlooking the sea. The bathrooms are reasonable. The communal rooms have period furniture and the elegantly welcoming public areas – bar, sitting rooms, restaurant, small television lounge with vaulted ceiling – are reached by means of a lovely old black and white tiled staircase. There is a garden, swimming pool and private beach.

RECOMMENDED IN THE AREA

RESTAURANTS:
Il Vascello Fantasma *and* Baia del sole

LOCAL SPECIALITIES:
Olive oil; pesto *sauce; dried tomatoes; olive paste*

VISIT:
Parish church of San Matteo

$\mathcal{C}$à Peo

Amongst the hillside olive groves,
on the gulf of Tigullio

☎ 0185 319671
via dei Caduti 80
16040 LEIVI (Genova)
Ref map 3, E5
A12, Chiavari exit, towards Leivi
3 rooms, 2 apartments; **££**
Credit cards: ☰ ☰ ☰ ⓪, bancomat

$\mathcal{C}$à Peo, or 'Peter's house', set on the hillside and surrounded by olive groves, has a wonderful panoramic view over the gulf of Tigulio; that is, the *Cinque Terre* (five lands), Portofino, Camogli, forming an amphitheatre of natural beauty and with pretty little villages with their multicoloured houses. The restaurant has only a few tables set well apart, so that diners may enjoy an uniterrupted view through the windows. The light shines on antique furniture and 18th-century wooden statues of the Maragliano school. The wine cellar, which nowadays houses great wines, was once an olive press used by the family and by neighbours, and the press is still there. For the guests, apart from the pleasure of tasting the splendid cooking of the restaurant, there are two apartments and three small suites encircled by a large terrace. Around them is the garden, the silver colour of the olive trees and the pale blue of sky and sea.

RECOMMENDED IN THE AREA

RESTAURANT:
Pepen

LOCAL SPECIALITIES:
Hand-worked slate, Fontanabona; hand-woven velvet fabric, Zoagli

VISIT:
Fieschi Basilica; route from Portofino to San Fruttuoso and from Portofino Vetta to Chiappa Point

Shelley e delle Palme

In an enchanting position on the Poets' gulf

☎ 0187 967127
lungomare Biaggini 5
19032 LERICI (La Spezia)
Ref map 3, F6
A12, Sarzana exit, S.S. 331 as far as Lerici
49 rooms; ££
Credit cards: AE VISA SI ⬤, bancomat

RECOMMENDED IN THE AREA

RESTAURANTS:
Miranda, Calata *and* Conchiglia

LOCAL SPECIALITIES:
Wine and extra virgin olive oil from the Cinque Terre

VISIT:
Ancient villages of San Terenzio and Tellaro

*T*his hotel has a central position and is opposite the sea, on the enchanting *golfo dei Poeti* (Poets' gulf). The building is modern its atmosphere is traditional. The hotel is very well known and loved by Italians and foreign guests alike.

Nearly all bedrooms face the sea and their furnishings are elegantly simple, with practical bathrooms. The sitting rooms have a secluded atmosphere and are decorated with panelling which gives them much warmth and character. There is a terrace equipped with large sun shades and sun loungers for guests' use in summer. The hotel belongs to the *Charme & Relax* chain.

Florida

With huge windows and on the Poets' gulf

☎ 0187 967332
📠 0187 967344
✉ florida@tamnet.it
lungomare Biaggini 35
19032 LERICI (La Spezia)
Ref map 3, F6
A12, Sarzana exit, S.S. 331 as far as Lerici
37 rooms; ££
Credit cards: AE VISA SI ⬤, bancomat

RECOMMENDED IN THE AREA

RESTAURANTS:
Due corone *and* La Barcaccia

VISIT:
The castle and ancient oratory of San Rocco

*T*he modern building of the hotel is completely white with large expanses of window. It faces the gulf beloved of Byron, Shelley and Virginia Woolf which, for this reason, is called the *golfo dei Poeti* (Poets' gulf).

Most of the bedrooms have sea views and are bright and elegant, with modern furniture and pale curtains, large windows and, in some cases, one wall that is almost all glass. Guests are welcomed into the little reception hall on the ground floor where the reflection of the sea can be seen even inside. The communal rooms are not large, but they provide for all the guests' needs: a restaurant, a small sitting room and a charming bar panelled in wood.

The beach, and beach equipment, in front of the hotel are reserved for guests, as are the swimming pool and tennis court 50 metres away. A little further away is a 9-hole golf course.

Stella Maris

In a fin de siècle *atmosphere*

☎ 0187 808258 F 0187 807351
✉ renza@hotelstellamaris.it
via Marconi 4
19015 LEVANTO (La Spezia)
Ref map 3, F6
A12, Carrodano-Levanto exit
15 rooms; ££/£££
Credit cards: AE VISA SI Ⓞ

A love story haunts this beautiful 18th-century palace. The two women who inherited it were unable to overcome their rivalry, and so the property was divided and today one part forms this charming hotel. The building stands in the historic centre. Guests go up to the first floor where they are welcomed into a lovely dining room with frescoes on the ceiling, tall windows and everything pervaded with a *fin de siècle* atmosphere. The rooms are large and a number still have frescoed ceilings and period stucco-work. Some of the furniture is antique and comes from the former owners of the palace. The hotel also has an annexe with more modern comforts only 50 metres from the sea.

RECOMMENDED IN THE AREA

RESTAURANTS:
Hostaria da Franco *and* Loggia

LOCAL SPECIALITIES:
Wine; extra virgin olive oil; honey; culinary and medicinal herbs

VISIT:
The villages of Monterosso, Corniglia, Vernazza, Manarola and Rio Maggiore, and the Via dell'Amore, *Cinque Terre; parish church of Sant' Andrea, Levanto*

Eden

In a garden shaded by orange trees

☎ 0185 269091
F 0185 269047
✉ eden@promix.it
Vico Dritto 20
16034 PORTOFINO (Genova)
Ref map 3, E5
A12, Rapallo exit, S.S. 227 towards Portofino
12 rooms; ££/£££
Credit cards: AE VISA SI Ⓞ, bancomat

Y ou go down lanes to get here, or rather through steep little alleyways. Everything has a character of its own, for the old buildings still remain. It is also quiet and, despite the international fame of Portofino, many corners are sheltered from busy crowds. The hotel is in a typical early 19th-century Ligurian house. Small and secluded, its entrance is through a garden shaded by orange trees and lovely bougainvillaea where guests take breakfast during the summer. The rooms are furnished very simply, in white with modern furniture, but there are thoughtful touches in the decoration and some rooms have their original floors. Apart from the restaurant on the terrace, there are few public areas, but nevertheless the atmosphere of the hotel has a delightful air of a private house.

RECOMMENDED IN THE AREA

RESTAURANTS:
Puny *and* Da U Batti

LOCAL SPECIALITIES:
Pillow lace; crafts in slate; paintings and sculptures by local artists

VISIT:
Castle of San Giorgio, Paraggi

$\mathcal{R}$oyal Sporting Hotel

On a hillside facing the sea

☎ 0187 790326
📠 0187 777707
✉ royal@royalsporting.com
via dell'Olivo 345
19025 PORTOVENERE (La Spezia)
Ref map 3, F6
A15, La Spezia exit, S.S. 530
towards Portovenere
61 rooms; **££/£££**
Credit cards: AE VISA SI ◉, bancomat

$\mathcal{P}$ortovenere is a small and typical medieval village that overlooks the sea. The hotel faces the *golfo dei Poeti* (Poets' gulf) in a quiet area and is surrounded by a garden. It is in a low modern, building that follows the slope of the hillside. The bedrooms are large and nearly all of them have sea views. Many also have a little terrace and the furniture is in warm-toned walnut wood. There is a private beach reached through an underground passage from the hotel, and a landing stage for mooring boats. In summer the restaurant serves a hot and cold buffet around the salt-water swimming pool. During other seasons meals are taken in the restaurant with its panoramic view. There is a garage for the use of guests and a tennis court.

RECOMMENDED IN THE AREA

RESTAURANTS:
Taverna del Corsaro *and* Antica Osteria

VISIT:
Boat trips to the islands of Palmaria and Tino

$\mathcal{R}$iviera

Near the old port in a busy, lively area

☎ 0185 50248
📠 0185 65668
✉ hotelriviera@tigullio.net
piazza IV novembre 2
16035 RAPALLO (Genova)
Ref map 3, E5
A12, Rapallo exit
20 rooms; **££/£££**
Credit cards: AE VISA SI ◉, bancomat

$\mathcal{T}$he building recalls the Art Nouveau style. In fact it dates back to the beginning of the 20th century. Its graceful form is moderate in size and it stands in the centre of the town in a busy, lively area on the seafront, a short distance from the old port. There is a terrace in front of the hotel and from this guests have a front-row view of events in the little town.

Inside guests are welcomed into modern rooms by friendly staff under the direction of the family that has owned the hotel since 1939. The lift is the very latest in design – all glass and technology. The rooms have recently been refurbished and are large, with good modern furniture, lovely parquet flooring and well-planned fittings. The bathrooms are good. The restaurant is open to non-residents. A garage (not free) is a kilometre from the hotel.

RECOMMENDED IN THE AREA

RESTAURANTS:
U Giancu *and* Roccabruna

LOCAL SPECIALITIES:
Craft in slate; pillow lace and filigree; pesto *sauce;* trofie *(home-made pasta);* vegetable cake and pansotti *(a variety of filled pasta)*

VISIT:
Madonna de Montallegro Sanctuary

Negro

In an ancient Ligurian village

☎ 0183 34089 📠 0183 324991
via Canada 10
località Cenova
18020 REZZO (Imperia)
Ref map 2, F3
A10, Albenga exit, towards Pieve di Teco
12 rooms; £/££
Credit cards: AE VISA SI OD, bancomat

RECOMMENDED IN THE AREA

RESTAURANT:
Baita, *Borghetto d'Arroscia*

LOCAL SPECIALITIES:
Insalata di stoccafisso *(dried cod salad);*
stewed snails with potatoes

VISIT:
Village of Triora

*S*ituated on the hills of the Ligurian hinterland which have been inhabited from the earliest times, this area was once a refuge from the dangers of the sea. Nowadays it has delightful holiday places that have been preserved almost untouched, far away from the more famous noisier resorts. Cénova is a Ligurian village in the high Arroscia valley with the characteristics of a mountain village, built in stone of typical architecture. The hotel building dates back to the 13th century. It was refurbished in 1988 when tastefully furnished, simple bedrooms were created. These vary in size to fit the ancient exterior walls. Throughout the building there are atmospheric features which recall its old origins: wooden ceilings and stone arches or walls. There is a swimming pool in the garden. The hotel restaurant, *I Cavallini* is highly recommended.

Palazzo Fieschi

The charm of antique and noble origins in exclusive surroundings

☎ 010 9360063 📠 010 936821
✉ fieschi@busalla.it
piazza della Chiesa 14
16010 SAVIGNONE (Genova)
Ref map 3, E5
A7, Busalla exit, S.S. 226,
then left for Savignone
20 rooms; ££/£££
Credit cards: AE VISA SI OD

*T*his 16th-century mansion, once the residence of the lords of Savignone, forms one side of the town-square like an enormous backdrop. Inside there are beautiful large rooms with high painted ceilings. A great staircase ascends to the floors above, and light enters through an inner courtyard. The sitting room was originally part of an old courtyard, and the dining room features a big fireplace. The bedrooms are simpler, but still have period furnishings, plus vaults, alcoves and ogives in the walls. If the main façade is a backdrop, behind the palace the ancient park sloping down to the valley is like a green sea. The hotel management can supply information and maps with descriptions of trips to make on bicycle or on horseback, or organise wine-tasting excursions.

RECOMMENDED IN THE AREA

RESTAURANT:
Ferrando, *Serra Riccò*

VISIT:
Scrivia Valley Historical Museum in San Bartolomeo

$\mathcal{V}$illa Balbi

*In the noble residence of an
aristocratic family*

☎ 0185 42941
🖷 0185 482459
viale Rimembranza 1
16039 SESTRI LEVANTE (Genova)
Ref map 3, E5
A12, Sestri Levante exit
99 rooms; **££/£££**
Credit cards: AE VISA SI Ⓞ, bancomat

Standing right on the seafront, this villa in the Genoese style was built in 1600. The hotel is made up of various parts. The original and most romantic section was the main family house of the marquis of Brignole. The height and great size of its reception hall is impressive with its large wooden mantlepiece. From here one passes into large frescoed sitting rooms with many pieces of antique furniture, and into a period bar and a lovely dining room with a veranda.

The bedrooms are spacious and maintain the character of a private home, adorned with period furniture and blending with the rest of the house. The bathrooms are equipped with every comfort.

On the private beach there are facilities for bathers and restaurant service. During the summer the bar, with its elegant décor featuring panelling and leather, transfers service to the terrace overlooking the well-tended garden, where there is also a heated swimming pool.

RECOMMENDED IN THE AREA

RESTAURANTS:
El Pescador, San Marco *and* Mandrella
VISIT:
La Baia delle Favole *(Fairytale Bay) and* la Baia del Silenzio *(Bay of Silence)*

Baja Benjamin

A crescent-shaped little bay with tropical colours

☎ 0184 38002 🖶 0184 38027
corso Europa 63
località Grimaldi Inferiore
18036 VENTIMIGLIA (Imperia)
Ref map 2, F2
A10, Ventimiglia exit
5 rooms; £££
Credit cards: AE VISA SI ⓪

*T*his is a place of rare charm, a jewel hidden in greenery by the sea where it is easy to relax. On arrival guests leave their cars in the private car park and walk down a short path.

The hotel stands on the gentle slopes of a hill running down to the sea, in a little crescent-shaped bay that seems like a tropical beach because of its colours and plants. The hotel is a modern building that blends well with the countryside around. Its restaurant is renowned for its cooking and for its refined service.

The few bedrooms were recently renovated, have period and period-style furniture and are elegant and welcoming. Curtains, lighting, trimmings and details are all carefully chosen. Terraces enable guests to spend time relaxing as they enjoy the panoramic view and the serenity of the place. A private beach adds to the charm of this hotel.

RECOMMENDED IN THE AREA

RESTAURANT:
Nanni

VISIT:
Palaeolithic grottos of the Balzi Rossi; Villa Hanbury with its famous garden

La Riserva di Castel d'Appio

Built on the ruins of an old farmhouse

☎ 0184 229533 🖶 0184 229712
✉ info@lariserva.it
via Pleidaigo 71
VENTIMIGLIA (Imperia)
Ref map 2, F2
A10, Ventimiglia exit
25 rooms; ££/£££
Credit cards: AE VISA SI ⓪, bancomat

*T*he original building, in a commanding position controlling the territory, was erected in AD 185 by the Roman consul Appio Claudio. In the 13th century the Genoese rediscovered the importance of this position high on a hill dominating the gulf. The hotel and restaurant have the same incomparable view. They were built on the ruins of an old farmhouse belonging to the family that still runs the hotel. The building is surrounded by greenery and its bedrooms are furnished in a romantic style. In the garden there is a swimming pool, playground, *bocce* (bowls) and *carambola* (type of billiards). The hotel belongs to the *Charme & Relax* chain.

RECOMMENDED IN THE AREA

RESTAURANTS:
Balzi rossi; La trattoria Re *and* Gastone, *Dolceacqua*

LOCAL SPECIALITIES:
Olive oil; pesto sauce made from olives; tomatoes in oil; bottled artichokes

VISIT:
Montecarlo and Monaco Aquarium; village of Grimaldi

149

Emilia-Romagna

In terms of its geography this is one of the simplest regions to describe: to the north is the River Po, to the south the ridge of the Apennines and on a third side the Adriatic coast from Lidi Ferrarese to Cattolica. Dividing it in half, from north-west to south-east, is the long diagonal of the Roman military road, the via Emilia. This separates the plain furrowed by rivers to the east from the hills and Apennine mountains, which are crossed by almost parallel valleys. Almost all the cities except Ferrara and Ravenna are positioned along this road.

The attractions for tourists are strong and diverse. The Italian Riviera is one of Europe's leading summer holiday destinations. There is an unbroken array of private beaches, hotels, aquatic parks, villages and little towns. Even towns that are famous mainly for their history and art reserve a special welcome for visitors. Hospitality is a business here, but it is also part of the culture. The Po delta offers fascinating, enchanting landscapes of water and countryside. The unspoilt Apennines – green,

secluded and sometimes harsh – are a haven for those looking for natural beauty and relaxation. The towns and cities have an unmistakable, original character which in some cases is unique – as with wonderful Byzantine Ravenna, glittering with mosaics, or aristocratic Ferrara that was the court of the Estensi family for three centuries. Parma is a small but great capital (the ancient capital of Parma and Modena in the 19th century) with a delightful French and Austrian atmosphere. Bologna is one of the most important Italian cities of art and in some senses is one of the richest. There are some splendid examples of Romanesque architecture at Modena, Parma, Fidenza, Piacenza and Ferrara; the *comunale* (pre-Renaissance) era shines at Bologna, and the Renaissance at Rimini, Bologna, Parma and Ferrara.

The highlight to any visit will be the gastronomy that is pure and rich, and as inviting as the people of the region.

The castle of Torrechiara in the Parma area

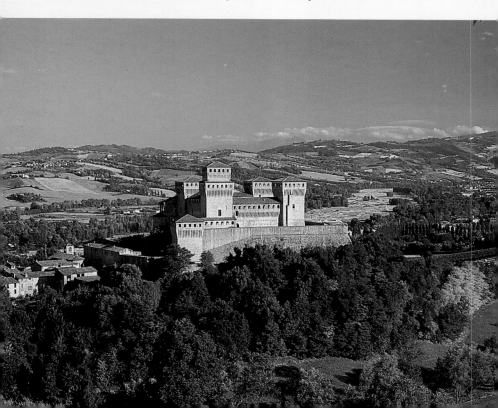

$\mathcal{V}$illa Reale

In the heart of the countryside and Emilian tradition

☎ 0532 852334
🖷 0532 852353
✉ villareale@villareale.it
viale Roiti 16/A
44011 ARGENTA (Ferrara)
Ref map 7, B5
A13, Ferrara Sud exit, S.S. 16 Adriatica,
towards Ravenna
50 rooms; ££
Credit cards: AE VISA SI ◉, bancomat

Argenta is a small town on the Adriatic trunk road for Ravenna, near Reno. The residential and historic centre of the town is reached via a lovely tree-lined avenue bordered by gracious houses dating from the beginning of the 20th century.

The hotel is in a small villa in the Art Nouveau style and surrounded by a large garden. Inside, the reception hall and sitting room have the delightful atmosphere of a private house furnished elegantly with period furniture. A lovely staircase leads to the upper floors.

The bedrooms are spacious and, on the top floor, they are attic-style. All are furnished along modern lines, in cherry-coloured wood that is both pretty and of good quality. The bedcovers and curtains are chosen with care, the beds are queen size and the floors have fitted carpets.

The bathrooms are medium-sized and all have showers with hydromassage. Breakfast is normally served in a modern room, but in high season may be taken in the garden. In addition, there is a modern, attractive annexe, built in keeping with the charm of the hotel itself.

RECOMMENDED IN THE AREA

RESTAURANTS:
Giannina, *Campotto;* Gastone, *Traghetto;*
La Locanda della Tamerice, *Ostellato*

VISIT:
Church of San Domenico, Santa Croce Oratory, Argenta; Campotto oasis in the regional park of the Po delta

Bentivoglio

An elegant hotel in the style of an old country residence

☎ 051 6641111
📠 051 6640997
via Marconi 18
40010 BENTIVOGLIO (Bologna)
Ref map 6, B4
A13, Bologna Interporto exit, turn right and go on for 4 km
50 rooms; **££/£££**
Credit cards: AE VISA SI ⓪, bancomat

*T*he mansion that now houses this delightful hotel was built in 1880 and was once a country residence. It stands opposite the 16th-century castle of Bentivoglio.

Intelligently refurbished in 1992, the hotel welcomes its guests into a very elegant interior: there are Venetian-style floors in the entrance hall and antique paintings and a few well-chosen 19th-century furnishings in the rooms. The pleasant and gracious atmosphere is maintained on all the floors, each of which is decorated in a different colour. This colour is reflected in the co-ordinating fabrics used in the simple but tasteful furnishing of the bedrooms. These have every comfort and the bathrooms are large and well equipped.

In the delightful breakfast room a varied and copious buffet is served.

A pleasant restaurant is also available to guests.

RECOMMENDED IN THE AREA

RESTAURANTS:
Torre dè Galluzzi *and* Pappagallo

VISIT:
Civiltà Contadina Museum (dedicated to farming history and culture) in the Villa Smeraldi, San Marino di Bentivoglio; historic centre of Cento

*A*l Cappello Rosso

*T*his hotel has a very long history, for it begins in 1375 when Cardinal Albornoz provided the building as guest quarters for the architects and artists who had been summoned to erect the nearby basilica of San Petronio. Then in 1550 it was used as accommodation reserved for Jews. Over time it continued as an inn, famous for its cooking, until the end of the 19th century. Then it took the name *Cappello*, to recall the cardinal in its history, and was the only hotel in the town to have bathrooms in each room with hot water. After the Second World War its illustrious past was forgotten and it became a hostel.

Finally, after careful restoration, it was reborn as a sophisticated and elegant hotel in the historic centre of Bologna, a few steps away from the basilica of San Petronio. Nowadays the hotel offers guests well-furnished rooms, endowed with every comfort, and with very special touches such as the provision of white silk kimonos for summer evenings. The meeting rooms and sitting rooms, bar and breakfast room are elegantly furnished and welcoming and in every respect are of the quality to be expected of a hotel which belongs to the *Charme & Relax* chain.

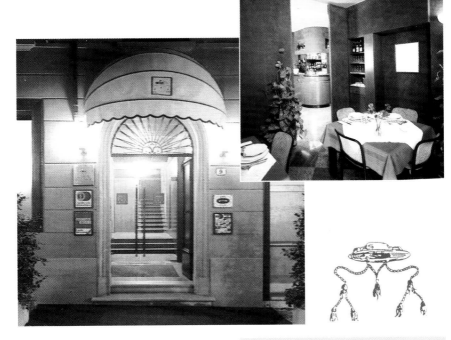

RECOMMENDED IN THE AREA

RESTAURANTS:
Carlo, *vai Marchesana 6, and* Buca San Petronio, *via dei Musei 4*

VISIT:
The town art collection in the palazzo comunale; piazza Maggiore with the Nettuno fountain and the basilica of San Petronio

In a historic mansion

☎ 051 261891
🖷 051 227179
via De' Fusari 9
40123 BOLOGNA
Ref map 6, B4
A1, Bologna Centro exit
35 rooms; £££
Credit cards: AE VISA SI ①

Orologio

A special address for those who want to stay in the heart of the city

☎ 051 231253 ☏ 051 260552
✉ hotoro@tin.it
via IV Novembre 10
40123 BOLOGNA
Ref map 6, B4

A1, Bologna-Casalecchio exit, from the Bologna *tangenziale* (by-pass) follow the signs for the Centro and piazza Maggiore
35 rooms; £££
Credit cards: AE VISA SI ◑

*T*his is a delightful small hotel in an old building facing the town clock-tower from which it gets its name. We are in the heart of Bologna.

In the little entrance hall guests will be struck immediately by the staff's kind and courteous welcome. The hotel has attractive bedrooms, some of them with a view over the splendid piazza Maggiore and the Asinelli tower. The rooms, equipped with safes and satellite television, are extremely comfortable and romantic. Charming floral motifs decorate the walls, and the curtains and furniture are chosen tastefully on old-fashioned lines. The bathrooms vary in size but are all more than just practical and have scales and hair-dryers.

On the first floor there is a sitting room and breakfast room. Newspapers are available to guests from early morning and the excellent buffet breakfast includes both savoury and sweet dishes. On special holidays or feast days, typical sweets are also offered. Both the management and the atmosphere guarantee a pleasant stay.

RECOMMENDED IN THE AREA

RESTAURANT:
L'Hostaria Don Camillo, *via San Gervasio5/d*

VISIT:
The sanctuary of the Madonna di San Luca

$\mathcal{D}$ei Commercianti

*T*his welcoming hotel stands in a little road running alongside the basilica of San Petronio, in the very central piazza Maggiore. Recent restoration work has brought to light parts of the original *Domus* building of the Bologna city-state that had its rooms here from the 12th century. Restoration has intelligently united practicality and the conservation of a warm and pleasing atmosphere. Furnishings have been chosen with great care, and antiques have been brightened with the elegant matching of vivid colours. Many of the bedrooms have a terrace, and they all look over the wonderful stained glass windows of the *Duomo* (Cathedral). They vary in size but all are welcoming and equipped with modern comforts. Buffet breakfast is especially well prepared. Morning newspapers are available to guests. Members of staff are helpful and friendly.

RECOMMENDED IN THE AREA

RESTAURANTS:
Grassilli, *via dal Luzzo 3, and* Nuovi Notai, *via de' Pignattari 1*

VISIT:
Asinelli and Garisenda towers; Mercanzia Palace

First seat or Domus *of the Bologna city-state*

☎ 051 233052
📠 051 224733
✉ hotcom@tin.it
via de' Pignattari 11
40124 BOLOGNA
Ref map 6, B4
A1, Bologna-Casalecchio exit, follow the signs for Questura centrale
34 rooms; £££
Credit cards: AE VISA SI ⓘ

$\mathcal{T}$ouring

A courteous and gracious atmosphere, with a view over the city rooftops

☎ 051 584305
📠 051 334763
✉ hoteltouring@hoteltouring.it
via de' Mattuiani 1/2
40124 BOLOGNA
Ref map 6, B4
A1, Bologna Fiera exit
38 rooms; ££/£££
Credit cards: AE VISA SÌ Ⓞ, bancomat

The Touring hotel in Bologna stands next to the well and storehouses where provisions for the Benedictine monastery of San Procolo were gathered. It was built around the middle of the 11th century and became powerful and influential through its estates and through sheer hard work. Situated in the historic centre, a few steps away from piazza Maggiore and the church of San Domenico, the hotel has comfortable rooms with well-chosen fabrics and modern furniture. The bathrooms are excellent. Walls are decorated in pale colours, and mouldings and light stucco-work form a background to the furnishings which have been recently renovated for the comfort of both business and holiday guests. A terrace roof garden looks over a charming view of roofs and churches, and one can see as far as the Bolognese hills. The hotel has a private garage.

RECOMMENDED IN THE AREA

RESTAURANTS:
Biagi, *Casalecchio di Reno;* Sole-Antica Locanda, *Trebbo di Reno;* Campagnola, *San Lazzaro di Sàv*

VISIT:
Palazzo Baciocchi, church of San Dominico and adjacent museum, Sanuti-Bevilacqua Museum, Bologna; sanctuary of the Madonna di San Luca, San Michele Monastery in Bosco; church of San Vittore

San Vitale

*T*his hotel is only 400 metres from Bologna city centre – a distance that guests can cover on foot as they enjoy the beauty of the city with its classical monuments, friendly inhabitants and mouth-watering food.

The hotel is near the university, which is one of the oldest in Italy, and is beneath the porticoes that are another famous feature of the city.

The bedrooms are simple in appearance, and each differs from the others in size and furnishing. The old architecture does not allow for functional design – hence there are big rooms and smaller rooms, all with modern, fairly standard furniture. A delightfully unexpected internal garden provides guests with an enjoyable quiet corner to relax in during spring and summer. The family management is both helpful and friendly.

Beneath Bologna's porticoes and near the university

☎ 051 225966
🖷 051 239396
via San Vitale 94
40125 BOLOGNA
Ref map 6, B4
A1, Bologna-Casalecchio exit, Bologna *tangenziale* (by-pass) exit 11, go on in the direction of Centro
17 rooms; **££**
Credit cards not accepted

RECOMMENDED IN THE AREA

RESTAURANTS:
Buca San Petronio, *via dei Musei 4, and* Duttòur Balanzon, *via Fossalta 3*

WINE CELLAR:
Bottega del Vino, *via Altabella 15b*

VISIT:
Certosa Monastery including the church of San Girolamo

157

Roma

The flavour of times past, in an old mansion

☎ 051 226322
📠 051 239909
via Massimo d'Azeglio 9
40123 BOLOGNA
Ref map 6, B4
A1, Bologna-Casalecchio exit
85 rooms; **££/£££**
Credit cards: AE VISA SI ⓪, bancomat

Right in the historic centre of the city, this pleasingly cosy hotel is in an old mansion. Its flavour is that of times past: from the marble staircase to the antique furniture which adorns every room. The sitting room is in distinctly classical style, and is large and bright. The bedrooms, some with terrace and others looking out on the little streets and roofs of the city, are comfortable and welcoming and well furnished, with pretty curtains. Each of the four suites is made even more pleasing by the addition of an elegant small sitting room, equally well designed. An ample English breakfast is served as a buffet in a charming Victorian-style room. There is also a restaurant for the use of guests.

RECOMMENDED IN THE AREA

RESTAURANT:
Rosteria Luciano, *via Sauro 19*

I Due Foscari

A stay in Verdi country

☎ and 📠 0524 91625
piazza Carlo Rossi 15
43011 BUSSETO (Parma)
Ref map 6, A2
A21, Castelvetro P. exit, S.S. 588
20 rooms; **££**
Credit cards: AE VISA SI ⓪, bancomat

A privileged destination for artists and music lovers making a pilgrimage in the land of Verdi, the hotel is in a wonderful little mansion in the Moorish style. The celebrated tenor Carolo Bergonzi had this establishment built in 1965.

All the rooms, from the *taverna* cellar to the dining room and from the sitting room to the bar, are furnished in the original style, with antique furniture and every comfort necessary for a peaceful stay.

The bedrooms are spacious and attractive and have recently been redesigned. All have air conditioning. Furniture is classical in design and reflects the good taste displayed throughout the hotel.

The restaurant serves traditional Emilian cooking, above all dishes from the Parma area.

RECOMMENDED IN THE AREA

RESTAURANTS:
Sole *and* Ugo; Palazzo Calvi, *Samboseto;* Vecchio Parco, *Salsomaggiore Terme*

LOCAL SPECIALITIES:
Culatello *(a kind of ham)* and *Parma ham (cured ham)*

$\mathcal{L}$ocanda Solarola

A family atmosphere in the country

☎ and ✆ 0542 670222

✉ solarola@imola.queen.it

via Santa Croce 5

40023 CASTEL GUELFO (Bologna)

Ref map 6-7, B4-5

A14, Castel San Pietro Terme and turn right towards Medicina, go on for about 5 kms and turn right again in via San Paolo, then follow the signs for the hotel

15 rooms; £££

Credit cards: AE VISA SI, bancomat

*T*his hotel is a real country house with a warm family atmosphere surrounded by a lush green garden. A short gravel road framed by a neat avenue of trees leads to the hotel. A pretty, very well-presented building in early 20th-century style greets guests. Inside it has the warmth of an old house. It is romantic and full of charming objects, the family's period furniture, paintings and carpets. All the bedrooms are named after flowers and are real little gems of a welcoming and poetic past. The lovely restaurant, serving meals of high quality, is only one of the pleasing communal rooms: the sitting room with its fireplace and the billiards room are ideal places for friendly conversations.

RECOMMENDED IN THE AREA

RESTAURANTS:
Naldi *and* E parlaminté, *Imola*

$\mathcal{L}$ocanda del Sole

In an old post house

☎ 051 4178111 ✆ 051 4178200

✉ ilsolebo@tin.it

via Lame 65, Trebbo di Reno

40060 CASTEL MAGGIORE (Bologna)

Ref map 6, B4

A1, Bologna-Arcoveggio, Bologna *tangenziale* (by-pass), exit 5, follow signs for Castel Maggiore-Trebbo di Reno

23 rooms; ££/£££

Credit cards: AE VISA SI Ⓞ

*U*ntil the 19th century, the building was one of Bologna's post houses, with lots of horses all ready for departure. Since then sympathetic restoration and restructuring work has conserved its architectural features and the characteristic colour of Bolognese buildings.

Surrounding the hotel are a charming garden and the delightful countryside of Emilia. Guests are struck by the quiet simplicity of the interior. The furnishings are charming and well chosen. Similarly, the large bedrooms all have every comfort and their gracious simplicity is very pleasing. Pale colours predominate on the walls and bedcovers with brighter curtains to match, and the little wooden writing desks have antique lines. In some rooms there are still beamed ceilings. The hotel's restaurant serves light modern dishes with great attention to detail.

RECOMMENDED IN THE AREA

RESTAURANT:
Da Sandro-al Navile, *via del Sostegno 15*

WINE CELLAR:
Bottega del Vino, *via Altabella 15b, Bologna*

VISIT:
15th-century castle, Bentivoglio

Marconi

S eafaring tradition and attention to detail are the essential features of this hotel's warm atmosphere. Its position in a shady avenue only a short distance from the sea is a perfect combination. The bedrooms have light modern furniture, and the whole effect is bright and charming. The dining room is large and furnished in a garden style with flowered tablecloths, curved wrought-iron furniture in white and a little *taverna* for breakfast. The garden itself is cool and sheltered from the din of the town, and it provides guests with somewhere quiet to rest or chat. The restaurant takes care over the smallest details and has the same management as the hotel. Every day there is a different special dish, created from the varied and imaginative cuisine.

In a quiet position a few steps from the sea

☎ 0541 962219 🖷 0541 967533
via Marconi 68
47841 CATTOLICA (Rimini)
Ref map 7, C6
A14, Cattolica exit
47 rooms; £/££
Credit cards not accepted

RECOMMENDED IN THE AREA

RESTAURANT:
Stazione

VISIT:
The arch of Augustus and Malatestiano Temple, Rimini

Britannia

Efficiency and graciousness in an Art Nouveau building

☎ 0547 672500 🖷 0547 81799
✉ hbritannia@linknet.it
viale Carducci 129
47042 CESENATICO (Forlì)
Ref map 7, C6
A14, Cesena exit and, once at the junction for the S.S. 161 towards Rimini, follow the signs for Cesenatico-viale Trento
40 rooms; ££/£££
Credit cards: AE VISA SI OD, bancomat

T his delightful Art Nouveau building was constructed in the 1920s and is surrounded by a lovely garden a few steps from the sea. The unfussy bedrooms are large and light, and equipped with air conditioning, safe, mini-bar and satellite television. The rooms are large and have charming furnishings and elegant details from the early 20th century. Breakfast is a buffet that can also be served outside on the terrace. Access to the beach, reserved for hotel guests, is across the wide terrace and beneath the olive trees which form a green screen between the beach and the hotel. Here there is bar service for quick snacks at lunchtime.

RECOMMENDED IN THE AREA

RESTAURANTS:
La Buca, Bistrot No Code *and* Lido Lido

VISIT:
The floating Marineria Museum, Cesenatico

Locanda del Passo Pompos

*O*n the old pilgrims' route to Rome near the very beautiful Pomposa abbey, is a pretty little building that has been reconstructed into a welcoming inn. It is a particularly charming place in a corner of the world where nature, art and peace blend together. The hotel rises up from the water on the left bank of the River Po at Volano in the national park of the Po delta, and has private mooring for boats.

The bedrooms are very new and attractive, with tasteful fabrics and furniture to match the rustic architecture of the house. A few bedrooms have a private terrace. The bathrooms all have bath or shower with hydromassage. Excursions with hired boats can be made from the private landing stage and guests may choose to go on the lagoon or as far as the sea where they can fish from the boat. Otherwise they may go on foot or bicycle along the lovely routes through the Delta park. There is a little tower in the inn from where birds, including rare varieties, may be observed on the Po delta.

On the old pilgrims' road

☎ 0533 719131
via Provinciale per Volano 13
44020 CODIGORO (Ferrara)
Ref map 7, A5
A13, Ferrara Sud exit, *superstrada* for Cormacchio, Migliarino-Portamaggiore exit, then left towards Massa Fiscaglia-Codigoro
26 rooms, 2 suites; **££**
Credit cards: ᴀᴇ 𝚟𝚒𝚜𝚊 𝚂𝚒 ⓪, bancomat

RECOMMENDED IN THE AREA

RESTAURANT:
La Capanna de Eraclio, *Ponte Vicini*

Caravel

In the Comacchio marshlands

☎ 0533 330106 🖷 0533 330107
viale Leonardo da Vinci 56
località Lido di Spina
44024 COMACCHIO (Ferrara)
Ref map 7, B6
A13, Ferrara sud exit, *superstrada* for Cormacchio, then S.S. 309 for Ravenna
22 rooms, 3 apartments; **£/££**
Credit cards: ᴀᴇ 𝚟𝚒𝚜𝚊 𝚂𝚒 ⓪, bancomat

*T*his little hotel amidst greenery is in a modern building with a lovely garden and is situated 200 metres from the sea. It has cheerful bedrooms with modern furniture and pale pink quilts: the whole effect is fresh and romantic. The sitting rooms are welcoming, mainly decorated in white along with a few panels with floral details. Together they create peaceful corners for comfortable moments of relaxation. The dining room is simple and elegant. The outside areas and terraces are equally well equipped. Hotel management is friendly and attentive to the requirements of guests. There is a tennis court and bicycles for hire.

RECOMMENDED IN THE AREA

RESTAURANT:
Osteria dalla Giulia
LOCAL SPECIALITIES:
Comacchio eels; Ferrara salamina da sugo*;*
Bosco Ericeo wine

161

Monte del Re

In an 18th-century monastery

☎ 0542 678400 🖷 0542 678444
📧 montedelre@mail.asianet.it
via Monte del Re 43
40050 DOZZA (Bologna)
Ref map 7, B5
A14, Castel San Pietro Terme, S.S. 9 towards
Imola, after 6 kms turn left
38 rooms; **££/£££**
Credit cards: ᴀᴇ 𝗩𝗜𝗦𝗔 𝗦𝗜 ⓓ

*T*he beautiful and imposing building, now an enchanting hotel but once a religious house, stands out on a hill and is surrounded by a great park. It belongs to the *Abitare la storia* hotel chain. Built in the 13th century, it was a monastery in the 18th century and has now been wonderfully restored. Large comfortable bedrooms have furnishings in the style of their surroundings. The sitting areas, which are indeed showpieces, consist of areas dedicated to reading (reading room and attached library), and others dedicated to meetings. A room has been created out of the former chapel, and the cloisters and refectory have also been transformed for conference hospitality. There is a bar, a winter garden and internal courtyard, and a restaurant. The reception rooms are gracious, with period furniture and paintings, lovely carpets and arrangements of flowers. Outside is a football pitch and a tennis court.

RECOMMENDED IN THE AREA

RESTAURANT:
Canè

VISIT:
15th-century sanctuary of the Madonna di Piratello; Imola, with its little 13th-century rock fortress

*C*lasshotel

Comfort, friendliness and a warm welcome

☎ 0546 46662 ✆ 0546 46676
✉ classfa@tin.it
via San Silvestro 171
48018 FAENZA (Ravenna)
Ref map 7, B5
A14, Faenza exit
69 rooms; ££
Credit cards: AE VISA SI ⓪

A modern-style hotel, located outside the city and easily reached from the motorway, this is a practical stopping point. Guests are welcomed into a large neat entrance hall with elegant furnishings: comfortable designer armchairs arranged in corners for quiet conversation. The bedrooms are spacious and attractive, all with fitted carpets, simple modern furniture and a careful choice of colour. They are equipped with every modern comfort: key card to open the door, satellite and pay television, safe and perfect soundproofing. There is a choice between smoking and non-smoking rooms. The bathrooms all have showers but no window and are very

RECOMMENDED IN THE AREA

RESTAURANT:
San Domenico, *Imola*

LOCAL SPECIALITY:
Faenza ceramics

practical with convenient washbasins and worktops. Various sizes of meeting rooms are available. The restaurant, which is not under the hotel management, looks on to a pretty courtyard interior that is decorated with plants. Both typical food from the Romagna region and international dishes are served, and speciality grills are prepared on the big barbecue in the centre of the room.

---

*T*orre

RECOMMENDED IN THE AREA

RESTAURANTS:
La Cantinetta; Al Tramezzino, *Parma*

LOCAL SPECIALITIES:
Langhirano prosciutto *(cured ham); Felino salami;*
San Secondo shoulder ham; Zibello culatello *ham;*
Grana cheese

In a romantic 17th-century mansion

☎ and ✆ 0521 831491
via A.Ghirardi 8
località San Michele Tiorre
43030 FELINO (Parma)
Ref map 6, A-B3
A1, Parma exit, after the city go south towards the hills
12 rooms, 3 suites; ££/£££
Credit cards: AE VISA SI ⓪

A great stone portal spans the entrance and opens into the courtyard in front of the building. In 1100 this was already the seat of the little community of Benedictine monks and in 1600 it took on the definitive appearance it has today. It has been a romantic little hotel for only a short while. The bedrooms differ in shape and decor. They are adorned with 18th- and 19th-century furniture and some still have working fireplaces. On the ground floor the hall, bar/sitting room and breakfast room are all furnished in the style of a family house. The cellars have been transformed into a *taverna* for gastronomic tastings: samples of the best cheeses, salamis and wine from the region. Around the hotel is a park through which runs a little stream. Guests may make use of both the La Rocca golf club only four kilometres away and the nearby riding school.

Annunziata

The Annunziata hotel has faced Estense Castle for four centuries, ever since it was the Annunziata inn beloved of Casanova. This charming hotel is undoubtedly one of the best in the Emilia region. Not only is it closely connected with the artistic and cultural life of the city, but the hotel itself has rich treasures. Paintings, signed ceramics, books and catalogues on the art exhibitions in the Diamanti palace enrich the rooms and help give them warmth and charm.

The bedrooms and suites, with views of Estense Castle or the Duchesse garden, have the atmosphere of an elegant private house and are endowed with every comfort. On the walls pastel tints are the background to sketches, all dedicated to the city of Ferrara, and in every room there is a book of stories as a welcome gift for guests. Very good breakfasts are served in a well-furnished lovely little room. Bicycles are available free of charge to guests, and there are Internet facilities in the hall.

Opposite Estense castle

☎ 0532 201111 📠 0532 203233
✉ annunzia@tin.it
piazza Repubblica 5
44100 FERRARA
Ref map 7, A5

A13, Ferrara Nord exit, direction of *centro città* (town centre), go towards Castello Estense
22 rooms; ££/£££
Credit cards: AE VISA SI ⓪

RECOMMENDED IN THE AREA

RESTAURANTS:
Max, *piazza della Repubblica;* Provvidenza, *corso Ercole I d'Este 92;* Riparestaurant, *via Ripagrande 21/B;* Torre dei leoni, *via Montebello 79/A*

LOCAL SPECIALITIES:
Ceramics from Ferrara; wines from the forest; Ferrarese bread and handmade grissini breadsticks

VISIT:
Estense Castle; Schifanoia Palace; the cathedral; Diamanti Palace and Nazionale Picture Gallery

Duchessa Isabella

*T*he façade of the Renaissance period, the unadorned bricks and pilasters are all simple and perfectly proportioned. The luxurious interior reflects the life of a noble family of that time. There are painted ceilings, grand fireplaces and a sumptuous staircase leading up to the great reception rooms on the upper floor reserved for the aristocrats. The Ercole I, Duchessa Isabella and Eleanora d'Aragona rooms contain the restaurant which is beautifully appointed, even in the modern furnishings and the positioning and setting of the tables. The rooms are equally elegant and decorated in a romantic fashion with a theme of red roses and flowers in the curtains and furnishings, in the tassels of the keys, the breakfast china and in many other details. The lady of the house is responsible for these charming touches. A lovely garden completes this little place of perfection. The hotel is in the *Relais & Chateaux* chain.

The culture and graciousness of noble Renaissance families

☎ 0532 2202121 📠 0532 202638
✉ isabelld@tin.it
via Palestro 70
44100 FERRARA
Ref map 7, A5
A13, Ferrara Nord exit, direction of *centro città* (centre of town), the hotel is in the historic centre, near piazza Ariostea
28 rooms; £££
Credit cards: AE VISA SI ◉

RECOMMENDED IN THE AREA

RESTAURANTS:
Romantica, via Ripagrande 34/40; Centrale, via Boccaleone 8; Il Bagattino, via Correggiari 6; Lanzagallo, Gaibana

VISIT:
Roman necropolis, Voghenza

Ripagrande

*L*iving in the historic centre of Ferrara means enjoying a calm not imaginable in other towns in the province. Here the noise of traffic is replaced with the odd bicycle bell or the conversation of passers-by.

The old mansion that houses the hotel stands in the middle of the historic centre, a short distance from all the major cultural and artistic attractions. The bedrooms, which are really suites, are elegant and welcoming. Each is different and all are equipped with the most modern comforts. In the entrance hall there are fragments of frescoes and wooden beams. There is an inner courtyard with Renaissance architecture where guests may take lunch in high season, rooms with tapestries, beautiful original antique furniture, and a high-class restaurant which offers very good local and regional dishes.

The hotel belongs to the *Abitare la Storia* chain.

RECOMMENDED IN THE AREA

RESTAURANT:
Provvidenza, *corso Ercole I d'Este 92*

LOCAL SPECIALITIES:
Ferrarese bread; pumpkin cappellacci *(filled pasta);* salama al sugo*; panpepato* cake*; hand-made* graffite *ceramics*

VISIT:
Estense Castle; Duomo *(cathedral); Diamanti Palace; Spina Museum*

A Renaissance palace in medieval Ferrara

☎ 0532 765250
📠 0532 764377
via Ripagrande 1
44100 FERRARA
Ref map 7, A5
A13, Ferrara Nord exit, direction of
centro città (town centre)
20 rooms; **£££**
Credit cards: AE VISA SI ◑

$\mathcal{T}$ouring

In the midst of Ferrarese life

☎ 0532 206200

🖷 0532 212000

viale Cavour 11

44100 FERRARA

Ref map 7, A5

A13, Ferrara Nord exit, direction of *centro città* (town centre)

57 rooms; **££**

Credit cards: AE VISA SI ⑩, bancomat

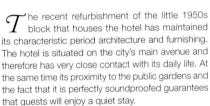

$\mathcal{T}$he recent refurbishment of the little 1950s block that houses the hotel has maintained its characteristic period architecture and furnishing. The hotel is situated on the city's main avenue and therefore has very close contact with its daily life. At the same time its proximity to the public gardens and the fact that it is perfectly soundproofed guarantees that guests will enjoy a quiet stay.

The bedrooms are very comfortable and well furnished and seem like elegant rooms in a private house with its own history. The large public rooms are all very well lit and enable guests to enjoy a comfortable stay and delightful moments of relaxation. Tickets for the important exhibitions that take place each year in the city may be purchased from the hotel's reception.

RECOMMENDED IN THE AREA

RESTAURANT:
Il Bagattino, *via Correggiari 6*

VISIT:
Estense rock fortress, Finale Emilia

Locanda Borgonuovo

A 17th-century mansion, formerly a religious house in Ferrara's historic centre

☎ 0532 211100
📠 0532 248000
via Cairoli 29
44100 FERRARA
Ref map 7, A5

A13, Ferrara Nord exit, direction of *centro città* (centre of town). Go towards Estense Castle
4 rooms; ££
Credit cards: AE VISA SI

*T*his inn was formerly the religious house and theological school of the Teatini fathers. Situated in the historic centre of Ferrara, a few steps from the castle, the theatres and the cathedral, it is identified only by a little door. This is the entrance to a welcoming and elegant place where guests are treated like family friends and where care is taken to maintain a close link with the cultural and commercial aspects of city life. In fact the inn offers a series of suggestions on how to enjoy the city: information about exhibitions, and special arrangements with restaurants, pizzerias, selected shops, golf courses and tennis courts. On the other hand, those who want a restful stay will find the inn is above all a welcoming and relaxing place. The single and double bedrooms are furnished with period furniture and ornaments. All have a private bathroom and air conditioning. There is a pretty garden in which to relax or take breakfast.

RECOMMENDED IN THE AREA

RESTAURANTS:
Centrale, *via Boccaleone 8,* Quel Fantastico Giovedì, *via Castelnuovo 9, and* L'oca giuliva

---

Locanda della Tamerice

Original cooking that draws on many sources, with contemporary recipes too

☎ 0533 680795, 0533 681811
📠 0533 681962
✉ iglesco@tin.it
via Argine Mezzano 2
località Valli di Ostellato
44020 FERRARA
Ref map 7, A5

A13, Ferrara Sud exit, junction with *autostrada* (motorway) in Portogaribaldi direction, Ostellato exit, then follow the signs for Valli di Ostellato and Locanda della Tamerice
4 rooms, 2 apartments; ££/£££
Credit cards: AE VISA SI ◉, bancomat

*F*or those who love the mix of scenic beauty deep in the peace of the countryside and good cooking, this inn is certainly an obligatory destination. It is lovely to glide in a boat between the reeds along the canals, watching the various species of birds that nest in this area, or fishing the numerous types of fish characteristic of the Po delta and waiting for the sunset to set fire to the calm waters. Afterwards the Emilian dishes prepared by the inn's manager who is a very good cook, will taste all the better. The accommodation consists of delightfully and practically furnished rooms, all with air conditioning. The restaurant offers mostly recipes from contemporary cuisine, prepared in an eclectic and very personal style.

RECOMMENDED IN THE AREA

RESTAURANT:
La Capanna de Eraclio, *Codigoro*
VISIT:
Po delta; Mesola forest; Pomposa Abbey

*I*mperiale

Delightful Art Nouveau hotel by the sea

☎ and 🖷 0547 86875
✉ hotelimperiale@icot.it
viale G. Cesare 82
47043 GATTEO A MARE (Forlì)
Ref map 7, C6
A14, Rimini Nord exit, S.S. 16, towards
Bellaria-Gatteo a Mare
37 rooms; **£/££**
Credit cards: AE VISA SÌ ⓪

*I*t is painted pink, with a few oriental-style details, and faces the sea. Once this was a private residence; now graceful restructuring has transformed it into a hotel with a bright interior, where modern furnishing combines with the floral features characteristic of Art Nouveau. The medium-sized bedrooms all have a terrace and simple but attractive furnishings. The wrought-iron beds and borders on the walls make the rooms bright and give them personality. The bathrooms are reasonably practical and all have a shower and a window. The communal rooms have, arranged on various levels, white and coloured furnishings and some Art Nouveau-style details. Bicycles are available to guests, together with a children's games room, garage (with just three car spaces), American bar, and summer activities.

RECOMMENDED IN THE AREA

RESTAURANT:
Dolce Vita

LOCAL SPECIALITY:
Typical piadina romagnola *flat bread*

---

*C*analgrande

*T*he hotel is in a magnificent 16th-century building right in the centre of Modena. The neo-classical lines of the exterior and interior are embellished by numerous frescoes and stucco-work in nearly all the rooms. A wonderful garden with a fountain and luxuriant greenery adds to the atmosphere of peace and harmony. The bedrooms and suites are elegantly furnished and very comfortable, with classically tasteful furniture. The hotel's restaurant is housed in the 17th-century basement. Dishes served are typical of the Emilia region: *tortellini* (pasta), *lesso di carne* (stewed meat), *zamponi con fagioli* (stuffed pig's trotters with beans), *gnocco fritto* (fried dumplings) and *tigelle*.

RECOMMENDED IN THE AREA

RESTAURANT:
Cucina del Museo, *via Sant'Agostino 7*

LOCAL SPECIALITIES:
Balsamic vinegar from Modena, Lambrusco Rubino red wine, parmigiano reggiano *cheese and* prosciutto *cured ham from Modena*

VISIT:
Duomo *(cathedral); Ghirlandina Tower and historic rooms of the Palazzo Comunale*

Frescoes and stucco-work in a 16th-century palace

☎ 059 217160 🖷 059 221674
✉ info@canalgrandehotel.it
corso Canalgrande 6
41100 MODENA
Ref map 6, B4
A1, Modena Sud or Modena Nord exit,
towards *centro storico* (historic centre)
69 rooms; **£££**
Credit cards: AE VISA SÌ ⓪

$\mathcal{M}$ini Hotel Le Ville

In a farmhouse built in the classic style of the Emilian countryside

☎ 059 510051
📠 059 511187
✉ leville@tin.it
via Giardini 1270
41100 MODENA
Ref map 6, B4

A1, Modena Nord exit, *tangenziale* (by-pass) towards Sassuolo, Baggiovara exit
46 rooms; **££/£££**
Credit cards: AE VISA SI OD, bancomat

RECOMMENDED IN THE AREA

RESTAURANT:
Fini, *rua Frati Minori 54*

VISIT:
Historic centre with the Duomo *(cathedral); Accademia and gardens; Ferrari car factory, Maranello*

Originally Le Ville was a late 19th-century farmhouse built in the classic style of the Emilian countryside. Refurbishment has preserved the external architecture and improved the facilities and practicality of the interior. The hotel is surrounded by the green of a large park and is only a few kilometres from the historic centre of Modena. The bedrooms are very large and light with pleasant modern furniture creating an overall elegance The communal rooms, too, are very large and welcoming. Outside, the areas around the swimming pool are well equipped. Sauna, gym and hydromassage are possible diversions for enjoyable hours of relaxation. The restaurant is under different management and offers typical Emilian and classic dishes, all prepared creatively by the chef.

$\mathcal{P}$alazzo Viviani

A hotel that is magically timeless

☎ 0541 855350 📠 0541 855340
via Roma 38
47837 MONTEGRIDOLFO (Rimini)
Ref map 7, C6

A14, Pesaro-Urbino exit, S.S. 423 towards Urbino, turn left at Montecchio for Montegridolfo
22 rooms; **££**
Credit cards: AE VISA SI OD

The castle is enclosed within walls and has a watchtower, and its medieval centre is perfectly conserved. A great portal leads inside. Like all Malatesta rock fortresses, it stands high on a hill dominating the countryside and inside are wonderfully atmospheric buildings. The hotel is within the Viviani Palace, magically detached from the present, from noise and tourism, and has beautiful areas of enormous character. There are lovely bedrooms and suites, all different, have antique furniture that fit perfectly with the surroundings. The communal rooms are large and airy and include the *Sala del Grande Camino* (the room with the big fireplace) and the *Sala di Lettura* (reading room) with a well-stocked library. There are also five little houses in the *Casa del Pittore* (painter's house) outbuilding, which are situated in the palace garden in a charming corner of the village.

RECOMMENDED IN THE AREA

RESTAURANTS:
Il Ristoro di palazzo Viviani, L'Osteria dell'Accademia *and* Ristorante dell'Agrumaia

VISIT:
"The Madonna with Child and Saints" by Guido Cagnacci in the church of San Rocco

$\mathcal{V}$illa Belfiore

RECOMMENDED IN THE AREA

RESTAURANT:
Locanda della Tamerice

LOCAL SPECIALITIES:
Pasta filled with nettles; pumpkin; chicory; cakes and tarts

VISIT:
Comacchio valleys; Po delta; Campotto haven

Quiet and rest, respecting nature

☎ 0533 681164 📠 0533 681172
via Pioppa 27
44020 OSTELLATO (Ferrara)
Ref map 7, A-B5
A13, Ferrara Sud exit, motorway junction
towards Portogaribaldi, Ostellato exit
10 rooms; **££/£££**
Credit cards: 📧 📧 📧 ⓞ, bancomat

*T*his is in a family villa, in one of the peninsula's most unpolluted areas of natural beauty. A large park full of native plants and medicinal herbs surrounds the hotel. Dunes, lagoons and marshes form a unique and poetic background.

Inside, the hotel is furnished in classic style with antique and rustic furniture, ensuring the utmost tranquillity. All the little sitting rooms and bedrooms are comfortable and elegant, and are equipped with air conditioning. The restaurant serves food prepared by the same *agrituristismo* business that runs the hotel: vegetables from the organically cultivated land and vegetarian dishes with herbs, as well as traditional Emilian recipes.

$\mathcal{V}$erdi

In an elegant little Art Nouveau mansion

☎ 0521 293539, 0521 293549
📠 0521 293559
via Pasini 18
43100 PARMA
Ref map 6, A3
A1, Parma exit, in the *centro* direction, then
follow the signs for the parco Ducale
20 rooms; **££**
Credit cards: 📧 📧 📧 ⓞ, bancomat

RECOMMENDED IN THE AREA

RESTAURANTS:
Antica Osteria Fontana, *via Farini 24/A;*
Palazzo Calvi, *Samboseto*

VISIT:
Church of San Giovanni Evangelista with frescos by Coreggio and Parmigianino

*F*acing and surrounding the hotel that was once the home of Maria Luigia d'Asburgo is the green and shady Ducale park with its ancient trees. An elegant Art Nouveau façade, an entrance in the style of a private residence, and a well-tended *parterre* flower garden greet guests on their arrival. The small, secluded living rooms are furnished with antique and period-style furniture, and the breakfast room tastefully combines Empire-style tables with floral decoration on the walls. The bedrooms are well appointed and have modern furniture chosen to blend with the early 20th-century architecture. Next to the hotel is the Santa Croce restaurant that has been created out of the former stables. The management is different, but the two establishments work together well and pay the same attention to detail.

$\mathcal{L}$e Quattro Piume

A simple but welcoming hotel

☎ 051 6861500 📠 051 974191
via XXV Aprile 15
40066 PIEVE DI CENTO (Bologna)
Ref map 6, B4
A14, before the Bologna junction with the A14,
S.S. 568, then immediately right towards Cento
16 rooms; **£/££**
Credit cards: AE VISA SI Ⓜ, bancomat

RECOMMENDED IN THE AREA

RESTAURANTS:
Buriani *and* Caimano

$\mathcal{T}$his unusual name kindles memories of the musketeers with their duels, and of the stories of their adventures. In fact it is all very quiet here. The hotel is in a little white house with dark shutters, a well-tended courtyard garden, and neat and spacious bedrooms with mini-bars, colour televisions, ceiling fans, simple modern furniture in light wood, white bedcovers and spotless curtains at the windows.

The bedrooms are on two floors (there is no lift) and those on the second floor are attic style. The bathrooms are small but very practical. This is an altogether simple establishment situated on the edge of the historic centre of a town that has conserved its medieval layout, is marked out by porticoes and symmetrical streets, and is rich in works of art.

$\mathcal{A}$l Vecchio Convento

Suroundings that are both rustic and refined

☎ 0543 967053 📠 0543 967157
📧 vecchioconvento@mail.asianet.it
via Roma 7
località Portico di Romagna
47010 PORTICO
E SAN BENEDETTO (Forlì)
Ref map 7, C5
A14, Forlì exit, then continue on the S.S. 67
towards Firenze (Florence)
15 rooms; **££**
Credit cards: AE VISA SI Ⓜ, bancomat

$\mathcal{A}$ winding panoramic road leads to this hotel which has been created out of a careful piece of restoration work. The 19th-century building has been transformed into a charming establishment for providing hospitality, and has conserved the original unspoilt atmosphere.

On arrival guests are welcomed into an interior that is rustic and refined at the same time: there are white walls, terracotta floors, hand-painted ceramics and hand-worked wrought iron. Accommodation is in bedrooms that are furnished simply and tastefully. The communal rooms with their pleasing architecture still

have the old arches and large fireplaces, and are furnished partly with antiques. The establishment bears the name of Giovanni Carmeli and Marisa Raggi: this married couple, with the help of their children, share their duties between careful preparation of typical regional dishes using ingredients in season, and the friendly and attentive care of guests.

RECOMMENDED IN THE AREA

RESTAURANT:
Mulino San Michele, *Tredozio*

I Tre Re

A building which dates back to the 1300s, a short distance from the sea

☎ 0541 629760 📠 0541 629368
via F.lli Cervi 1
47824 POGGIO BERNI (Rimini)
Ref map 7, C6
A14, Rimini Nord exit, towards Sant'Arcangelo di Romagna-Poggio Berni
13 rooms, 1 suite; ££
Credit cards: AE VISA SI ◑, bancomat

Some parts of this hotel date back to the 14th century. It stands in a peaceful rural area only a few kilometres from the sea and the popular beaches. The low building is rustic, typical of the area, and made of stone. The bedrooms are carefully furnished, with features reflecting the ancient origins of the hotel. In some, wooden beams and fireplaces add to the charm of the interior, and all have a splendid view stretching as far as the sea. In the part of the hotel which was a watch-tower during the 14th century, a cosy little room has been created for discreet meals, and the place is full of character. In summer the restaurant provides service outside in the garden and on the patio under a big canopy, with romantic lighting. The wine cellar, which has been built in stone and brick in accordance with the original style, contains old oak casks and selected wines.

RECOMMENDED IN THE AREA

RESTAURANTS:
Osteria La Sangiovesa, *Santarcangelo;* Zanni, *Verruchio*

*C*asa Matilde

*T*he feminine name recalls Matilda of Tuscany who dominated these lands from the Canossa stronghold. The bedrooms of the hotel, too, are named after other famous women, historical figures who inspired poets: there is an Isabella Gonzaga room, another dedicated to Lucrezia Borgia who was the wife of Alfonso I of Este, and yet another called the Beatrice d'Este room. The graceful villa stands in the middle of a beautiful park and is reached by avenues bordered with roses and flanked by cypresses.

Inside, the sitting rooms and salons are formal in appearance but softened by flower arrangements, cretonne curtains and large fireplaces. The rooms are big and full of character, the antique furniture perfectly suited to the interior. The ceilings are sometimes attic style, the high beds are made of brass or wrought iron, the armchairs are comfortable and there is warm parquet flooring. The restaurant is in the Carpineti room and local dishes inspire the cooking; at breakfast there is home-made cake. A large terrace and garden 'lounge' are ideal for moments of relaxation.

In an old patrician villa, with rooms named after immortal women

☎ and 📠 0522 889006
via Ada Negri 11
località Puianello
42030 QUATTRO CASTELLA (Reggio Emilia)
Ref map 6, B3

A1, Reggio Emilia exit, S.S. 63 towards la Spezia as far as Puianello, then go on in the direction of Quattro Castella and before Montecavolo turn right for the hotel

4 rooms, 2 suites; £££
Credit cards: AE VISA SI ⓄⒹ, bancomat

RECOMMENDED IN THE AREA

RESTAURANTS:
Mammarosa, *San Polo;* Il Picchio, *Neviano degli Arduini*

LOCAL SPECIALITIES:
Prosciutto *cured ham,* culatello *ham and farm-produced salami;* cappelletti *pasta,* erbazzone *and* tortelli *(filled pasta)*

VISIT:
Canossa Castle; castles of Parma and Reggio nell' Emilia

Cappello

In an elegant little 16th-century mansion

☎ 0544 219813 📠 0544 219814
via IV Novembre 41
48100 RAVENNA
Ref map 7, B6
A14, then A14 straight on to the end
9 rooms; ££/£££
Credit cards: AE VISA SI Ⓞ

This hotel is in a little 16th-century mansion in a pedestrian zone in the historic centre of Ravenna. There are only a few bedrooms but these are beautiful with panelled ceilings, co-ordinated décor, lovely parquet flooring and period furniture. The marble bathrooms are large and sumptuous – all have windows and five of them have bathtubs. The rooms open onto a gallery that is often used to display paintings or modern sculpture. The reception hall is in the same style as the rest of the hotel, and here more sculpture and ornaments have been tastefully blended with the refined antique surroundings. The restaurant is both cosy and elegant, and is also open to non-residents.

RECOMMENDED IN THE AREA

RESTAURANTS:
Trattoria al Gallo, Tre Spade *and* Trattoria Capannetti

Park Hotel

A peaceful and very hospitable atmosphere

☎ 0522 292141
📠 0522 292143
via De Ruggero 1
42028 REGGIO NELL'EMILIA
Ref map 6, B3
A1, Reggio Emilia exit, towards
centro storico (historic centre),
from which go on towards Passo
Cerreto
41 rooms; ££
Credit cards: AE VISA SI Ⓞ, bancomat

The hotel is in a large park in the neighbourhood of Reggio nell'Emilia, outside the city but close enough to the centre to reach it by car in a few minutes. The interior is furnished in the 'English country' style, which is certainly unusual in this area, but nevertheless is charming and relaxing. The bedrooms and mini-suites are pretty and welcoming. They all have a balcony, and the delightful flowered bedcovers in restful colours match the wallpaper and fitted carpets. They are equipped with air conditioning, satellite television and mini-bar. The small but comfortable restaurant offers traditional Emilian cooking and classic dishes.

RECOMMENDED IN THE AREA

RESTAURANTS:
Cinque Pini-Da Pelati, *viale Maritiri di Cervarolo 46 and* Capriolo, *via Tassoni 223*

LOCAL SPECIALITIES:
Balsamic vinegar; Parmigiano Reggiano *cheese*

VISIT:
Palaces of Banco di San Gimignano and San Prospero; cloisters of the Santa Maria delle Grazie Monastery; Teatro Comunale (theatre); Reggio nell' Emilia; Canossa and the lands of Matilda, ruins of the famous castle there

Posta

In the Capitano del Popolo palace

☎ 0522 432944
🖷 0522 452602
✉ hotelposta@citynet.re.it
piazza del Monte 2
42100 REGGIO NELL'EMILIA
Ref map 6, B3

A1, Reggio nell'Emilia exit, towards *centro storico* (historic centre)

43 rooms; £££
Credit cards: AE VISA SI Ⓞ, bancomat

RECOMMENDED IN THE AREA

RESTAURANTS:
Caffè Arti e Mestieri, *via Emilia San Pietro 16;*
Enoteca Morini, *via Passo Buole 82*

LOCAL SPECIALITIES:
Balsamic vinegar; Parmigiano Reggiano *cheese*

VISIT:
Duomo *(cathedral), baptistery, Teatro Municipale and San Prospero Basilica*

P lazzo del Capitano del Popolo (the palace of the people's captain) is a splendid medieval building situated in Reggio's historic centre. Four centuries of hotel tradition are discernible, not only in the beauty of the interior but also in the utmost professionalism of the staff – which is never too formal but always very attentive to the needs of guests.

The rooms inside have become even more practical after recent restoration work that has managed to preserve intact the charm of the medieval building. The bedrooms and suites are elegantly furnished and care is taken over the slightest detail. All are equipped with air-conditioning and mini-bars. There is also a wonderful meeting room, with frescoes on the walls and beautiful large windows. The hotel restaurant serves Emilian and classic dishes.

Nabila

In an old country residence

☎ 0522 973197
🖷 0522 971222
via Marconi 4
42046 REGGIOLO (Reggio nell'Emilia)
Ref map 6, A3

A22, Reggiolo-Rolo
26 rooms, 6 apartments; £/££
Credit cards: AE VISA SI Ⓞ, bancomat

T he villa is surrounded by a large park and stands in the historic centre of Reggiolo, a typical town of the River Po lowlands. At the end of the 17th century it was a country residence, which was subsequently enlarged. Now transformed into a hotel, it has maintained the character and delightful atmosphere derived from its history. The bedrooms are in the old stables and are carefully furnished in pastel colours and classic designs, with beautiful hangings and upholstery. The bathrooms are modern and practical. Communal rooms are large and attractive, with period features that give personality to the comfortably modern interior. The restaurant, in the main building, also has lovely rooms suitable for banquets and ceremonies: normal service is in a room with decorated ceilings and antique furniture. The kitchen prepares specialities of the Emilian region.

RECOMMENDED IN THE AREA

RESTAURANT:
Buriani dal 1967, *Pieve di Cento*

VISIT:
Medieval rock fortress

$\mathcal{A}$tilius

A brightly coloured building for a holiday with every comfort

☎ and 🖷 0541 647624
via Boito 3
47838 RICCIONE (Rimini)
Ref map 7, C6
A14, Riccione exit,
go on towards the sea
51 rooms; £££
Credit cards: AE VISA SI ⓪

The marble bathrooms are impeccable, with complimentary toiletry set and accessories. The communal rooms and reception hall are light and attractive.

Guests, particularly families with young children, receive a warm welcome. Cyclists, too, are well catered for.

*T*his is a construction in a cheerful modern style, with a bright fuchsia and petrol blue exterior. Recently refurbished, it uses the latest hotel design technology – hence there is perfect soundproofing, air conditioning of course, and every other comfort.

Restructuring has reduced the number of bedrooms from 66 to 51: they are now large with modern navy-style furniture in mahogany, with carefully chosen upholstery and hangings, comfortable interior-sprung divan beds, attractive fittings and lovely parquet flooring.

RECOMMENDED IN THE AREA

RESTAURANTS:
Birreria Hops, Azzurra *and* Casale

LOCAL SPECIALITIES:
Prints on modern and antique canvases

Acasamia

Kind attentiveness in a delightful atmosphere

☎ 0541 391370

📠 0541 391816

✉ acasamia@iper.net

via Parisano 34

47900 RIMINI

Ref map 7, C6

A14, Rimini Sud exit, towards the sea

40 rooms; ££

Credit cards: 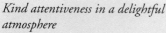, bancomat

The hotel is in a modern block in a quiet street that is bordered by little mansions evoking Rimini in the early 1900s. The bedrooms have simple but pleasing furniture. The communal rooms have the charming atmosphere of a private house. The hotel's restaurant is open from June until September and serves typical, mainly fish, dishes of the area. The management takes care of guests with thoughtful attention.

RECOMMENDED IN THE AREA

RESTAURANTS:
Acero Rosso, *viale Tiberio II, and* Embassy, *viale Vespucci 35*

LOCAL SPECIALITIES:
Tagliatelle *(ribbon-shaped pasta) and* strozzapreti *(spinach dumplings); ceramics, turned clay products and terracotta products; hand-printed pictures*

VISIT:
Malatestino Temple; for children: Mirabilandia Amusement Park, Italia in miniatura *(model of Italy), Dolphin park*

Grand Hotel Porro

A haven of silence in the heart of the city of thermal baths

☎ 0524 578211 🖷 0524 577878
viale Porro 10
43039 SALSOMAGGIORE TERME (Parma)
Ref map 6, A2
A1, Fidenza exit, towards Salsomaggiore, *centro storico* (historic centre)
81 rooms; **££/£££**
Credit cards: AE VISA SI ⓜ, bancomat

S tanding on the lowest slopes of the Appennine mountains and a few minutes away from the thermal baths, the hotel is in a large private park full of trees yet is only 100 metres from the lively centre of the little town.

A totally relaxing stay awaits both regular visitors to the baths and more occasional guests. In fact the thermal cures increasingly include fitness and beauty treatments in their programmes, and so also attract young clients who want a break in elegant surroundings. The hotel bedrooms and suites have air conditioning, television and mini-bar. The hotel is equipped with a sauna, solarium and indoor swimming pool: in short everything necessary to boost wellbeing and promote relaxation. The restaurant offers classic and Emilian dishes, in a perfect combination of traditional flavours and original recipes.

RECOMMENDED IN THE AREA

RESTAURANTS:
Querce; Antica Trattoria del Duomo, *Fidenza*

LOCAL SPECIALITIES:
Parmigiano Reggiano *cheese;* Parma ham; Felino salami; Zibello culatello *(ham)*

VISIT:
Berzieri thermal baths, *Terme;* Stirone regional river park

Locanda Calori

A historic spot in the centre of the village

☎ 051 811111
🖷 051 818818
piazza Calori 16
40018 SAN PIETRO IN CASALE (Bologna)
Ref map 6, B4
A13, Altedo exit
11 rooms; **££/£££**
Credit cards: AE VISA SI ⓞ

RECOMMENDED IN THE AREA

RESTAURANTS:
Dolce e salato; L'800, *Argelato*

VISIT:
Gastronomic route through the Bolognese lowland;
Argelato wine cellars with quality wines;
museum of farming life, San Marino di Bentivoglio

The towers one comes across in this territory used to control a close network of canals under Bologna's authority. These marshy areas, which had been drained since the 18th century, were subject to regular flooding by the River Reno. San Pietro in Casale has an old centre, with 18th-century porticoes around its central square. The inn is in a period building that has been well refurbished and is in this historic centre. The place is old, but the furnishings are attractively modern. The rooms still have wooden beams. But it is the inn's restaurant that has made this place famous. The cooking is well known, especially the pasta: there are a thousand and one forms of pasta of every shape and colour, and we are not exaggerrating! But not only the first courses are delicious, for imagination and care are taken over the preparation of main courses and sweets.

Il Povero Diavolo

A simple, welcoming hotel and top-class cuisine

☎ 0541 675060
via Roma 30
47030 TORRIANA (Rimini)
Ref map 7, C6
A14, Rimini Nord exit, towards
Sant'Arcangelo de Romagna-Torriana
5 rooms; **££**
Credit cards: AE VISA SI

RECOMMENDED IN THE AREA

VISIT:
In the last week of November a national seminary on Fossa cheese, including tasting sessions

Standing at the foot of the ancient rock fortress, this pretty refurbished inn is in an 18th-century house in the historic village of Torriano.

The building is on more than one level: on the upper floor is the inn, where the attractive bedrooms have antique furniture worn with the patina of age and panelled ceilings. A little sitting room and breakfast room are just as welcoming. On the ground floor the doors, designed by Tonino Guerra, open into the restaurant. Served here are authentic local dishes using 500 recipes drawn from local sources, both oral and written. The territory around is the area of the rocky Valmarecchia hills dominated by historic castles and by the spurs of the Montefeltro region. And only 18 kilometres away are the sea and Rimini with its nightlife.

Cà Monduzzi Zocca

An old farmhouse dating back to the 17th century, in the midst of enchanting quiet

☎ 059 9876206
via Vignolese 1130 D
41100 ZOCCA (Modena)
Ref map 6, B4
A1, Modena Sud exit, S.S, 623 towards Spilamberko-Vignola-Giuglia-Zocca
7 apartments; £/££
Credit cards not accepted

*T*his is a farmhouse dating back to the 17th century and completely restructured in 1990. The work created three one-roomed and four two-roomed apartments. The rooms are rustic and attractive; the pleasing furniture looks as though it belongs in someone's home and is well arranged in its surroundings. We are on the hillside, the view is of the upper valley of the Panaro River and there are oak trees and chestnuts as far as the eye can see. There are no roads visible to interrupt the beauty of the landscape and the charm of the silence. Quiet roads take one to parish churches and sanctuaries, castles, rocks and ancient villages or to discover the gastronomic treasures that are abundant in this area. The establishment is open during July and August, but only at weekends for the rest of the year.

RECOMMENDED IN THE AREA

RESTAURANTS:
Giusti, *vicolo Squallore 46, and* Cucina del Museo, *via Sant'Agostino 7, Modena*

Locanda dell'Artista

Elegant, modern surroundings

☎ 0549 996024 ℻ 0549 996024
via del Dragone 18
località Montegiardino
47898 REPUBBLICA DI SAN MARINO
Ref map 7, C6
A14, Rimini Sud exit, take the *superstrada* (dual-carriageway) for San Marino
3 rooms; ££
Credit cards: 𝔸𝔼 𝗩𝗜𝗦𝗔 𝗦𝗜 ⓪

*S*tanding in the historic centre of Montegiardino, is this early-20th-century building. It has been completely refurbished, retaining the murals in the bedrooms and adding reproductions of modern art (Picasso, Grosz, Severini, Magritte, Domenico Bianchi and still more), for this is the owner's passion.

The hotel has three bedrooms and two suites. Needless to say the rooms are as carefully tended as porcelain and as elegant as Tiffany glass. The furniture is inspired by that of the early 20th century, with cream-coloured carpets and floors which are either original or else in the style of that era. Bathrooms are large and very well appointed, all with hydromassage baths.

It would not be possible for such a refined house to lack attractive corners for conversation and rest, and a bar. The restaurant has stone walls, and is furnished in an elegantly sparse manner, with lighting designed to set off the modern paintings decorating the walls.

RECOMMENDED IN THE AREA

RESTAURANTS:
Righi la Taverna, *piazza Libertà 10, San Marino;* La Sangiovese, *Santarcangelo di Romagna;* L'Osteria del Povero Diavolo, *Torriana;* Zanni, *Villa Verrucchio*

*T*itano

In the monumental centre of the old republic

☎ 0549 991006 📠 0549 991375
✉ hoteltitano@omniway.sm
contrada del Collegio 31
47890 SAN MARINO
Ref map 7, C6
A14, Rimini Sud exit, take the *superstrada* (dual-carriageway) for San Marino
47 rooms; **££**
Credit cards: AE VISA SI ◑, bancomat

*T*he hotel is in the historic centre amidst the monuments of this ancient republic. It sets out to provide a restful place for lazy holidays as well as a chance stopping point for those travelling without any prearranged programme.

It was inaugurated on 30 September 1894, the same day as the *Palazzo Pubblico* (public palace or town hall), and therefore has always been in close contact with the institutional and social life of the tiny state of San Marino. Many illustrious men have stayed here.

All the bedrooms are different and are equipped with every comfort. They have antique or period-style furniture that blends perfectly with the architecture of the building.

The hotel has more than one restaurant, and the rooms are delightfully old. From the terrace of the restaurant on the top floor there is an enchanting view over the Appenines and the rock fortress, and for romantic candle-lit dinners there is a little balcony which is set apart and overlooks the panorama.

In addition the hotel has a garage and a solarium.

HOTEL TITANO

RECOMMENDED IN THE AREA

RESTAURANTS:
Hosteria La Botte, *Gradara;* Ristorante Rocca, *Verrucchio*

LOCAL SPECIALITIES:
Hand-made ceramics and examples of goldsmith's craft

Tuscany

In Tuscany the hills succeed one another with shadows that change according to the light and the colours of the seasons

Moderation, balance, sublime simplicity, civilised landscape, nature that becomes art: hundreds of descriptions have attempted to define the enchantment of Tuscany. The best way to experience the heart of Tuscany is to spend time there. The welcome and hospitality of the region is a very strong tradition and many people from other places have adopted it as their home.

A region usually remembered as a single entity actually comprises several areas with clearly distinct geography and landscapes. The sea and the Apennines, rivers and scattered heights such as the Metallifere hills enclose basins between mountains, hilly districts and plains. Lunigiana, Gargagnana, Mugello, Chianti, Casentino, Valdarno, Valdichiana and fascinating Maremma are just some of these.

The coastline extends in long sandy stretches as far as Mount Agentario; and the islands of the archipelago – from Elba to Giglio – are a world of their own, as are the harsh Apuan Alps with white peaks in the Versilia area. Many Tuscan places are paradigms of Italian landscape and art, tourist shrines since the time of the Grand Tour. One need only think of Chianti – vines, olives and cypresses, and farmhouses – or the rhythmic flow of hills around Siena that changes according to the time of day and the colour of the season.

There are towns wherever there is a square, a church and a palace. Apart from the universally famous Florence, Siena, Pisa and Lucca, other delightful examples of urban art include Pienza and Certaldo, Pitigliano and Montepulciano, Cortona and Volterra. The areas of natural beauty – the Crete Senesi and mountains of Uccelina, the lagoons and surviving pinewoods of the *tomboli*, the oak forests and fir woods of Casentino, the peaks of the Apuan Alps – all offer rare charm.

Medieval and Renaissance art has many highlights in this region and is diffused widely in the parish churches, walls, religious houses and villas of both the countryside and the towns. Long visited and studied, Tuscany has not been exhausted: every successive visit brings new and astonishing discoveries.

*I*l Paretaio

In an 18th-century farmhouse between woods, vineyards and olive groves

☎ 055 8059218 📠 055 8059231
✉ ilparetaio@tin.it
strada delle Ginestre 12
50021 BARBERINO VAL D'ELSA (Firenze)
Ref map 6, D4

A1, Firenze-Certosa exit, *superstrada* (dual-carriageway) for Siena, Tavarnelle exit, past Barberino Val d'Elsa, turn right for San Filippo
6 rooms, 2 apartments; £
Credit cards not accepted

A large 18th-century farmhouse in an isolated position with a wonderful view, three kilometres from the village. There is a friendly, family

atmosphere and the Tuscan cooking is very good. Meals are taken together around a big larch table in the old dining room. The bedrooms are in the main house and all are attractive, tastefully furnished and have private bathrooms. One, in what was the old pigeon-loft, is very romantic. The owners manage the hotel, helped by their two sons plus a staff of four. Their main business is their riding school, which is run with great professionalism. However, the hotel is also a good place for any tourist to stay. The riding school has 25 horses and there are courses at every level. The hotel has a swimming pool and children's playground.

RECOMMENDED IN THE AREA

RESTAURANT:
paese dei Campanelli, *Petrognano*
LOCAL SPECIALITIES:
Wine and oil produced by the farm
VISIT:
Parish church of Sant'Appiano

---

*I*l Fienile

An elegant residence in the countryside

☎ and 📠 0575 593396
✉ zetaemme@technet.it
località Gresse
52011 BIBBIENA (Arezzo)
Ref map, 7 D5

A14, Cesena exit, then S.S. 71 towards Passo Mandrioli
6 rooms; £/££
Credit cards: AE VISA SI

RECOMMENDED IN THE AREA

RESTAURANTS:
Il Bivio; Buca di Michelangelo, *Caprese Michelangelo*
LOCAL SPECIALITIES:
Fabrics from the Casentino area including cashmere, Stia; old weaving workshop, Anghiari; locally produced honey

*T*his old barn has been restructured with traditional materials and transformed into a welcoming inn with a few bedrooms. It is on a hill with panoramic views close to the national park of the Casentinesi forests, an unspoilt expanse of fir and chestnut forests that is centuries old. Here there are guided tours along hidden paths.

The bedrooms are elegantly furnished in rustic period-style furniture and have ceiling beams of characteristic chestnut wood. On the ground floor comfortable sofas and a large stone fireplace invite guests to linger in enjoyable and lazy conversation; the windows open on to a big garden and a lovely swimming pool. A short distance away there is a golf course, indoor swimming pool, sports facilities, riding schools and a little lake for fishing.

La Ripolina

Charming solitude on a hillside

☎ and ✆ **0577 282280**
località Pieve di Piana
53022 BUONCONVENTO (Siena)
Ref map 6, E4
A1, at the Firenze-Certosa junction with the Firenze-Siena motorway, take S.S. 2 towards San Quirico d'Orcia
6 rooms, 2 apartments; **£/££**
Credit cards not accepted

Surrounded by a wonderful panorama, this complex is 200 metres above sea level on a hill. Not far away, in charming solitude on an elevated site dominating the clay hills of Siena, is the Monte Oliveto Maggiore abbey where Giovanni Tolomei withdrew from the world. All around, and only a few kilometres away, are the attractions of important cities of art.

This *agriturismo* (farm accommodation) has bedrooms and two little apartments, each sleeping four people, plus four larger apartments for up to 10 people. Accommodation is in an old 19th-century parish church or else in 16th- and 19th-century typical Tuscan farmsteads. The exterior is in warm-coloured stone and inside there are beamed ceilings, late 19th-century furniture and a simple family atmosphere. All the apartments have a fireplace. Available to guests

are laundry facilities, a barbecue, children's playground, bicycles, table tennis and two artificial lakes for fishing. In the immediate vicinity there are also a swimming pool, tennis courts and riding school.

RECOMMENDED IN THE AREA

RESTAURANT:
La Torre, *Monte Oliveto Maggiore*

LOCAL SPECIALITIES:
Nobile di Montepulciano and Brunello de Montalcino wines; Sienese sweets; terracotta and ceramic products

VISIT:
Montalcino; Siena; Murlo; Monte Oliveto Maggiore Abbey

Locanda Le Monache

The best gastronomic cooking using traditional ingredients

☎ 0584 989258
📠 0584 984011
✉ lemonache@caen.it
piazza XXIX Maggio 36
55041 CAMAIORE (Lucca)
Ref map 6, C3
A12, Viareffio exit, towards Camaiore
13 rooms; £/££
Credit cards: AE VISA SI ⓄⒹ, bancomat

RECOMMENDED IN THE AREA

RESTAURANT:
Il Centro Storico

LOCAL SPECIALITIES:
Coppa *(cured neck of pork); wine tasting*

VISIT:
Sant'Anna di Stazzena; Lake Puccini Tower

*T*he inn is in an old building in the historic centre of Camaiore, facing the town's main street, a street that was once the pilgrims' route. The inn is named after a nunnery of the enclosed order of Carmelite sisters that stood next to the palace.

The simple, pretty hotel has been recently refurbished: it has attractive comfortable bedrooms furnished on modern lines. The practical bathrooms have showers and hair-dryers.

The busy restaurant is run by the owners, and since 1923 has served regional dishes of a high standard. Guests are required to stay for a minimum of three days, full board.

Capo Sud

Wonderful greenery close to the sea

☎ 0565 964021 📠 0565 964263
via Capo del Marinaro 311
57037 CAPOLIVERI (Livorno)
Ref map 6, F3
A12, Rosignano M., *superstrada* (dual-carriageway) Roma-Livorno, Venturina exit for porto di Piombino; then *traghetto* (ferry) for Portoferraio, leave the port towards Porto Azzurro, and turn right for Lacona
42 rooms; ££
Credit cards not accepted

RECOMMENDED IN THE AREA

RESTAURANT:
Il Chiasso

LOCAL SPECIALITIES:
Aleatico, Elba bianco and Elba rosso wines

VISIT:
View of the 'three seas'; Napoleon's summer residence at San Maritno and Portoferraio home; Mount Capanne, the highest point of Elba

*H*ere there are pine, eucalyptus and olive trees, shades of green and of the blue of the sea. The Capo Sud hotel is both amidst the greenery and on the sea, in the enchanting Stella gulf on the island of Elba, surrounded by a park in which the little buildings containing the bedrooms nestle peacefully. These rooms are modern and painted the colours of the sea, with ceramic tiled floors, private terraces and bathrooms with showers and hair dryers. In the main hotel are the communal rooms, including a small library and the restaurant. There is another restaurant beside the lovely swimming pool facing the sea. There are also bicycles free to guests, a tennis court with synthetic grass and illumination at night, and boat and canoe hire on the large private beach.

$\mathcal{S}$alivolpi

*On a hill in the Chianti area, with a view
over Siena, Volterra and San Gimignano*

☎ 0577 740484 📠 0577 740998

📧 info@hotelsalivolpi.com

via Fiorentina 89

**53011 CASTELLINA IN CHIANTI
(Siena)**

Ref map 6, D4

A1, Firenze-Certosa exit, S.S. 222 towards
Greve in Chianti, then Castellina in Chianti

19 rooms; **££**

Credit cards: AE VISA SI

$\mathcal{A}$n old rural building that has been recently
converted into a hotel without changing
the original characterisics that gave it such a unique
atmosphere. This hotel is situated on a hill where the
ancient Etruscan settlement of Castellina stood, and
the gently rolling panorama opens on to the Elsa
valley and the towers of San Gimignano as far as
Volterra; surrounding it is Gallo Nero ('black
cockerel') country, or rather Chianti.

The hotel's bedrooms are furnished to complement
the building, with period or period-style furniture,
wrought iron and wooden beds that shine with the
patina of age, not varnish. The sitting rooms are large
and welcoming with original arches, bricks and
beams recalling the time when the building had a
rural use. Outside there are pleasant terraces and a
large swimming pool.

RECOMMENDED IN THE AREA

RESTAURANTS:
Albergaccio di Castellina *and* Antica Trattoria La Torre

VISIT:
*Rock fortress, parish church and Ugolini Palace,
Castellina in Chianti*

*B*elvedere di San Leonino

RECOMMENDED IN THE AREA

RESTAURANTS:
Osteria del Laghetto; Galleria, *Poggibonsi*

LOCAL SPECIALITY:
Wine tasting, Castellina

A large country house in the heart of the Chianti region

☎ 0577 740887
🖷 0577 740924
📧 info@hotelsanleonino.com
località San Leonino
53011 CASTELLINA IN CHIANTI (Siena)
Ref map 6, D4

Al, at Firenze-Certosa, junction with Firenze-Siena motorway, Badesse exit, go on for Lornano
28 rooms; **££**
Credit cards: AE VISA SI, bancomat

*I*n classic Gallo Nero ('black cockerel') Chianti territory, vineyards, wooded areas, cultivated fields and pretty villages are to be found in the harmonious countryside. The old Romanesque parish church of San Leonino, with its medieval appearance now restored, is not far from the country house that is the hotel. The buildings date back to the 15th century and have maintained their architectural character and original atmosphere. Surrounded by forests and pine woods, the hotel enjoys a spendid view from Siena as far as Volterra, San Gimignano and the Elsa valleys. The bedrooms are large with terracotta floors, old wooden beamed ceilings and period furniture. The communal areas are welcoming and, being formed out of the old structure, have character and personality. The complex is surrounded by a lovely garden and the open-air swimming pool is in a panoramic position.

Casa Ranieri

*O*riginally Casa Ranieri was an old small holding. Then it was refurbished as an *agriturismo* farm with accommodation, maintaining the style of traditional Val d'Orcia architecture. It is composed of three rustic buildings around a typical little square paved in Sienese terracotta. Accommodation consists of seven bedrooms (all non-smoking) and a two-roomed apartment. These have period-style furniture and are well appointed. During their stay here, guests may take part in riding activities in the covered school or on the obstacle course, and they may go for excursions on foot or on horseback with expert guides. These walks can even last for more than a day. Courses are organised on horse behaviour, the environment, bridge, ceramics, and gardening. Qualified cooks teach the history and art of cooking and in the autumn hold courses on fungi. Available to guests are a swimming pool, *bocce* (bowls), table tennis and a children's playground.

An old farm in the setting of a picturesque village

☎ and 🖷 0577 872639
📧 naranier@tin.it
podere la Martina
località Campiglia d'Orcia
53020 CASTIGLIONE D'ORCIA (Siena)
Ref map 7, E5
A1, Chiusi-Chianciano exit, towards Chianciano Terme, follow the signs for Monte Armiata
7 rooms, 1 apartment; £/££
Credit cards not accepted

RECOMMENDED IN THE AREA

RESTAURANT:
Castello di Ripa d'Orcia

LOCAL SPECIALITIES:
Wine and extra virgin olive oil; sausages; honey; herb liqueurs; cheeses

---

Castello Ripa d'Orcia

In a 13th-century rock fortress with the descendants of the Piccolomini

☎ 0577 897376 🖷 0577 898038
📧 info@castelloripadorcia.com
via della Contea 1/16
località Ripa d'Orcia
CASTIGLIONE D'ORCIA (Siena)
Ref map 7, E5
A1, at Firenze-Certosa, junction with Firenze-Siena motorway, S.S. 2 towards Roma (Rome), San Quirico d'Orcia exit
6 rooms, 7 apartments; ££
Credit cards: VISA SÌ

RECOMMENDED IN THE AREA

RESTAURANT:
Cantina il Borgo, *Rocca d'Orcia*

LOCAL SPECIALITIES:
Products from the castle's farm: extra virgin olive oil; Orcia red wine; Orcia Bianco del Castello white wine; grappa spirit; jam and honey

*T*he castle of Ripa d'Orcia and the typical little village houses grouped inside the 14th-century rock fortress make up this architectural scene in the heart of the Orcia valley. The whole group has remained almost intact since it was built at the beginning of the Middle Ages. In 1274 the fortress and village were sold to the Salimbeni, a powerful Sienese family who strenthened its defensive structure. In 1483, the fortress and village were bought by Francesca Piccolomini from whom the current owners are descended. They have recently transformed the castle and now the ancient walls contain comfortable bedrooms and some little apartments, a meeting room, a chapel for ceremonies and a wine cellar, children's playroom and a lovely reading room.

Grand Hotel Terme

Friendly professionalism for an enjoyable and relaxing stay

☎ 0578 63254 📠 0578 63524 ✉ ghotelterme@ftbcc.it

piazza Italia 8

53042 CHIANCIANO TERME (Siena)

Ref map 7, E5

A1, Chiusi-Chianciano Terme, towards Chianciano as far as the main square,
then follow the signs for the hotel

64 rooms, 8 suites; ££

Credit cards: AE VISA SI ⓪

*S*et in the Tuscan countryside with its gentle hills and old villages is the modern city of Chianciano. The green and shady thermal baths are celebrated in the black-and-white images of one of Federico Fellini's films.

A gentle slope from the thermal park leads up to the main square, and not far from here is the hotel. The building is elegant and modern, and enjoys a central position whilst remaining far from noise and traffic.

Guests are welcomed by lovely rooms, shining parquet flooring, big windows opening on to the garden and, in cold seasons, a fireplace that is always in use. The bedrooms are furnished in different ways, some with period furniture, others in a pleasingly modern way, and the pretty hangings and upholstery are carefully chosen. The new and practical marble bathrooms all have windows.

The kitchen pampers guests with an abundance of specialities and delightful contrasts.

The hotel has a fitness centre with heated swimming pool and hydromassage, sauna and gym; beauty treatments are available. There is also a solarium terrace in the garden. In addition for the guests, are a projection room and a piano bar three times a week. During the summer the restaurant serves meals on the terrace.

RECOMMENDED IN THE AREA

RESTAURANTS:
Il Patriarca, *Chiusi;* La Frateria di Padre Eligio, *Cetona*

VISIT:
Montepulciano; Pienza; Monticchiello

Relais della Rovere

In an old 16th-century abbey

☎ 0577 924696 📠 0577 924489
📧 dellarovere@chiantiturismo.it
località La Badia
53034 COLLE DI VAL D'ELSA (Siena)
Ref map 6, D4

A1, at Firenze-Certosa, junction with
Firenze-Siena motorway, Colle Val
d'Elsa exit
30 rooms; £££
Credit cards: AE VISA SI Ⓞ

RECOMMENDED IN THE AREA

RESTAURANTS:
Il Cardinale *and* La Cartiera

VISIT:
Church of Sant'Agostino; Duomo *(cathedral) and*
Palazzo pretorio *(magistrate's palace), including the*
Bianchi Bandinelli museum of archaeology

*T*his building and its occupants have changed
over time. In the 16th century it began as an
abbey, a place of meditation and prayer; then it
became the home of Cardinal Giuliano della Rovere,
a place perhaps of meditation but certainly of rest
and recreation. Nowadays it is an inn for recreation,
rest and holidaying. The building is beautiful and, as
has already been said, very old. It is noble in
appearance with many graceful details, moulded
stone and bricks vaults.

The bedrooms are attractive and rich in
atmosphere. There is period or period-style furniture
made of walnut or warm-toned wood for both
aesthetic value and comfort. The restaurant has
similar furnishing and decoration, and the kitchen
uses ingredients from the nearby countryside and
serves good-quality Tuscan wines. A park
surrounds the hotel and a swimming pool adds
further enjoyment.

La Vecchia Cartiera

In a 13th-century building which was once a paper mill

☎ 0577 921107

📠 0577 923688

📧 cartiera@chiantiturismo.it

via Oberdan 5/7/9

53034 COLLE DI VAL D'ELSA (Siena)

Ref map 6, D4

A1, at Firenze-Certosa, junction with Firenze-Siena motorway, Colle Val d'Elsa exit

38 rooms; ££

Credit cards: AE VISA SI ⓪, bancomat

*D*uring medièval times a paper-making industry developed at Colle. The first paper-makers began in the 10th century, using the River Elsa for power. This activity grew and soon the city became one of Italy's foremost producers of paper.

The hotel is in an 18th-century building that used to be a paper mill. With complete restoration, new parts on attractive modern lines have been added alongside the original structure. Several bedrooms have been created, and these have modern furnishings and are attractively light, with air conditioning, satellite television and mini-bar. The bathrooms are good. Communal rooms reflect the the former establishment in form and size, but with modern furnishings. The hotel has a garage, and there is a conference room.

RECOMMENDED IN THE AREA

RESTAURANT:
Arnolfo

LOCAL SPECIALITIES:
Crystal procuced as a craft and also on an industrial scale; locally produced furniture and wrought iron

VISIT:
Chianti area; San Gimignano; Siena; Volterra

193

$\mathcal{P}$odere La Vecchia Fornace

In rustic surroundings on a hillside

☎ 0575 692245/0368 3039300
🖷 0575 692245
📧 vecchiafornace@technet.it
San Lorenzo 257, località San Lorenzo
52042 CORTONA (Arezzo)
Ref map 7, E5
A1, Valdichiano exit, towards Perugia, exit for San Lorenzo-Montepulciano towards Cortona
4 apartments; ££
Credit cards not accepted

*I*n a beautiful hilly position there is an old stone farmhouse with an outbuilding as an annexe. The buildings have been restored without spoiling the original features. This *agriturismo* (farm accommodation) has four apartments: three in the farmhouse and one in the annexe. The apartments are attractive and comfortable, with central heating but also with working fireplaces in stone, and they are furnished in rustic style with original furniture. The separate entrances open directly on to the garden/park that is shaded by big oak trees and has a children's playground, a lovely swimming pool and various sporting facilities: basket ball, volley ball, *bocce* (bowls), archery and table tennis. The complex is under family management. A short distance away is a golf course, tennis courts and riding facilities.

RECOMMENDED IN THE AREA

RESTAURANTS:
La Fonte dei Frati, *località Il Sodo, and* Club Ippico il Comanchero, *località Piazzanella*

LOCAL SPECIALITY:
Ceramics of Cortona, marked with a sunflower

$\mathcal{F}$attoria Maiano

An elegant welcome in splendid surroundings

☎ 055 599600   🖷 055 599640
📧 fattoriadimaiano@dada.it
via Benedetto da Maiano 11
località Maiano
50016 FIESOLE (Firenze)
Ref map 6, C-D4
A1, Firenze Nord exit, follow the signs for the *stadio* (stadium), then for Fiesole, as far as the crossroads for la Fattoria di Maiano
7 apartments; ££
Credit cards: 💳, bancomat

*T*he Maiano villa, on the hills between Fiesole and Settignano, was built by the Pazzi family during the course of the 15th century. In the 1800s it and the adjacent religious house and nearby estates were bought by an English aristocrat and on his death by an Italian nobleman. Director James Ivory chose the interior of the villa, which is furnished with original 18th- and 19th-century furniture, for the film 'A Room with a View'.

In the farmhouse that forms part of the farm business it is possible to rent apartments, some of which are very large. These have period furniture and are equipped with the most modern comforts. They may also be rented for short periods. In addition there are a car park, open-air swimming pool and garden.

RECOMMENDED IN THE AREA

RESTAURANT:
Le Cave di Maiano

LOCAL SPECIALITIES:
Local produce; extra virgin oil from organic olives, Località Maiano

VISIT:
Fiesole; historic centre of Florence

Cimabue

A hearty buffet breakfast

☎ 055 471989 ☏ 055 475601
via Bonifacio Lupi 7
50129 FIRENZE (FLORENCE)
Ref map 6, D4
From piazza della Libertà go into via
Cavour, turn right at the first road,
then again first right, next first left
and again first left
16 rooms; **££**
Credit cards: AE VISA SI ⓪⃝, bancomat

A charming and welcoming family-run hotel which takes great care over service and detail. The result is an establishment with the right balance between quality and price. It is situated in a 19th-century mansion that has recently been completely refurbished and is in the historic centre of Florence, but in a quiet area which is only a short distance from the city's principal monuments. The attractive bedrooms have character and are all furnished with period and period-style furniture. Some of them have frescoed ceilings. The communal rooms have a pleasing atmosphere and management is attentive to guests' requirements.

RECOMMENDED IN THE AREA

RESTAURANT:
La Taverna del Bronzino, *via delle Ruote 25-27/R*

VISIT:
Medici villas in Careggi and Petraia

Hermitage

Facing the River Arno with a view over the Ponte Vecchio

☎ 055 287216 ☏ 055 212208
✉ florence@hermitagehotel.com
vicolo Marzio 1
50122 FIRENZE (FLORENCE)
Ref map 6, D4
From the wide *circonvallazione* (ring road),
follow the signs for *centro* and Ponte Vecchio
28 rooms; **£££**
Credit cards: VISA SI

This former house/hotel for the guests of the archbishopric was destroyed during the Second World War and then rebuilt, first serving as a club run by an English colonel, then as a hotel. It is in a unique position, both very central and also secluded, a few metres from the Ponte Vecchio. Reception, the beautiful sitting room and the roof terrace are on the fifth floor, facing the River Arno and seeming almost to touch it. The bedrooms differ but all have parquet flooring and are furnished in English style: much of the furniture is of the original period, the wallpaper is in the same style; the matching bedcovers and curtains are in pastel-coloured patterns. Bathrooms vary in size but nearly all have a hydromassage bath and almost all have a window. Altogether the hotel is very well presented and welcoming.

RECOMMENDED IN THE AREA

RESTAURANTS:
Oliviero, *via delle Terme 51/R;* Cavallino, *via delle Farine 6/R, F;* Omero, *Arcetri*

*I*l Guelfo Bianco

Relive the atmosphere of the Florence of the Medici in this late 15th-century building

☎ 055 288330 📠 055 295203

via Cavour 29

50129 FIRENZE (FLORENCE)

Ref map 6, D4

From the *statione centrale* (central station) in Florence, follow the signs
for the *Duomo* (cathedral) along via Cavour

29 rooms; £££

Credit cards: AE VISA ST, bancomat

*T*he hotel is very central and is a short distance from the *Duomo* (cathedral), piazza San Marco (St Mark's square), Accademia Museum and Medici Chapels.

From here it is walk of a few metres or a cycle ride through the pedestrian zone to the city's principal monuments.

The hotel was originally an old 15th-century palace. It has been carefully restored and has preserved many details of the original architecture.

The different-sized bedrooms are in the old building and are pretty and full of character. Some have panelled ceilings and others have impressive windows. All of them have furniture in the style of the period to blend with the old building, but the careful restoration work has also included effective soundproofing, modern practical bathrooms and the most up-to-date facitlities: some rooms have video recorders and modem points.

On arrival guests are welcomed into the little reception hall and carefully presented communal rooms that are bright and well furnished. The breakfast room has a vaulted ceiling, panelling on the walls and faces a small courtyard.

Newspapers are available each morning and guests receive friendly attention.

RECOMMENDED IN THE AREA

RESTAURANTS:
Terrazza Brunelleschi, *piazza Unità Italiana 6;*
Al lume di candela, *via delle terme 23/R*

Mario's

☎ 055 216801 📠 055 212039
✉ hotel.marios@webitaly.com
via Faenza 89
50123 FIRENZE (FLORENCE)
Ref map 6, D4
A1, Firenze Centro Città
16 rooms; £££
Credit cards: AE VISA SI ⑩, bancomat

An old palace is the setting for this pretty hotel that displays the features of a delightfully welcoming private house. From the street there is almost nothing to show that this is a hotel. Guests go up to the first floor and are welcomed into a large salon furnished in the Florentine style with high panelled ceilings, beautiful and genuine Persian carpets, paintings on the walls and diffused lighting: the surroundings and atmsosphere are indeed charming.

The bedrooms are carefully furnished and bear the same stamp of a personal welcome. They have brass beds, and the walnut-coloured furniture is traditional Tuscan style. There is a country-style, secluded breakfast room as well as a bar/reading room. The owner is a very attentive host who looks after his guests with great care.

RECOMMENDED IN THE AREA

RESTAURANTS:
Il Saso di Dante, *piazza delle Pallottole 6/R;*
I Quattro amici, *via degli Orti Oricellari 29;*
l' Toscano, *via Guelfa 70/R*

Residenza Johanna II

☎ and 📠 055 473377
via delle Cinque Giornate 12
50129 FIRENZE (FLORENCE)
Ref map 6, D4
A1, Firenze Nord exit, towards *centro città*
(city centre), *stazione* and Fortezza da Basso
6 rooms; ££
Credit cards not accepted

The owners of the Residenza Johanna I were successful with their first hotel, which combined attentive hospitality with low prices, and have recently opened this second hotel in a very central position a few steps away from the Fortezza da Basso (Basso Fortress). The building is a little mansion of the early 20th century, with a garden. The large bedrooms are charmingly furnished. Some of the rooms have air conditioning and the three that look on to the street have double glazing and good soundproofing. All have television, no telephone though guests are given a mobile phone for calls in Italy as well as keys to the hotel's front door. On the ground floor there is a reading room with a large choice of books on Florence and on Italian art.

RECOMMENDED IN THE AREA

RESTAURANTS:
Sabatini, *via de' Panzani 9/A, and* Mamma Gina,
borgo San Jacopo 37/R

LOCAL SPECIALITIES:
Many exclusive shops in Florence, for example:
international 19th-century books, gold jewellery and
jewellery made with coral, pearls and gems

$\mathcal{V}$illa Le Rondini

On one of the most charming Tuscan hills, a few minutes from the centre of Florence

☎ 055 400081 ☏ 055 268212
✉ mailbox@villalerondini.it
via Bolognese Vecchia 224
località Trespiano
50139 FIRENZE (FLORENCE)
Ref map 6, D4
A1, Barberino and via Bolognese exit,
towards Firenze (Florence)
43 rooms; **£££**
Credit cards: AE VISA SI Ⓞ, bancomat

The road leading to the hotel on the outskirts of Florence is between lovely private houses and large gardens. The villa stands within a park that is part cultivated with vineyards and in part forested. The different-sized bedrooms have antique and period-style furniture, and a delightful atmosphere that is full of character. One bedroom has a lovely loggia with a view over Florence and the countryside. Bathrooms are of different sizes and of a reasonable standard; nearly all have showers and windows. The communal rooms are large, and arranged with corners for conversation and reading.

The dining room faces the green garden. In the high season it is possible to have meals outside and by the swimming pool there is a snack service. Breakfast is in the loggia looking over the garden. In addition there are tennis and riding facilities, a heliport and meeting rooms.

RECOMMENDED IN THE AREA

RESTAURANTS:
Enoteca Pinchiorri, *via Ghibellina 87, and*
Alle murate, *via Ghibellina 52/R*

$\mathcal{L}$iana

In a 19th-century villa in a quiet part of the city

☎ 055 245303
☏ 055 2344596
✉ hotelliana@dada.it
via Vittorio Alfieri 18
50121 FIRENZE (FLORENCE)
Ref map 6, D4
A1, Firenze Nord exit, take the
circonvallazione (ring road) and follow the
signs for *centro* (town centre)
24 rooms; **££**
Credit cards: AE VISA SI Ⓞ, bancomat

During the brief period in which Florence was the capital of Italy, this mansion was the seat of the British Consulate. It is situated in a peaceful position that is easily reached by car from the ring road. It has spacious rooms with high ceilings, many of which are decorated with pretty 19th-century paintings. The furnishing is simple, but in the style of the surroundings, and there are still some beautiful original floors. The bathrooms are practical. The breakfast room has frescoes, period furniture and the lovely atmosphere of times past. A few antique pieces of furniture in the wide corridors give a more personal and private atmosphere. Behind the hotel is a pretty garden, part of which is used as a car park. Guests receive a friendly welcome.

RECOMMENDED IN THE AREA

RESTAURANTS:
Enoteca Pinchiorri, *via Ghibellina 87;*
Cibreo, *via dei Macci 118/R;* Bar Gelateria Vivoli *in central Florence sells superlative ice-cream*

$\mathcal{M}$orandi alla Crocetta

Secluded, refined and comfortable surroundings

☎ 055 2344747 📠 055 2480954
✉ welcome@hotelmorandi.it
via Laura 50
50121 FIRENZE (FLORENCE)
Ref map 6, D4

Take the signs for *centro* in Florence and follow the *circonvallazione* (ring road) as far as piazza Donatello, go on through via Alfieri, piazza d'Azeglio, via Giusti, Borgopinti and via Laura
10 rooms; **££**
Credit cards: AE VISA SI ⓪

*T*his hotel is situated in the heart of the historic centre, five minutes from the *Duomo* (cathedral) and Florence's main monuments. The building once housed the Crocetta religious house. The bedrooms, which differ in size and type, have parquet flooring, individually controlled air conditioning and safes. They are furnished with care, mostly using period furniture. Those bedrooms created out of what was once the chapel still have some of the original frescoes. The bathrooms have good fittings. The communal rooms are quiet and the high ceilings with wooden beams give these too a special charm. Management is attentive and kind.

RECOMMENDED IN THE AREA

RESTAURANTS:
Il Cibreo, *via dei Macci 118/R; delicious coffee at* La via del thé *in central Florence*

$\mathcal{P}$oggio San Felice

The pleasure of staying near Florence and yet feeling as if you're in a private home

☎ 055 220016
📠 055 2335388
✉ ilpoggio@tin.it
via San Matteo in Arcetri 24
50125 FIRENZE (FLORENCE)
Ref map 6, D4

A1, Firenze Sud exit, towards piazza Ferrucci, go up the viale dei Colli for piazzale Michelangelo; after 500 metres turn left
4 rooms; **£££**
Credit cards: AE VISA SI ⓪, bancomat

spacious with high ceilings and parquet flooring. They are furnished with care and all have private bathrooms. There is also parking for guests' cars. A courtesy shuttle bus connects the hotel with Florence.

*T*he proprietors of this family villa between the hills of Pian dei Giullari have transformed it into an elegant hotel. It is only a short distance from the city and gives one a sense of being at home. An avenue lined with old roses leads through an olive grove to a 19th-century garden. The ground-floor sitting rooms looking on to this are furnished with antique furniture typical of Florentine aristocratic homes. On the first floor the bedrooms are

RECOMMENDED IN THE AREA

RESTAURANTS:
Sabatini, *via de' Panzani 9/A;* Omero, *Arcetri*
LOCAL SPECIALITIES:
Oil; Vinsanto *sweet white wine and* grappa *spirit*
VISIT:
Stena; San Gimignano; Monteriggioni

Villa Calcinaia

Between woods and olive groves in the heart of the Chianti region

☎ and 🖷 055854008
✉ capponis@ftbcc.it
via di Citille 84
località Greti
50022 GREVE IN CHIANTI (Firenze)
Ref map 6, D4
A1, Firenze Sud exit, then *strada regionale* (regional road) 222 from Grassina
3 apartments; ££
Credit cards: 🖃 🖃

*I*n 1524 the family of the Capponi counts bought Villa Calcinaia. They gave it its present appearance and are still the proprietors. The building stands in the middle of 170 hectares of olive groves, vines and woods in the heart of the Chianti area, a few kilometres from Florence and Siena. The village of San Pierino is between these hills, and here two apartments have been created out of the 13th-century presbytery of the church of San Piero al Pino. Another apartment, Le Refie, was originally a typical Tuscan farmhouse and is on the hillside surrounded by chestnut woods on the edge of the San Michele Nature Park. It looks on to a delightful garden. Inside the apartments retain many of the architectural features of the era. An open-air swimming pool is also available to guests.

RECOMMENDED IN THE AREA

RESTAURANT:
Trattoria del Montagliari, *Ponzano*

LOCAL SPECIALITIES:
Products from the Villa Calcinaia's farm

VISIT:
Medieval village of Montefioralle

Castello di Querceto

A medieval castle surrounded by the enchanting Chianti countryside

☎ 055 85921
🖷 055 8592900
via Dudda 61
località Dudda-Lucolena
50022 GREVE IN CHIANTI (Firenze)
Ref map 6, D4
A1, Incisa-Valdarno exit, go through Incisa and Figline Valdarno, then to Greve in Chianti
5 apartments; ££
Credit cards: 🖃, bancomat

A short distance from Greve in Chianti, in a quiet place amidst the olive groves and vineyards of the farm and surrounded by oak and chestnut woods stands the Castello de Querceto, an old Lombard castle. This still has a medieval appearance with its watch-tower at the centre of the façade. Within the property are various types of apartment, some next to the castle opposite the cellars where wine is aged and others in a farmhouse with barn, surrounded by vineyards. All have been recently refurbished, maintaining their unspoilt rustic Tuscan character. They have independent central heating, television, and some also have a fireplace.

RECOMMENDED IN THE AREA

RESTAURANTS:
Il Vescovino, *Greve;* Da Omero, *Passo dei Pecorari*

LOCAL SPECIALITIES:
Tuscan terracotta; wine from the castle's farm; wild boar salami

VISIT:
Greve in Chianti; Siena

Castello di Lamole

From 1200 Lamole Castle has dominated the Chianti hills, in its strategic position 600 metres above sea level, and in charming scenery of vineyards and oak and chestnut woods.

Reaching here, the heart and spirit grow calm and feed on the panorama of the hills around. The castle was built to be an observation post defending the Florentine borders in the time of war with Siena. Despite having changed over the centuries so that it was used more by farmers than soldiers, nowadays as a little village it preserves the medieval layout and character, and contains some lovely little nooks.

Eight two-roomed apartments have been created out of castle rooms and much attention has been paid so as not to lose the personality and charm of the old building. The apartments are furnished with antiques, have terracotta floors, ceilings adorned with beams made from chestnut wood, light pastel-coloured plaster or plain stone walls. Pretty windows open on to the countryside, a lovely open-air swimming pool has been introduced within this old structure, and paths for excursions through the woods are being made.

The hotel management organises concerts of traditional music and Tuscan folklore and vigil nights recalling the old farming custom of staying up late, sitting around the fire telling true or imaginary stories. Children too used to stay up for this and would learn the legends and traditions from the old people.

RECOMMENDED IN THE AREA

RESTAURANTS:
Trattoria del Montagliari *and* Cernacchie, *Ponzano*

VISIT:
Abbeys at Passingano and at Coltibuono; church of San Cresci, Montefioralle; Brolio Castle, Gaiole in Chianti

---

Where old traditions of Medieval and then Renaissance times are respected and maintained

☎ 055 630498 📠 055 630611 ✉ castellodilamole@arscanora.it

via di Lamole 82, località Lamole

50022 GREVE IN CHIANTI (Firenze)

Ref map 6, D4

A1, Incisa-Valdarno exit, go through Incisa and Figline Valdarno, take direction of Greve in Chianti

8 apartments; ££

Credit cards: AE VISA SI ⓪

Villa San Michele

*O*n the highest hill of Florentine Chianti, 900 metres above sea level, stands the imposing building that was once the San Michele convent, built in the 10th century. Inside the chapel there are still some valuable frescos.

Nowadays the old group of buildings is a villa/farm in the midst of a green public park, and it is also a hotel offering simple accommodation in six bedrooms and three apartments that can cater for large numbers.

The hotel has a billiards room, football pitch, children's playroom, and bicycles available for hire. There is family management, and the food is typically Tuscan.

The beautiful park around the hotel is very extensive, and affords many glimpses of the panorama. There are several paths in the park for walks.

A villa and farm surrounded by green hills

☎ and 🖷 055 851034
località Monte San Michele
50020 GREVE IN CHIANTI
(Firenze)
Ref map 6, D4

A1, Incisa-Valdarno exit, go through Incisa and Figline Valdarno, then take direction of Greve in Chianti
6 rooms, 3 apartments; **£/££**
Credit cards: VISA SÌ

RECOMMENDED IN THE AREA

RESTAURANTS:
Cernacchie, *località La Panca*;
Da Omero, *Passo dei Pecorari*

VISIT:
Parish church of Santa Croce, Greve in Chianti; castle ruins, Montefioralle; parish church of Santa Maria, Impruneta

Pardini's Hermitage

A house on an island, far from other habitations and directly facing the sea

☎ **0564 809034**
🖷 **0564 809177**
📧 **hermit@ats.it**
località Cala degli Alberi
58013 ISOLA DEL GIGLIO (Grosseto)
Ref map 8, C1

This hotel can only be reached by motor-launch from Giglio Porto
12 rooms; **£/££**
Credit cards: 📇 📇

The villa is in a wonderful position by the sea, far from the crowds. The path up to the hotel is inconvenient and the walk along it takes about an hour and a half; but boatmen can take visitors there across the sea from Giglio Porto – a journey of 20 minutes. Accommodation is in attractive, charmingly furnished bedrooms, together with communal rooms, a library and a *taverna* where sociable meals are served. Outside, on the well-equipped beach, there are *bocce* (bowls), table tennis, archery, slipways for boats, windsurfing, and more besides.

There are rowing boats and motor boats, an astronomical observatory and a gazebo with gym facilities. Besides this, guests may take courses on watercolours and ceramics. Donkeys are the means of transport for excursions within the island. There is a simple agrarian business on the property and animals are reared here. Goat's milk is used to make cheeses or yoghurt for delicious breakfasts. Guests are asked to stay for at least two nights.

RECOMMENDED IN THE AREA

RESTAURANT:
Da Santi, *Giglio Castello*

VISIT:
Medieval walls, Giglio Castello

Romantica

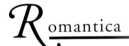

An Art Nouveau villa at Lucca

☎ **0583 496872**
🖷 **0583 957600**
📧 **villaromantica@lunet.it**
via N. Barbantini 246
località San Marco
55100 LUCCA
Ref map 6, C3

A11, Lucca exit, signs for *Stadio* (stadium)
4 rooms, 2 apartments; **££**
Credit cards: 📇 📇 📇 📇

Within the well-tended garden around the house are an open-air swimming pool and a barbecue with a pergola for evening meals outside during hot weather. It is possible to hire bicycles and a very short distance away, but not under the same ownership, are four tennis courts.

Walls enclose this medieval city with a dense web of streets and old houses that is almost intact. Within this, Renaissance and 18th-century palaces and noble houses blend harmoniously. Near the walls, now transformed into green ramparts that make lovely walks, stands the elegant form of the villa built in the Art Nouveau era.

There are rooms, suites and two apartments (each with two rooms), with air conditioning, modem points and satellite television. The interiors have English and French furniture. Breakfast is served as a buffet.

RECOMMENDED IN THE AREA

RESTAURANT:
Mora, *Ponte a Moriano*

LOCAL SPECIALITIES:
Olive oil from Lucca; spelt wheat from Garfagnana; wine from the hills of Lucca

VISIT:
Lucca; tower on Lake Puccini; Puccini's house

*D*a Caino

*M*ontemerano is a little town standing on top of a hill surrounded by olive trees. The house containing the hotel is noted for its restaurant. But the love for detail that has made its food famous is also evident in the care taken over the accommodation. The bedrooms are very pretty, warm and welcoming. There are beamed ceilings in lovely pale stripped wood, and floorboards that have been waxed not varnished. The antique furniture has been lovingly and carefully collected and arranged over the years. The restaurant is on the ground floor: here too, there is a clever contrast between the rustic building and the elegant crystal and silverware.

Cuisine that takes care over every detail and a very good wine cellar

☎ 0564 602817 📠 0564 602807
✉ caino@ftbcc.it
via Chiesa 4
località Poderi di Montemerano
58050 MANCIANO (Grosseto)
Ref map 6, F4
A12, Rosignano M. exit, then S.S. 1 Aurelia for Grosseto-Albinia; from here S.S. 74 for Manciano
3 rooms; £££
Credit cards: AE VISA SI OD

RECOMMENDED IN THE AREA

RESTAURANT:
Antica Trattoria Aurora, *Magliano in Toscana*

WINE CELLAR:
Perbacco, *Manciano*

VISIT:
L'Argentario mountain; Maremma Nature Park

---

*L*e Macchie Alte

*T*his large farm is set in 420 hectares of oak woods alternating with expanses of olive trees, organically cultivated cereals and fodder crops. Situated in the Maremma 420 metres above sea level, it is a short distance from Montemerano, a town that still has its medieval walls, which were nearly all rebuilt in the 15th century. Set in this countryside, the accommodation is in two stone farmhouses. These have been reconstructed while respecting the rural architecture of the Maremma and now have 12 bedrooms, all with bathrooms and characteristic regional furnishings. This *agriturismo* (farm with accommodation) also houses the Centro Ippico Macchie Alte riding centre and is a departure point for trekking. Yoga courses are also organised. Delicious food of the Maremma region is prepared using products from the farm.

This *agriturismo* belongs to the *Andar per Ville* chain.

Deep in the countryside between wild woods and organically farmed land

☎ 0564 620470 📠 0564 629878
✉ lemacchiealte@laltramaremma.it
frazione Poderi di Montemerano
58050 MANCIANO (Grosseto)
Ref map 6, F4
A12, Rosignano M. exit, then S.S. 1 Aurelia for Grosseto-Albinia; from here S.S. 74 for Manciano
12 rooms; £/££
Credit cards: VISA SI, bancomat

RECOMMENDED IN THE AREA

RESTAURANTS:
Due cippi-Da Michele *and* Caino

VISIT:
Saturnia thermal baths

*L*e Pisanelle

An old farmhouse deep in the gentle green hills

☎ 0564 628286
📠 0564 625840
✉ lepisanelle@laltramaremma.it
S.P. 32 al km 3,8, località Le Pisanelle
58014 MANCIANO (Grosseto)
Ref map 6, F4

A12, Rosignano M. exit, then S.S. 1
Aurelia for Grosseto-Albinia; from here
S.S. 74 for Manciano
5 rooms; ££
Credit cards: ⧉ ⧉ ⓪, bancomat

RECOMMENDED IN THE AREA

RESTAURANT:
Caino

VISIT:
Rock fortress, with archaeological museum

*I*n a panoramic position deep in the green tranquillity of the Maremma countryside, this old farmhouse of 1786 has been transformed into an attractive and hospitable residence. The comfortable bedrooms have 19th-century furniture that blends with the old structure of the house. The communal rooms have the warmth of a private home with fires burning in the hearths and corners for reading. In the garden full of ornamental plants, fruit trees, olives and vines, there are sauna and hydromassage baths. The managers organise guided tours of the neighbouring environmentally protected areas and nature reserves. There is also a special arrangement with the nearby Saturnia thermal baths.

*C*astello di Gargonza

*T*he complex belongs to the *Abitare la storia* ('living history') chain, and this concept has never been more fitting: Gargonza castle, a 13th-century fortified village, is still enclosed within its circle of ancient walls in a harmonious blend of colours and architecture. The entrance is through the Sienese portal and the reception area is in the little square with its octagonal well and watch-tower. Inside the village the houses are close together and preserve the rustic, agricultural character of the former dwelling

places. The hotel has apartments for between two and ten people with private bathroom, living room and kitchen. There is also a guest house with seven double bedrooms, a restaurant with stone walls and arches outlined in brick. A big fireplace heats the old mill. The swimming pool is in the area just outside the walls, surrounded by olive trees. Guests may hire bicycles for trips to the surrounding area.

RECOMMENDED IN THE AREA

RESTAURANT:
Le antiche sere, *Ambra*

Elegant hospitality in a converted castle

☎ and 📠 0575 847054
✉ gargonza@teta.it
52048 MONTE SAN SAVINO (Arezzo)
Ref map 7, D5

A1, Monte San Savino exit, then S.S. 73 towards Siena
12 apartments; ££
Credit cards: ⧉ ⧉ ⧉ ⓪

*F*attoria di Petrognano

RECOMMENDED IN THE AREA

RESTAURANT:
Antica Trattoria Sanesi, *Lastra a Signa*

LOCAL SPECIALITIES:
Wine, olives and honey from the farm

VISIT:
Archaeological and Ceramics Museum, Montelupo Fiorentino; Vinci, San Miniato and Certaldo

*T*his is a big private house with simple Tuscan architecture set amidst rows of vines and olives. Within this lovely property two 18th-century farmhouses have been transformed, after careful restructuring, into cosily furnished apartments equipped with every comfort. There is an open-air swimming pool, hydromassage bath, tennis court, *bocce* (bowls) court, table tennis and mountain bikes. The old barn with its lovely portico is used as a meeting room, as a place for tasting products from the farm, and for evening occasions. Courses are organised on decorating ceramics, in collaboration with Montelupo museum, as well as courses in watercolours, history of art and bonsai.

A peaceful environment amidst vineyards and olive groves

☎ 0571 913795
🖷 0571 913796
via Bottinaccio 116
50056 MONTELUPO FIORENTINO (Firenze)
Ref map 6, D4
A1, Firenze-Certosa exit, Firenze-Pisa-Livorno *superstrada* (dual carriageway), Montelupo Fiorentino exit, follow signs for Bottinaccio
2 apartments; **££**
Credit cards: AE VISA SI, bancomat

Tenuta San Vito in Fior di Selva

Old farm buildings in peaceful countryside

☏ 0571 51411 📠 0571 51405
✉ sanvito@san-vito.com
via San Vito 32, località San Vito
50056 MONTELUPO FIORENTINO (Firenze)
Ref map 6, D4
A1, Firenze-Certosa exit, Firenze-Pisa-Livorno *superstrada* (dual carriageway), Lastra a Signa exit
14 apartments; **££**
Credit cards: AE VISA SI ⓪, bancomat

RECOMMENDED IN THE AREA

RESTAURANT:
Delfina, *Artimino*

LOCAL SPECIALITIES:
Ceramics and terracotta

VISIT: *The Medici Ambrogiana Villa*

Situated among the hills of Chianti, a few kilometres from Florence, in an area of very beautiful quiet countryside. Le Querce, il Frantoio and il Podere Casanova are three farmhouses which have been refurbished to offer hospitality. The apartments created out of farm buildings still preserve their original character. They have independent central heating, terracotta floors and modern rustic furnishings. The agricultural business to which the farmhouses belong has used organic methods since 1982. The lovely buildings are scattered among neat vineyards, woods and olive groves, and on offer are a restaurant, tasting of farm products, mountain bike hire, and organised courses in cookery, ceramics and painting. There is also a swimming pool.

Borgo Trerose

RECOMMENDED IN THE AREA

RESTAURANTS:
La Grotta, *Montepulciano;*
Acquario, *Castiglione del Lago*

VISIT:
City of Pienza

Skilful restoration in a medieval village

☏ 0578 724231 📠 0578 724227
via Palazzi 5
località Valiano di Montepulciano
53040 MONTEPULCIANO (Siena)
Ref map 7, E5
A1, Valdichiana exit, Siena-Perugia towards Perugia, Cortona Montepulciano-*statale* (trunk road) Lauretana exit, turn left following the signs for Borgo Trerose-Tenuta Trerose
19 apartments; **££/£££**
Credit cards: AE VISA SI ⓪

La Casina ('the little house'), il Frantoio ('the press'), le Botteghe ('the workshops'), la Loggia, il Poggio ('the hillock') and la Villa all make up this medieval village that has been restored with great care to offer modern facilities and welcoming hospitality. The complex contains different kinds of apartments, all with independent entrances and lovely furnishing, some with a fireplace.

There is also a hotel for guests. Facilities for activity and relaxation are: swimming pool, tennis court with night lighting, table tennis, riding school a kilometre away, and competitive fishing in the private lake.

Castel Bigozzi

An old castle-fortress of the 12th century

☎ 0577 300000
📠 0577 300001
località Bigozzi
53035 MONTERIGGIONI (SIENA)
Ref map 6, D4
At Firenze-Certosa, junction with the Firenze-Siena motorway, Monteriggioni exit, follow the signs for Strove
16 apartments; ££
Credit cards AE VISA SI ⓄⒹ

a swimming pool and a solarium in the garden. The hotel has a lift and a meeting room for around 50 people.

RECOMMENDED IN THE AREA

RESTAURANTS:
Casalta; Il Cardinale, *Colle Val d'Elsa*
VISIT:
The medieval walls of the village

*T*he Bigozzi castle, at the port of Monteriggioni, is an old medieval fortress which, after careful and skilful restoration work, has been transformed into a hotel. There are various apartments, each able to accommodate between two and four people, and they are well furnished and equipped with most modern comforts: air conditioning, satellite television, mini-bar and safe. The modern, practical bathrooms all have a bathtub or shower with hydromassage. In addition, there is

Tenuta della Selva

Near the Francigena pilgrim's road

☎ and 🖷 **0577 377063**
✉ **fabioin@tin.it**
La selva 34, località Ville di Corsano
53010 MONTERONI D'ARBIA
(Siena)
Ref map 6, E4
At Firenze-Certosa, junction with Firenze-Siena motorway, Siena Ovest exit, towards S.S. Aretino; in località Costafabbri follow signs for Ville di Corsano
5 apartments; **£/££**
Credit cards: 🆅🆂🅸

RECOMMENDED IN THE AREA

RESTAURANT:
La Mencia, Asciano

LOCAL SPECIALITIES:
Farm products: pork, sausages, red and white wine, extra virgin olive oil, grappa *(spirit), cheeses and honey*

VISIT:
Museum of sacred art and Etruscan museum, Asciano

The estate's land extends over 1000 hectares, of which 700 are Mediterranean woodland where wild boar, deer, foxes, pheasants, hares, porcupines and very many species of birds are found in the wild. The heart of the estate is a village of old farm dwellings surrounding the main house built on the ruins of an 11th-century castle. In the surrounding hills among farmhouses, fortified buildings and churches is this stone house that has been perfectly renovated and has both antique furniture and modern comforts. The apartments for guests are of various kinds and can accommodate from two to ten people. In the estate there is an open-air swimming pool, 20 kilometres of roads and paths for nature walks, three lakes for fishing, and a centre where horses are bred and trained and where it is possible to follow courses in Western-style riding from beginner to competitive level.

Quattro Gigli

Genuine Tuscan atmosphere in the magistrate's palace

☎ and 🖷 **0571 466879**
✉ **quattro.gigli@galli.it**
piazza Michele da Montopoli 1
56020 MONTOPOLI
IN VALDARNO (Pisa)
Ref map 6, D3
A1, Firenze-Signa exit, Firenze-Pisa-Livorno *superstrada* (dual carriageway), Montopoli-Valdarno exit
24 rooms; **£/££**
Credit cards: 🅰🅴 🆅🆂🅰 🆂🅸 ⓄⒹ, bancomat

created partly out of old warehouses, and is decorated with typical Montopoli ceramics. During the summer meals are served outside on the panoramic terrace. An *enoteca* (place for tasting vintage wines) underneath the old palace stocks very good wines, not just from Tuscany.

From as far back as the 8th century, Montopoli was a stronghold in a dominating position with a view as far as the hills of Livorno and the Apuan Alps. The hotel, owned by the same family since 1930, is in the historic centre of the village, in a 15th-century mansion that was once the magisterial seat. Inside it has been skilfully restored and there is an atmosphere of genuine Tuscan hospitality. The bedrooms look onto countryside or characteristic village streets. The restaurant has been

RECOMMENDED IN THE AREA

RESTAURANTS:
Trattoria dell'Orcio Interrato; Bianconi, *Empoli*

LOCAL SPECIALITIES:
White truffles; pecorino *(sheep's milk cheeses); extra virgin olive oil; Varramista wine*

VISIT:
Diocesan museum of sacred art, San Miniato

Eden

Within the framework of the Apuan Alps

☎ 0585 807676 📠 0585 807594
✉ eden@bicnet.it
via A. Gramsci 26
località Cinquale
54030 MONTIGNOSO (Massa)
Ref map 6, C2

A12, Massa exit, towards *Viale a mare*
(avenue to the sea), then Viareggio
27 rooms; **££/£££**
Credit cards: AE VISA SI ⓂⒸ, bancomat

*T*his recently refurbished modern building is surrounded by a large, well-tended garden with many corners for relaxing under the shady pine trees. Bedrooms are spacious, many with terraces, equipped with individually controlled air conditioning, satellite television and mini-bar. Bathrooms are very practical. The communal rooms are light, with big windows opening on to the surrounding greenery. The hotel has a mini-club for children, organised candle-lit evenings for tasting local dishes, and bicycles that may be hired. Eighty metres away are the sea and sporting facilities, and the hotel has special arrangements for using the beach, swimming pool and tennis court.

RECOMMENDED IN THE AREA

RESTAURANTS:
Ruota, *Massa;* Oca Bianca *and* Romano, *Viareggio*

VISIT:
Trips into the region's marble caves and marble works; boat excursions to the Cinque Terre and Portovenere; trekking in the Apuan Alps

La Cerbana

Farmsteads among gentle hills and patches of woodland

☎ and 🖷 0587 632058
via delle Colline per Legoli 35
56036 PALAIA (Pisa)
Ref map 6, D3
A12, Collesalvetti exit, *superstrada* (dual carriageway) towards San Miniato, then before reaching Montopoli in Valdarno turn right for Palaia
12 rooms, 2 apartments; ££
Credit cards: AE VISA SI ⓪, bancomat

sheep and fish, where hunting (following the rules of the reserve) is allowed. The restaurant, in rustic rooms with a large hearth to give warmth to the surroundings, serves homely and satisfying cooking. There are spaces for camper vans and caravans, and a large swimming pool.

RECOMMENDED IN THE AREA

RESTAURANT:
Pettirosso

VISIT:
Parish church of Sant' Andrea

*T*he scene is one of typical Tuscan countryside where there is a charming alternation of gentle hills and cultivated areas, a few rustic buildings and patches of woodland, and every now and then an elegant cypress stands out. Within a 600-hectare *agriturismo* (farm accommodation) are some estate houses dating back to the early years of the 20th century. These have been restructured to provide accommodation in double bedrooms and small apartments. A hunting reserve in the land stretching from Palaia to Peccioli breeds deer, pheasants and hares, wild boars, mouflon mountain

213

*L*ocanda Senio

Warm, elegant hospitality and exquisite, unusual food

☎ 055 8046019 🖷 055 8046485
✉ locanda.senio@newnet.it
borgo dell'Ore 1
50035 PALAZZUOLO SUL SENIO (Firenze)
Ref map 6, C4
A14, Imol-Via Emilia, Castelbolognese-Palazzuolo sul Senio crossroads
6 rooms; **££**
Credit cards: AE VISA SI ⓪, bancomat

*P*alazzuolo is in the heart of the little valley of the River Senio, and is 400 metres above sea level. The inn is in the lovely stone house at the entrance to the medieval village, facing the *Capitano del popolo* mansion. It is skilfully rustic in style, with welcoming bedrooms furnished in an early- 20th-century manner. During winter the restaurant is in a little room, and in summer meals are served on the veranda in the garden. There are only a few tables and much care is taken with presentation. Dishes served are strictly regional and seasonal, with the flavour of herbs, together with mushrooms and chestnuts in season and meat from the medieval swineherd reared in the *Le Panare* farm. There is family management.

RECOMMENDED IN THE AREA

RESTAURANTS:
Camino, *Marradi*

LOCAL SPECIALITIES:
Salami from the inn's own larder

---

*L*a Casellina

Holiday in the green hills of Tuscany

☎ 055 8398498 🖷 055 8395007
✉ lacasellina@tiscalinet.it
via Colognolese 28
50065 PONTASSIEVE (Firenze)
Ref map 6-7, D4-5
A1, Firenze Sud exit, S.S. 67 towards Pantassieve, then follow the signs for Rufina
5 rooms, 1 apartment; **££**
Credit cards: AE VISA SI ⓪

A few kilometres from Florence is an old farmhouse, surrounded by lovely vineyards, within the large Galiga and Vetrice farm on the *Vie del Vino* (wine roads) of classified Chianti di Rufina.

Accommodation is in simple, rustic-style bedrooms (only one with a bathroom) and an apartment. The hotel's sitting room has a large *contadino* fireplace with seats set into the stone walls inside it; in times past when there was no central heating, people would stay up all night relaying news and telling

stories. The hotel's terrace looks over a view embroidered with rows of vines. The adjoining restaurant, *La Casellina*, has a young friendly management and serves traditional Tuscan dishes.

RECOMMENDED IN THE AREA

RESTAURANT:
Cave di Maiano, *Maiano*

VISIT:
Parish church of San Giovanni Battista a Remole, Sieci

$\mathcal{V}$illa Emilia

VILLA EMILIA
BED AND BREAKFAST

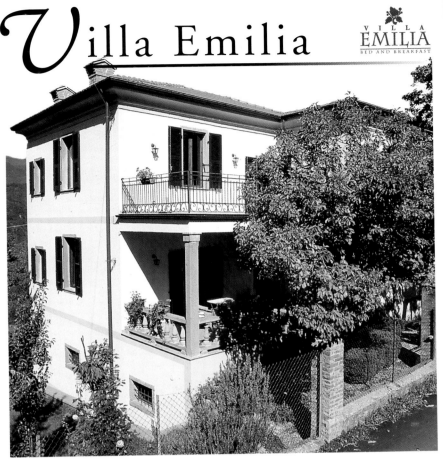

In the quiet green of unspoilt Valdantena

☎ and 📠 0187 836455
✉ info@villaemilia.com
via Versola 4, località Versola
54027 PONTREMOLI (Massa)
Ref map 6, B2
A15, Pontremoli exit
2 rooms; **£/££**
Credit cards not accepted

$\mathcal{A}$round the year AD 1000, pilgrims and merchants began to cover great distances in order to reach holy places: the walk to Rome, along the Francigena road, went through Lunigiana. The castles, parish churches and fortified villages scattered around the area still tell of that past time. The villa is a refined home of the 1920s surrounded by a large garden and is situated a short distance from Pontremoli on the slopes of lower Cisa, in the little village of Versola. Refurbishment has brought out many pretty details, and has carefully conserved the original characteristics that give the building personality. Accommodation is in bedrooms with period and period-style furniture. The original floors in the bedrooms have been preserved, and the windows open on to radiant countryside. The sitting and reading rooms are on the ground floor, together with an attractive kitchen with a fireplace.

Guests who stay here can go and discover many of Lunigiana's treasures or may simply enjoy the peace in the green and secluded jewel of Versola, and the garden and lovely terrace offer the chance of rest and contemplation.

A minimum of two nights' stay is requested.

RECOMMENDED IN THE AREA

RESTAURANTS:
Da Bussè, *and* Ca' del Moro

LOCAL SPECIALITIES:
Porcini *mushrooms in season*

VISIT:
Villages and medieval castles in historic Lunigiana

215

Castelvecchi

A romantic and unforgettable holiday in a farmhouse

☎ 0577 738050 📠 0577 738608
località Castelvecchi 17,
53017 RADDA IN CHIANTI (Siena)
Ref map 6, D4

A1, Valdarno exit, towards Montevarchi,
then Cavriglia, Radda in Chianti
7 rooms, 13 apartments; £
Credit cards not accepted

The rustic architecture of the splendid farmhouses, grouped together like a small village around a lovely big main house, is so cleverly designed that the scene appears to be part of a stage set. The village has an illustrious past. In the early Middle Ages it was already a defensive settlement, then it became the castle of the parish of Santa Maria Novella below. Towards 1700 it took the name of Castelvecchi from the aristocratic family of Vecchi that still owns it.

Accommodation is in little apartments and bedrooms in rustic village style. All the rooms have been created from the very characteristic old buildings, with details and furnishings inspired by the place itself. Other more elegant bedrooms are in the 18th-century villa and have access to the reading room and the adjoining terrace. In the large park are two swimming pools, tennis courts, table tennis and riding schools offering excursions on horseback.

RECOMMENDED IN THE AREA

RESTAURANT:
Vignale

VISIT:
Rock fortress, parish church and Ugolini Palace, Castellina in Chianti; farmhouses, dating back to the 19th-century grand-ducal era, in surrounding region

$\mathcal{F}$attoria Solaio

In the green hills between villages rich in history

☎ 0577 791029 ❻ 0577 791015
località Solaio,
53030 RADICONDOLI (Siena)
Ref map 6, E4
A1, at Firenze-Certosa, junction with the
Firenze-Siena motorway, colle Val d'Elsa
Nord exit, then S.S. 541
6 rooms, 3 suites; **££**
Credit cards: ᴀᴇ ᴠɪꜱᴀ ꜱɪ ⓞ, bancomat

$\mathcal{T}$he panorama is of gentle hills that are sometimes covered with dense patches of oak woods, sometimes with orderly rows of vines or olive trees, or else with yellow corn or sunflowers. Here roads curve sharply, but views are extensive and the villages rich in history, dominated by castles and enclosed by walls. There is a wonderful vista over the Cecina valley and the upper part of Pomarance. Bedrooms and suites are in a 16th-century villa. In addition, some attractive old farmhouses have been restructured to provide three apartments. There is a large garden with open-air swimming pool and tennis court for the use of guests. The minimum stay requested varies according to the season.

RECOMMENDED IN THE AREA

RESTAURANT:
La Mencia, *Asciano*

VISIT:
Parish church of San Vittore, Radicondoli;
Archaeological Museum, località Campo Muri

$\mathcal{V}$illa Buoninsegna

A 17th-century villa among oak woods

☎ and ❻ 0577 724380
località Buoninsegna
53040 RAPOLANO TERME (Siena)
Ref map 6, E4
A1, Val di Chiana exit, S. S. 326
towards Sinalunga-Siena
4 apartments; **££/£££**
Credit cards: ᴠɪꜱᴀ ꜱɪ

RECOMMENDED IN THE AREA

RESTAURANT:
Trattoria La Patria

LOCAL SPECIALITIES:
Products from the farm: Tuscan red wine, extra virgin olive oil, Chianti wine; local craft work and other crafts using travertine marble from Rapolano

VISIT:
Two thermal establishments with open-air swimming pool, Rapolano Terme; medieval elliptical-shaped plan of the village

$\mathcal{S}$ituated between the Valdichiana valley and the Ombrone valley, in a panorama of hills covered with oak forests. This large farm is surrounded by vineyards, olive groves and sunflowers. At the heart of the farm is a large 17th-century villa with imposing and attractive architecture. Recently the old outbuildings have been restored and transformed into little apartments for guests at this *agriturismo* (farm accommodation). They have modern comforts and carefully chosen furnishings. Each apartment has its own space outside, allowing guests to enjoy the surrounding countryside. At the foot of the olive grove is the open-air swimming pool and barbecue.

*I*l Crocicchio

In characteristic Tuscan countryside among vineyards and olive groves

☎ 055 8667262
📠 055 869102
✉ info@crocicchio.com
via San Siro 133
50066 REGGELLO (Firenze)
Ref map 7, D5
A1, Incisa-Valdarno exit, towards Reggello
2 rooms, 9 apartments; **££**
Credit cards: AE VISA SI Ⓞ

*A*s far as the eye can see lies a fabric woven of olive groves and vineyards, a masterly work dating from ancient times. The fame of this place is undisputed for the quality of its products and for its delightful countryside. Once it was a farmhouse and now it is a charming holiday place. The old building has been restructured, conserving a characteristic rustic atmosphere that makes the rooms particularly welcoming. Accommodation is in little apartments and well-furnished bedrooms. Here modern comforts blend with terracotta, wooden beams, fireplaces and antique-style furnishings. The communal rooms also have a rustic appearance. Outside the architecture is typically Tuscan, with some unplastered stone walls and stone-framed windows, and lemon trees in big *cocci* pots adorning the courtyard. In addition there is a swimming pool and children's playground in the garden. Throughout the year, specialists give riding lessons and accompany guests on rides in the vicinity.

RECOMMENDED IN THE AREA

RESTAURANT:
Archimede, *Pietrapiana*

VISIT:
Vallombrosa Abbey

*Q*uerce

*T*he historic centre is found inside a 19th-century fortified village. A short distance away the thermal baths, famed from Roman times, get their health-giving water from 42 neighbouring springs. The hotel stands right at the entrance to the village, in oak woods dating back centuries. At first it was an inn, then it was restored with care to keep to the original structure. Its particular charm has been preserved, despite the addition of all modern comforts. The bedrooms are equipped with satellite television, modem points, air conditioning and mini bar. The bathrooms are modern and practical and, in the suites, they also have hydromassage. This little hotel welcomes its guests and surrounds them with furnishings in the Tuscan tradition, canopied beds, bright upholstery, and the agreeable atmosphere of a private house with stone walls, vaulted ceilings, large fireplaces and distinctive little details and corners.

An old building inspired by traditional Tuscany

☎ 0578 58174 ☻ 0578 58172
✉ settequerce@krenet.it
viale Manciati 215
53040 SAN CASCIANO DEI BAGNI (Siena)
Ref map 7, E5
A1, Chiusi-Chianciano Terme exit, towards San Casciano
9 rooms; **££/£££**
Credit cards: AE VISA SI, bancomat

RECOMMENDED IN THE AREA

RESTAURANT:
Daniela

VISIT:
Chiusi; Montepulciano; Pienza; Montalcino; Cortona; Siena

---

*F*attoria Poggio Alloro

An old farmhouse where the surrounding countryside is exceptionally beautiful

☎ 0577 950153
☻ 0577 950290
via Sant'Andrea 23
53037 SAN GIMIGNANO (Siena)
Ref map 6, D4
Firenze-Siena *superstrada* (dual carriageway), Poggibonsi exit, towards San Gimignano, then Certaldo, at first crossroads right for Ulignano, then follow the road signs for the *agriturismo*
8 rooms, 2 apartments; **££**
Credit cards: AE VISA SI

*T*he farmhouse is set amid green countryside, where in the distance the towers of San Gimignano can be seen. Peaceful holidays may be spent in this area of natural beauty, surrounded by the farm's land which extends over more than 90 hectares, and consists of vineyards, olive groves, orchards and pasture (Chianina cattle are reared here, chosen for their very good steaks in the Florentine style). An old barn and farmhouse have been restructured to provide bedrooms and two small apartments: furnishings are simple but attractive. Lavish meals are organised in the *taverna* and restaurant using products from the farm: local wine, oil, meat and salami (these may also be purchased). There is a buffet breakfast with milk from the farm. For horse-riding enthusiasts there is a riding school 300 metres away.

RECOMMENDED IN THE AREA

RESTAURANT:
Leonetto, *Pancole*

LOCAL SPECIALITIES:
Classified Vernaccia di San Gimignano wine; Chianti wine and oil from the hills around Siena; saffron from San Gimignano; ceramics, glass and alabaster

$\mathcal{V}$illa Anna Maria

An 18th-century country villa within a botanical park

☎ and 📠 050 850139
S.S. 12 dell'Abetone
località Molina di Quosa 146
56010 SAN GIULIANO TERME (Pisa)
Ref map 6, D3
From San Giuliano take the S.S. 12 from Abetone, towards Lucca, along the S.S. 46 in località Molina di Quosa
5 rooms, 2 suites, 3 apartments; **££**
Credit cards not accepted

RECOMMENDED IN THE AREA

RESTAURANT:
Sergio a Villa di Corliano, *Rigoli*
VISIT:
Certosa di Calci (Carthusian monastery)

$\mathcal{S}$ituated on the road between Pisa and Lucca, at the foot of the Pisa hills, is a lovely 18th-century country villa on three floors and surrounded by about a hectare of botanical park. Recent refurbishment work has returned the villa to its original form and all the frescos adorning the interior have been completely restored. The villa is furnished with original antiques and the rooms are very welcoming and agreeable.

Accommodation is in bedrooms and suites, all with private bathrooms, satellite television and mini-bar. In addition there are three two-roomed apartments that can each take four people and are equipped with washing machines, dishwashers and refrigerators. Lovely rooms for the use of all guests include a library, billiards room and video library. A swimming pool is in the process of being built. There are bicycles for hire.

Il Molino

In the shelter of the castle walls, with a view over the city's towers

☎ and 📠 0577 897278
via Sano di Pietro 9
53027 SAN QUIRICO D'ORCIA (Siena)
Ref map 7, E5
A1, at Firenze-Certosa, junction with the Firenze-Siena motorway, Siena Sud exit, follow the sign for Roma on the S.S. 2
2 apartments; **£/££/£££**
Credit cards not accepted

$\mathcal{T}$he medieval village is Etruscan in origin and 460 metres above sea level in the hills around Siena. Here there are il Molino and il Molinetto, two apartments within old buildings. The architecture of il Molino is typical of a medieval dwelling. Formed from the restructuring of a 15th-century mill, and in the shelter of the castle walls with a view over the city's towers, it has its own entrance and is on two floors. The sitting room with fireplace, kitchen and bathroom are on the ground floor; three bedrooms with bathrooms are on the first floor. On the second floor is a wide terrace with a panoramic view, equipped as a solarium.

All the rooms are carefully presented, pretty and comfortable: there are terracotta floors, wooden beams, period furniture and furnishings to blend with

the old surroundings. Il Molinetto is adjacent. This is a large one-roomed apartment; the living room sleeps two, and there is a little fitted kitchen and bathroom. A minimum stay of a week is requested.

RECOMMENDED IN THE AREA

RESTAURANTS:
Il Tinaio, Il vecchia Forno *and* Pizzeria le 4 Contrade
LOCAL SPECIALITIES:
Ceramics; charcuterie; cheeses; wine and oil
VISIT:
Collegiate church, Horti Leonini Gardens, feast of the Rosary (first Sunday in October), San Quirico d'Orcia; feast of Saint Biagio (first Sunday after 3 February), Vignoni

$\mathcal{P}$odere Violino

$\mathcal{D}$eep in the green valley of the Tiber, Podere Violino has a lovely farmhouse at its centre with arches and loggias opening on to a lush garden. The building has been carefully refurbished to preserve the distinctive characteristics of the original. All the bedrooms have bathrooms and are furnished pleasingly with 19th-century furniture.

For horse-riding enthusiasts there is a centre in the estate which includes 20 stone stalls, 25 permanent covered places, outside manège, obstacle course, covered manège, dressage area, sand ring, cross-country field and pony club. In addition there is a large garden, and open-air swimming pool, outside playground and indoor children's playroom, and bicycles are available. During the winter a stay of three nights includes one free night.

Time and space for exercise and relaxation

☎ and 🖷 0575 720174
✉ violino@technet.it
Gricignano 99, località Gricignano
52037 SANSEPOLCRO (Arezzo)
Ref map 7, D6
Superstrada (dual carriageway) E45, Sansepolcro Sud exit, then S.S. 73
8 rooms; ££
Credit cards: VISA SI ⑪, bancomat

RECOMMENDED IN THE AREA

RESTAURANTS:
Oroscopo di Paola e Marco *and* La Balestra

LOCAL SPECIALITIES:
Chianina *meat, truffles, mushrooms, sausages*

VISIT:
Tiber valley

$\mathcal{A}$ntico Casale di Scansano

Traditional cooking and riding horses from the farm's stables

☎ 0564 507219
località Castagneta
58054 SCANSANO (Grosseto)
REF MAP 8, B2
A12, Rosgnano M. exit, then S.S.1, Grosseto Est exit, from here S.P (*strada provinciale*) 322 for Scansano
15 rooms; ££
Credit cards: AE VISA SI ⑪

RECOMMENDED IN THE AREA

RESTAURANT:
Il Caino, *Montemerano*

LOCAL SPECIALITIES:
Morellino di Scansano wine; local cheeses; organic extra virgin olive oil; jam and honey

VISIT:
Saturnia thermal baths; Maremma Park

$\mathcal{T}$he hotel started business in 1989 and arose out of the refurbishment of an early 19th-century country house. This is an entirely stone building with characteristically angular architecture standing in open countryside and surrounded by rich vegetation and a lovely flower garden. There is a fully equipped stable and riding school with around 30 horses: excursions in the vicinity can be organised. The restaurant serves typical dishes of the region, home-made pasta and grilled meat. The *taverna* is open every day for snacks, *bruschette* (pieces of toasted bread spread with oil, garlic and sometimes tomato) and wine tasting. In addition there is an open-air swimming pool, and bicycles for hire.

221

Santa Caterina

Warm traditional Tuscan style in Siena

☎ 0577 221105
📠 0577 271087 ✉ hsc@sienanet.it
via E. S. Piccolomini 7
53100 SIENA
Ref map 6, E4
A1, at Firenze-Certosa, junction with the
Firenze-Siena motorway
19 rooms; £££
Credit cards: AE VISA SI ⓪, bancomat

with furnishings that have charm and character, and flower arrangements by the lady of the house.

The garden is both large and faces a beautiful panorama of the Siena countryside with a veranda where buffet breakfast is served. The owners manage the hotel with kindness and attentiveness.

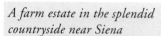

*T*his is an 18th-century patrician residence situated a few metres from the Porta Romana, the old entrance to the city of Siena, and a few steps from the historic centre. The hotel's bedrooms are all carefully furnished in period style and some have panelled ceilings. A lovely imposing staircase goes up from the pretty little reception area to the first floor. The bathrooms are good, the communal rooms small but very attractive

RECOMMENDED IN THE AREA

RESTAURANT:
Guido, *viccolo Pier Perrinaio 7*

LOCAL SPECIALITIES:
Typcial sweet dishes from Siena: ricciarelli *(marzipan cakes),* panforte *(flat nougat-type delicacy)*

VISIT:
Squares, churches and museums of Siena

Torrenieri

A farm estate in the splendid countryside near Siena

☎ and 📠 0578 748112
✉ piramide@bccmp.com
località Sant'Anna in Camprena
53020 TREQUANDA (Siena)
Ref map 7, E5
A1, Chiusi exit, towards Chianciano-
Montepulciano-Pienza, go on for San
Quirico d'Orcia, turn right towards the
monastery of Sant'Anna in Camprena
3 rooms, 1 house; ££/£££
Credit cards not accepted

*T*he monastery of Sant'Anna was founded in Camprena by Bernardo Tolomei, a descendant of one of the most powerful Siena families and founder of the Monte Oliveto Maggiore abbey. Situated a few kilometres from Pienza, in peaceful countryside where vineyards and woods alternate with villages. It was in this setting that the little farmhouse was built in 1934. The bedrooms have terracotta floors, wooden beams and pretty furniture that is antique but not grand. The kitchen/sitting room is arranged around a hearth and has wooden furniture and a big rustic table. Outside the garden is equipped for guests to spend time relaxing.

RECOMMENDED IN THE AREA

RESTAURANTS:
Buca delle Fate *and* Falco, *Pienza*

VISIT:
Pienza

Villa Campestri

This 12th-century villa with its harmonious Tuscan architecture is within a 140-hectare park in an isolated position on a hill surrounded by green countryside and silence. The rooms are big and some of them are in the main house, others in little outbuildings scattered over the property. They are furnished with antique or early 20th-century furniture. All the bathrooms have windows and are very spacious, practical and with particularly large bathtubs. The main salon on the first floor can accommodate small conventions.

The communal rooms are also furnished with beautiful period furniture and face on to a big terrace. The restaurant is divided into little rooms and serves dishes with a Tuscan influence that are embellished and developed with great care. From the lovely swimming pool outside guests can admire the wonderful Mugello valley.

In a great park with history, tradition, beauty and nature

☎ 055 8490107 📠 055 8490108
✉ villa.campestri@villacampestri.it
via di Campestri 19, località Campestri
50039 VICCHIO DI MUGELLO (Firenze)
Ref map 6, C4
A1, Barberino di Mugello exit, follow the signs for via Faentina, then for Sagginale and Campestri
21 rooms; £££
Credit cards: AE VISA SI, bancomat

RECOMMENDED IN THE AREA

RESTAURANT:
Il Feriolo, *Polcanto*

LOCAL SPECIALITIES:
Oil; wine; cheeses and charcuturie; knives from Scarperia

VISIT:
Borgo San Lorenzo

The Marches

The region is enclosed between the Apennine mountains of Umbria on the eastern side and, from Gabicce Mare to San Benedetto del Tronto, the low and sandy Adriatic coastline interrupted only by the Conero headland. Thus it is a mainly hilly region where the lengthy connection between the Apennine ramparts and the plain is seen in a varied, bright rural landscape with austere villages and rocks overlooking valleys from woody spurs above.

A visit here could have at least three strands, without any one excluding another because places are relatively close. There are seaside holidays in well-organised, welcoming places which, like Fano or Senigallia, are often notable for historic and artistic interest as well as good seafood. Mount Conero is a nature park with rare flora and fauna and contrasting views of the Adriatic sea and the hills. The hilly regions of Montefeltro to the slope of the Sibillini mountains are amongst the most undulating and enchanting in Italy. Villages huddled on the ridges retain their medieval layouts and appearance.

In the 18th and 19th centuries two noble families, the Montefeltro and the Malatesta, exercised great power here, and there is still evidence of this in the splendid rock fortresses such as Cradara and San Leo. The fine towns include Urbino – celebrated as a centre of Renaissance art (Piero della Francesca was one of the artists who worked here) – Pesaro and Macerata, Ascoli Piceno (more monumental and severe) and the main city, Ancona, with its historic centre grouped beneath the San Ciriaco basilica.

The golden age of art (including the famous local majolica), was the Renaissance period, and the artists Bramante and Raphael were from the Marches. Hotels and inns are often housed in historic buildings, in both city and countryside, throughout this region.

A typical farmhouse near Jesi

$\mathcal{L}$e Piane

Deep in the green park of the Sibillini mountains

☎ 0736 847641

🖷 0736 848557

✉ marcosel@tin.it

villa Piane 21, fraz. Taccarelli

63021 AMANDOLA (Ascoli Piceno)

Ref map 7, E8

A14, Porto San Giorgio exit,

S.S. 210 towards Fermo-Amandola

7 apartments; ££

Credit cards not accepted

$\mathcal{A}$maldola is an old village, the place for holidays with a view of the Sibillini mountains. Here, in a big estate 700 metres above sea level within the Monte Sibillini national park and in a panoramic position in an unspoilt area of great beauty, is this *agriturismo* (farm accommodation). The 18th-century village has recently been restored, maintaining its original features, and a number of dwellings – some very large – have been created within it. These have separate entrances with private space outside. Each apartment has a kitchen area, its own garden, heating and parking. In addition there is a swimming pool and guests may hire bicycles. The management organises excursions in the vicinity.

RECOMMENDED IN THE AREA

RESTAURANT:
Cantina dell'Arte, *Ascoli Piceno*

VISIT:
Church of San Francesco, Amandola;
Santi Rufino e Viale Abbey

Oasi San Benedetto

The ideal place for experiencing the natural beauty of the Pesaro Apennines

☎ 0722 80133 🖷 0722 80226

✉ oasi@info-net.it

via dell'Abbazia 7, località Lamoli

61040 BORGO PACE (Pesaro e Urbino)

Ref map 7, D6

A14, Fano exit, *superstrada* (dual carriageway) towards Rome, Fossombrone exit, S.S. 73bis to Urbania-Sant'Angelo in Vado-Borgo Pace

15 rooms; £

Credit cards: VISA SI

$\mathcal{T}$his reserve is run by a co-operative of young people and stands in the heart of the woods and paths of the Alpe della Luna. The surrounding countryside is exceptionally beautiful, with ancient woods of beech and spruce, and the accommodation complex for guests at the reserve is very attractive. Nearby is the Benedictine abbey of San Michele Arcangelo which was built at the beginning of the 11th century and faithfully restored over the years. Within the stone walls there are attractive rooms with a friendly atmosphere. The reception area, with its eye-catching big stone fireplace, acts also as the restaurant. This is the perfect place to sit and discuss the day's excursions. The simple and lovely bedrooms have all been refurbished. They have reasonable bathrooms and are furnished with rustic antiques.

RECOMMENDED IN THE AREA

RESTAURANT:
Big Ben, *Urbania*

LOCAL SPECIALITIES:
Ceramics in natural shades

VISIT:
Medieval village of Alta Valle del Metauro; Sansepolcro

Casale Torre del Sasso

A restructured house in the Apennines of Umbria and the Marches

☎ 0721 782655
✆ 0721 701336
✉ torresasso@info-net.it
61043 CAGLI (Pesaro e Urbino)
Ref map 7, D6
A14, Fano exit, *superstrada* (dual carriageway) towards Rome, Cagli exit
4 apartments; **££/£££**
Credit cards not accepted

RECOMMENDED IN THE AREA

RESTAURANT:
Taverna del Lupo, *via Ansidei 6, Gubbio*

VISIT:
Archaeological Museum in the Palazzo pubblico della cittadina (town hall)

*T*his farmhouse is situated between Umbria and the Marches, at the foot of the Apennines. The building was developed around a sentry post and a tower with a pigeon coop which, in the 15th century, were part of a well-constructed defence system throughout the territory of Cagli. Accommodation is in apartments of different sizes, which sleep from two to ten people. They are equipped with heating, safes and satellite television. Recent refurbishment has emphasised the old structure, and the stone walls, wood-beamed ceilings and pleasant rooms give the place its character. Materials used are in harmony with the age and function of the original building. Furnishings have been chosen according to the same criteria, with rustic pieces and also antiques. The result is attractive, welcoming and agreeable. Around the hotel are a large park and a flower garden. Within the park guests can enjoy a swimming pool, archery, bird watching and jogging, and there are paths as far as the river with its many loops and natural little beaches that allow for swimming.

Il Giardino degli Ulivi

RECOMMENDED IN THE AREA

RESTAURANT:
Due Torri, *San Severino Marche*

WINE CELLAR:
Enoteca Belisario, *Matelica (for Verdicchio di Matelica wine)*

LOCAL SPECIALITIES:
Truffles and Pecorino *cheese*

VISIT:
18th-century watch-tower, the Rocca d'Ajello

A medieval country lodge

☎ 0737 642121 ✆ 0737 640441
via Crucianelli 54
località Castel Sant'Angelo
62022 CASTELRAIMONDO (Macerata)
Ref map 7, E7
A14, Porto Recanati exit, S.S. 77 and 361 as far as Castelraimondo, from here take the road for Matelica, then turn left for Rustano-Santa Maria-Castel Sant'Angelo
5 rooms; **£/££**
Credit cards: AE VISA

*I*n the valley of the River Potenza, on the borders of Umbria and Tuscany, this area is rich in art, natural beauty and gastronomic novelties. This *agriturismo* (farm accommodation) has been created out of a medieval lodge, with elegantly austere architecture. It has been lovingly refurbished to maintain its character, and is situated 600 metres above sea level, deep in the countryside in peaceful surroundings. All the bedrooms have bathrooms and are furnished with late 19th-century pieces. The farm cultivates organically, and produces barley, honey and spelt wheat. There are bicycles for guests to hire .

$\mathcal{V}$illa Amalia

📞 071 9160550 📠 071 912045
📧 villa.amalia@fastnet.it
via degli Spagnoli 4
**60015 FALCONARA MARITTIMA
(Ancona)**
Ref map 7, D8

A14, Ancona Nord exit, *superstrada* (dual carriageway) as far as Falconara-Aeroporto exit, follow signs for Falconara Centro
7 rooms; **££**
Credit cards: AE VISA SI ⑩, bancomat

RECOMMENDED IN THE AREA

RESTAURANT:
Il Camino

WINE CELLARS:
Enoteca dell'Angelo *(Conero wines)*

VISIT:
Church of Santa Maria delle Grazie, Falconara Alta

$\mathcal{T}$his quiet and welcoming small hotel is in a charming villa dating from the early 20th century and surrounded by a lovely garden. The family that owns it receives guests in the three little rooms on the ground floor or, during the summer, on the delightful veranda. The bedrooms are comfortably sized and are furnished with warmth and simplicity. Adding to the guests' enjoyment is the care taken over the cooking. In fact the restaurant serves very good local dishes but with a touch of innovation: vegetables from the Marches accompany main courses of fresh fish from the Adriatic. Everything is enhanced by a good selection of local and national wines.

Corallo

📞 0721 804200
📠 0721 803637
📧 corallo@mobilia.it
via Leonardo da Vinci 3
61032 FANO (Pesaro e Urbino)
Ref map 7, C7

A14, Fano Centro exit, then follow signs for the *zona mare Sassonia* (Sassonia sea area)
34 rooms; **££**
Credit cards: AE VISA SI ⑩

RECOMMENDED IN THE AREA

RESTAURANTS:
Pesce Azzurro *and* Ristoriantino da Giulio

LOCAL SPECIALITIES:
Matta *sausage from Fano;* bozzotto *cheese;* moretta *(brandy-based liqueur); anisette and rum (which fishermen added to their coffee)*

VISIT:
Rocca Malatestiana fortress, Fano

$\mathcal{T}$his small hotel is well cared for and has comfortable rooms and attentive service. It is situated a short distance from the centre of the little town, facing the sea, and is in a simple modern building that has been completely refurbished. The bedrooms are equipped with every comfort, furnished with light wood furniture and each has a terrace overlooking the sea. The bathrooms are very practical. Buffet breakfast is particularly abundant and is served in the restaurant. Main meals are specialities based on local seafood, and over the years the hotel kitchen has gained a local reputation for its gastronomy. The owners are welcoming and attentive. The hotel has some garage spaces for guests' cars.

Grand Hotel Michelacci

A hotel where hospitality is a whole culture

☎ 0541 954361 📠 0541 954544

✉ michelacci@gabiccemare.com

piazza Giardini Unità d'Italia 1

61011 GABICCE MARE (Pesaro e Urbino)

Ref map 7, C6-7

A4, Gabicce Mare exit

80 rooms, 4 suites; ££

Credit cards: AE VISA SI ◯, bancomat

With its sunny white architecture typical of the Mediterranean, this hotel stands by the sea in a central but quiet position. Its medium-sized bedrooms are well presented and attractive, all with balconies overlooking the sea, with lovely upholstered furniture, and equipped with satellite television, safes, mini-bars and air conditioning. The bathrooms are very practical, with scales, hair-dryers, courtesy toiletry sets and sinks with pink marble surrounds. The communal rooms are large, spacious, welcoming and well furnished. The dining and breakfast rooms have sea views. In addition there are three swimming pools, including one indoor heated pool with hydromassage and water jet, a beauty salon with sauna, Turkish bath and various types of massage. An external terrace overlooking the sea is equipped for relaxation and there is bar service here. The uniformed members of staff in reception are welcoming and the owner is both vigilant and in evidence.

RECOMMENDED IN THE AREA

RESTAURANTS:
La Boccia *and* Il Traghetto

LOCAL SPECIALITIES:
Gabicce ceramics

Locanda San Rocco

In the midst of woods and vineyards

☎ and 📠 0737 642324

via Collaiello 2

62020 GAGLIOLE (Macerata)

Ref map 7, E7

A1, Orte exit, S.S. 3 for Foligno, then S.S. 7 towards Muccia, then S.S. 256 fro Camerino, Castelraimondo, Gagliole

6 rooms; ££

Credit cards: VISA, bancomat

Built around 1700, this big country house stands in the heart of the region that produces the famous Verdicchio di Matelica wine and is surrounded by green hills covered with vineyards and woods. The inn has recently been refurbished according to the original architectural principles: two storeys of unplastered stone accommodate the few bedrooms (all with balconies) and the communal rooms with their old-world charm. The stone walls both outside and inside, the terracotta floors and wood-beamed ceilings create a warm and attractive atmosphere. There is simple and refined period furniture in all the rooms in this quiet inn with its elegantly rural character. The building is part of a farm estate of 55 hectares that supplies the inn's restaurant with its own vegetables, fruit, cheeses, meat, wine and oil.

RECOMMENDED IN THE AREA

RESTAURANT:
La mia cucina, *San Severino Marche*

WINE CELLARS:
Enoteca Simoncini, *Macerata*

LOCAL SPECIALITIES:
A few kilometres away, direct factory outlets for some of Italy's most important designer clothes

$\mathcal{A}$rena

Central, but in a quiet corner

☎ 0733 230931 📠 0733 236059
via Sferisterio 16
62100 MACERATA
Ref map 7, E8

A14, Civitanova Le Marche exit, then
superstrada (dual carriageway) for Macerata,
Macerata-Sud-Corridonia exit,
then continue to Macerata Centro
22 rooms; £
Credit cards: AE VISA SI ⓪, bancomat

RECOMMENDED IN THE AREA

RESTAURANTS:
Osteria dei Fiori, via Lauro Rossi 61, Macerata;
Osteria dei Ricordi and Agriturismo le Case, Pollenza

VISIT:
Villa Potenza, a small archaeological site on the ruins
of a Roman city, 'Helvia Ricina'

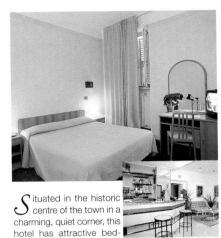

$\mathcal{S}$ituated in the historic centre of the town in a charming, quiet corner, this hotel has attractive bed-rooms and some in particular, having been recently renewed, are particularly fine. Nearly all have safes, air conditioning and double-glazing. The bathrooms are practical, with hair-dryers and towel heaters. Altogether this is a simple, friendly place where nothing is overlooked and guests receive a kind and attentive welcome. During the Arena opera season, many artists choose to stay here.

$\mathcal{V}$illa Quiete

In a hunting lodge dating back to the end of the 18th century

☎ and 📠 0733 599559
località Vallecascia
62010 MONTECASSIANO (Macerata)
Ref map 7, D8

A14, Loreto-Porto Recanati, S.S. 77,
towards Macerata
38 rooms, 2 suites; ££
Credit cards: VISA

$\mathcal{A}$ nobleman called Domenico Perozzi had this lovely little palace built at the end of the 18th century as a meeting and resting place during the shooting parties that he used to have in the surrounding area. Over the centuries the building has been gradually transformed yet has always maintained the original charm that even today is evident in every room and in the countryside around.

A very beautiful park surrounds this welcoming and relaxing country hotel, and not far away can be seen the old and still recognisable stables. The refurbished bedrooms face the park and are equipped with every comfort. They are furnished in different ways but all with good taste and simple elegance. The two suites are more ornate. The communal rooms, such as the reception hall and the various small reading rooms, have a special atmosphere. Here old-fashioned elegance welcomes the guest who wishes to enjoy peace and quiet.

RECOMMENDED IN THE AREA

RESTAURANT:
Secondo, via Peschiera Vecchia 26, Macerata

VISIT:
Palazzo comunale (town hall); parish church of
Assunta

229

La Ginestra

A splendid example of rural architecture put to new uses

☎ 0734 780449 📠 0734 780706
✉ info@laginestra.it
**63020 MONTELPARO
(Ascoli Piceno)
Ref map 7, E8**

A14, Pedaso exit, continue for the Valdaso *statale* (trunk road) towards Comunanza, after 27 km crossroads for Montelparo
13 rooms, 15 apartments; **£/££**
Credit cards: AE VISA SI ①

RECOMMENDED IN THE AREA

RESTAURANTS:
Osteria Mercuri-Da Quintilia, *Montefalcone Appennino;* Damiani e Rossi, *Porto San Giorgio*

*T*his hotel comprises an old farmhouse and its outbuildings, together with a few low buildings constructed in the stone and tiles typical of rural architecture in the Marches. They are delightfully situated among the green hills of the lovely countryside extending from the Sibillini mountains to the Adriatic sea. Accommodation consists of 13 bedrooms and 15 apartments: all are spacious with pleasingly rustic furniture and majolica floors or fitted carpets. The bathrooms have windows and showers, and are very practical.

The dining room has a brickwork ceiling, and the flames of the log fire burning in a big fireplace are reflected in the copper pots and pans hung on the walls. The bar extends on to a veranda looking over the green countryside. Here breakfast is served. The apartments are in separate little buildings of 90 square metres on one or two floors, each with a big sitting room and kitchen area, two bedrooms and two modern bathrooms. The apartments are attractive and well fitted, and have small gardens in front of the sitting rooms. They may also be hired by the day.

Around the hotel are large green spaces with six clay tennis courts, an open-air swimming pool and football pitch. Guests may take advantage of facilities for volley ball, riding, mini golf, *bocce* (bowls) and table tennis, and mountain bikes are available. There is also a children's playground and a car park.

$\mathcal{U}$illa Torraccia

The fascination of an old building

☎ and ✆ 0721 21852
strada Torraccia 3
61100 PESARO
Ref map 7, C7
A14, Pesaro exit, then S.S. Urbinate for
about 1.5 kilometres as far as the Torraccia
private road
5 suites; ££
Credit cards: AE VISA SI

RECOMMENDED IN THE AREA

RESTAURANTS:
Scudiero, *via Baldassini 2, and* Alceo, *via Panoramica Ardizio 101*

VISIT:
Ceramics Museum, Pesaro

*C*onstructed around the 13th century as a watch-tower, this was transformed into a private villa in the 15th century. All restoration work since has been done by faithfully conserving its architectural features. The villa is composed of two buildings: the tower and the *Frontale* ('front') with its monumental entrance. The interior is charming, and guests are welcomed into attractive rooms and suites: the pink suite, the blue, the Monsignore suite on the top floor, and the two suites facing the mountain and the sea are in the *Frontale* building. Each is different and each is a little haven: a secluded space enhanced by antique furniture and terracotta flooring, attics with wood-beamed ceilings, a charming atmosphere and yet with nothing incompatible with modern comfort. Everything has the mark of care and charm.

$\mathcal{U}$illa Serena

An 18th-century villa that was once an aristocratic residence

☎ 0721 55211 ✆ 0721 55927
via San Nicola 6/3
61100 PESARO
Ref map 7, C7
A14, Pesaro exit
8 rooms; ££
Credit cards: AE VISA SI ⓓ, bancomat

RECOMMENDED IN THE AREA

RESTAURANTS:
Teresa, *via Trieste 180, and* Scudiero, *via Baldassini 2*

LOCAL SPECIALITIES:
Cartoceto *extra virgin olive oil;* fossa *cheese;* Bianchello del Metauro *wine;* berlingozzi *(typical little cakes)*

VISIT:
Italian garden of Villa Caprile

*T*his 18th-century building on the hillside in the centre of a park/garden was the residence of the Pinto de Franca y Vargas counts, and it still belongs to descendants of the same family.

The villa has large rooms with high ceilings, inviting areas heated by big fireplaces and furnished with original furniture. The breakfast room is particularly charming with a beautiful terracotta floor that is original and worn down with time, a panelled ceiling and paintings of the period. The dining room is modern and built of brick with load-bearing wooden beams and large windows. In the garden there is a lovely swimming pool amongst the trees, in quiet green surroundings.

Giardino

☎ 0721 776803 📠 0721 735323
📧 massimo@netforce.it
via Mattei 4
61047 SAN LORENZO IN CAMPO
(Pesaro e Urbino)
Ref map 7, D7
A14, Morotta exit, then S.S. Pergolese,
towards Pergola for about 25 kilometres
20 rooms; **££**
Credit cards: 🆎 📇 📇 ⓞ, bancomat

*E*njoying a view of the beautiful hills around, this small family-run hotel is in a modern building about 1.5 kilometres from the residential centre. In addition to the prettiness and good taste of the furnishings, there are various facilities including a large bar, a good restaurant and a delightful swimming pool (open in summer only) that is surrounded by a little garden. The bedroom furnishings have recently been renewed, and the rooms are practical and furnished in a warm simple style; they have comfortable bathrooms. Of particular note is the cooking. The various dishes are all prepared with care in the choice of their ingredients, and are served at beautifully laid tables. An ample and up-to-date wine cellar completes the experience. The owners welcome guests warmly and are attentive to their requests.

RECOMMENDED IN THE AREA

RESTAURANT:
Il Giardino

VISIT:
Medieval castle and Renaissance Campiano Palace,
Castellone di Suasa

Locanda dei Comacini

A delightful view over
the hills of the Marches

☎ 0733 639691
via San Francesco 2
62027 SAN SEVERINO LE
MARCHE (Macerata)
Ref map 7, E7
A14, Porto Recanati-Loreto exit, in direction of
Macerata, then towards Villa Potenza-San Severino
5 rooms; **£**
Credit cards not accepted

*A*round the year 1200, the medieval master builders and stone-cutters of Como constructed a girdle of walls around the old village. Right outside the walls, still in the high part of the small town and encircled by a garden, is the little building of the *locanda*. It is rural in character but there are also two new buildings reserved for guests of the *agriturismo* (farm accommodation). The view from here sweeps over the beautiful surrounding hills.

Inside, there are simple ornaments and furniture typical of country houses. All the bedrooms have bathrooms and are plainly furnished. A corner of the restaurant is warmed by a brick fireplace, and the room maintains the character of the old building. The tables are set with particular care. Here relaxation is guaranteed at the end of a day's visit to the historical and natural sights of the area.

RECOMMENDED IN THE AREA

RESTAURANT:
Due Torri

WINE CELLAR:
La Bottega dell'Africano

VISIT:
Archaeological museum, art gallery, castle and
monumental area

Duchi della Rovere

*T*his building is modern with striking architecture, and is in a strategic position a short distance from the historic centre and the sea, not far from the station and from the main roads. Its bedrooms are nicely presented, all with parquet flooring. The bathrooms are fairly practical and have showers and hair-dryers. The communal rooms are well furnished, very bright and – in the hotel's spirit of efficiency – are aimed particularly at business clients. On the top floor the roof garden with swimming pool faces the sea and the imposing Rovere rock fortress. The restaurant has big windows on to the garden. The kitchen serves good quality national and international dishes. The hotel also has a garage and bicycles for the use of guests.

RECOMMENDED IN THE AREA

RESTAURANTS:
Uliassi, La Madonnina del Pescatore *and* Bano

VISIT:
Church of Santa Maria delle Grazie; museum of sharecropper history

Efficiency, practicality and good cooking

☎ and 🖷 071 7927784
✉ hduchi@indi.it
via Corridoni 3
60019 SENIGALLIA (Ancona)
Ref map 7, D7A14, Senigallia exit, towards the sea
44 rooms; £££
Credit cards: AE VISA SI ⓪ bancomat

Villa Pina

A small villa from the early 1900s

☎ 071 7926723
🖷 071 65558
via F. Podesti 158
60019 SENIGALLIA (Ancona)
Ref map 7, D7
A14, Senigallia exit
15 rooms, 2 apartments; ££/£££
Credit cards: AE VISA SI

RECOMMENDED IN THE AREA

RESTAURANTS:
La Madonnina del Pescatore *and* Al cuoco di bordo

VISIT:
Rovere rock fortress

A large part of Senigallia is made up of small-scale buildings with pleasing architecture dating from the early 1900s when taking holidays began to be part of normal life. Here, in contrast to much of the Adriatic coast, nearly all the town remains unchanged and Villa Pina is no exception. This home that has become a hotel is situated a short distance from the sea and about one kilometre from the centre. It has large bedrooms with simple dark wood furniture that are charming and individual in appearance.

The bathrooms are adequate, most have showers and many have windows. The communal rooms are delightful and some rooms retain their original early 20th-century floors. Outside is a big garden that in summer is equipped with sunshades, and there is a *bocce* (bowls) pitch and table tennis. The hotel does not have a lift. The proprietors run the hotel, and pay careful attention to their guests' requirements.

*D*e' Conti

Deep in the silent countryside of the Marches

☎ and ✆ 0731 879913
via S. Lucia 58
60030 SERRA DE' CONTI (Ancona)
Ref map 7, D7
A14, Senigallia exit, the S.S. 360 towards Sassoferrato, next turn off for Montecarotto
14 rooms; **£/££**
Credit cards: AE VISA SI ⓓ, bancomat

RECOMMENDED IN THE AREA

RESTAURANTS:
Alla Bona Usanza; Hostaria Santa Lucia, *Jesi*

WINE CELLARS:
Enoteca Brunori *and* Osteria Forno Ercoli, *Jesi;*
Ancona Vini, *Ancona*

VISIT:
At the end of November, feast of the cicerchia *plant; medieval walls; Pianetti Palace, art gallery and Signoria Palace, Jesi*

*T*his well-designed and charming modern hotel is a delightful place to stay. The very comfortable, white building is situated 300 metres above sea level in a panoramic and 'strategic' position. It is amongst the Verdicchio hills, in a great wine-producing area where tradition still plays an important part and care is taken to recreate dishes of the past. The graceful lines of the exterior are replicated inside the hotel: the lighting is carefully planned and the rooms are very bright, understated and furnished with comfortable modern sofas. The bedrooms are spacious with designer details.

There is a garden and a panoramic terrace with a view over the gentle hills of the Marches, where there is bar service and breakfast. The restaurant serves dishes with a traditional emphasis.

Casa Oliva

An old palace with a medieval atmosphere

☎ and ✆ 0721 891500
via Castello 19
61030 SERRUNGARINA (Pesaro e Urbino)
Ref map 7, D7
A14, Fano exit, then *superstrada* (dual carriageway) to Fano-Grosseto, towards Bargni, Serrimgarina
16 rooms; £
Credit cards: ⟨AE⟩ ⟨VISA⟩ ⟨SI⟩ ⟨DC⟩

*T*he windows look on to the small square of the little medieval village: from here the view extends over hills covered with olive trees, vines and woods as far as the sea. The old noble palace containing the hotel has been harmoniously restructured: respect for the architectural features is reflected inside, with elegant furniture gracing comfortable and relaxing rooms. The bedrooms are divided between the main building and an outbuilding, and are all equipped with the most modern comforts: fitted carpets, terracotta floors and designer fittings. The bathrooms are a comfortable size, modern and practical. The communal areas are well furnished and charming. The restaurant, which offers a carefully chosen menu of regional specialities, is in another of the village houses. It has a delightful terrace overlooking the valley below.

RECOMMENDED IN THE AREA

RESTAURANTS:
Il Symposium-Quattro stagioni, *Cartoceto*

LOCAL SPECIALITIES:
Handbags; pecorini cheeses (made from sheep's milk); fruity olive oil particular to this region

---

VillaFederici

In a park of ancient trees

☎ and ✆ 0721 891510
✉ federici@mobilia.it
via Cartoceto 4, località Bargni
61030 SERRUNGARINA (Pesaro e Urbino)
Ref map 7, C-D7
A14, Fano exit, *superstrada* (dual carriageway) tp Fano-Cagli, towards Serrungarina, then go on towards Bargni
5 rooms; ££
Credit cards: ⟨AE⟩ ⟨VISA⟩ ⟨SI⟩ ⟨DC⟩, bancomat

*T*his old house has spacious rooms and an interior that is warm and full of atmosphere: wood-beamed ceilings, terracotta floors, simple decorations enriched by 19th-century antique furniture. A park containing many age-old trees surrounds the building. The villa was built in 1683 by Domenico Federici, one of Emperor Leopoldo I's diplomats, and it has been completely restructured. This refurbishment has remained faithful to the original building. Breakfast is served around a large table in a lovely room which during the day becomes a reading and sitting room. The dining room has antique furniture and elegantly set tables. A pretty little adjacent room can accommodate social occasions and family parties, and is surrounded by the beautiful garden. Adding to the calm and tranquillity is the great care taken over every detail by the proprietors.

RECOMMENDED IN THE AREA

RESTAURANT:
Teresa, *Pesaro*

LOCAL SPECIALITIES:
Fossa *cheese and truffles*

VISIT:
Gola del Furlo (a narrow ravine)

Conchiglia Verde

Old authenticity and healthy traditions

☎ 071 9330018
🖷 071 9330019
via Giovanni XXIII 14
60020 SIROLO (Ancona)
Ref map 7, D8
A14, Ancona Sud exit, follow signs
for Sirolo
26 rooms; **££**
Credit cards: AE VISA SI ⒹⒹ, bancomat

*A*dorned by plants and flowers, this is a modern white building with several terraces. All the bedrooms, with central heating, mini-bars and ceiling fans, are furnished with wrought iron beds and lovely bed linen to make guests feel welcome and at home. The communal rooms have stylish furnishings, signed paintings and a warm atmosphere. There is also a room for meetings and conferences. The restaurant has a menu specialising in fish and is very well furnished: the floor tiles were hand-decorated by a specialist in Faenza ceramics. The swimming pool's walls imitate rocks, and the heated hydromassage area has a natural theme with stalactites, stalagmites and waterfalls. On the top floor the lovely panoramic terrace is equipped for relaxation. In addition there is a garden and the hotel has a garage.

RECOMMENDED IN THE AREA

RESTAURANT:
Il Saraghino

WINE CELLAR:
Enoteca Solaria

VISIT:
Conero mountain in the centre of Conero Nature Park

Monteconero

*T*he building's fascination derives from its history. The hotel was born from the transformation of an old Benedictine abbey, and its original appearance was faithfully conserved in the recent restructuring. The severe lines of the exterior are softened by the small square with a well and a little church, around which the whole building is arranged, and by the beautiful panorama. The restaurant and all the bedrooms, most with a balcony, open on to this view. Situated on the summit of Conero mountain, 500 metres above sea level, the building is surrounded by the green hills of the Marches and not far from the Adriatic beaches. The bedrooms are large, light and extremely welcoming: there are frescoes on the walls, parquet or terracotta floors and period furniture. The communal rooms, many with vaulted ceilings, are charming and full of romantic elegance. There is a lovely swimming pool encircled by trees for guests' use.

RECOMMENDED IN THE AREA

RESTAURANT:
Locanda Rocca

VISIT:
San Pietro Abbey

A relaxing holiday in charming surroundings

☎ 071 9330592
🖷 071 9330365
via Monteconero 26
60020 SIROLO (Ancona)
Ref map 7, D8
A14, Ancona-sud exit, first follow signs for
Sirolo, then for Monte Conero
50 rooms; **££**
Credit cards: AE VISA SI ⒹⒹ, bancomat

*I*l vecchio Granaio

RECOMMENDED IN THE AREA

RESTAURANTS:
Il Vecchio Granaio, *San Severino Marche;* La Rocca dei Borgia, *Camerino;* Il Giardino degli Ulivi, *Castelraimondo*

LOCAL SPECIALITIES:
Wine and olive oil from local cellars and presses

VISIT:
Church of Santa Maria de Rambona

The atmosphere of an old private country house

☎ 0733 8434488
🖷 0733 541312
contrada Chiaravalle 49
62010 TREIA (Macerata)
Ref map 7, D8
A14, Porto Recanati-Loreto, towards Macerata; at Villa Potenza follow the signs for San Severino
19 rooms, 17 apartments; ££
Credit cards: AE VISA SI ⓓ, bancomat

*T*he complex, which is surrounded by tree-lined avenues in an old park of six hectares and at the heart of a large agricultural estate, arose out of the refurbishment of farmhouses, granary, wine store, stables and other 18th-century farm outbuildings. These buildings have lovely walls made of terrracotta and river stone and inside the ceilings have the original beams. A sense of history and the character of the whole complex make this a fascinating place.

The little guest apartments are extremely practical and comfortable, and are furnished in the taste of old private country houses in the Marches: the large rooms embellished with floral wallpaper or painted vaulted ceilings have simple period furniture.

The atmosphere is particularly welcoming and elegant on the delightful big open veranda, set in the green of the old trees, and in the restaurant. This is in the 16th-century main house and, with its wooden beams and brick arches, preserves the atmosphere of the past.

Raffaello

In the pedestrian zone of the historic centre of Urbino, this palace is a few steps away from the 15th-century house of the artist Raphael (Raffaello Sanzi). Here the proprietors have created a hospitable and comfortable hotel that blends a refined modern use of space and furnishings with the ancient walls of the building.

Built by Valadier to house Urbino's first seminary, it was transformed into a hotel in 1984 and in 1995 was refurbished with simple modern elegance. There are lovely marble floors and carpets in the reception halls. The bedrooms are equipped with every comfort and furnished in modern style with well-designed furniture. They also enjoy the wonderful view stretching from the city's most important monument, the Ducal palace (which is the archetype of a Renaissance non-fortified home), to the gentle hills of the Marches.

The bathrooms are small but quite practical. A buffet breakfast is served in a tiny, pretty room and includes home-made cakes. It is worth noting that, for clients, there is a convenient shuttle service to the main car parks and to the bus station.

A former seminary just a few steps from Raphael's house
☎ 0722 4784
🖷 0722 328540
via Santa Margherita 38
61029 URBINO
Ref map 7, D6
14 rooms; **££**
Credit cards: Æ VISA SI, bancomat

RECOMMENDED IN THE AREA

RESTAURANT:
Il Cortegiano, *via Puccinotti 13*

LOCAL SPECIALITIES:
Caciotta *from Urbino (a speciality cheese)*

VISIT:
Church of San Bernarndinodegli Zoccolanti

Umbria

The monastery and basilica of St Francis, at Assisi

This rather small, secluded inland area contains a formidable concentration of art, history and natural beauty. The landscape resembles Tuscany's and anticipates that of Lazio in a succession of hills, fields, olive trees, vines, outlines of villages and towns with imposing mountains in the background. 'There is not an inch of land between these hills,' noted Montaigne in the 16th century; he exaggerated, but not much. Between the mountains and hills sloping down to the west there are the Umbra valley basin between Perugia and Spoleto, the Tiberina valley basin with Città di Castello, and then briefly the plains of Gubbio, Norcia and Terni.

History and art are linked with spirituality – it could not be otherwise for places associated with St Benedict of Norcia, St Francis of Assisi, and Jacopone of Todi. The wonderful synthesis of this link must be the basilica at Assisi in which Giotto – with Cimabue, Simone Martini and Pietro Lorenzetti – made landmarks in the story of Italian art. Perugia, Orvieto, Spello, Gubbio, Todi, Spoleto, Bevagna and Montefalco display extraordinarily vivid medieval fragments. A visit to Umbria provides images of incredible beauty: the Gothic cathedral at Orvieto, Gubbio's piazza della Signoria, and the Maggiore fountain at Perugia.

Natural beauty is found in a variety of forms, and often very close to the major centres of art, and is now usually protected in nature parks: Gubbio's Mount Cucco, Norcia's Sibbillini mountains, Assisi's Mount Subasio, and the fluvial park of Trevere. Lake Trasimeno tempts visitors to explore its banks and bathe in its waters. Old inns and palaces, farmhouses amidst olive trees or in panoramic villages all provide accommodation and hospitality.

Castello di Casigliano

A copybook castle of the 17th century

☎ 0744 943428 📠 0744 944056
📧 casigliano@mail.caribusiness.it
piazza Corsini 1
05021 ACQUASPARTA (Terni)
Ref map 8, B4

A1, Orvieto exit, S.S. 448 as far as Todi,
then S.S. E45 towards Terni
6 rooms; ££
Credit cards: VISA SI Ⓞ, bancomat

This big castle stands on a hill in slightly rolling countryside dominated on the horizon by the green mass of the Marani mountains. It was built in the 17th century by Antonio da Sangallo the younger. In the shadow of the palace that guaranteed protection and shelter, stands the old village composed of low stone houses. A short time ago this place discovered a new vocation as a haven for tourists, and a small, attractive inn has been created in the old castle wine stores. Here the rustic atmosphere is warmed by a large fireplace, and by traditional cooking (and barbecues) using fresh herbs, precious truffles and game. Within the village some of the houses have been restructured to provide accommodation and are now attractive little apartments equipped with air conditioning, satellite television and mini-bars. In addition there is a car park, garden and solarium.

RECOMMENDED IN THE AREA

RESTAURANT:
Umbria, *Todi*

VISIT:
San Faustino thermal baths; San Faustino Abbey

Villa Stella

With the atmosphere of a private house

☎ and 📠 0744 930063
via G. Marconi 37
05021 ACQUASPARTA (Terni)
Ref map 8, B4

A1, Orvieto exit, S,S, 448 as far as Todi,
then S.S. E45 towards Terni
10 rooms; ££
Credit cards: VISA SI Ⓞ

This hotel is in a villa that was constructed in 1923 in the graceful Art Nouveau style with a slim little turret and lovely wrought-iron railings. Transformed into a hotel, it still has the style of a private residence. The large bedrooms have the atmosphere of a home rather than a hotel: the ceilings are high, the windows look on to the garden. The bathrooms are small but quite good, each with a window, and all except one have showers rather than a bath. The sitting room and little breakfast room are furnished with authentic early 20th-century furniture. Breakfast is continental style. Guests receive a friendly welcome from the family who run the hotel. In the large garden surrounding the hotel there is an area equipped for relaxation and also a car park. There is no lift.

RECOMMENDED IN THE AREA

RESTAURANT:
Martini

LOCAL SPECIALITIES:
Hand-crafted furniture in the Renaissance style, Todi; ceramics, Deruta; lace, Città di Castello

VISIT:
Monteluco

Carleni

RESTAURANT:
Alfio, *via Galilei 4*

LOCAL SPECIALITIES:
Local oil and wine

The atmosphere of an old, welcoming home

☎ 0744 983925 🖷 0744 978143
✉ carleni@tin.it
via Pellegrino Carleni 21
05022 AMELIA (Terni)
Ref map 8, C4
A1, Orte exit, then *superstrada* (dual
carriageway) 204 for Terni, Amelia exit
7 rooms, 3 apartments; ££
Credit cards: AE VISA SI ①

S ituated at the heart of Amelia's historic centre, this hotel arose out of the restructuring of an old palace dating back to the 18th century. Surrounded by a charming little garden that is very luxuriant and encircled by lovely stone walls, it retains all the atmosphere of an attractive old dwelling. The dark wood doors stand out against the high walls inside, as does the beautiful furniture with its character and simple and traditional style. Big fireplaces warm the communal areas which are decorated with glass showcases and tasteful ornaments. The bedrooms are comfortable and elegantly simple, maintain the same style and, like the other rooms, have wood-beamed ceilings.

The excellent restaurant serves refined cooking that mixes traditional Umbrian flavours with those of French cuisine.

Dal Moro

In the land of Saint Francis of Assisi

☎ 075 8043688
🖷 075 8041666
✉ dalmoro@perugioaonline.com
località Santa Maria degli Angeli
05021 ASSISI (Perugia)
Ref map 8, B4
A1, then Perugia junction, next *superstrada*
(dual carriageway) 75 and S.S. 147 for Assisi
4 rooms; ££
Credit cards: AE VISA SI ①, bancomat

RECOMMENDED IN THE AREA

RESTAURANTS:
Buca di San Francesco *and* Il Frantoio

LOCAL SPECIALITIES:
Local tastings of Umbrian olive oil, cheeses and home-produced charcuterie

N ot long ago this hotel was restructured in an original and delightful way. It stands next to the basilica of Santa Maria degli Angeli. In its large and attractive reception hall there are many statues and rich carpets. Red runners cover the stairs.

The bedrooms are large and well lit, some with a panoramic view over the nearby basilica and the cupola by Vignola. They have large beds with shaped headrests, and blue and light red upholstery. The bathrooms are comfortable and equipped with hair-dryers and courtesy toiletry sets.

Breakfast is carefully prepared and served as a buffet.

Malvarina

A small but welcoming stone farmhouse

☎ and 🖷 075 8064280
✉ malvarina@umbria.net
via Malvarina 32, località Viole
06081 ASSISI (Perugia)
Ref map 8, B4

A1, then Perugia junction, next *superstrada* (dual carriageway) 75 and S.S. 147 for Assisi
7 rooms, 3 apartments; **££**
Credit cards: 🆅🆂🄰 🆂🄸

D eep in the green of the garden and the surrounding countryside, this lovely stone farmhouse with its pleasantly rustic shape has a welcoming family atmosphere. The management of the *agriturismo* (farm accommodation) is relaxed yet efficient. The location is enchanting and has the advantage of being well placed for visits to the area's sites of historical importance and natural beauty.

The few bedrooms are in various buildings and are individual, comfortable and practical. Terracotta floors and fresh white walls dominate, and in the restaurant and the communal areas there are little dressers and late 19th-century prints of rural scenes, ornaments and rustic furnishings that stand out against the white background. Guests may relax in the garden by the swimming pool, or else can go riding in the vicinity.

RECOMMENDED IN THE AREA

RESTAURANTS:
Il Viaggiatore *and* Pozzo della mensa

VISIT:
Santa Maria degli Angeli Basilica (where St Francis founded the order of Franciscan monks)

Villa Bellago

A large villa on Lake Corbara

☎ 0744 950521 🖷 0744 950524
località Pian delle monache 138
05023 BASCHI (Terni)
Ref map 8, B-C3

A1, Orvieto exit, then S.S. 448 for Todi, after the motorway bridge turn left for Baschi
10 rooms; **££**
Credit cards: 🄰🄴 🆅🆂🄰 🆂🄸 ⓄⒹ, bancomat

T his hotel stands in a very panoramic position with a lovely view over Lake Corbara and is surrounded by wide green spaces that slope down towards the river. Its low, precise architecture of tiles and bricks is that of a large villa.

The bedrooms are in two little buildings in the garden, and they are spacious and furnished with delightful aniline-painted furniture and equipped with mini-bars, satellite television and ceiling fans. There are also two small suites with fireplaces, parquet flooring and rustic furniture. The breakfast room and communal rooms are in the main house and still have some of the original features of the farmhouse it once was. In the large garden is an open-air swimming pool with solarium terrace, a pitch for five-a-side football, beach volleyball, and table tennis. The hotel also has sauna, gym and mountain bikes available to guests. The restaurant is under different management but in the same building, and has a winter area, and a terrace for summer dining under a portico with an enchanting view. The dishes are Umbrian specialities.

RECOMMENDED IN THE AREA

RESTAURANT:
Trippini, *Civetella del Lago*

VISIT:
Alviano Nature Reserve

Il Poggio degli Olivi

A warm welcome in a delightful area

☎ and 🖷 075 9869023
✉ poggiodegliolivi@edisons.it
frazione Passaggio di Bettona
località Montebalacca
06084 BETTONA (Perugia)
Ref map 8, B4
A1, Perugia junction as far as Ponte San
Giovanni, then E45 towards Todi,
Ponte Nuovo exit, go on for Bettona
6 rooms, 10 apartments; **££**
Credit cards: 🝗 🝗 🝗 ⓪, bancomat

*A*n elegant rural complex dating back to the 17th century, surrounded by olive trees and vines, that stands on a little hill dominating one of Umbria's most beautiful green areas. From here there is a view of places famous for their history, culture and natural beauty. Large ceilings with wooden beams characterise the big elegant areas inside. The rooms are tastefully decorated and have rustic, stylish furniture. Both bedrooms and apartments are comfortably large. Terracotta, dark wood furniture and fabrics recall farming traditions with their delightful warm earthy colours. A lovely fireplace warms the communal rooms, while the restaurant's large windows open onto the valley. The airy spaces are elegantly simple and welcoming. In the garden there is a tennis court and swimming pool. The bedrooms are warm and comfortable, furnished in the mountain style, and have balconies and big windows.

RECOMMENDED IN THE AREA

RESTAURANT:
Poppy Inn-Locanda del Papavero, Petrignano

LOCAL SPECIALITIES:
Sagrantino di Montefalco wine, truffles and olive oil

VISIT:
Wine museum, Torgiano

Palazzo Brunamonti

Elegant rooms and old frescoes

☎ 0742 361932
🖷 0742 361948
✉ p.brunamonti@mclink.it
corso Matteotti 79
06031 BEVAGNA (Perugia)
Ref map 8, B4
A1, then Perugia junction, then S.S. 75
as far as Foligno, Bevagna exit
16 rooms; **£**
Credit cards: 🝗 🝗 🝗 ⓪, bancomat

*T*he name is evidence of the Renaissance past of this aristocratic palace which also displays the ancient ruins of an even older history, Roman and medieval. The building is a couple of steps away from the wonderful piazza Silvestri. Skilfully refurbished, some of the communal rooms are adorned with elegant 18th- and 19th-century frescoes, and old, sought-after furnishings embellish the light and elegant interior. In the airy, pale-coloured bedrooms there are terracotta floors and vaulted brick ceilings, comfortable beds with brass bedsteads, arrangements of flowers, and copies of drawings by the poetess Alinda Brunamonti who loved this place. The *amaro* liqueur that the proprietor offers guests is made by him personally from an infusion of 13 herbs. The communal rooms can also accommodate small conferences.

RECOMMENDED IN THE AREA

RESTAURANTS:
Ottavius *and* El Rancho

LOCAL SPECIALITIES:
Wrought iron; ceramics; fabrics; truffles; olive oil; wine; charcuterie and cheeses

VISIT:
Town walls and piazza Silvestri, with Consoli Palace and churches of San Silvestro and San Michele Arangelo

243

*I*l Poggio dei Pettirossi

*T*he harmonious buildings that make up this little village are a successful blend of old (intelligently restored) and new (built on characteristic traditional lines). The village, with well-tended fields, gravel paths, lovely swimming pool and a summerhouse with tables and sunshades, stands on the top of the hill from which it takes its name. From here there is a vast panorama of the rich valley beneath and of the historic small town of Bevagna.

The comfortable bedrooms are furnished in a delightfully co-ordinated way: coloured fabrics match the rustic furniture, and there are also modern, practical touches. The high-ceilinged suites on two levels have a cooking area. Charming verandas overlooking the garden complement the interior. In the main building there is a welcoming entrance hall adorned with antique furniture. The restaurant serves authentic dishes based on products from the farm.

RECOMMENDED IN THE AREA

RESTAURANT:
Villa Roncalli, *Foligno*

LOCAL SPECIALITIES:
Wine and typical products of the region: pecorini cheeses, truffles, oil and meat

VISIT:
Hand weaving of hemp on special looms using the medieval method; church of San Michele Arcangelo

An atmosphere of culture and freedom

☎ 0742 361744 📠 0742 360379
✉ albergo@ilpoggiodeipettirossi.com
vocabolo Pilone 301
06031 BEVAGNA (Perugia)
Ref map 8, B4
A1, Perugia junction, then S.S. 75 as far as Foligno, Bevagna exit
24 rooms, 3 suites; **££**
Credit cards: AE VISA SI OD , bancomat

$\mathcal{L}$ocanda Enoteca Piazza Onofri

In the old tradition of Italian taverns

☎ and 🖷 0742 321290
piazza Onofri 2
06031 BEVAGNA (Perugia)
Ref map 8, B4
A1, Perugia junction, then S.S. 75
as far as Foligno, Bevagna exit
13 apartments; ££
Credit cards: AE VISA SI ⓪, bancomat

$\mathcal{B}$evagna offers visitors its wonderful monuments, streets with an unmistakable medieval character, and a little gem of a historic centre. In a lovely stone palace with austere architecture is this *enoteca/locanda* (wine shop/inn), inspired by the tradition and warm hospitality of Italian taverns. Inside there is a big fireplace, lovely brick vaults and simple rustic furnishings. The wine cellar has a list of 400 labels that represent the best of local production and a very good choice of Italian and foreign wines. The *minialoggi* (the name given to little apartments) has a character deriving from the details that only old buildings possess: thick walls, beamed ceilings and arches framing the windows. The furnishings are simple but pretty and in keeping with the whole atmosphere of the place.

RECOMMENDED IN THE AREA

RESTAURANTS:
Locanda del Cavaliere che no c'è, *Foligno;*
La Taverna del pescatore, *Trevi*

VISIT:
Gaite market (last week in June); Foligno

$\mathcal{L}$a Casina Bassa

A rustic building in the midst of organic groves and orchards

☎ and 🖷 075 9527213
via Poggio del Sole 3
frazione Villastrada Umbra
06060 CASTIGLIONE DEL LAGO (Perugia)
Ref map 8, B3
A1, Chiusi-Chianciano exit, S.S. 71, then
10 km from Castiglione del Lago turn left
for Villastrada
5 apartments; £
Credit cards not accepted

$\mathcal{A}$n old farmhouse on the green hillside surrounded by ancient trees and only ten kilometres from Lake Trasimeno. The building has been refurbished but its architectural proportions and original materials have been maintained. Visitors see a delightful building made of warmly attractive materials. It is in the centre of a large agricultural area where olive and fruit trees and also vegetables are cultivated organically. Accommodation is in apartments each containing two or three bedrooms and a cooking area, bathroom and fireplace. For guests there is an open-air swimming pool, table tennis, children's playground, equipment for outside leisure and meals, and bicycles for hire.

RECOMMENDED IN THE AREA

RESTAURANTS:
Cantina *and* Acquario

*C*asal de' Cucchi

Amongst woods, pines and olive trees

☎ 075 9528116 ✆ 075 5171244
✉ dinfani@tin.it
località Petrignano del Lago
**06060 CASTIGLIONE DEL LAGO
(Perugia)**
Ref map 8, B3
A1, Chiusi-Chianciano exit, S.S. 71,
then 10 km from Castiglione
del Lago, next go towards Pozzuolo
4 rooms, 6 apartments; **££/£££**
Credit cards not accepted

Situated on the border between Umbria and Tuscany, this hotel is deep in restful countryside with beautiful views, in the green of woods and pine trees interspersed with olive groves and rows of vines – this is an area where table and selected wines are produced.

Accommodation is in typically harmonious buildings: the main one, in stone, was the old family house and around it are a number of agricultural outbuildings that have been refurbished. The whole complex has four bedrooms (without private bathrooms) and six apartments of various types, each with two to four rooms.

RECOMMENDED IN THE AREA

RESTAURANTS:
Merletti, *isola Maggiore;* Il Falconiere, *Cortona*
VISIT:
Castiglione del Lago

The restaurant has the original stone walls and some charming details, and the kitchen serves traditionally based dishes using typical products from the farm and the local area. There is also a wine cellar. In the big garden around the house is a children's playground and table tennis. Bicycles can be hired. In addition there is an open-air swimming pool.

$\mathcal{M}$iralago

On a promontory overlooking the lake

☎ 075 951157 e 🖷 075 951924
✉ miralago@ftbcc.it
piazza Mazzini 6
06061 CASTIGLIONE DEL LAGO (Perugia)
Ref map 8, B3
A1, Chiusi-Chianciano exit, towards Chiusi, then S.S. 71 as far as Castiglione del Lago
19 rooms; ££
Credit cards: Ⓐ Ⓥ Ⓢ Ⓜ

$\mathcal{T}$his attractive hotel is in the centre of the small town in a delightful little mansion dating from the end of the 19th century. The interior, which has been recently refurbished, has the fresh style of Art Nouveau, with marble and floral-patterned carpets in the pretty hall. The spacious bedrooms all face the historic square or have a beautiful view over Lake Trasimeno and are furnished simply in classic style. No comfort is lacking, so an agreeable and relaxing stay is guaranteed. An ample and tempting buffet breakfast is the prelude to the good food served by the ground-floor restaurant. During summer, meals are served in the little garden with a view of the lake. Local specialities are accompanied by wine of the region.

RECOMMENDED IN THE AREA

RESTAURANT:
Acquario

VISIT:
Trasimeno a tavola *(display of local gastronomy with tastings) in June; Tuscan and Umbrian towns with their artistic, historic, archaeological and religious treasures*

$\mathcal{T}$iferno

Wine and good food to enjoy in a small medieval village

☎ 075 8550331
🖷 075 8521196
✉ hoteltiferno@lineanet.net
piazza Raffaello Sanzio13
06012 CITTÀ DI CASTELLO (Perugia)
Ref map 8, A3
E45, towards Perugia, Città di Castello
38 rooms; ££
Credit cards: Ⓐ Ⓥ Ⓢ Ⓜ, bancomat

$\mathcal{O}$riginal features have been retained in the complete renewal of this hotel which stands in the historic centre of the lovely little town and is one of Umbria's oldest places of hospitality. Once it was a 17th-century palace and before that the religious house of the nearby church of St Francis. Now the hotel maintains a perfect balance between the gracious atmosphere created by period furniture and paintings and the modern comfort that distinguish the charming bedrooms with their elegantly coloured walls, fabrics and furnishings. The communal rooms are refined and decorations carefully chosen. A few valuable works by Burri (a contemporary local artist) decorate the walls, whilst panelled ceilings, sofas in antique shapes and valuable furniture are the visible sign of the attention to detail that distinguishes this historic hotel. There is also a conference room.

RECOMMENDED IN THE AREA

RESTAURANTS:
Il postale di Marco e Barbara *and* Bersaglio

$\mathcal{A}$bbazia dei Collemedio

In the peace of an old abbey

☎ 075 8789352
🖷 075 8789324
via Convento
località Collepepe
06050 COLLAZZONE (Perugia)
Ref map 8, B4
E45, Ripbianca exit
52 rooms; ££
Credit cards: AE VISA SI OD, bancomat

This complex was founded in 1200 by the counts of Collemedio, and later was a Benedictine abbey. After 1860 it no longer belonged to the monks and was abandoned for a long time. Restoration began in 1990 and was finished four years later. The building was transformed into a hotel with a delightful atmosphere. Lovely architecture and well-furnished sitting rooms welcome visitors. In winter open fires heat the rooms, whilst in summer guests can enjoy the breeze on the terrace by the swimming pool. The bedrooms used to be the monks' cells, and they are different sizes but all furnished stylishly with rustic furniture. The church has been transformed into a room to accommodate shows and conferences.

RECOMMENDED IN THE AREA

RESTAURANT:
Le Tre Vaselle, *Torgiano*

LOCAL SPECIALITIES:
Ceramics from Deruta

VISIT:
The church of Madonna di Bagno

$\mathcal{C}$onca del Sole

Deep in a forest in the heart of Umbria

☎ 075 5171149
🖷 075 5170777
via Pascarella 13
località Ellera
06074 CORCIANO (Perugia)
Ref map 8, B4
A1, Perugia junction, Corciano exit
32 rooms, 11 apartments; ££
Credit cards: AE VISA SI OD, bancomat

A short distance (six kilometres) from Perugia in a big park is this hotel composed of various accommodation units distributed over the green surroundings.

Reception and the main facilities are in the main house. Separate little buildings contain the bedrooms and the apartments with their own entrances. There are terracotta floors, white or rustic-style simple modern furniture, and large windows overlooking the park. The restaurant serves meals outside in the high season. There is also an open-air swimming pool, tennis court, five-a-side-football pitch and beach volleyball, children's playground and a discothèque and piano bar. The hotel asks for a minimum of a week's half-board stay.

RECOMMENDED IN THE AREA

RESTAURANT:
Enoteca Giò, *via R. Andreotto 19*

LOCAL SPECIALITIES:
Majolica, copper and wrought iron from Deruta

VISIT:
Corciano; antiques markets at Todi and Perugia

$\mathcal{L}$a Mandorla

Sport and relaxation in the open air

☎ and ✆ 075 5140643
via Venturi
località San Mariano
06073 CORCIANO (Perugia)
Ref map 8, B4
A1, Perugia junction, Corciano exit
8 apartments; ££
Credit cards not accepted

$\mathcal{A}$ lovely grey stone building that dominates the hill and looks onto a green Umbrian valley. The garden encloses the well-maintained house, and has a big swimming pool surrounded by a luxuriant green area in which the peace of the neighbourhood can be enjoyed. The hotel's interiors are typically rustic in character: there are different mini-apartments arranged in a number of buildings and all are furnished simply. The bedrooms are large, welcoming and comfortable in their design and furnishings.

A visit here is all about open-air life, sport and relaxation: not far away are golf, tennis and squash clubs as well as a riding centre. Guests can also visit the historical and natural sites nearby.

RECOMMENDED IN THE AREA

RESTAURANTS:
Aladino, *via delle Prome 11, and* Da Giancarlo, *via dei Priori 36, Perugia*

$\mathcal{L}$a Casella

An old country fiefdom

☎ 0763 86588 ✆ 0763 86684
✉ lacasella@tin.it
strada La Casella 4
05016 FICULLE (Terni)
Ref map 8, B3
A1, Fabro exit, towards Parrano, the sign for the *agriturismo,* is on the right after 7 km and before going up the hill to the village
15 rooms; ££
Credit cards: AE VISA SI ⓜ, bancomat

$\mathcal{I}$n this little medieval village a number of old farmhouses have been restructured and transformed into small hotels scattered over a green valley of 450 hectares. The bedrooms are carefully furnished, simple, large and bright, some with characteristic old details. In the main part of the *agriturismo* (farm accommodation) there are two tennis courts, mountain bikes, open-air swimming pool and a small health centre, billiards, table tennis and grass volleyball court. Near the farm is a riding centre that teaches riding and organises excursions and treks. The restaurant looks out on to the greenery and serves traditional dishes at large tables.

RECOMMENDED IN THE AREA

RESTAURANT:
Il Giglio d'Oro, *Orvieto*

LOCAL SPECIALITIES:
Terracotta from Ficulle; ceramics from Orvieto

VISIT:
Abbey of Saints Severo and Martirio

La Locanda del Gallo

Green hills as far as the eye can see

☎ and ✆ 075 9229912
✉ locanda.del.gallo@infoservice.it
località Santa Cristina
06020 GUBBIO (Perugia)
Ref map 8, A4
E45, Umbertide exit, towards Gubbio
10 rooms; £
Credit cards: 💳 SI, bancomat

This inn started as a noble residence: in fact it belongs to the Capranica del Grillo family and dates from the 17th century. It stands in a panoramic position surrounded by green hills dotted with stone farmhouses and villages as far as the eye can see. The old building has been restructured to create ten bedrooms, all with bathrooms. Under the high beamed ceilings antique and oriental furniture contrast well with the terracotta floors and the pastel tones of the walls. The carefully prepared cooking includes vegetarian dishes and draws its inspiration from the tradition and products of the area. There are well-equipped terraces in the large green areas around the house.

RECOMMENDED IN THE AREA

RESTAURANTS:
La Fornace di Mastro Giorgio, *via Mastro Giorgio 12;*
Federico da Montefeltro, *via della Repubblica 35;*
Villa Montegranelli, *località Monteluiano*

LOCAL SPECIALITIES:
Ceramics from Gubbio, Orvieto and Deruta

Gattapone

In an austere palace with a view over the roofs and bell towers of Gubbio

☎ 075 9272489 ✆ 075 9272417
via Ansidei 6
06024 GUBBIO (Perugia)
Ref map 8, A4
E45, Umbertide exit, towards Gubbio
18 rooms; ££
Credit cards: AE 💳 SI ⓪, bancomat

Visitors climb the hill surrounded by the medieval architecture of narrow streets and stone houses up to this austere-looking old palace. The bedrooms are not very big but they are pretty, all with fitted carpets, carefully chosen upholstery and bedcovers, and light-coloured stylish furniture; many look out on to old roofs and bell towers. The bathrooms are new and very practical, nearly all with showers and windows. The communal rooms are small, full of character and are furnished with care; retaining much of the lovely period detail.

A tiny garden enables guests to take breakfast in the open air during the high season, and to relax with bar service outside.

RECOMMENDED IN THE AREA

RESTAURANT:
Funivia, *Monte Ingino*
LOCAL SPECIALITIES:
Eugubine ceramics

*O*derisi
e Balestrieri

RECOMMENDED IN THE AREA

RESTAURANTS:
La Taverna del Lupo, *via Ansidei 6;* La Fornace di Mastro Giorgio, *via Mastro Giorgio 12*

LOCAL SPECIALITIES:
Game, hare and wild boar

VISIT:
Sant'Ubaldo Basilica

In the medieval heart of Gubbio

☎ 075 9220662
📠 075 9220663
via Mazzatinti 2-12
06024 GUBBIO (Perugia)
Ref map 8, A4
E45, Umbertide exit, towards Gubbio
35 rooms; £
Credit cards: AE VISA SI ①, bancomat

*T*wo separate buildings with a common reception area make up this hotel in the medieval heart of the town. In the past this was perhaps Gubbio's first inn: now recent refurbishment has brightened and modernised the large rooms.

Breakfast is served in a charming little room that is also a bar. This is furnished with small square tables rather like an attractive modern teashop.

The bedrooms are equipped with essential comforts and are light and welcoming. They are furnished in various styles, but all with restraint and warm simplicity. Some of them still have their original wooden beams and look out on to a panorama of old rooftops and green countryside that is typical of this region of Umbria.

The distinguishing feature of this owner-managed hotel is the kind attention guests receive.

$\mathcal{V}$illa Montegranelli

An elegantly refined villa amongst age-old trees

☎ 075 9220185
🖷 075 9273372
✉ montegra@tin.it
località Montelviano
06024 GUBBIO (Perugia)
Ref map 8, A4
E45, Umbertide exit, towards Gubbio
21 rooms, 4 apartments; ££
Credit cards: AE VISA SI ⓪, bancomat

$\mathcal{D}$ ating back to the 13th or 14th century, this beautiful villa has an illustrious past. The elegant interior has the patina and atmosphere of times gone by. The austere façade is softened by the avenue of old cypresses that lead right up to the entrance and by the lovely garden with a maze cut into the hedge, which is typical of an 18th-century Italian garden. Inside the rooms have high ceilings adorned with stucco, antique furnishings and prints, and marble pillars frame the doors and walls. Lovely carpets give warmth to the large rooms. The large light bedrooms share the refined elegance of the communal areas, and their simplicity does not detract from the special character of this establishment.

RECOMMENDED IN THE AREA

RESTAURANT:
Taverna del Lupo, *via Ansidei 6*

LOCAL SPECIALITIES:
Traditional ceramics and wrought iron

$\mathcal{V}$illalago

A farmhouse on the border between Umbria and Tuscany

☎ 075 848200
🖷 075 848050
via Montivalle
località Sant'Arcangelo
06060 MAGIONE (Perugia)
Ref map 8, B3
A1, Perugia junction,
exit for Magione
13 rooms; £/££
Credit cards: AE VISA SI ⓪, bancomat

$\mathcal{T}$ his farmhouse has the architecture characteristic of the area between Umbria and Tuscany, and is built of stone finished with terracotta. It stands 200 metres away from the shore of Lake Trasimeno where it has its own private beach for guests. It is surrounded by greenery, in a peaceful and delightful position, a short distance from the important cities of artistic treasures, and near the Valle del Trasimeno Nature Reserve and the Santa Sabina golf course. And for those who love thrills, there is a parachuting school only three kilometres away. The hotel has 13 bedrooms with modern furnishing, air conditioning and television. Bathrooms are practical. There is no restaurant. The large and well-tended garden has an open-air swimming pool and solarium, tennis court and gym.

RECOMMENDED IN THE AREA

RESTAURANT:
Settimio

VISIT:
Passignano sul Trasimeno; island of Maggiore del Trasimeno with Salvatore Church

Le Casette

A refurbished old farmstead standing amidst of fields and woods

☎ 0744 957645
📠 0744 950500
località Le Casette
05020 MONTECCHIO (Terni)
Ref map 8, C4
A1, Orvieto exit, S.S. 448 for Todi, turning for Baschi and Montecchio
16 rooms; ££
Credit cards: VISA SÌ

RECOMMENDED IN THE AREA

RESTAURANT:
Trippini, *Civitella del Lago*

LOCAL SPECIALITIES:
Truffles and wild boar; lace, ceramics, hand-worked articles in wood, Orvieto

VISIT:
Marshy area of nearby Alviano Nature Reserve where migrating birds can be observed

Standing at the foot of the Croce di Serra mountain looking across the Tevere valley, and extending over a hilly area between woods and wide open spaces where sheep are kept is this *agriturismo* (farm accommodation). Scattered around the estate there are little buildings, old farmhouses and typical rural stone constructions, which have been transformed into small apartments furnished in simple style. Each has a fitted kitchen, bathroom with shower, and its own space outside. Some of them have a view over nearby Lake Corbara. The restaurant, which is in the main house, is rustic and welcoming. At the heart of the *agriturismo* is a big swimming pool surrounded by terraces for the use of guests, and by panoramic green areas.

Maitani

In a 16th-century palace in the centre of Orvieto

☎ 0763 342011 📠 0763 342012
via L. Maitani
05018 ORVIETO (Terni)
Ref map 8, B3
A1, Orvieto exit
30 rooms; £/££
Credit cards: AE VISA SÌ ⓄⒹ,
bancomat

RECOMMENDED IN THE AREA

RESTAURANTS:
Maurizio, *via Duomo 68, and* Dell'ancora, *via di Piazza del Popolo*

LOCAL SPECIALITIES:
Ceramics

Let's start our visit to this little hotel from the top. The building is 16th century and stands right opposite the *Duomo* (cathedral). The hotel's delightful terraces give wonderful glimpses of the majestic façade of the *Duomo* and breakfast is served here.

All the bedrooms are different and are furnished in a harmonious blend of different styles, with both antique furniture and that of the more recent past. All are a comfortably size and their bathrooms are quite good and have hair-dryers. The reception area has comfortable sofas and colourful carpets adorning the marble floors.

There is a very calm atmosphere here, and the place is delightfully welcoming.

253

$\mathcal{V}$alentino

A Renaissance palace in the vicinity of the Duomo *(cathedral)*

☎ and 🖷 0763 342464
via Angelo da Orvieto 30
05018 ORVIETO (Terni)
Ref map 8, B3
A1, Orvieto exit
19 rooms; **££**
Credit cards: AE VISA SI OD, bancomat

RECOMMENDED IN THE AREA

RESTAURANT:
Il Giglio d'oro, *piazza Duomo 8*
VISIT:
Civita Bagnoregio, Corbara Lake

$\mathcal{A}$ few steps away from the *Duomo* (cathedral), in a typical medieval street in Orvieto's historic centre, is the Renaissance palace that now houses this little hotel. The 19 bedrooms are of various sizes and often irregular in shape since they follow the line of the old building. All have parquet flooring, pleasing modern furniture and carefully chosen bedcovers. Bathrooms are medium-sized, nearly all with showers but few have a window. The communal rooms are small but attractive and characterful. Marble predominates in the reception hall – light coloured for the floor and grey-green for the bar counter. Coloured sofas, plants and cream walls give this communal area a simple but refined appearance. Breakfast is served as a buffet.

$\mathcal{V}$illa Ciconia

A villa which has preserved the atmosphere of the Renaissance

☎ 0763 305582/3
🖷 0763 302077
via dei Tigli 69
05019 ORVIETO (Terni)
Ref map 8, B3
A1, Orvieto exit
10 rooms; **££/£££**
Credit cards: AE VISA SI OD, bancomat

RECOMMENDED IN THE AREA

RESTAURANT:
I7 consoli, *piazza Sant'Angelo 1/A*
VISIT:
Etruscan burial site, Crocifisso del Tufo;
Abbeys of Saints Sever and Martirio

$\mathcal{T}$his elegant 16th-century villa is surrounded by a very old park and inside has preserved all its splendid history. Careful restoration has kept architectural features intact: there are thick walls, great beams and terracotta floors, and a truss beam made of chestnut wood more than 12 metres long adorns the sitting room. The communal rooms have large fireplaces and are furnished with antiques. The main rooms still have panelled carved wood ceilings and murals depicting landscapes and allegorical scenes. Accommodation is in ten large bedrooms furnished in antique style, and some of the larger rooms have canopied beds and original period furniture. Nearly all the fairly practical bathrooms have showers and windows. The bedrooms reflect the villa's beauty and the refined history of the building, but not at the expense of modern comforts. The dining room and meeting rooms also have lovely architecture.

*P*oggio
del Belveduto

POGGIO del *Belveduto*

On horseback on the gentle hills
near to Lake Trasimeno

☎ 075 829076
📠 075 8478014
via San Donato 65
**06065 PASSIGNANO
SUL TRASIMENO (Perugia)**
Ref map 8, A3
A1, Perugia junction, Passignano Est
exit
14 apartments; **££**
Credit card: AE

*A*n *agriturismo* (farm accommodation) situated in peaceful green countryside overlooking Lake Trasimeno and offering recreational facilities for horse-riding enthusiasts and others. Various kinds of apartments are available and these are pleasantly furnished in rustic style and equipped with every comfort.

Within the *agriturismo* there is a riding school, numerous equipped stalls, a manège with night lighting, horse boxes, five hectares of fenced pasture, swimming pool, archery, practice golf course, beach volleyball, orienteering, mountain bike hire and excursions on horseback.

There are many suggested tours to satisfy those interested in sport, art and gastronomy. These include a trip round the three lakes, a visit to local castles and a tour of producers of selected wines.

RECOMMENDED IN THE AREA

RESTAURANTS:
La Corte, *Passignano sul Trasimeno;* Locanda della Rocca, *Paciano*

LOCAL SPECIALITIES:
Extra virgin olive oil from the farm; direct sales outlets of many clothes manufacturers around Perugia; cashmere fabric

*I*l Covone

A medieval villa with a watch-tower

📞 075 694140

📠 075 694503

✉ covone@mercurio.it

strada Fratticiola 2

località Ponte Pattoli

06085 PERUGIA

Ref map 8, B4

A1, Perugia junction, go past the town in a northerly direction, towards Ponte Pattoli

10 rooms; £/££

Credit cards: AE VISA SI ◑, bancomat

*T*his is a villa dating from medieval times with a watch-tower at its centre and set in a big park sloping down to the river bank. It is on a 50-hectare estate in the Tevere valley about 15 kilometres from Perugia. Watch-towers defended the territory along the River Tevere. Over the centuries, the villa was enlarged and changed by successive refurbishments and the addition of other buildings. The last of such works was in 1930. The villa has a sitting room, dining room, library and music room. These are large rooms with high ceilings, internal loggias and balconies that look onto the salon, period furnishings and big old fireplaces that give them a particular character. The ten guest bedrooms are in a nearby former farmhouse and are attractive and comfortable. In the immediate vicinity are sports centres where tennis, swimming pool and horse riding is possible. A minimum stay of two days is requested.

RECOMMENDED IN THE AREA

RESTAURANTS:

Enoteca Giò, *via R. d'Andreotto 19, and* Osteria del Gambero, *via Baldeschi 17*

---

*R*elais San Clemente

The air of the Umbrian hills – pure, clean and redolent with history

📞 075 5915100

📠 075 5915001

✉ info@relais.it

località Bosco

06080 PERUGIA

Ref map 8, B4

A1, Perugia junction, then towards Gubbio as far as Bosco

64 rooms, 1 suite; ££

Credit cards: AE VISA SI ◑

A historic little train links this inn with the centre of Perugia. The hotel, which was skilfully and carefully transformed from an old private residence, was a Benedictine monastery in 14th century and the small church from this time has been perfectly preserved. The charm of the place derives from the imposing building, surrounded and enhanced by a large and well-equipped park. The gracious interior has a noble atmosphere, with elegant furniture, parquet flooring and beautiful carpets. The bedrooms are very spacious, all with individually-controlled air conditioning, and have the same simple elegance as the communal areas. The bathrooms are very practical. There are many opportunities for social gatherings and relaxation: open-air swimming pool, tennis courts, five-a-side football pitch, volleyball and basketball, archery, gymnastic trails and mountain bicycles available for hire. The restaurant's reputable cuisine ranges from traditional Umbrian dishes to international menus.

RECOMMENDED IN THE AREA

RESTAURANT:

Fortebraccio, *via Palermo 88*

LOCAL SPECIALITIES:

Wine; oil; truffles; ceramics from Gubbio and Deruta

VISIT:

Ipogeo dei Volumni, a noble Etruscan tomb

La Cerqua

O riginally, in the 14th century, this large stone farmhouse was the monastery of San Salvatore. It stands on a hill in a panoramic position between the Carpina and Carpinella valleys, two kilometres from the medieval village and the Pietralunga state forest.

The farmhouse is part of an organic farm business of 70 hectares. The guest bedrooms are large and well furnished and all have bathrooms. There are also reading, music and television rooms. Outside there is a swimming pool for children and adults, a playground and a family restaurant with organic food. Guests staying at the *agriturismo* (farm accommodation) can enjoy horse riding, guided nature walks, archery and cycling. There is an open-air laboratory, run in collaboration with the natural history museum of Candeleto, for studying plants and observing animals without disturbing them.

An organic farm business

☎ and 🖷 075 9460283
✉ lacerqua@krenet.it
case San Salvatore 27
06026 PIETRALUNGA (Perugia)
Ref map 8, A3
E45, Città di Castello, towards Umbertide as far as the turning for Pietralunga
8 rooms; **££**
Credit cards: AE VISA SI ⓓ

RECOMMENDED IN THE AREA

RESTAURANT:
La Taverna del Lupo, *via Ansidei 6, Gubbio*

LOCAL SPECIALITIES:
Products from the farm business: cereals, fruit, Pietralunga potatoes and white truffles

VISIT: *Sant'Ubaldo Basilica*

La locanda di Carsulae

Relaxation and a flavour of the past just a few steps away from the thermal baths

☎ 0744 630163 📠 0744 333068
✉ ascassi@tin.it
via Tiberina 2
05029 SAN GEMINI (Terni)
Ref map 8, C4

A1, Orte exit, *superstrada* (dual carriageway) 204 towards Terni, Palombare exit, go on as far as San Gemini
9 rooms; ££
Credit cards: AE VISA SI ⓓ, bancomat

RECOMMENDED IN THE AREA

RESTAURANTS:
Alfio, *via Galileo Galilei 4, Terni*

VISIT:
Historic/folk displays in medieval costume in the old medieval village between the end of September and the beginning of October ending with the famous Palio della Giostra dell'Arme (jousting tournament)

*T*his inn has been completely refurbished and is situated near the thermal springs that are the source of the renowned Sangemini mineral water. It is also close to the ruins of the Roman town from which the inn takes its name. Surrounded by a pleasant garden and large terrace, it provides hospitality centred around relaxation and a flavour of the past. There are nine attractive big bedrooms, showing an attention to detail with their simple furniture, terracotta floors, carefully chosen curtains and bedcovers and some ceramics from nearby Deruta. The bathrooms are practical, most have a window and all have a shower or bath. There is an attractively rustic restaurant and a little bar with a veranda, but no sitting rooms. The restaurant serves homely cooking with the flavours of the area: truffles, *porcini* mushrooms, home-made bread and seasonal delights.

La Bastiglia

In the little roman town of Spello, in a peaceful Umbrian valley

☎ 0742 651277
📠 0742 301159
✉ fancelli@labastiglia.com
via dei Molini 17
06038 SPELLO (Perugia)
Ref map 8, B4

A1, Perugia junctionn, then *superstrada* (dual carriageway) 75 for Foligno as far as Spello
33 rooms, 2 apartments; ££
Credit cards: AE VISA SI ⓓ, bancomat

RECOMMENDED IN THE AREA

RESTAURANT:
Il Molino

VISIT:
Church of Santa Maria Maggiore

*T*he town of Spello, at the foot of mount Subasi and enclosed within walls, is full of Roman, medieval and Renaissance history. A delightful place to stay here is La Bastiglia, an old mill that has been skilfully restructured and nowadays houses a little hotel and restaurant. The bedrooms have peaceful views of Umbrian valleys. The walls are stone and there are rustic materials and furnishings to blend with the old building, but the bedrooms have modern facilities such as air conditioning, television, mini-bar and practical bathrooms. During winter the restaurant is in a big room with a fireplace, but in summer meals are served on the lovely panoramic terrace. Food is prepared with care using traditional recipes that are adapted imaginatively. The chef offers seasonal and daily menus.

Le due Torri

At the foot of a medieval watch-tower

☎ 0742 651249
🖷 0742 352933
via Torre Quadrano 1
località Limiti di Spello
06038 SPELLO (Perugia)
Ref map 8, B4

A1, Perugia junction, then *superstrada*
(dual carriageway) 75 for Foligno as far
as Spello
4 rooms, 1 suite, 5 apartments; **££**
Credit cards:

*I*n the countryside between Spello and Assisi, on
a 200-hectare farm estate, are two stone
farmhouses providing hospitality in this *agriturismo*
(farm accommodation). The larger of these is at the
foot of a medieval watch-tower which controlled the
city-state borders of Spello, Bevagna and Cannara.
The second looks over a panorama that includes a
view of the basilica of Saint Francis of Assisi. Skilful
restoration has made the most of the original
construction, and wooden beams of oak and
chestnut, panelled ceilings and floors made of brick
and pink and white limestone have been restored.
Accommodation is in two-roomed apartments, a
suite and bedrooms. These are carefully furnished
with antiques to blend with the architecture. A rustic
restaurant is reserved for the guests. Outside is a
lovely swimming pool and a children's playground.

RECOMMENDED IN THE AREA

RESTAURANT:
Cacciatore

LOCAL SPECIALITIES:
*Organically produced classified extra virgin olive for
sale at the* agriturismo*; jam; legumes; truffles; wine*

L'Ulivo

In a panorama of olive and pine trees

☎ 0743 49031 🖷 0743 222527
📧 agrulivo@tin.it
via Bazzanese 63
località Bazzano di Sotto
06049 SPOLETO (Perugia)
Ref map 8, B4

A1, Perugia junction, then *superstrada* (dual
carriageway) 75 for Foligno, then S.S. 3
towards Spoleto, after San Giacomo turn off
for Bazzano di Sotto
2 rooms, 4 apartments; **£/££**
Credit cards not accepted

*T*he two refurbished farmhouses are only six
kilometres from Spoleto, in delightful natural
surroundings at the foot of a big terraced olive grove.
They are on the edge of the characteristic little village
of Bazzano di Sotto and here the view is of woods,
olive and pine trees.

The buildings are adjacent to the main house which
is the home of the owners of the farm business. As
a result of the restructuring work two bedrooms and
a number of one- and two-roomed apartments have
been made. These are equipped with televisions and
fitted kitchens, and the larger apartments have
fireplaces. The furniture is rustic style. The outside
swimming pool is located halfway up a hill in a very
sunny position from which the wonderful view may
be enjoyed.

RECOMMENDED IN THE AREA

RESTAURANT:
Tartufo, *piazza Garibaldi 24*

LOCAL SPECIALITIES:
Extra virgin olive oil; naturally reared veal and pork

*C*harleston

E quipped with many comforts, this recently refurbished small hotel is part of a 17th-century palace in the heart of Spoleto's historic centre.

The bedrooms are large, all with wooden-beamed ceilings and with modern furnishings and original paintings. They are equipped with televisions, video recorders, mini-bars and air conditioning. The attractive communal areas are furnished simply and arranged in several rooms, including a lounge with a fire always burning in the hearth during winter and an *enoteca* wine cellar with mainly Umbrian wines. There are frequent art exhibitions in these communal areas. Buffet breakfast is served in two little rooms during the winter and outside under the pergola during the high season. In addition there is a private garage, sauna, gym and conference room.

RECOMMENDED IN THE AREA

RESTAURANT:
Il Pentagramma, *via Martani 4*

LOCAL SPECIALITIES:
Truffles; extra virgin olive oil

A cultural atmosphere and an excellent wine cellar

☎ 0743 220052 ✆ 0743 221244
✉ hotelcharleston@krenet.it
piazza Collicola 10
06049 SPOLETO (Perugia)
Ref map 8, B4

A1, Orvieto exit, then S.S. 448 for Todi, next E45 for Terni, Acquasparta exit, 418 to Spoleto
18 rooms; £
Credit cards: AE VISA SI OD, bancomat

*L*a Porta del Tempo

Great comfort in a 16th-century palace

☎ 0744 608190
📠 0744 430210
✉ info@portadeltempo.com
via del Sacramento 2
05039 STRONCONE (Terni)
Ref map 8, C4

A1, Orte exit, *superstrada* (dual carriageway)
204 for Terni, then in the direction of
Stroncone
8 rooms; ££
Credit cards: AE VISA SI ⓪, bancomat

RECOMMENDED IN THE AREA

RESTAURANT:
Taverna de Porta Nova

VISIT:
Marmore Falls

*T*his fortified village on a hill was built in the 10th century and belonged to the abbey of Farfa. It was destroyed in the relentless battles against Farfa and reconstructed in 1215 according to the wishes of Pope Innocent III. It was reconstructed as a castle-fortress and the little square, which is reached through the gate to the village, still has the features of a medieval castle and stands out in the landscape that extends from Narni to the Amelia mountains.

The hotel is in an old 16th-century palace that was recently refurbished with great care and attention. It has only eight bedrooms, all with satellite television and mini-bar, and with a very delightful atmosphere. The rooms are furnished with stylish furniture, little canopies over the beds, and bright upholstery. The attic bedroom has a fireplace and a lovely ceiling. The communal rooms, too, are charming. The hotel is run by its owners.

*C*astello di Porchiano

*Situated in a medieval village
on top of a hill that looks
over the Tevere valley*

☎ 075 8853127
📠 0635 347308
✉ maxbern@tin.it
località Porchiano
06059 TODI (Perugia)
Ref map 8, B4

A1, Orvieto exit, S.S. 448 as far as the
crossroads for San Sisto, after San Sisto
turn right for Porchiano
5 apartments; ££
Credit cards: VISA SI

RECOMMENDED IN THE AREA

RESTAURANT:
Martini, *Acquasparta*

LOCAL SPECIALITIES:
Regional specialities from the agriturismo

*T*he *agriturismo* (farm accommodation) stands on a hill overlooking the Tevere valley and 300 metres above sea level, and is inside the medieval village of Porchiano. This is an outlying village under the administration of Todi, seven kilometres away, and its castle dates back to between the 10th and 11th centuries. The apartments in the *agriturismo* have been created from disused 19th-century buildings that were once lived in by farm workers or were stables. They are fully furnished, with private bathrooms, central heating, kitchen and rustic furniture. The village is deep in the lovely green hilly countryside of Umbria, and here visitors may spend relaxing holidays walking and going on excursions by mountain bicycle or on horseback.

Tenuta di Canonica

An old building that bears the signs of an eventful past

☎ 075 8947545
🖷 075 8947581
📧 tenutadicanonica@tin.it
località Canonica 75
06059 TODI (Perugia)
Ref map 8, B4
A1, Orvieto exit, S.S. 448 as far as Prodo-Titgnano crossroads, then for Cordigliano
11 rooms, 2 apartments; **£/£££**
Credit cards not accepted

Nowadays the surrounding landscape provide peaceful places for recreation and calm, but they draw their fascination also from the many handsome, rough defensive structures that are reminders of a troubled past. To get to Canonica you go through Prodo, where there is a lovely castle that has perfect ramparts for controlling the whole valley. Canonica was another outpost with a medieval tower for keeping watch and guarding the territory. These defensive structures have been transformed into elegant accommodation. Today the complex is full of charm. There are big rooms with vaulted ceilings, wooden beams, antique fireplaces in working order, period furniture and elegant decorations. The few rooms inside have great atmosphere. Outside is the peaceful countryside of Umbria that is depicted in the clear landscapes painted by Perugino. There are big green spaces, a modern swimming pool and quiet corners.

RECOMMENDED IN THE AREA

RESTAURANTS:
Umbria, *via San Bonaventura 13*, Cavour, *corso Cavour 21/23, and* Jacopone, *piazza Jacopone 5*

LOCAL SPECIALITIES:
Sagrantino di Montefalco wine; pork sausages; extra virgin olive oil; hand-crafted ceramics from Orvieto and Deruta

I Mori Gelsi

A pleasing stay in the countryside

☎ and 🖷 075 982192
✉ fspinola@host.dex.net.com
via Entrata 37
06089 TORGIANO (Perugia)
Ref map 8, B4
A1, Perugia junction, then E45,
Torgiano exit
3 apartments; **£/££/£££**
Credit cards not accepted

RECOMMENDED IN THE AREA

RESTAURANTS:
Le Tre Vaselle

LOCAL SPECIALITIES:
*Grechetto Bianco and Sangiovese classified red wine
produced by the farm; ceramics from Torgiano and
Deruta*

VISIT:
Perugia, Assisi and Corciano

*I*n the centre of a quality wine-producing farm in the Tevere valley, well situated for access to the Umbrian cities of art, is this group of old farm buildings. The main farmhouse and an annexe have been transformed into two small apartments and one rather larger. These can accommodate between six and eight people, and are furnished with antique and period-style furniture and equipped with washing machines, dishwashers, safes and irons. Outside the apartments have pretty pergolas with illumination and barbecues to enable guests to enjoy themselves in the open air. They are surrounded by the garden with swimming pool and fruit trees. A large organic summer vegetable garden belonging to the Spinola farm is free for the use of guests who, on arrival, also have a welcoming basket of wine and all that is necessary for breakfast (honey, milk, coffee etc.). The managers can suggest and advise on itineraries and excursions in the vicinity.

L a Dogana

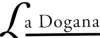

*A nature reserve on the shore of
Lake Trasimeno*

☎ 075 8230158
🖷 075 8230252
località Dogana 4
**06069 TUORO SUL TRASIMENO
(Perugia)**
Ref map 8, B2-3
A1, Perugia junction, Tuoro exit
13 apartments; **£/££**
Credit cards not accepted

*T*his historic 16th-century building was used as the customs house between the Papal State and the Grand Duchy of Tuscany, and was an obligatory stopping place for travellers to Rome. Those who stopped here included Michelangelo, Goethe, Byron and Stendhal. The old stone farmhouses that surround this building on a farm of more than 50 hectares have been recently restructured in order to accommodate visitors in apartments that are prettily furnished with antiques. There are apartments of various sizes from one-roomed apartments through to apartments of 200 square metres that can take from six to ten people. All have modern comforts. The farmhouses are on a hilltop between olive groves that slope down to the nature reserve on the shore of Lake Trasimeno. This is a destination for keen bird watchers. Guests may use horses bred on the farm to ride along the paths used by Hannibal or follow routes through the Mount Casteluccio park.

RECOMMENDED IN THE AREA

RESTAURANT:
La Corte, Passignano sul Trasimeno

LOCAL SPECIALITIES:
Olive oil from the farm; wine from the Trasimeno hills

VISIT:
Maggiore island on Lake Trasimeno

Lazio

What happens in Lazio happens in all regions where a central city of exceptional importance acts as a pole of attraction that makes everywhere else seem insignificant – and in this case the central city is no less than Rome: one of the world's most endlessly beautiful cities for its history, art, culture, colour and gentle climate.

Acquaintance with the rest of Lazio tends to be superficial, a brief visit or even simply an overnight stop. This is a pity because Lazio offers an unusual variety of atmosphere and scenery, not least that of the Roman countryside so often depicted in literature. And if the history of the region is mainly Roman, its artistic wealth extends well beyond it. Behind the long, sickle-shaped stretches of coastline, regularly broken by headlands, are three plains: part of the Maremma, Agro Romano and Agro Pontino. This landscape of marshes and coastal lakes, Mediterranean vegetation and forest is protected by the Circeo National Park.

Also inland are four volcanic complexes with craters filled by the lakes of Bolsena, Vico, Bracciano, Albano and Nemi. These sites are full of woods, and offer a wealth of archaeological remains and history. Then there is the complex structure of the Ante-Apennines with mountains that are occasionally sheer, but more often slope gently down to plains cultivated with corn. In the middle are thousands of river loops, and rolling hills that are sometimes bleak, sometimes green with meadows and woods. Here there is art from several wonderfully different eras: Etruscan remains in the north (at Veil, Tarquinia and Cerveteri), pre-Roman in the south (at Norma, Ferentino and Alatri) and Roman (at Palestrina, Tivoli and Ostia). You can see Romanesque examples at Anagni, Tuscania and Tarquinia; Gothic at Viterbo and Subiaco and Renaissance at Caprarola, Tivoli, Civitavecchia and Civita Castellana.

There are many hospitable inns with leafy branches outside, and gastronomic/wine-tasting tours are available in the Castelli Romano area. Authentic flavours, and sometimes real surprises can be enjoyed in Lazio.

Left: fresco from an Etruscan tomb at Tarquinia.
Below: panorama of the Imperial Fori, Rome

La Riserva Montebello

Harmony between the beauty of the countryside and distinctive old buildings

☎ 0761 798965 📠 0761 799492
località Montebello
01023 BOLSENA (Viterbo)
Ref map 8, C3
A1, Orvieto exit, turn into the S.S. 71 towards Montefiascone, then turn right for Bolsena: 2.5 km before the town at a wide horseshoe curve are the signs for the farm
12 rooms; **£/££**
Credit cards: AE VISA SI ⓪, bancomat

buildings in its surroundings. The old farmhouses of the farm business are in a panoramic position. They have been well refurbished and contain a few pretty and welcoming bedrooms, all with a view and furnished with antique traditional farm and wicker furniture.

These characteristic buildings, in the centre of an area full of woods and artistic charm, offer a base for a number of sporting and cultural recreations. Swimming and archery courses are organised for guests, as well as sailing on the lake and horse rides. Then there is the swimming pool, riding school and mountain bikes.

*L*ake Bolsena is a sparkling mirror that shines in its setting among high hills. On its shores there are little villages full of lovely reminders of the past.

Here there is a reciprocal, magical balance: the lake gives beauty to the countryside and is itself enhanced by the lovely and distinctive old

RECOMMENDED IN THE AREA

RESTAURANTS:
Da Picchitetto, *Bolsena;* I sette consoli, *Orvieto*

LOCAL SPECIALITIES:
Antique and modern ceramics; hand-made lace

$\mathcal{T}$enuta La Vita

One of Europe's most beautiful and unspoilt places in Lake Vico's nature reserve

☎ and 🖶 0761 612077
località La Vita, Valle di Vico
01032 CAPRAROLA (Viterbo)
Ref map 8, C3
A1, Orte exit, then S.S. 204 as far as Viterbo, from here go on southwards
on the S.P. Cassia Cimina following the signs for Lake Vico
until reaching the *agriturismo* (farm accommodation)
5 rooms; ££
Credit cards: AE VISA SI ⓪, bancomat

$\mathcal{T}$he estate stands within the nature reserve of Lake Vico, a reserve that is surrounded by chestnuts and hazels, by age-old woods with streams/ponds full of fish and aquatic birds. The sparkling air and pungent fragrances of the countryside, together with the numerous possibilities for sports and leisure activities, refresh both body and mind.

RECOMMENDED IN THE AREA

RESTAURANTS:
Richiastro, *via della Marrocca 16/18 and* Grottino, *via della Cava 7*

VISIT:
The hazelnut feast with allegorical floats (last Sunday in August); Farnese Palace in historic centre of Caprarola; collegiate church, Fabrica di Roma

The same management for three generations, with unchanged enthusiasm

The farm business is in a completely restructured farmhouse. The five guest bedrooms are tastefully and elegantly furnished, all equipped with bathroom, refrigerator, television and telephone, and they enjoy a lovely view over the lake.

The family who own it has worked on the estate for three generations, keeping traditions alive with great enthusiasm for open-air life and authentic food.

The healthy cooking provided by the *agriturismo* (farm accommodation) uses fresh ingredients every day from the farm, from local shooting and fishing, together with local wine and oil. Meanwhile the area around offers interesting historic and nature trips.

The pastry kitchen within the farm is worthy of note, and produces cakes using hazelnuts and chestnuts.

Ida

The sign of practicality and comfort

☎ and 🖷 0775 950040
✉ hotelida@flashnet.it
via Caragno 27
03024 CEPRANO (Frosinone)
Ref map 9, E6
A1, Ceprano exit
44 rooms; ££
Credit cards: AE VISA SI ⓄⒹ

modern hotel with 35 large, comfortable bedrooms, with completely renewed furnishings and electronic controls, doors operated with magnetic entry cards, smoke alarms, individually controlled air conditioning and full soundproofing. They also have pleasing modern furniture, and are equipped with satellite televisions and mini-bars. All the bathrooms are new and very practical; the showers and sinks have convenient surrounds, and are fitted with hair-dryers and heated towel rails. There is a large green area around the hotel with a lovely wooden pavilion to accommodate receptions and conferences; there is also a children's playground in the park. The hotel's restaurant has a traditional appearance and in summer meals are served in the open air.

Guests receive a friendly family welcome, and the ratio between quality and price is good. The hotel also has a garage with spaces for 14 cars.

RECOMMENDED IN THE AREA

RESTAURANT:
Quadrato, *Frosinone*

LOCAL SPECIALITIES:
Cannate *amphorae and vases made of unvarnished clay;* mozarello *buffalo cheese and* ricotta *cheese*

Casale di Gricciano

Natural beauty and culture

☎ 06 9941358
località Gricciano Quota 177
00052 CERVETERI (Roma)
Ref map 8, D3
A12, Ceveteri exit, follow the signs for the *Necropoli etrusca* (Etruscan burial site)
11 rooms; ££
Credit cards: VISA SI, bancomat

t the foot of the Ceretani mountains is one of Italy's most important Etruscan burial sites. Nearby is a hill amidst natural beauty that gives no hint of the proximity of such a big urban centre as Rome. On the contrary, there is a genuine sense of the country and the Lazio woods, and is only 20 minutes' drive from the coast. This is a snapshot of the historic and naturally beautiful area in which this farmhouse is immersed. There is a family atmosphere and the rustic furnishings are similar to that found in old farm-workers' houses of the upper Lazio region.

The delicious cooking is typical of the area: the wooden benches and farm implements in the restaurant are a decorative framework for the traditional dishes that are prepared each day from the freshest ingredients (wine olive oil, vegetables and fruit) that come from the farm.

RECOMMENDED IN THE AREA

RESTAURANT:
Da Alfredo, *Bracciano*

LOCAL SPECIALITIES:
Etruscan-style terracotta vases from the agriturismo

VISIT:
Banditaccia Etruscan burial site

Casa Ciotti

In an old post-house

☎ 0761 513090
📠 0761 599120
✉ agriciot@tin.it
via Terni 14
01033 CIVITA CASTELLANA (Viterbo)
Ref map 8, C4
A1, Magliano Sabino exit, via Flaminia as far as Sassacci, then signs for Civita Castellana
11 apartments; £
Credit cards: AE VISA SI ⓓ, bancomat

*V*arious signs of Etruscan, Roman and medieval civilisations are interwoven into this corner of Lazio, with its very old history and very beautiful surroundings.

The story of Civita Castellana is old, as are its walls and its cathedral, and as is the history of this 17th-century post-house that has been skilfully refurbished to maintain its structure and traditions. The various buildings that comprise it stand in the middle of a large and well-tended park with olive trees, old roses and ancient oak trees on a carpet of English lawn. The swimming pool is in a corner of the park, shielded by shrubs.

Guest accommodation consists of large one- and two-roomed apartments furnished in the simple style of past times, and with wood-beamed ceilings and terracotta floors. The two three-roomed apartments enjoy a lovely portico that leads directly on to the garden. This is a real haven for relaxation to return to after walks in the woods and visits to the ruins, not far away, of an early medieval castle.

RECOMMENDED IN THE AREA

RESTAURANTS:
L'Altra Bottiglia *and* Giaretta

LOCAL SPECIALITIES:
Locally produced ceramics

VISIT:
The ruins of Falerii Novi (a Roman city)

La Tana dell'Istrice

An elegant palace dating back to medieval times and restructured in the 16th century

☎ 0761 914501 📠 0761 914815
✉ mottura@isa.it
piazza Unità d'Italia 12
01020 CIVITELLA D'AGLIANO (Viterbo)
Ref map 8, C3
A1, Orvieto exit, go on for Castiglione in Teverina
8 rooms; ££
Credit cards: AE VISA SI, bancomat

RECOMMENDED IN THE AREA

RESTAURANT:
I sette consoli, *piazza Sant'Angelo, Orvieto*

LOCAL SPECIALITIES:
Wines, olive oil and jam produced by the farm

*T*his is an enchanting hotel far away from the most frequented destinations. The medieval palace stands in the heart of Civitella d'Agliano's historic centre: a little agricultural town on the borders between Lazio, Umbria and Maremma. The proprietor, who also produces wine, has transformed the palace into a romantically elegant hotel, preserving the unspoilt atmosphere of a high-class country home where elegance and attention to detail are combined with simple antique furnishing. The bedrooms are all different and have lovely furniture. The bathrooms are in marble with heated towel rails, hair-dryers and lovely towels. The restaurant prepares dishes with care, and the library is well stocked. On the ground floor are an *enoteca* (wine cellar) and piano wine bar that are open in the evenings. The hotel is part of a farm business and takes advantage of seasonal foods which guests can enjoy, including an ample selection of wines.

*I*lle Roif

In the peace of the wonderful Sabine countryside

☎ 0765 386749/0765 386783
📠 0765 386783
località Coltodino
02030 FARA IN SABINA (Rieti)
Ref map 8, C4
A1, Fiano Romano exit, S.S. 4 towards
Rieti, after 5 km turn left for
Fara in Sabina
12 rooms; ££
Credit cards: AE VISA SI ⓪, bancomat

*T*he name may be deceptive, but this is an unusual *agriturismo* (farm accommodation) not run by strangers who have been transplanted into Italy. Read it backwards and the mystery will be revealed. The Fiorelli family is responsible for this jewel where the bedrooms all differ from each other, and are furnished creatively and with unerring taste.

The washbasins are a particular feature: all are hand-made, beautifully sculpted and coloured. The bedrooms are large (those on the ground floor contain pieces of rock to add to the fantasy) and the furnishing consists of fine fabrics, pale colours in unusual tones, designer furniture and cupboards. The bathrooms are furnished with the same care.

RECOMMENDED IN THE AREA

RESTAURANT:
Bistrot, *Rieti*

VISIT:
Farfa Abbey

LOCAL SPECIALITIES:
Herbal products, liqueurs and digestive liqueurs from the herbalist at Farfa Abbey, made according to ancient recipes

*I*l Voltone

RECOMMENDED IN THE AREA

RESTAURANT:
Caino, *Manciano*

LOCAL SPECIALITIES:
Caciotta, ricotta *and* pecorino *cheeses; extra virgin olive oil; wine; ceramics from Valentano*

VISIT:
Barabbata festival on 14 May, Marta; Papal Palace, Viterbo

Farm accommodation in a perfectly-restored 17th-century village

☎ and 📠 0761 422540
località Voltone
01010 FARNESE (Viterbo)
Ref map 8, C3
A1, Orvieto exit, go on for
San Lorenzo Nuovo-Latera-Volotone
30 rooms; ££/£££
Credit cards: VISA SI, bancomat

*T*he name comes from Fanum Voltumnae, the old temple dedicated to the Etruscan deity Voltumna. This is a little 17th-century village that has been perfectly restored and was the property of the Chigi-Della Rovere family.

The location is in upper Lazio, in the Selva del Lamone Nature Park which is an ideal habitat for squirrels, porcupines and badgers. The farm covers 465 hectares of green countryside. The elegantly rustic bedrooms within the lovely building are harmonious and well proportioned. A delightful atmosphere welcomes guests in the sitting rooms where the arrangement of antique furniture creates little islands for conversation and the warmth from the fireplace draws guests together. The restaurant's dishes are prepared with care and bear the stamp of local gastronomic traditions.

$\mathcal{V}$illa Irlanda

In the exclusive surroundings of an old villa

☎ 0771 712581
🖷 0771 712172
✉ villairlanda@villairlanda.com
via Lungomare Caboto 6
04024 GAETA (Latina)
Ref map 9, F6

A1, Cassino exit, *superstrada* (dual carriageway) for Formia-Gaeta
54 rooms, 6 suites, 5 apartments; **££/£££**
Credit cards: AE VISA SI ⓄⒹ

$\mathcal{T}$he hotel is composed of four buildings that stand in a big park, with a view of the sea, on the road linking Gaeta and Formia. The buildings date from various eras and tell different stories. The villa, in neoclassical style, was constructed in 1912 by Count Stenbock, a cousin of the last Tsar. The religious house, of 1930, was built by the Irish Papal College. The convent is more recent and is decorated with Neapolitan hand-painted tiles; the reception stands on the site of an old house with its Roman walls forming an integral part of its structure. Restructuring has created attractive bedrooms and large suites. These are furnished in classically elegant style, with air conditioning, mini-bars, satellite televisions and internal video circuit. The dining room is in the former chapel of the Irish college, and has characteristically large proportions. In the park there is an Olympic-sized swimming pool and another with hydromassage; bicycles and scooters may be hired. In addition there are rooms available for meetings.

RECOMMENDED IN THE AREA

RESTAURANTS:
Antico Vico; Chinappi, *Formia*

LOCAL SPECIALITIES:
Olives from Gaeta; fish from the gulf for sale in the market on the sea shore; Falerno and Falanghina classified wine

Castello di Santa Cristina

On horseback in the green countryside of upper Tuscany

☎ and 🖷 0763 78011
✉ cardinale@tin.it
località Santa Cristina
01025 GROTTE DI CASTRO (Viterbo)
Ref map 8, C3

A1, Orvieto exit, towards Castelgiorgio, towards San Lorenzo Nuovo and then Grotte di Castro
10 rooms; **££**
Credit cards not accepted

$\mathcal{A}$ real castle dating back to the 19th century, or rather, a delightful little village immersed in green upper Tuscany, in a strategic position between Lazio, Umbria and Tuscany. The village is a special place set deep in countryside surrounded by age-old trees in peaceful woods and cultivated fields. There is a big garden with an open-air swimming pool for the use of guests, as well as a tennis court under the old walls and a riding school for agreeable rides in the neighbourhood. The castle interior is warm and welcoming: cream-coloured walls go well with the wood-beamed ceilings and floral patterned curtains and sofas. The furnishing is authentic – that of the late 19th century. The bedrooms, too, are simple and elegant, all with bathrooms.

RECOMMENDED IN THE AREA

RESTAURANT:
I sette Consoli, *Orvieto*

$\mathcal{A}$xel

In green countryside facing Lake Bracciano

☏ and ✆ 0761 699535
località Macchia del Cardinale
01030 MONTEROSI (Viterbo)
Ref map 8, D4
A1, Magliano Sabina, then S.S. 3
as far as Civita Castellana, from here
S.S. 311, towards Nepi-Monterosi
6 rooms, 1 apartment; £/££
Credit cards not accepted

*I*n an area full of Etruscan relics and papal architecture, at Bracciano near Viterbo, but also close to the Vallelunga motor-racing track and Le Querce golf course, this elegant *agriturismo* (farm accommodation) is in a modern one-storey building facing the lake. It has big terraces with windows overlooking a lawn that slopes down among ancient oak trees.

The complex has six bedrooms (two are reserved for non-smokers) and an apartment that can accommodate up to six people, with fitted kitchen and reserved parking space. Within the *agriturismo* is an attractive restaurant and a television room; outside there is a large garden with an open-air swimming pool and solarium. There is a riding school and also bicycles for hire.

RECOMMENDED IN THE AREA

RESTAURANTS:
Da Righetti, *Campagnano di Roma*

VISIT:
The cathedral and rock fortress of Civita Castellana

La Chiocciola

*History and tradition in a
15th-century farmhouse*

☎ 0761 402734
🖷 0761 490254
località Seripola
01028 ORTE (Viterbo)
Ref map 8, C4

A1, Orte exit, towards *Orte città* (Orte town), after
3 km turn right towards Amelia and, 300 m
further, turn left towards Penna in Teverina
8 rooms; **££**
Credit cards: 🆅🆂🅰 S̄Ī, bancomat

A 15th-century farmhouse and the old farm
worker's cottage annexed to it on a large
estate form this small and very pleasant *agriturismo*
(farm accommodation). Both have been restored
and are faithful to the original character in every
detail: from the old log stove to the little stone well in
the garden. All the bedrooms are different, and are
furnished carefully with period furniture making them
particularly welcoming. Breakfast is served on a
charming veranda, amongst the greenery that
surrounds the entire complex, whilst lunch and
dinner are in the lovely rustic restaurant with its
strikingly imposing fireplace dating from the 17th
century. The cooking, too, reflects history in its links
with traditional fare. For guests who, apart from the
tranquil setting and the historic neighbourhood, are
looking for healthy physical activity, there is a
swimming pool and mountain bicycles to hire for
delightful expeditions.

RECOMMENDED IN THE AREA

RESTAURANT:
Carleni, *Amelia*

LOCAL SPECIALITIES:
Majolica from Deruta

VISIT:
Mostri Park and sacred wood at Bomarzo

Sant'Ilario sul Farfa

*In the valley of the River Farfa,
in the heart of the Sabine region*

☎ and 🖷 0765 872410
📧 silario@ats.it
via Colle
02030 POGGIO NATIVO (Rieti)
Ref map 8-9, C4-5

A1, Fiano Roman Exit, S.S. 4 towards Rieti,
after about 70 km, turn left towards Frasso
Sabino, after 3 km turn left again for Poggio
Nativo
6 rooms; **£**
Credit cards not accepted

RECOMMENDED IN THE AREA

RESTAURANT:
Bistrot, *piazza San Rufo 25, Rieti*

LOCAL SPECIALITIES:
*Hand woven fabrics; home-made pasta;
terracotta crockery*

VISIT:
Farfa Abbey

T he two completely refurbished farmhouses look
on to the valley of the River Farfa and make up
this *agriturismo* (farm accommodation) that enjoys a
very beautiful panorama of the Sabine region with its
rich history and delicious culinary traditions. The
agriturismo is a few kilometres from Farfa Abbey and
from places where Saint Francis of Assisi lived: a land
that is only an hour from Rome yet where the
countryside is unspoilt. The bedrooms of the
agriturismo are tastefully furnished with simple late
19th-century furniture and warm chestnut wood
beams and terracotta floors, and are set in the greenery
of the large garden that surrounds both buildings.
Guests may enjoy not only the pleasant swimming pool
but also typical local dishes that are carefully prepared
using products from the farm: home-made jam, oil and
vinegar, and the freshest fruit and vegetables.

*A*ugustea

An exclusive palace of the late 19th century

☏ 06 4883589 📠 06 4814872
via Nazionale 251
00184 ROMA (ROME)
Ref map 8, D4
A1, gyratory system, towards Nomentana,
Nomentana-Roma Centro exit, signs for
Centro and *Stazione Termini* (Termini station)
20 rooms; ££
Credit cards: AE VISA SI ⓞ

*T*he noise from the busy via Nazionale does not disturb the quiet of this little hotel on the second and third floors of an exclusive late 19th-century palace, a few steps from piazza Esedra and via Veneto.

In a very central position (Termini station, shops and museums are within walking distance), the hotel has recently been completely refurbished but it retains its period atmosphere. There are pink walls, stylish furniture in pastel colours, armchairs and sofas that make the bedrooms look attractive and well cared for. Altogether there are 20 comfortably large bedrooms.

Nearly all the bathrooms have windows and showers and they are medium sized and completely practical. The communal rooms are simple but not without adornment. The hotel is run with care and attention that guarantees a service to satisfy the demands of guests.

RECOMMENDED IN THE AREA

RESTAURANT:
Agata e Romeo, *via Carlo Alberto 45*

---

*B*orromeo

An attractive hotel in a strategic location

☏ 06 485856
📠 06 4882541
via Cavour 117
00184 ROMA (ROME)
Ref map 8, D4
A1, A1 direction, gyratory system, towards
Nomentana, Nomentana-Roma Centro exit,
signs for *Centro* and *Stazione Termini*
(Termini station)
30 rooms, 3 suites; £
Credit cards: AE VISA SI ⓞ, bancomat

*T*he position of this attractive hotel is decidedly strategic, being situated between the station and the imperial forums, close to the ancient Roman slum quarters. This lively area with its workshops and open-air markets has always retained a strong popular character and has continued to thrive, with local craftsmen and small shopkeepers continuing their typical working life. The hotel is in a period mansion, has an elegantly presented reception hall

with a beautiful inlaid floor, and communal areas which are particularly neat and charming. The bedrooms are spacious and practical, with lovely furniture and equipped with televisions, mini-bars, safes and magnetic key cards. The bathrooms are delightful and have telephones, hair-dryers and heated towel rails. Guests may request satellite television and modem points. There is a roof garden with a lovely view over the roofs of the city.

RECOMMENDED IN THE AREA

RESTAURANT:
Monte Caruso, *via Farini 12*
WINE CELLAR:
Cavour 313
VISIT:
The network of little streets on either side of via Cavour with their craft workshops

Casa in Trastevere

Situated in a typical lane running parallel to the 16th-century via della Lungara, at the foot of the green Giancolo hill in the Trastavere quarter, this is a convenient guest-house. It is on the first floor and looks on to the street and on to a private garden. The apartment has recently been restructured, retaining the original features of vaulted ceilings and octagonal-tiled marble floors. This bed and breakfast accommodation can take up to six people and has a living room with kitchen area, two bedrooms and two bathrooms. Furnishing is in a modern style with a few antique features; the upholstery and some details evoke the atmosphere of the surrounding gardens. A minimum stay of three nights is requested.

A house with garden in the Trastevere quarter

☎ 0335 6205768
📠 06 69924722
via della Penitenza 19
00165 ROMA (ROME)
Ref map 8, D4

A1, A1 direction, enter the gyratory system in the direction of Fiumincino, enter the city from *uscita* (exit) 30, follow signs for Trastevere
3 rooms, 1 apartment; **£££**
Credit cards not accepted

RECOMMENDED IN THE AREA

RESTAURANTS:
Romolo *(very close to the apartment);* Sabatini, *piazza Santa Maria in Trastevere 13,* Paris, *piazza San Callisto 7/A, and* Pastarellato, *via San Crisogono 33, Trastevere*

Cesàri

In the middle of Rome, a few steps from the political centre

☎ 06 6792386 📠 06 6790882
📧 cesari@venere.it
via di Pietra 89/A
00186 ROMA (ROME)
Ref map 8, D4

A1, A1 direction, enter the gyratory system, Salaria-Roma Centro exit, follow the signs for *Centro-piazzale Flaminio*
47 rooms; **£££**
Credit cards: 🆎 💳 SI ⓪, bancomat

This old building dating from 1787 is situated in the narrow and ancient via di Pietra (stone road) in the Colonna district. The stone referred to is that of the columns in the Adriano temple: 11 imposing pillars introduced into the façade of this building in the 18th century. The building was a customs house and then the seat of the commodities exchange, and is in the centre of Rome, a few steps from the big shops and the political centre. The mansion was completely

refurbished in 1999 but has kept the unspoilt charm that comes from age. This is a hotel that combines good position with reasonable cost. The rooms have double-glazing and are large and tastefully furnished; all have satellite television, air conditioning and mini-bars. The bathrooms are new and equipped with hair-dryers. The communal areas are simple but welcoming. Management is professional.

RECOMMENDED IN THE AREA

RESTAURANT:
Quinzi e Gabrielli, *via delle Coppelle*

WINE CELLAR:
Cul de Sac, *piazza Pasquino*

Domus Aventina

In the charming setting of ancient Rome

☎ 06 5746135 🖷 06 57300044
✉ domus.aventina@flashnet.it
via di Santa Prisca 11/B
00153 ROMA (ROME)
Ref map 8, D4

A1, A1 direction, enter the big ring junction, towards Napoli *uscita* (exit) 15, go on as far as the centre
26 rooms; **£££**
Credit cards: AE VISA SI ◑, bancomat

RECOMMENDED IN THE AREA

RESTAURANTS:
Luna Piena, *via Luca della Robbia, and* Felice, *via Mastro Giorgio*

VISIT:
Piazza dei Cavalieri di Malta

*O*f the seven hills of Rome, Aventino is the most peaceful and residential. The roads are lined with trees, and bordered with elegant small buildings, deep in a haven of quietness, peace and little traffic. The hotel has an 18th-century façade and is a particularly suitable stopping place for those who want their stay to be near the centre but without losing tranquillity. Well cared for and simple, it has spacious bedrooms that are tastefully furnished and nearly all look on to the 17th-century cloisters of the nearby Santa Prisca church. Many of the bedrooms have delightful balconies from which to enjoy the lovely view, and are equipped with mini-bars, satellite television and modem points. The bathrooms are comfortable, with showers or baths, and fitted with hair-dryers. The communal areas are agreeably and carefully furnished and embellished with *trompe-l'oeil*. The hotel has a lovely terrace with a view over the centre of ancient Rome.

Due Torri

In a lively and popular area

☎ 06 68806956 🖷 06 6865442
vicolo del Leonetto 23/25
00186 ROMA (ROME)
Ref map 8, D4

A1, A1 direction, go on to the big ring junction, towards Napoli uscita (exit) 15, go on as far as the centre
26 rooms; **££/£££**
Credit cards: AE VISA SI ◑

*T*his is in the heart of old Rome, a very short distance from the Pantheon, piazza Navona and St Peter's. Notwithstanding these nearby tourist attractions, it is an area of the city not frequented by tourists and has preserved its shops and craftsmen, little antique shops, small local markets that each morning display fresh fruit and vegetables on the stalls. This part of the city is alive, lived in, and has not been taken over by tourism.

The hotel looks on to a narrow, very old and characteristic street where, in 1518, the old Campana inn stood. The building was for a long time the residence of cardinals and bishops and today is a hotel that has been completely renewed. The rooms are light, comfortable, furnished stylishly and all vary. The rooms on the top floor have little balconies with panoramic views over the roofs of the city. The sitting rooms are small and attractive, and are furnished with antiques. Guests receive a warm welcome.

RECOMMENDED IN THE AREA

RESTAURANTS:
La Campana, *vicolo della Campana 18,* Caffè Mercedes, *piazza San Silvestro, and* Caffè Vitti, *piazza San Lorenzo in Lucina*

VISIT:
Daily local market, Campo de' Fiori

$\mathcal{G}$regoriana

On the site of an old religious house

☎ 06 6794269
🖷 06 6784258
via Gregoriana 18
00187 ROMA (ROME)
Ref map 8, D4

A1, A1 direction, go on to the big ring junction, towards Napoli *uscita* (exit) 15, go on as far as the centre
19 rooms; £££
Credit cards not accepted

*V*ia Gregoriana is an elegant and very beautiful street that today is the address of fashion houses, just as the parallel via Sistina was frequented by artists and intellectuals at the beginning of the 20th century. The two roads meet at the little *loggia* of Zuccari Palace in piazza Trinità dei Monti. From there begins the Spanish Steps down to the Barcaccia fountain, Keat's house and smart shopping streets. The hotel stands on the site of an old religious house, and is small but quiet, despite its very central position. The bedrooms are furnished in a simple but elegant style, are light and attractive, and some have terraces. The bathrooms are comfortable and have complimentary toiletry sets. During summer breakfast is served on the lovely terrace, but at other times of the year is brought to guests' bedrooms as the hotel has no breakfast room. Professional and attentive service ensures that guests enjoy their stay.

RECOMMENDED IN THE AREA

RESTAURANTS:
La Terrazza dell'Eden, *via Ludovisi 49,* George's, *via Marche 7, and* Da Babington, *piazza di Spagna*

$\mathcal{L}$ocarno

RECOMMENDED IN THE AREA

RESTAURANT:
El Toulà, *via della Lupa 29/B, and* Caffè Greco, *via Condotti*

VISIT:
Piazza del Popolo, Pincio terrace with panoramic view from Mount Mario to the Vatican to Gianicolo; via del Babuino and via del Corso for shopping; via Margutta, the artists' road

An atmosphere of striking individuality

☎ 06 3610841 🖷 06 3215249
✉ info@hotellocarno.com
via della Penna 22
00186 ROMA (ROME)
Ref map 8, D4

A1, A1 direction, enter the big ring junction, Flaminia-Roma Centro *uscita* (exit), follow signs for piazzale Flaminio, piazza del Popolo
48 rooms, 2 suite; £££
Credit cards: 📇 📇 📇 ⑪, bancomat

*T*his is an intimate and elegant hotel with a striking personality. The furnishings of all the communal areas are chosen with refined taste and where everything helps recreate a delightful and original Twenties atmosphere. The dining room, bar and winter drawing room for breakfast all have fireplaces, and the dining room has a number of interesting pieces of Thonet-style furniture. The bedrooms all differ but all are equally attractive and well furnished: here too the atmosphere has the mark of Art Deco in furnishings and ornaments. Attention to detail is enriched by the most modern comforts. The hotel allows guests the free use of bicycles for exploring the historic centre and the zones where cars are forbidden.

Montreal

A few metres from the basilica of Santa Maria Maggiore, this attractive and well-presented hotel is in an elegant mansion dating from the beginning of the 19th century. It also contains private homes.

Uniformed members of staff welcome guests. The reception hall is small but recently refurbished. The bedroom walls are painted in cheerful pastel colours, there is some stucco-work, the furniture is stylish, and the effect altogether fresh and pretty. All the bathrooms are equipped with showers (five also have baths) and are very practical. The communal rooms are small, and without air conditioning but are carefully though simply presented, with some individual character deriving from the period floors and the attention paid to detail.

An exclusive mansion in the centre of Rome

☎ 06 4457797/06 4460514/
06 4464701

🖷 06 4465522

✉ Info@hotelmontrealroma.com

via Carlo Alberto 4

00185 ROMA

Ref map 8, D4

A1, A1 direction, go on to the big ring junction, towards Napoli *uscita* (exit) 15, continue as far as the centre, follow the signs for Stazione Ferroviaria and then Santa Maria Maggiore

22 rooms; £££

Credit cards: AE VISA SI ⑩, bancomat

RECOMMENDED IN THE AREA

RESTAURANT:
Agata e Romeo, *via Carlo Alberto 45*

WINE CELLAR:
Wine Bar Trimani

VISIT:
Market in piazza Vittoria Emanuele II (one of the oldest and most lively markets in Rome)

$\mathcal{P}$arlamento

RECOMMENDED IN THE AREA

RESTAURANTS:
Entoteca Capranica, *piazza Capranica 99/100*,
Convivio Troiani, *via dei Soldati 28, and*
La Campana, *vicolo della Campana 18*

A terrace overlooking the roofs of Rome

☎ and 🖷 06 69921000
via delle Convertite 5
00187 ROMA
Ref map 8, D4

A1, A1 direction, go on to the big ring
junction, via Flaminia towards Roma Centro;
follow the signs for *Centro* (centre), then Ponte
Cavour (Cavour bridge), Corso Umberto
23 rooms; **££**
Credit cards: AE VISA SI OD, bancomat

$\mathcal{S}$ituated on the third and fourth floors of a lovely
17th-century mansion, the hotel has a warm
family atmosphere. Everything is simple but carefully
presented. The furniture is stylish, and the entrance
is embellished with an airy *trompe-l'oeil* that
reproduces the roofs and domes of Rome.

The bedrooms are well furnished and practical with
simple furnishings on antique lines; and those with
double-glazing are particularly quiet. They also have
air conditioning, satellite televisions, modem points,
electronic safes and hair-dryers. There is a delightful
terrace that enjoys a lovely view over the roofs of
Rome and where, during the hot months, guests
may take buffet breakfast. The hotel is in a restricted-
traffic zone, but has an arrangement for parking a
few metres away.

$\mathcal{T}$urner

A refined and exclusive atmosphere

☎ 06 44250077 🖷 06 44250165
✉ info@hotelturner.com
via Nomentana 29
00161 ROMA (ROME)
Ref map 8, D4

A1, A1 direction, go on to the big ring
junction, exit at via Nomentana in towards
Centro (centre), then follow all of via
Nomentana as far as Porta Pia
47 rooms, 4 suites; **£££**
Credit cards: AE VISA SI OD

RECOMMENDED IN THE A

RESTAURANTS:
Giovanni, *via Marche 64,*
Papà Baccus, *via Toscana 36, and*
Cantina Cantarini, *piazza Sallustio 12*

$\mathcal{T}$his refined hotel is in a lovely 19th-century
mansion a few minutes from via XX settembre
and via Veneto. The hotel's name is a reference to the
English painter, Joseph Turner, and was chosen to
signify the combination of beauty, harmony and
atmosphere. Guests are welcomed into an elegant
reception hall that is furnished with late 18th-century
furniture. A lovely marble staircase leads up to the
breakfast room and small bar, both agreeably attractive
rooms decorated with stucco-work and well furnished.
The large, carefully furnished bedrooms are individual
in their colours and moiré upholstery fabric, with
valuable rosewood period furniture. All the
bedrooms are equipped with video, safes and
satellite television. The bathrooms are very practical
and have hair-dryers and complimentary toiletry sets.
Breakfast is served as a buffet with pastries and food
fresh from the oven.

𝒰illa Borghese

RECOMMENDED IN THE AREA

RESTAURANTS:
Andrea, *via Sardegna 28, and* Piccolo Mondo, *via Aurora 39/D*

LOCAL SPECIALITIES:
Yoghurt from the Yogobar *in via Lucania (can be sweet or savoury)*

𝒯he hotel is in a small pretty villa, and stands at the entrance of the Vila Borghese Park, a few steps away from the art galley of the same name, a matchless collection made by Cardinal Scipione Borghese. In this villa the twentieth-century novelist Alberto Moravia was born and lived for a long time. He wrote some of his books and received many representatives of Italian culture here.

The architectural style of the building is agreeable, and the interior and communal rooms have a pleasing character and are personalised with many Art Nouveau features. The hotel was recently completely refurbished. However all the rooms, including the large, attractive and tastefully-furnished bedrooms, maintain the family atmosphere and a flavour of cultural traditions combined with the most modern comforts.

There is a pleasant private garden for moments of relaxation, and under a pergola there is bar service and breakfast. Guests can use a small meeting room and a convenient garage.

𝒰illa Paradiso

𝑅eminiscent of the houses which climb up the cliff on the Amalfi coast, this large, comfortable villa looks on to a little bay on the Tyrrhenian Sea, and is constructed on four levels. Three of these are raised and have big terraces overlooking the bay, and the other is at sea level and has a lovely Mediterranean-style courtyard with direct access to the beach. Typical Mediterranean vegetation provides shade, whilst in front of the villa guests can enjoy the natural and ever-changing views of the sea. The rooms are warmly welcoming and tastefully furnished by the lady of the house who is always ready to receive guests as friends. There are three bedrooms and one suite for guests, all different but all light and looking on to the very beautiful panorama of terraces and the sea.

RECOMMENDED IN THE AREA

RESTAURANTS:
Antica Trattoria dei Cacciatori 'Dal 1884', *Santa Marinella;* Il Barracuda, *Santa Severa*

VISIT:
Odescalchi Castle, Santa Marinella

$\mathcal{L}$ocanda della Mirandolina

The best specialities of Mediterranean cooking

☎ and 🖷 0761 436595
✉ info@mirandolina.it
via del Pozzo Bianco 40/42
01017 TUSCANIA (Viterbo)
Ref map 8, C3
A1, Orte exit, then *superstrada* (dual carriageway) 204 towards Viterbo, next S.S. in the direction of Tuscania
5 apartments; **££**
Credit cards: VISA SI, bancomat

RECOMMENDED IN THE AREA

RESTAURANT:
Al Gallo
VISIT:
Etruscan burial sites in the neighbourhood

$\mathcal{E}$ ven from a distance Tuscania is beautiful, with its towers and Romaneque churches of San Pietro and Santa Maria Maggiore. Enclosed within walls, high on a hill, it has an unspoilt and charming historic centre. The very small house containing this simple and pretty hotel is in one of the town's typical medieval streets. On the ground floor guests are welcomed into a tiny winter restaurant with five tables delightfully covered with Provençal printed cloths. On the floor above the bedrooms are furnished simply but carefully, each in a different colour. The pale tints are reflected in the patterned material of the upholstery, the duvets and bedspreads. The bathrooms are very small. During summer the restaurant serves meals outside, a few steps away, next to the ancient walls of the city. The cooking is strictly seasonal and Mediterranean, with a few touches of Sicilian inspiration.

$\mathcal{A}$l Gallo

In an old 17th-century residence

☎ 0761 443388 🖷 0761 443628
✉ gallotus@tin.it
via del Gallo 22
01017 TUSCANIA (Viterbo)
Ref map 8, C3
A1, Orte exit, then *superstrada* (dual carriageway) 204 towards Viterbo, next S.S. in the direction of Tuscania
13 rooms, 2 suites; **££/£££**
Credit cards: AE VISA SI ⓪, bancomat

RECOMMENDED IN THE AREA

RESTAURANTS:
La Zaffera *and* Richiastro, *Viterbo*

LOCAL SPECIALITIES:
Pecorini *cheeses; extra virgin olive oil from Canino*

$\mathcal{T}$ uscania is reached by way of a charming panorama through deep *calanques* that cut into the tufa porous rock in a dramatic way. The city, which was Etruscan, Roman and medieval, has an authentic and compact historic centre. This is where the hotel is, made out of an old 17th-century residence with windows opening on to a wide view of old roofs. Its few bedrooms are all different, but all are decorated in pale colours and with 19th-century period furniture. The bathrooms are finished in marble.

The restaurant is well known and popular, being one of the best in the area, and it is delightfully rustic. Its style is partly that of a French bistro and partly that of a country home, with checked tablecloths, painted decorations, white floors and light furniture. There is a tennis court for the use of guests.

Abruzzo

The landscape of the Abruzzo is predominately two coloured: the pale blue of the sea and the green of the plains and mountains. Its coast extends for about 300 kilometres between the mouths of the Tronto and Trigno rivers. It is sandy as far as Pescara, then becomes stonier with stretches of rocks and little bays between the beaches. Typical fishing huts built on piers stretch out into the sea, like the antennae of insects. The seaside holiday resorts around Alba Adriatica, Pescara, Ortona and Vasto are well organised and peaceful. Sometimes villages by the sea are divided into two, with the older, original part on the hillsides.

From the coast, valleys and rolling hills rise towards the mountains. There are austere stone villages and panoramic views between oak and olive trees towards the Apennines or the sea. Nearly a third of the total area of the Abruzzo mountains is protected and it is the only region in Italy with three national parks: the Abruzzo, Gran Sasso and Laga mountains (with the highest Apennine peak and Europe's most southerly glacier), and Maiella. There are also a multitude of reserves and small parks.

Campo Imperatore (about 1,120 metres above sea level), a vast plateau within the Gran Sasso massif

The countryside is wonderfully varied with harsh limestone summits, forests, meadows, dramatic scenery, plateaux encircled by mountains, lakes and ancient lake-beds, and rivers. The brown bears of Marsica, the Abruzzo chamois, the Apennine wolf, the royal eagle – and equally rare plants – are aspects of the unusual wildlife that is now being skillfully promoted to develop tourism in this remote area. The natural beauty forms the basis of the history and art to be found in the villages, hermitages and towns.

The Abruzzo is a land that has its own self-confident individuality, which can be seen in the Italic archaeological finds displayed in museums, in the churches with their straight façades, and in certain crafts and customs that are more vibrant here than elsewhere in Italy. It is also true of the good food and open hospitality.

Zunica

A tradition that has lasted from 1880

☎ 0861 91319 ✆ 0861 918150
piazza Filippi Pepe 14
64010 CIVITELLA DEL TRONTO (Teramo)
Ref map 9, B6
A14, S. Benedetto d. T. exit, junction for Ascoli Piceno, S. S. 81 towards Civitella del Tronto
21 rooms; ££
Credit cards: AE VISA SI ⬤, bancomat

The small 17th-century mansion that houses this hotel stands in the central square of Civitella, in the shadow of the walls of the Bourbon fortress. The family management guarantees a sincere welcome and comfortable stay in a period atmosphere.

The elegant furnishings are early 20th century, the bedrooms and bathrooms look on to the characteristic lanes of this medieval village with charming views over the Fiori and Laga mountains. The family tradition is particularly evident in the attached restaurant where there is also a little rustic grotto, with a cross-vaulted ceiling, that can be used for romantic dinners and private gatherings. The high-quality cooking consists of typical regional dishes served tastefully and elegantly.

RECOMMENDED IN THE AREA

RESTAURANT:
Duomo, *via Stazio 9, Teramo*

WINE CELLARS:
Cantina del barone Cornacchia, *Torano Nuovo;*
Cantina Montori *and* La Credenza, *Controguerra*

VISIT:
Bourbon fortress, Civitella del Tronto; Scala Santa (Holy staircase), Campli;. Ascoli Piceno

Bellavista

On a hillside with a view of the sea

☎ 0861 70627 ✆ 0861 1700122
via Icona 3
64010 COLONNELLA (Teramo)
Ref map 9, B6
A14, S. Benedetto d. T. exit, junction for Ascoli Piceno, S. S. 16 towards Gliulianova, then turn off for Colonnella
24 rooms, 2 suites; ££
Credit cards: AE VISA SI ⬤

The building is late 19th century and has been recently refurbished. It is situated in the historic centre of the village that stands on the top of a hill with a wide view over the valley and the Adriatic coast that is only six kilometres away.

The hotel has large, carefully furnished bedrooms with parquet flooring, pleasing modern furniture, matching upholstery and wallpaper, safes, magnetic key cards to the doors, televisions and mini-bars. The furnishing is practical, new and carefully chosen. The bathrooms are medium sized and very practical, all with showers and most with windows, and they have hair-dryers. The communal rooms are light, and the large restaurant serves meals outside on a lovely panoramic terrace during summer. The cooking is based on regional dishes. Breakfast is served on a terrace with big windows. The hotel has a number of free parking spaces in the garage available to guests.

RECOMMENDED IN THE AREA

RESTAURANT:
Pasqualò, *Martinsicuro*

VISIT:
Church of Santa Maria a Vico

$\mathcal{V}$illa Maiella

At the foot of the Maiella Park

☎ 0871 809319
🖶 0871 809362
✉ info@villamaiella.it
via Sette Dolori 30
66016 GUARDIAGRELE (Chieti)
Ref map 9, C7

A14, Ortona exit, S.S. 538 towards Orogna, go on Guardiagrele
14 rooms; ££
Credit cards: AE VISA SI OD, bancomat

The restaurant serves typical food from the Abruzzi region, imaginatively adapted traditional dishes, seasonal dishes (those with mushrooms are excellent) and seafood specialities. There is a good wine cellar.

Management gives a kind welcome to guests and is very attentive to their requirements.

$\mathcal{S}$ tanding at the entrance to Guardiagrele, this is a modern, functional building at the foot of the Maiella Park and a few kilometres from the Adriatic Sea.

The proprietors manage this little hotel with love and enthusiasm. All bedrooms have air conditioning, minibars and satellite televisions, and are furnished with care to give a pleasing and welcoming atmosphere. The bathrooms are very practical, all with showers, hairdryers and heated towel rails.

RECOMMENDED IN THE AREA

RESTAURANT:
La Maielletta, *Lanciano*

LOCAL SPECIALITIES:
Tremonti *cakes from local pastry shop; wrought iron, copper, gold items from Guariagrele; home produced oil and honey*

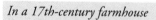

$\mathcal{L}$e Magnolie

In a 17th-century farmhouse

☎ and 🖶 0854 214473
contrada Fiorano
65014 LORETO APRUTINO (Pescara)
Ref map 9, C6

A14, after Pescara Nord, S.S. 16 and 151, from Loreto Aprutino continue in the direction of Penne, after 2.5 km at the Pianella crossroads turn left and after 1 km turn right for Le Magnolie
4 rooms, 3 apartments; £
Credit cards not accepted

The dining room and meeting room have brick ceilings, arches and welcoming interiors. The kitchen prepares simple dishes using farm ingredients, and guests receive a friendly welcome. There is also an open-air swimming pool, bikes, table tennis and fishing.

$\mathcal{S}$ urrounded by a large garden featuring a fountain of the same age as the house, this is a delightful, carefully restored 17th-century farmhouse. The building is on a hillside 300 metres above sea level and a short distance from the sea and from the historic Abruzzi park. It is also near the Gran Sasso-Monti della Laga and Maiella Park, the regional park of Sirente-Velino and 30 nature reserves. This *agriturismo* (farm accommodation) has four carefully furnished bedrooms: one of these is on two floors, some have rustic furnishings, and others have antique furniture.

RECOMMENDED IN THE AREA

RESTAURANTS:
Il Celliere, *Loreto Aprutino;* Tatobbe, *Penne*

LOCAL SPECIALITIES:
Extra virgin olive oil; pecorino *cheese; products preserved in oil; pickles*

VISIT:
Parish church of San Pietro Apostolo; Acerbo Gallery with antique Abruzzi ceramics; religious house of Saint Francis containing ethnographic and archaeological museums

$\mathcal{F}$attoria Cerreto

Surrounded by unspoilt natural beauty

☎ 085 8061579 ☏ 085 8062227
✉ cerreto@net-uno.it
Colle Cerreto 9
**64023 MOSCIANO SANT'ANGELO
(Teramo)**
Ref map 9, B6
A14, Teramo-Giulianove exit, then S.S. 80
for Teramo and turn off for Mosciano
Sant' Angelo
60 rooms, 1 suite, 1 apartment; **£/££**
Credit cards: AE VISA SI ⑩, bancomat

*I*n lovely hilly countryside eight kilometres from the
Adriatic coast, stand some new farmhouses
grouped around a modern complex with the traditional
agricultural style of architecture. The reception,
restaurant, bar and billiards room are in the centre, and
around these are small and characteristic buildings
containing the light and spacious bedrooms with their
simple modern furnishings. Available for guests are an
open-air swimming pool, covered *bocce* (bowls) pitch
with illumination, sauna, beach volleyball court, a

modern and well-equipped beauty/health centre, gym
with fitness club, and bicycles for hire. The stables have
qualified instructors to give individual and group
lessons and to accompany guests on rides on the
nearby Laga and Gran Sasso mountains. The
restaurant serves local dishes using organic products.

RECOMMENDED IN THE AREA

RESTAURANT:
Da Beccaceci, *Giulianova Lido*

LOCAL SPECIALITIES:
*Farm-produced wine, extra virgin olive oil, jam, honey
and* pecorino *cheese*

VISIT:
Church of Santa Maria a Mare; Teramo

$\mathcal{C}$arlton

*T*his modern building on the town's waterfront is
always a holiday destination for those who love
the sun and the sea, but also for business travellers
who want high standards and professionalism. The
bedrooms are practical and comfortable, all
completely soundproofed and looking onto the wide
beach. The reception hall is spacious and the
communal areas are furnished with modern simplicity.
The restaurant has managed to make a name for itself
in the town's gastronomic hierarchy, serving the best
of Abruzzi cooking with a rich selection of national and
international cuisine.

The best of Abruzzi cooking

☎ 085 373125 ☏ 085 4213922
✉ hcsdiol@tin.it
viale della Riviera 35
65123 PESCARA
Ref map 9, C7
A14, Pescara Nord-Città Sant' Angelo, go on in
the direction of *Riviera* for about 6 km
71 rooms, 2 suites; **££**
Credit cards: AE VISA SI ⑩, bancomat

RECOMMENDED IN THE AREA

RESTAURANTS:
La Cantina di Jozz, *via delle Caserme;* Taverna 58,
corso Manthoné 58; Regina del Porto, *via Paolucci 65*

LOCAL SPECIALITIES:
*Wrought-iron products from Guardiagrele; sugared
almonds and sweets from Sulmona*

VISIT:
Birthplace of Gabriele D'Annunzio, corso Manthoné

*P*aradiso

A warm and welcoming mountain-style atmosphere in the heart of the Bruzzo national park

☎ 0863 910422
🖷 0863 910498
✉ a.paradiso@ermes.it
via Fonte Fracassi 4
67032 PESCASSEROLI (L'Aquila)
Ref map 9, D6

A25, Pescina exit, S.S. 83 as far as Pescasseroli
20 rooms; ££
Credit cards: 𝖵𝖨𝖲𝖠 𝖲𝖨

RECOMMENDED IN THE AREA

RESTAURANT:
Peppe di Sora

LOCAL SPECIALITIES:
Pillow lace; filigree jewellery

VISIT:
Parish church of Saints Peter and Paul

*T*his small hotel in typical mountain style is deep in the woods and about a kilometre from the centre of Pescasseroli. Guests are welcomed with all the warmth and attention that come with friendly, family management. It has been recently refurbished, and has retained the atmosphere of a mountain home. All the rooms have white walls and warm terracotta floors, with some antique Abruzzi furniture and wooden chests painted with floral and Tyrolean-style decorations.

The guest bedrooms, too, are warmly welcoming, with checked duvets, pine or decorated wood furniture, iron beds and lace curtains at the windows. Some rooms also have a balcony. The bathrooms are quite practical and nearly all are new. The communal rooms have benches, armchairs and comfortable sofas pleasantly arranged in front of the fireplace. Around the hotel is a little terrace and a lovely garden where guests may enjoy the heart of the Abruzzi national park and the peace of this charming quiet corner among the mountains.

$\mathcal{L}$e Georgiche Country House

*A*n old mill dating from the 19th centtury that was abandoned and forgotten until 1992 when the present owner saw it and fell in love with it. Today it has been completely restructured and is the main house at the centre of a farm business where fields of wheat and soya alternate with rows of vines and orchards. Padiglione is a short distance away, and this is a little building surrounded by flower meadows, with a tiled roof, whitewashed walls, blue shutters and Mediterranean-style architecture that make visitors feel happy just to see it.

The bedrooms and suites are light, bright and welcoming, and have pretty period furniture. Fireplaces warm the communal areas, and guests meet round the communal rustic tables for breakfast and other meals. The guest-house is a member of Country Club, a cultural association that brings country lovers together with the aim of promoting the environment, organic food and farm working traditions.

Recreational facilities consist of: herbalist and cookery courses, a tennis court, *bocce* (bowls), swimming pool and health farm. A garden and private wood are available for walks.

Farming tradition combined with organic food

☎ 085 412500
🖷 085 299216
🖂 tcolavi@tin.it
contrada Santa Maria
65019 PIANELLA (Pescara)
Ref map 9, C6
A25, Pescara-Villanova exit,
S.S. 602 towards Penne,
then turn off for Pianella

1 room, 3 suites; **££**
Credit cards not accepted

RECOMMENDED IN THE AREA

RESTAURANTS:
Nonna Elisa, *via P. Bentivoglio 2, Chieti;*
Guerino, *viale della Riviera 4, Pescara*

Miglia

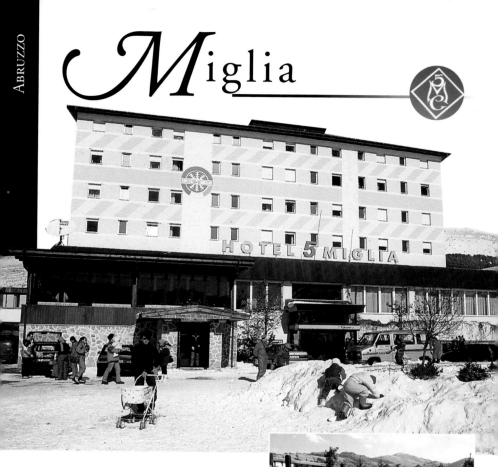

*T*his modern building stands alone on the 'five-mile plain', a charming plateau that is naturally and beautifully framed, in the Abruzzi region a short distance from Rivisondoli and from the ski lifts. The bedrooms are large and well cared for, with pleasing modern furniture and convenient cupboards. All the bathrooms have windows, showers, and washbasins with convenient surrounds. The communal rooms are large and arranged as delightful separate areas, and there is a bar with veranda and a large dining room. A big garden around the hotel has facilities for several sports: an indoor heated swimming pool, tennis, gym, children's playground, mini-golf, *bocce* (bowls), football, five-a-side football, volleyball, archery, and well-equipped solarium areas. The proprietors have been in the hotel business for three generations and welcome guests warmly. The hotel has a garage.

RECOMMENDED IN THE AREA

RESTAURANT:
Da Giocondo

LOCAL SPECIALITIES:
Cheeses including mozarella; *saffron from Navelli plain*

VISIT:
Parish church

On the most noted and charming of the main plateaux in the Abruzzi region

☎ 0864 69627
🖷 0864 69628
✉ hotel5miglia@cyberia.avc.it
67036 RIVISONDOLI (L'Aquila)
Ref map 9, D6-7
A25, Pratola Sulmona exit, then S.S. 17 towards Sulmona, at Santa Maria della Portella turn left for Rivisondoli
64 rooms, 2 suites; **£/££/£££**
Credit cards: VISA SI

La Meridiana

The quiet and tranquillity of the most unspoilt rural spots

☎ and 📠 **0861 786336**
Santa Maria a Vico
64027 SANT'OMERO (Teramo)
Ref map 9, B6
A14, Val Vibrata exit, S.S. 259,
towards Nereto and Sant' Omero
13 rooms, 6 apartments; **££**
Credit cards not accepted

*T*he simplicity of the building, an old and typical farmhouse that has been completely refurbished, is mirrored in the rooms inside. Surrounded by a large garden and by cultivated fields belonging to the farm, this *agriturismo* (farm accommodation) reflects the natural customs and traditions of the Abruzzi region. There are large rooms where the essential furnishing is arranged in a careful, practical way. The light bedrooms and small apartments look on to cultivated land. The small apartments are equipped with everything necessary in order to prepare delicious meals with ingredients from the local area. The garden has a vegetable garden and an orchard, and in addition there is a barbecue. There is a friendly welcome for guests.

RECOMMENDED IN THE AREA

RESTAURANT:
Zunica, Civitella del Tronto

LOCAL SPECIALITIES:
Extra virgin olive oil; local wines; charcuterie and cheeses

VISIT:
Cathedral, Teramo

Mion

A holiday between olive groves and the sea

☎ 085 9350935 📠 085 9350864
📧 info@mionhotel.com
via Garibaldi 22
64029 SILVI MARINA (Teramo)
Ref map 9, C7
A14, Atri-Pineto exit, follow the signs for Silvi
64 rooms; **££**
Credit cards: 🆎 💳 SI 🅾️

*T*his hotel stands directly on the private beach by the Adriatic Sea. The rooms are attractive and extremely well presented: practicality and modernity go together with tasteful furnishings. Bedrooms are bright, light and comfortable, with antique furniture and many with terraces. The bathrooms are quite practical.

Attention to detail is evident in the service and in the carefully prepared candlelit dinners in the hotel restaurant. Here good Italian cooking features with fish freshly caught form the Adriatic and selected local and national wines. Guests are welcomed kindly.

RECOMMENDED IN THE AREA

RESTAURANTS:
Il Sanio *and* Vecchia Silvi

VISIT:
Silvi Paese, village of Roman origin

Molise

More than half of Molise – the second smallest Italian region – is mountainous: it incorporates the Apennine ranges of the Mainarde, Matese and part of Sannio. Most of the rest of the region is hilly, gently sloping eastwards towards 35 kilometres of Adriatic coast, where the centre is Termoli, the only port.

From the Apennine divide, rivers flow towards the Adriatic and Tyrrhenian seas. Molise is an unspoilt region with a history that is predominantly one of isolation. For visitors its charm lies in seeking out surprising and lovely places to visit.

The scenery is rough and mountainous, particularly in upper Molise, with great stretches of wood, panoramic views, plateaux, mountain lakes, basins and wide valleys and a few old villages. Mountains, snow and wood – the residual tip of the original Apennine forest – are the habitat of wild animals that have largely disappeared elsewhere. These include the eagle, sparrow hawk and buzzard, the wolf and the wild boar.

The highest Matese peak is Mount Miletto (2,050 metres) and the second highest is Livio, the *Tifernus Mons* at the foot of which

Above: a view of Venafro, with the medieval castle in the foreground
Top right: the village of Gambatesa in the south of Molise

the Samnites fought their final battle against the Romans. The Samnites were the ancient inhabitants of the region, a pastoral and warlike people who, for more that 50 years between the 4th and 3rd centuries BC, opposed Rome before being assimilated by it. Both the Samnites and the Romans left remains, examples of which can be found in the museums at Pietrabbondante, Sepino, Larino and Venafro.

The medieval period, when Molise was linked to events in the southern kingdom, left precious records in the frescos of San Vincenzo Abbey at Volturno, in the church of Santa Maria di Canneto, and in the cathedrals of Termoli and Larino.

Venafro, situated on the plain amongst the olive trees of Volturno's middle valley, was remembered by the Roman poet, Horace. Nowadays Molise offers nature and sporting holidays, from the ski slopes on the Matese mountains to the Adriatic beaches.

$\mathcal{A}$ntica Masseria Mastronardi dei Maranconi

A tradition dating back to the 18th century

☎ 0865 770002
🖷 0865 770086
✉ maranconi@tin.it
località Maranconi
86081 AGNONE (Isernia)
Ref map 9, D7
A1, Cassino exit, S.S. 630 for Cassino, S.S. 6 and 85 as far as Isernia, then S. S. 650 and turn off for Poggio Sannita-Agone
3 rooms, 6 houses; £££
Credit cards not accepted

*T*he first to settle here in the middle of the 18th century were Fabio and Perpetua Mastronardi from the Marches region. In 1923 the inhabitants of property, which had been enlarged by successive generations, numbered about 60 – all of them belonging to the Mastronardi family. After the Second World War, emigration depopulated the area. Nowadays, brought back to new life, the old stables have been transformed into a welcoming tavern, while the barns and part of the old farmhouse contain the bedrooms of this *agriturismo* (farm accommodation). Everything was restructured in 1996 but the original architecture has been preserved, as has the lovely façade and the mostly stone-walled rooms, the vaulted or wooden ceilings, the family furniture and harmonious atmosphere.

RECOMMENDED IN THE AREA

RESTAURANT:
Selvaggi, *località Staffoli*

LOCAL SPECIALITIES:
Fresh dairy products (trecce, burrate *and* scamorze*)
and matured cheeses* (caciocavallo *and* pecorino*)*

$\mathcal{A}$ljope

Well-tended and practical surroundings

☎ 0875 689500/02 🖷 0875 689503
via D. Alighieri 4
86034 GUGLIONESI (Campobasso)
Ref map 9, D7
A14, Termoli Molise exit, S.S. 16 towards Termoli, then turn off on the S.S. 483 for Guglionesi
35 rooms, 1 suite; £/££
Credit cards: 💳 💳 , bancomat

*T*his modern, small-scale hotel building was constructed in 1989, is well designed, and stands high up a short distance from the sea. From the hotel guests may admire a lovely panorama that extends from the Molise mountains to the sea beneath, to the Tremiti islands and down as far as Gargano.

The bedrooms are well furnished, light and modern and the bathrooms are very practical. The communal rooms provide a wide range of services: a restaurant with both traditional and vegetarian cooking, *pizzeria* with stone oven and disco, baby-sitting service, private beach and garage. Breakfast is served as a buffet including delicious local specialities. The management takes good care of guests and gives attentive service.

RECOMMENDED IN THE AREA

RESTAURANT:
Ribo, *contrada Malecoste 7*

LOCAL SPECIALITIES:
Fresh and matured cheeses; truffles; charcuterie

VISIT:
Church of Santa Maria Maggiore and church of San Nicola; medieval walled village, Termoli

Europa

An ideal base for discovering the beauty of upper Molise

☎ 0865 2126
🖶 0865 413243
✉ grandhot@tin.it
S.S. 17, n. 140
86170 ISERNIA
Ref map 9, E7

A1, Cassino exit, S.S. 630 for Cassino, then
S.S. 6 and 85 as far as Isernia
67 rooms, 6 suites, 6 apartments; **££/£££**
Credit cards: AE VISA SI ⓪

RECOMMENDED IN THE AREA

RESTAURANT:
Taverna, *via San Lazzaro 85*

LOCAL SPECIALITIES:
Local rich fruit cakes, sometimes iced with chocolate

Recently refurbished, this hotel is a short distance from the city and is decidedly modern in appearance, but practical and comfortable inside. The uniformed members of staff who welcome guests are not only experienced and professional but also warmly courteous. The hotel has large, light bedrooms with well-chosen furniture, air conditioning, automatic light switches and satellite televisions. The bathrooms have been well restructured with hair-dryers and telephones, all with baths and showers, floors finished in marble and convenient washbasin surrounds. The communal rooms are large, well furnished and arranged as comfortable separate areas. The hotel has a garage and two meeting rooms.

Strand

On the seashore

☎ 0873 803106 🖶 0873 803450
via Costa Verde
località Marina di Montenero
**86036 MONTENERO
DI BISACCIA (Campobasso)**
Ref map 9, D8

A14, Vasto Sud exit, S.S. 650
towards Isernia, then turn off to
left for Monternero di Bisaccia
36 rooms; **££/£££**
Credit cards: SI

The traffic goes fast along the coast, flashes of light blue appear through the vegetation and give just a hint of the sea and the shore without revealing their beauty and secrets. But just leave the road and go a short distance for peace and nature to prevail: noise gives way to silence.

The hotel is in a simple white building standing in a lovely position right on the beach. It has radiantly light rooms, some with balconies, that are furnished in a modern, neat and bright style. The sitting

RECOMMENDED IN THE AREA

RESTAURANT:
Corsaro, *Porto di Vasto*

rooms are airy and the restaurant has big windows opening on to the panorama. Leisure facilities available to guests are: a tennis court, swimming pool and private beach. There is an Internet connection in the reception hall.

Santa Maria del Bagno

On a hillside surrounded by natural beauty

☎ 0865 460136
🖷 0865 460129
viale Santa Maria del Bagno 1
86090 PESCHE (Isernia)
Ref map 9, E7
A1, Cassino exit, S.S. 630 for Cassino, then
S.S. 6 and 85 as far as Isernia, next S.S. 650
as far as the turn for Pesche
41 rooms, 41 apartments; **£/££**
Credit cards: AE VISA SI, bancomat

RECOMMENDED IN THE AREA

RESTAURANTS:
Letizia, *Monteroduni;* Antica Trattoria del Riccio,
Cantalupo nel Sannio

LOCAL SPECIALITIES:
*Dairy products from the Molise area; crafts in copper;
pillow lace*

VISIT:
Paleolithic Museum, Isernia

This hotel stands in a hilly position surrounded by natural beauty. Behind it is a panoramic outline of typical medieval village houses grouped on the steep slopes of the mountain, and of the Pesche Nature Reserve where a diverse ecosystem is preserved. A short distance away are many interesting routes for exploring natural beauty, history and archaeology.

The recently refurbished hotel building has simple architecture, with comfortable, practical bedrooms and a series of little apartments. Inside there are ceramic floors and practical furniture. The hospitality is simple, yet practical and courteous. The cooking consists of local specialities. Outside in the partly paved garden is a children's playground.

Lo Sciatore

A few metres away from the ski lifts

☎ and 🖷 0874 784137
✉ muccillihotels@net-point.it
località Campitello Matese
86027 SAN MASSIMO (Campobasso)
Ref map 9, E7
A1, Cassino exit, S.S. 6 for Isernia, then
S.S. 17, turn off for San Massimo,
go on as far as Campitello Matese
40 rooms; **£/££**
Credit cards: AE VISA SI ⓪

RECOMMENDED IN THE AREA

RESTAURANTS:
Antica Trattoria del Riccio, *Catalupo nel Sannio, and*
Vecchia Trattoria da Tonino, *corso Vittorio Emanuele 8*

VISIT:
*Cathedral at Bojano; ruins of megalithic walls and
Lombard castle, Civita Superiore*

A lovely broad and panoramic road winds upwards surrounded by woods, and after curves and turns opens unexpectedly on to the wide Campitello basin. The hotel stands close to the ski lifts, and is a modern building that recalls mountain architecture. The bedrooms look out on to a green and woody view and are in the classic mountain style, with wooden furniture, parquet floors, panelled wood ceilings and attics. The bathrooms are convenient and modern. The cosy sitting rooms combine fireplaces and stone arches with the pleasure of being able to enjoy the natural beauty outside. There is a garden, mini-club for children and a covered swimming pool. The restaurant serves meat dishes prepared with ingredients from the animal-rearing business owned by the same management.

La Taverna

An atmosphere combining the flavour of the past with a modern welcome

☎ 0874 79626
📠 0874 790118
contrada Piana d'Olmo 6
86017 SEPINO (Campobasso)
Ref map 9, E7-8
A1, Cassino exit, S.S. 6 for Isernia,
then S.S. 17, turn off for Sepino
14 rooms; £
Credit cards not accepted

RECOMMENDED IN THE AREA

RESTAURANT:
Potestà, *Via Persichillo 1, Campobasso*

VISIT:
Ruins of ancient Roman city, Saepinum

*A*long the ancient routes that linked Rome and Benevento stood taverns where horses were changed and where travellers found shelter and refreshment. The name of the inn has been chosen as a reminder of this past as is the building itself. A massive front door, the ancient protective screen from dangers outside, opens on to a very lovely interior. Carriages stopped here and then parked further on in what is today a garden with a pergola. The stone walls, low arches and vaults contain nowadays, as then, rustic tables for hungry wayfarers.

The atmosphere has the flavour of the past, although the comfort and welcome are that of the present.

A steep stone staircase goes up to pretty bedrooms painted in pale pastel colours and furnished with late 19th-century and period-style furniture. Completing them are modern bathrooms.

A stay here offers the chance to go for walks, horse rides or trips on mountain bikes in a very beautiful neighbourhood.

Somerist

*T*he castle of Federico II, surrounded by a mighty wall and built on high ramparts, juts out into the sea and the promontory contains the old town with characteristically narrow streets, ancient houses and a lovely cathedral. At the foot of the wall the new town extends along the coast, following the contours of the seashore. The hotel is situated away from the heavier traffic, in a residential area high up overlooking the sea. It is in a modern building with large bedrooms where tones of pale and dark blue dominate the colours of the walls, fitted carpets and modern furnishings. The bedrooms have small balconies or large terraces facing the sea: the Tremiti Islands decorate the horizon like pieces of stage scenery. The sitting rooms are modern and attractive, and the restaurant serves meals on the terrace during summer.

Facing the Tremiti Islands

☎ 0875 706760
📠 0875 706440
via V. Cuoco 14
86039 TERMOLI (Campobasso)
Ref map 9, D8
A14, Termoli Molise exit, follow signs for Termoli
20 rooms; ££/£££
Credit cards: AE VISA SI ◍, bancomat

RECOMMENDED IN THE AREA

RESTAURANTS:
Zi'Bass; Torre Sinarca, *Torre Saracena*

VISIT:
The Romanesque Duomo *(cathedral)*

Dimora del Prete di Bel Monte

ocuments conserved in the historic family archive relate that this old mansion was restructured in 1860. It stands in the heart of Venafro's historic centre. This is a little town surrounded by green olive trees. The mansion is a special place where the fascination of history and the life of the past have been protected and preserved unspoilt. Once past the large and distinguished entrance door, guests receive a friendly welcome from the owners of the house and are conducted through wide corridors with columns on the walls and cross-vaulted ceilings. The four

An old family residence in the heart of the Molise area

☎ **and** 📠 **0865 900159**
via Cristo 49
86079 VENAFRO (Isernia)
Ref map 9, E6-7

A1, Cassino exit, S.S. 630 as far as Cassino, then S.S. 6 for Isernia as far as Venafro
4 rooms; ££
Credit cards not accepted

guest bedrooms are all different and are furnished with original period furniture. These are spacious rooms full of atmosphere, and enhanced by the surrounding views. The frescoed public rooms, big terraces and the garden of this family mansion recall memories and traditions of times past.

RECOMMENDED IN THE AREA

RESTAURANT:
Bellevue

LOCAL SPECIALITIES:
Taralli *biscuits; sheep's milk,* scamorza *and* caciocavalli *cheeses; pillow lace; wicker baskets; wrought iron and copper*

VISIT:
Pandone Castle, Archaeological Museum and Romanesque Duomo *(cathedral); San Martino in Pensilis*

Campania

Those who have fallen under the spell of Campania date from antiquity to the present day. They have included many illustrious visitors, from rich Romans at the beginning of the Christian era (who built villas all over the island of Capri and the Phlegraean coast) to Goethe. Today this seductive magic affects all visitors. Famous places succeed each other along a coast that was colonised long ago by the Greeks, and they radiate the intensity, colours and flavours of the Mediterranean. Beyond the Campi Flegrei – the fascinating volcanic landscape, which continues in the islands of Ischia and Procida – is jagged, mountainous and green. Here there are vineyards, orchards and chestnut trees, and a view over the sea in the Gulf of Naples. That city, with its formidable concentration of natural beauty, culture, humanity and history, involves those who visit and live like few others in the world: 'See Naples and die,' as the Italian proverb says.

The cone of Vesuvius which dominates the gulf is green as far as the lava rock, and is now a protected environment. To the south the Sorrentine peninsula completes the crescent of the gulf, with high, sharp cliffs overhanging the sea. Opposite is Capri, its coast hollowed out by grottoes and bordered by strange cliffs with Mediterranean vegetation, and villages with arches and vaulted streets, and a cosmopolitan reputation. Beyond Campanella Point is the famous coast of Positano, Amalfi and Ravello with white houses and oriental touches, terraces overlooking the sea, olives trees and lemons.

Campania's archaeological and classical sites are extraordinary. In first place is Pompeii, an unparalleled vision of an ancient time that was frozen the instant Vesuvius errupted in AD 79. Then there are Herculaneum, Paestum, Cuma, and the Roman amphitheatres of Pozzuoli and Santa Maria Capua Vetere. Not far away, the royal residence and gardens of Caserta are reminders of 18th-century splendour. Less well known are centres of art like Capua, Benevento and Sant' Angelo in Formis; Sannio and Irpinia with its green mountains and valleys furrowed by rivers; and Cilento, a nature park with the Diano valley. This is a wild region with watch-towers and castles, charming hillsides and inaccessible, wooded countryside.

Sant' Angelo point, on the island of Ischia

La Colombaia

Amongst olive trees, facing the island of Capri

☎ 0974 821800
🖷 0974 823478
via Piano delle pere
84043 AGROPOLI (Salerno)
Ref map 10, E2
A3, Battipaglia exit, then S.S. 18 as far as the turn for Agropoli, entrance towards *Centro* (centre)
7 rooms; £
Credit cards: 〓 SÌ 〓

*T*his old villa is set amongst natural beauty and silence, surrounded by a big olive grove. A short while ago it was restructured and turned into a hotel. It enjoys a magnificent view over the gulf of Salerno and Capri. The bedrooms are bright and well furnished, with air conditioning and televisions. The bathrooms are equipped with hair-dryers and complimentary toiletry sets. The communal rooms are charmingly furnished with antiques; the dining room is cosy and welcoming with a family atmosphere. Service is attentive and members of staff are very helpful. Outside is a big garden and open-air swimming pool with solarium.

RECOMMENDED IN THE AREA

RESTAURANTS:
Il Ceppo; La Taverna del Pescatore, *Santa Maria di Castellabate*

LOCAL SPECIALITIES:
Oil; wine; limoncello *liqueur; fresh fish; terracotta*

VISIT:
Paestum Greek Temple of Poseidon and ruins

Grand Hotel Italiano

Courtesy and comfort in the historic centre

☎ 0824 24111
🖷 0824 21758
via Principe di Napoli 137
82100 BENEVENTO
Ref map 10, C2
A1, Caserta Sud exit, S.S. 265 and 7 for Benevento, Benevento Ovest exit, follow the signs for *Stazione* (station)
71 rooms, 2 suites; £
Credit cards: 〓 〓 SÌ 〇)

*S*ituated in a lovely tree-lined avenue close to the historic centre and the cathedral, this is the town's oldest hotel and it has been recently refurbished. The same family has run it since 1923, making courtesy a matter of pride.

The bedrooms are large and decorated simply: the furniture is in the pink shades of cherry wood, with modern panelling used for the headboards of the beds. The bathrooms are practical. The large communal rooms are of modern design and arranged as various spaces. There are also rooms where conferences can be held.

RECOMMENDED IN THE AREA

RESTAURANTS:
Pedicini, *via Grimoaldo Re 16;* Vecchie Carrozze, *piano Cappelle*

VISIT:
Duomo *(cathedral);* Diocletian Museum in the *Archbishop's Palace; Roman Theatre*

*V*illa Sarah

On the island of Capri, but far from its worldliness

☎ 081 8377817 📠 081 8377215
✉ info@villasarah.it
via Tiberio 3/A
80073 CAPRI (Napoli)
Ref map 10, E1

From Naples by hydrofoil or ferry; from the port of Capri take the cable railway to the *piazzetta* (little square) and from there on foot to the hotel
20 rooms; **££/£££**
Credit cards: AE VISA SI OD, bancomat

*T*he further one gets from the *piazzetta* (little square), the more muffled its noise becomes. Coloured tiles indicate the route, vivid bougainvillea lifts the heart and in a few minutes you reach the hotel. Originally this was a private home; today it is a little hotel surrounded by a large cultivated area with an orchard and vineyard. The building in the Capri style has broad arches opening on to the garden. Inside a private-house atmosphere is maintained and the light rooms are furnished with pretty, early 20th-century furniture. The bedrooms are simple, airy and cheerful, and some have terraces with a view of the sea. The furnishings are rustic.

A copious and very well-prepared breakfast is served in the garden, in guests' rooms or on their private terraces. The fruit and jam provided are home-made. The owners run the hotel kindly and attentively.

RECOMMENDED IN THE AREA

RESTAURANTS:
Da Paolino, *Marina Grande;* Rondinella, *Anacapri*
VISIT:
Villa San Michele, Anacapri

---

*G*iacaranda

A residence full of lovely details

☎ 0974 966130 📠 0974 966800
✉ giaca@costacilento.it
località Cenito, fraz. San Marco
84071 CASTELLABATE (Salerno)
Ref map 10, E2

A3, Battipaglia exit, S.S. 18 as far as the turn off for Agropoli, then S.S. 267 to the turning for Castellabate, go on as far as San Marco
6 rooms, 1 suite, 2 apartments; **££**
Credit cards: AE VISA SI OD

*S*urrounded by flowers, this white villa has the harmonious architectural form of the late 19th century and is set in a big olive grove. Accommodation is in bedrooms with 19th-century furniture and embroidered bed linen, and in two comfortable apartments. All the furnishings are carefully chosen and within the mainly white rooms there is a charming mix of modern design and the patina of antiques.

Breakfast includes home-made jams and is served

in the garden or the winter garden. During the course of the day there are aperitifs of prosecco from the Cenito vines and snacks of fried sage and ricotta with mint, then lunch with home-grown vegetables, traditional Neapolitan pasta and, after dinner, wonderful herb tea.

There is a reliable baby-sitting service. At the end of a stay complimentary pizza is served, accompanied by a concert of folk music.

RECOMMENDED IN THE AREA

RESTAURANTS:
La Taverna del Pescatore, *Castellabate;*
Gelso d'oro-Da nonna Sceppa *and* Nettuno, *Paestum*

La Mola

The old medieval village of Castellabate is a place for holidays combining both nature and art. The sandy shores of San Marco and Santa Maria stretch below the ancient municipality.

The little hotel was transformed from an old 12th-century palace and is in a dominating panoramic position. Skilful restoration has created new rooms out of the old interior, and all have a view of the gulf. They are comfortable and full of atmosphere, with pleasingly stylish furniture, and are equipped with safes, televisions and mini-bars.

The communal rooms are elegantly welcoming and have characteristic walls in unplastered stone. In addition there is a garden with charming terraced

Atmosphere and comfort in a period environment

☎ 0974 967053
📠 0974 967714
✉ lamola@mediatek.it.com
via A. Cilento 2
84048 CASTELLABATE (Salerno)
Ref map 10, E2

A3, battipaglia exit, then S.S. 18 as far as the turn off for Agropoli, then S.S. 267 as far as the turning for Castellabate
5 rooms, 3 suites; **££**

areas. The owners manage the hotel and also the restaurant which is only open in the evenings and serves mainly fish dishes using old recipes.

RECOMMENDED IN THE AREA

RESTAURANT:
Due Fratelli, *Santa Maria di Castellabate*

VISIT:
Rocca Cilento Castle, Agropoli

Villa Sirio

By the sea, close to the little fishing port

☎ 0974 960162
📠 0974 961099
✉ villa.sirio@costacilento.it
via Lungomare De Simone 15
località Santa Maria di Castellabate
84072 CASTELLABATE (Salerno)
Ref map 10, E2

A3, Battipaglia exit, then S.S. 18 as far as the turn for Agropoli, then S.S. 267 to the turning for Santa Maria di Castellabate
14 rooms, 5 suites; **££**
Credit cards: AE VISA SI Ⓞ

In a little bay with a typical small fishing port, where the road ends and on a rock jutting out into the sea, stands an elegant building dating from 1904. Originally a private villa belonging to an ancient Neapolitan family, it was transformed into a hotel and opened as such in May 1997. The bedrooms are large, with a view over the gulf, and have light-coloured stylish furnishings, small tables with decorative cloths, matching bedspreads and curtains. They are equipped with air conditioning, mini-bars, modem and fax power points and safes. The bathrooms have showers and hydromassage baths and hair-dryers. The communal rooms have particularly good-quality details, with original paintings from the early 20th century and lovely floors. In addition the hotel offers guests a panoramic terrace, a wide jetty, restaurant, piano bar and garage.

RECOMMENDED IN THE AREA

RESTAURANT:
Ceppo, *Agropoli*

LOCAL SPECIALITIES:
Mortella *(myrtle)* mozzarella *cheese, goats' cheeses; extra virgin olive oil*

Della Baia

'A home for each guest'

☎ 0823 721344
✆ 0823 721556
via dell'Erica
località Baia Domizia
81030 CELLOLE (Caserta)
Ref map 9, F6

A1, Cassino exit, S.S. 630 for Formia for 30 km, then left in the direction of Naples as far as the turning for Cellole
56 rooms; ££
Credit cards: AE VISA SI ⓘ, bancomat

RECOMMENDED IN THE AREA

RESTAURANTS:
Italo, Sirio *and* Il Garro e la Volpe, *Formia*

VISIT:
Teano

*T*he owners are three sisters of Venetian origin who were born and lived in Rome, and they love to describe this hotel as 'a home for each guest'. The building faces the sea and is typically Mediterranean, white both outside and inside, with floors made of terracotta. Period and modern furniture go together beautifully in the bright communal rooms. Everywhere there are arrangements of fresh flowers. In the bedrooms, too, there are some period-style furnishings, The bathroom tiles are hand-painted. The food is carefully prepared under the direction of a chef of 24 years' standing who comes from the Alfredo Beltrame school and the famous Toulà restaurant. The hotel has a private beach.

Villa De Pertis

A 17th-century residence in a quiet location

☎ and ✆ 0823 866619
via Ponti 30, località San Giorgio
81010 DRAGONI (Caserta)
Ref map 9, F7

A1, Capua exit, S.S. 7 for Capua, turning for Aiazzo, then for Alvignano, go on as far as Dragoni
5 rooms, 2 suites; £
Credit cards: AE VISA SI

*T*his old residence with its 17th-century Neapolitan architecture has now been transformed into a hotel. Its little courtyard and pergola open onto the main square in the historic centre of Dragoni. A lovely staircase goes up to the bedrooms, a staircase that appears to be both inside and outside the house.

The hotel has only five bedrooms, all large, with valuable antique furniture and some with antique stucco work and frescos. The bathrooms are of various sizes and are quite practical. The pretty and welcoming dining room has been created in a delightful area and is pleasingly furnished. There are many communal areas, some with fireplaces.

The owner participates in the day-to-day running of the hotel with great devotion.

RECOMMENDED IN THE AREA

RESTAURANT:
Il Generale, *Caiazzo*

VISIT:
Cathedral, Caiazzo

Hostaria di Bacco

RECOMMENDED IN THE AREA

RESTAURANT:
Cambusa, *Positano*

LOCAL SPECIALITIES:
Rosoli *and* limoncello *liqueurs; classified Costa d'Amalfi wine; sandals and clothes from Positano; cameos and coral from Ravello*

VISIT:
Parish church of Santa Maria Assunta, Positano

A haven for poets

☎ 089 830360
🖷 089 830352
via G.B. Lama 9
84010 FURORE (Salerno)
Ref map 10, D1-2
A3, Castellammare di Stabia fork,
then S.S. 366 for Pimonte-Agerola
19 rooms, 2 suites; **£**
Credit cards: AE VISA SI ⓓ, bancomat

*F*rom the coast the horizon widens as one goes up and around bends, past terraces and through little villages surrounded by natural beauty.

The hotel is 450 metres above sea level, with the Gulf of Salerno below. Originally it was a simple *trattoria* with a pergola that served as a place of rest and refreshment for people on foot or riding donkeys up the Agerola Pass. Nowadays it is composed of little Mediterranean-style buildings that are reached along paths and short flights of steps cut into gardens of orange and olive trees. The bedrooms are large and all have terraces. The bathrooms have showers and are quite big with white majolica tiles and yellow fittings. The communal rooms are simple but attractive. Buffet breakfast includes local breads and specialities. The restaurant serves simple natural food. The hotel is family run with great care.

Villa Angelica

RECOMMENDED IN THE AREA

RESTAURANTS:
Da Peppina di Renato *and* Il Melograno, *Forio*

Austrian cakes in a Mediterranean environment

☎ 081 994524 🖷 081 980184
via IV Novembre 28
80076 LACCO AMENO, ISCHIA (Napoli)
Ref map 12, A1
A1, Napoli exit, ferry for Lacco Ameno
20 rooms; **£**
Credit cards: AE VISA SI ⓓ, bancomat

*T*his is a pretty Mediterranean-style building in a quiet road a short distance from the sea and from the commercial centre of Lacco Ameno. The bedrooms are of various sizes, all with terraces and majolica floors, and they are well looked after and clean. There are fans, and televisions are available on request. All the bathrooms have showers and hair-dryers. The charming communal rooms look onto the thermal swimming pool and the little garden, and they are delightfully furnished. Breakfast includes cakes made by the lady of the house who comes from Austria. The hotel is on two floors and has an indoor swimming pool and a small massage room. Bicycles may be hired. Guests are welcomed very kindly.

Certosa di San Giacomo

Modern comfort in a medieval monastery

☎ 081 8240932
📠 081 8249743
✉ certosasangiacomo@octava.it
via Nazionale 1
83023 LAURO (Avellino)
Ref map 10, D2
Al, A30, Nola exit, then follow the signs
for Lauro
45 rooms, 10 suites; **££**
Credit cards: AE VISA SI ⓪, bancomat

RECOMMENDED IN THE AREA

RESTAURANTS:
Antica Trattoria Martella, *Avellino;*
Valleverde, *Atripalda*

*T*his imposing building is surrounded by a large park and has a very long history. On the edge of Lauro, a village with a medieval layout, the hotel began life at the end of the 12th century as a monastery. Then it was elevated to the rank of abbey, and after that became a splendid country residence. There has been very precise restoration work, and this has conserved the beauty of the rooms. These are now embellished with elegant modern furnishings that blend harmoniously with the historic building. The bedrooms are comfortable with satellite television, safes and video recorders. The very comfortable bathrooms are equipped with hair-dryers. One of the three restaurants for the use of guests is in the beautiful cloisters at the heart of the building. There is an abundant choice of dishes ranging from local specialities to national and international cuisine. As far as attentive and willing service and comfort are concerned, this is an ideal place to stay, whether guests are travelling for pleasure or for work.

Casa Raffaele Conforti

A holiday with a touch of class in a 19th-century palace

☎ 089 853547
📠 089 852048
✉ casaconforti@amalfinet.it
via Casa Mannini 10
84010 MAIORI (Salerno)
Ref map 10, D2
A3, Vietri sul Mare exit, S.S. 163
as far as Maiori
7 rooms, 2 suites; **££/£££**
Credit cards: AE VISA SI ⓪, bancomat

ceilings, and a few rooms preserve the *Costaioli* frescos by painters of the school of Maiori in the 19th century.

Meals may be taken in one of the numerous restaurants in the area that have a special arrangement with the hotel, with no limitations or pre-arranged set menus. The hotel also has a private beach and belongs to the *Abitare la Storia* chain.

*O*n the second floor of a noble 19th-century palace in the oldest street in Maiori, the doors open on to a residence that conserves the precious and romantic features of a lovely house overlaid with the patina of age.

This is now a little hotel that has been completely restructured and has seven bedrooms and two suites, all with terraces. The rooms are big and are steeped in tradition. They have period floors, high

RECOMMENDED IN THE AREA

RESTAURANTS:
Mammato; Eolo *and* Da Gemma, *Amalfi*

Taverna del capitano

Very imaginative cooking and the gentle sound of waves breaking on the shore

☎ 081 8081028 🖷 081 8081892
piazza delle Sirene 10
località Marina del Cantone
80061 MASSA LUBRENSE (Napoli)
Ref map 10, D1
A3, towards Castellammare di Stabia, S.S.
145, turning for Sant' Agata sui Due Golfi, go
on for Marina del Cantone
15 rooms; **££**
Credit cards: AE VISA SI ⓪

RECOMMENDED IN THE AREA

RESTAURANT:
Antico Francischiello-Da Peppino

LOCAL SPECIALITIES:
*Products from Sorrento peninsula and Amalfi coast:
extra virgin olive oil,* limoncello *liqueur, diary products*

VISIT:
Church of Santa Maria delle Grazie, Massa Lubrense

*M*arina del Cantone is a corner of paradise between the sea and the citrus orchards. It is a tiny village that was once inhabited by fishermen, and consists of white houses, narrow streets, characteristic little vistas, the beach and some cliffs. One of the old buildings has been restructured and turned into a restaurant with hotel rooms, and is lovingly managed by Captain Salvatore and his family. The small building almost sinks its foundations into the sea. The rooms, although very simple, are welcoming and attractive, nearly all with a superb view over the little bay. The cooking is carried out with skill and imagination, with dishes inspired by tradition and using the local products. The family, being very industrious, relaxes by preparing wonderful products in oil, preserves and jams, and these are served for breakfast along with home-made cakes and *brioche*.

Don Alfonso 1890

Where the love of cooking becomes an art

☎ 081 8780026
🖷 081 5330226
corso Sant'Agata 11
località Sant'Agata sui Due Golfi
80064 MASSA LUBRENSE (Napoli)
Ref map 10, D1
A3, towards Castellammare di Stabia,
S.S. 145, turning for Sant' Agata sui Due
Golfi, go on for Marina del Cantone
9 rooms, 2 suites; **££/£££**
Credit cards: AE VISA SI ⓪

The calmly refined elegance of the interior is shown in the linen tablecloths and the simple design of the silver, and again in the bedrooms and communal areas. Here the patterned fabrics of the sofas and bedcovers in colours ranging from pale to spring hues beautifully matches the valuable antique furniture. Livia and Alfonso have dedicated their lives to this work, and in each part of the little villa their love and attention to every detail are evident.

*T*he garden that surrounds the little pink-coloured villa is the first sign of the care with which Livia and Alfonso express their hospitality. Alfonso, cook of the year in 1999, astonishes guests with the quality of his dishes in which love of cooking has become an art. Meanwhile Livia is the perfect lady of the house as she welcomes guests to the hotel or to their famous restaurant.

RECOMMENDED IN THE AREA

RESTAURANTS:
Antico Francischiello-Da Peppino;
I Quattro Passi, *Nerano*

$\mathcal{M}$ercure

In a period mansion in the historic centre

☎ 081 5529500
📠 081 5529509
via Depretis 123
80133 NAPOLI (NAPLES)
Ref map 10, D1
A1, San Giovanni a Teduccio exit,
then towards the port
85 rooms; £££
Credit cards: AE VISA SI Ⓞ, bancomat

$\mathcal{T}$he hotel is in an entirely refurbished mansion with pleasing architecture that dates from the early 20th century. It is in a central position and is a suitable place whether for business or holiday travellers. The bedrooms all have fitted carpets and pleasing modern furniture in wood, as well as televisions and mini-bars. The small bathrooms are modern and very practical, equipped with hair-dryers and complimentary toiletry sets. The communal rooms are bright and welcoming.

Breakfast is served as a buffet, with plenty of typical Neapolitan specialities. There is room service until almost midnight. In the hall there is an Internet connection available for guests' use. Uniformed members of staff welcome guests kindly.

RECOMMENDED IN THE AREA

RESTAURANT:
Trattoria Medina, *via Medina*

LOCAL SPECIALITIES:
Buffalo mozzarella *cheeses;* sfogliatelle *pasta;*
pastiere *and* babà *cakes*

$\mathcal{P}$arker

*In an old hotel with a splendid view
over the gulf of Naples*

☎ 081 7612474
📠 081 663527
✉ ghparker@tin.it
corso Vittorio Emanuele 135
80121 NAPOLI (NAPLES)
Ref map 10, D1
A1 as far as Napoli (Naples), *tangenziale*
(by-pass), exit 9 for via Cilea
83 rooms, 10 suites; £££
Credit cards: AE VISA SI Ⓞ

$\mathcal{I}$n the heart of the city, in a panoramic position across the hillside and a few steps away from elegant piazza Martiri, is an old Neapolitan hotel that has been completely refurbished.

The rooms are large and well furnished in the Empire style, and have pastel-coloured walls bordered with white stucco, lovely upholstery, and satellite televisions and mini-bars. The large white marble bathrooms are well fitted and very practical, with hair dryers, complimentary toiletry sets and soft towels. The restaurant and breakfast room are on the top floor: this has a wonderful view and extends into a lovely terrace. A piano bar named 'Bidder's' has been recently inaugurated for guests. The reception and communal rooms on the ground floor are large and well furnished.

Members of staff are uniformed and professional, but they are very kind and not over-formal. The hotel has conference rooms and a garage.

RECOMMENDED IN THE AREA

RESTAURANT:
Vadinchenia, *via Pantano 21*

LOCAL SPECIALITIES:
*Antiques in the shops in and around piazza Martiri;
ties from via Riviera di Chiaia*

Villa Medici

An atmosphere of the 1900s

☎ and ✆ 081 7623949/081 7623040
✉ info@sea-hotels.com
via Nuova Bagnoli 550
80124 NAPOLI (NAPLES)
Ref map 10, D1
A1 as far as Napoli (Naples), *tangenziale* (by-pass), Agnano exit
15 rooms, 15 apartments; ££
Credit cards: 🆎 🆅🆂🅰 🆂🅸 ⓄⒹ, bancomat

*T*his is an early 20th-century villa in the Fuorigrotta district which has been restructured while remaining faithful to the original architecture. It is suitable for both holiday and business travellers, with hotel accommodation or residence in apartments for a minimum period of a week. The bedrooms have practical furniture, bathrooms with showers, hair-dryers and heated towel rails.

All the apartments are fitted with kitchen areas and guests may order meals from a nearby *trattoria*. There is an open-air swimming pool with hydromassage, plus a delightful garden and a free car park.

RECOMMENDED IN THE AREA

RESTAURANT:
Giuseppe a Mare, *via F. Russo, and* Poeta, *piazza S. Di Giacome 133, Posillipo*

Casa Pixos

RECOMMENDED IN THE AREA

RESTAURANTS:
Perbacco; Cantina del Marchese, *Marina di Camerota*

LOCAL SPECIALITIES:
Mozarella *cheese with myrtle; goats' cheeses; extra virgin olive oil*

VISIT:
Blue Grotto of Palinurodi Palinuro

Facing the limpid Sea of Palinuro

☎ and ✆ 0974 973792
✉ pixos@usa.net
via Canto del Gelso 22
**84066 PISCIOTTA
(Salerno)**
Ref map 10, E3
A3, Battipaglia exit, then S.S. 18 as far as Procoio, turning for Castellammare di Velia, go on as far as Pisciotta
4 rooms, 1 suite, 3 apartments; £
Credit cards not accepted

*S*ituated in the historic centre of Pisciotta, this 17th-century building faces the Palinuro sea. Each bedroom enjoys a panoramic view. There are also small apartments, with small kitchens, and these have been restructured in a way that is faithful to the original building. The areas created out of the old architecture are charmingly irregular and skilfully make the most of uneven surfaces, niches, sloping roofs and wooden beams. The result is an attractive interior full of character that opens on to a charming panorama. The furniture is very carefully chosen: modern pieces alternate with a few antiques. The owner is a sculptor and has completed the decorations with works of art. The exterior is a triumph of Mediterranean vegetation, hibiscus, shady pergolas and vivid bougainvillea on terraces and in the hanging garden.

Forum

A few steps away from the main archaeological sites

☎ 081 8501170
🖷 081 8506132
via Roma 99
80045 POMPEI (Napoli)
Ref map 10, D1
A3, Pompei exit, follow the signs for the
scavi (excavation sites)
24 rooms; **££**
Credit cards: AE VISA SI ⓄⒹ, bancomat

RECOMMENDED IN THE AREA

RESTAURANTS:
Da Andrea *and* Hostaria del Gallo Nero

LOCAL SPECIALITIES:
Coral and cameos produced in the nearby city of Torre del Greco

VISIT:
Excavation sites, Pompei

A short distance from the entrance to the excavation sites and from the cathedral, the hotel is in the heart of the town, but in a peaceful corner sheltered from the intense traffic. The building is modern, with large bedrooms that are pleasantly furnished with pastel coloured modern furniture and carefully chosen upholstery. Each room is fitted with air conditioning and a ventilator, television, electronic safe and mini-bar. The bathrooms are large, all with windows, hair-dryers and complimentary toiletry sets, and many also have bath-tubs. The sitting room is not big but is comfortable, and includes the reception area. The dining and breakfast room looks on to a very well tended garden with a raised terrace. Breakfast is served as a buffet. The owners run the hotel themselves, and guests are warmly welcomed. Use of the garage is included in the price of accommodation, and there is a roof garden equipped with a solarium.

Margherita

A terrace overlooking the sea, and surrounded by citrus orchards

☎ 089 874227 🖷 089 874628
✉ suelac@tin.it
via Umberto I 170
84010 PRAIANO (Salerno)
Ref map 10, D1-2
A3; fork for Castellammare di Stabia,
go on as far as Vico Equense, then S.S. 269
for Positano, then Amalfi coast road as far as
Praiano
28 rooms, 9 suites; **££**
Credit cards: AE VISA SI ⓄⒹ, bancomat

*T*he white, Mediterranean-style building stands out in the quiet, secluded street and has a delightful view over the gulf. The bedrooms are large and bright and in some there are wrought-iron beds and pieces of antique furniture. The whole effect is charmingly simple, and everything is very clean. The medium-sized bathrooms are well kept.

The communal area has large windows and corners for different uses, and is at one and the same time reception, restaurant, bar and sitting room. It is very light and opens on to a raised and well equipped terrace. The hotel is surrounded by a garden of citrus fruits: oranges and lemons are always on the breakfast table, together with home-made cakes. The restaurant is open only to hotel guests and the food is carefully prepared with a homely flavour. The hotel has a pay garage and a free parking area.

RECOMMENDED IN THE AREA

RESTAURANTS:
Open Gate; Brace, *Veltica Maggiore*

LOCAL SPECIALITIES:
Lemons and limoncello *liqueur*

VISIT:
Parish church of San Luca, Praiano

$\mathcal{V}$illa San Michele

Deep in the countryside, on a sheer cliff

☎ and 🖷 089 872237
✉ smichele@starnet.it
via Carusiello 2, località Castiglione
84010 RAVELLO (Salerno)
Ref map 10, D2
A3, Vietri sul Mare exit, Amalfi coast road for
Amalfi, turn off for Ravello
12 rooms; ££
Credit cards: AE VISA SI ◑, bancomat

RECOMMENDED IN THE AREA

RESTAURANTS:
Garden *and* Salvatore

$\mathcal{T}$his is a typical Mediterranean-style villa, white and pretty with arched windows, that is constructed on the edge of cliffs with a sheer drop to the sea. Only a gate on the road tells you that you have arrived. The villa is below the main road and you get there along little driveways under shaded pergolas, halting at panoramic viewpoints or on the little equipped terraces. Grass and flowers surround the villa, which faces the gulf.

Originally a private house, nowadays it is a hotel with bedrooms that are all different but every room has a view of the sea and some have a little terrace.

In place of a headboard for the bed, one room has a porthole with a lovely view.

The rooms are bright and cheerful, with Vietri majolica floors in white and blue and with attractive modern furnishings. The bathrooms are small but well presented. There is a pretty restaurant, but breakfast may also be taken on the terrace. A large garden slopes down to the sea and a wide jetty has been dug out between the rocks. Guests are welcomed kindly and thoughtfully in family style, with the spontaneous friendliness that is typical of southern Italians.

$\mathcal{F}$iorenza

Rooms with a view

☎ and 🖷 089 338800
✉ fiorealb@tin.it
via Trento 145
84161 SALERNO
Ref map 10, D2
A3, Salerno Centro exit, in the direction of the sea front going towards the south
30 rooms; ££
Credit cards: AE VISA SI ◑, bancomat

RECOMMENDED IN THE AREA

RESTAURANT:
Al Cenacolo, *piazza Alfano 14*

LOCAL SPECIALITIES:
Buffalo mozzarella *cheeses and quality dairy products;* limoncello *liqueur from the Amalfi coast; ceramics from Vietri*

VISIT:
Duomo *(cathedral); churches of Santa Maria delle Grazie, del Crocifisso and di San Pietro a Corte; Amalfi*

$\mathcal{T}$his hotel is a few steps from the sea front and is situated about three kilometres from the historic centre, in a modern area of the city. It has been completely renovated and is in a building that also houses apartments. The rooms have a comfortable appearance and all have balconies with sea views, good fitted carpets and modern furnishings, safes, mini-bars and televisions. The bathrooms are equipped with hair-dryers, heated towel rails and complimentary toiletry sets. They have been recently refurbished and are very practical. The public rooms are small but welcoming, well cared for and bright. The hotel also has a conference room. Breakfast is served as a buffet. The uniformed members of staff welcome guests very kindly. The hotel is on one upper floor of the building and has no lift.

La Minervetta

Dine on the terrace on the sheer cliff above the gulf of Sorrento

☎ 081 8073069
🖷 081 8773033
via Capo 25
80067 SORRENTO (Napoli)
Ref map 10, D1
A3, fork for Castellammare di Stabia, go on on the S.S. 145 as far as Sorrento
12 rooms; **££**
Credit cards: AE VISA SI ◍, bancomat

RECOMMENDED IN THE AREA

RESTAURANT:
Caruso

LOCAL SPECIALITIES:
Local crafts

VISIT:
Byzantine church in the Cattolica area

To anyone going along the coast road the hotel is practically invisible: the building is below the level of the road, clinging onto the cliffs and overhanging rocks on the Gulf of Sorrento. The panoramic position is very beautiful, with giddy drops from the hotel directly over the village and the fishing port, making it one of the most charming corners in Sorrento.

The bedrooms are spacious with very modern furnishings and large bathrooms with windows, nearly all with baths and equipped with hair-dryers. There is a large restaurant used in winter with big windows and traditional furnishing. In summer meals are served outside on the lovely terrace. The cooking is delicious and homely, with traditional dishes. The hotel is run in a kind, family style with friendly concern to give good service. Parking is on the hotel roof – that is, on the level of the road – and it is included in the price of accommodation.

Capo la Gala

A hotel carved out of the rock

☎ 081 8015758 🖷 081 8798747
S.S. Sorrentina al km 14
via L. Serio 8
80069 VICO EQUENSE (Napoli)
Ref map 10, D1
A3, Castellammare di Stabia, go on for Vico Equense
18 rooms; **£££**
Credit cards: AE VISA SI ◍, bancomat

RECOMMENDED IN THE AREA

RESTAURANTS:
Torre del Saraceno, *Stiano;* Nonna Rosa, *Pietrpiano;* Caruso, *Sorrento;* Don Alfonso 1890, *Sant' Agata sui Due Golfi*

LOCAL SPECIALITIES:
Limoncello *liqueur; citrus-flavoured cakes; ceramics*

The hotel stands above the sea, built out of the rock face, and looking over the Gulf of Sorrento. There are unforgettable views and sunsets, and romantic breakfasts on the balconies of the bedrooms that all face the sea. The rooms are light with simple bamboo furniture, ceramic floors, and upholstery in the colours of the sea and the sunshine. The predominant material is stone, which frames the bedroom windows, forms the walls of the communal rooms, and alternates with cement in the ceilings as a reminder that we are on a mountain. Gardens and terraces have been constructed out of the rock around the hotel to make a stay here yet more enjoyable.

There is a lovely swimming pool with sulphurous mineral water that provides an alternative to sea bathing.

Apulia

*Above: the Gargano sea;
left: Castel del Monte,
built on the orders and
possibly according to the
architectural design of
Federico II*

Apulia (Puglia) stretches eastwards, with the unmistakable outline of the Salentine peninsula confined on three sides by the Adriatic and the Ionian seas. Its physical characteristics are simple: it consists largely of an enormous lump of limestone. The 800 kilometres of coastline are mostly low and linear, apart from Gargano and the Otrantino coast. Few rivers are visible above ground but many flow underground, especially in the Murge mountains.

This mainly agricultural and seafaring region leaves unusually powerful and varied memories. These include the Romanesque cathedral of Trani silhouetted against the sea with its very high bell tower. There is also Federico II' s castle – white, symmetric and elegant – that from Castel del Monte looks over the rolling meadows and olive groves of the Murge. There is the sunny farmland of Tavoliere and the low terraces of the Murge mountains, thickly covered with olive and almond trees, vines, orchards and fields of vegetables. The big headland of Gargano offers sandy beaches between sheer cliffs, charming villages, Mediterranean vegetation, lakes and forests. In places like Monte Sant' Angelo and the remains of the lost Siponto,

visitors can enjoy the countryside and beaches without renouncing art and history. Then there is the thick pinewood of Salento and the spectacular stretch with cliffs and sea grottoes between Otranto and Sant Maria di Leuca; and the long Ionian coastline with the port of Taranto and the white village of Gallipoli jutting into the sea.

In the Murge mountains, little conical *trulli* houses are scattered around the countryside; they are more concentrated at Alberobello, around Gravina and Altamura and the grottoes of Castellana. Cathedrals in the Apulian Romanesque style dating from the happy Norman and Swabian period (with Byzantine flavours) – at Trani, Bari, Braletta, Bitonto, Ruvo di Puglia, Lucera, Troia and Otranto – can provide an itinerary for cultural holidays. Even the smallest towns, like Barletta, Martina Franca or Venosa, have artistic and historical interest. Churches rise out of the labyrinth of the old city of Bari or in the exuberant baroque of Lecce. Apulia has a generous Mediterranean, farming spirit and a refined culture; and the region displays both these characteristics in the best of its hospitality.

*A*bbondanza

Among olive groves and oak woods and near to the typical trulli *dwellings*

☎ and 🖷 080 4325762
✉ abbond@tin.it
contrada Lama Colonna 5
70011 ALBEROBELLO (Bari)
Ref map 11, D6
A14, Gioia del Colle exit, S.S. 604
for Noci and Alberobello
3 rooms, 3 apartments; ££
Credit cards not accepted

RECOMMENDED IN THE AREA

RESTAURANT:
Il Poeta contadino

LOCAL SPECIALITIES:
For sale from the farm: conserves, oil, wine, taralli *and other biscuits*

VISIT:
Area of trulli *dwellings; Castellana grottoes*

*T*his farm business is situated in the heart of the Barsento Nature Reserve, 450 metres above sea level and dominating the valley below. A recently built construction enlarges the conical stone *trulli* buildings, traditional to the Apulia (Puglia) region, that date back to the 17th century. It is all set within characteristic local countryside, surrounded by oak trees and big olive groves and completed by an old wood-burning stove and panoramic terraces. The interior is rustic and welcoming: there are unplastered stone walls around simple wooden furniture and a large fireplace, also in stone, that heats one of the two communal rooms. The choice of furnishings recreates the family atmosphere of a real country house. Guests are served with local dishes and wines.

*C*olle del Sole

In luxuriant countryside in the Apulian Murgia

☎ 080 4321814/080 4325649
🖷 080 4321370
✉ colledelsole@mailbox.media.it
via Indipendenza 63
70011 ALBEROBELLO (Bari)
Ref map 11, D6
A14, Gioia del Colle, S.S. 604 for
Noci and Alberobello
37 rooms; ££/£££
Credit cards: AE VISA SI ①, bancomat

RECOMMENDED IN THE AREA

RESTAURANT:
Il Trullo d'Oro

LOCAL SPECIALITIES:
Hand-made almond sweets and cakes

*I*n the immediate vicinity of the historic and fascinating *trulli* quarter of conical stone buildings, this modern hotel is run kindly and attentively to guarantee a delightful stay. It is furnished in a practical modern style, and has attractive and comfortable rooms, some recently fitted with air conditioning and double glazing.

The furniture is of light wood, the bathrooms very small (some with baths) but with hair-dryers and

quite practical; some have windows and other – the new ones – do not.

The restaurant and bar/sitting room are very simple but neat and clean. Breakfast is a buffet, while the hotel restaurant offers delicious menus with local and national dishes. The garden is equipped with outdoor furniture and there is bar service on the veranda and under the pergola.

*B*osco di Mudonato

Rediscover the countryside in a reserve abundant in greenery

☎ and ✆ 099 9704597
via per Salice Salentino, km 3
74020 AVETRANA (Taranto)
Ref map 11, E7
A1, to the end, S.S. 7, after Taranto, S.S. 7, after Manduria turning for Avetrana, then Salice Salentino direction
10 rooms, 4 apartments; **£/££**
Credit cards not accepted

A large estate with its own olive groves, orchards and vineyards surrounds this old fortified farmhouse. The guest quarters, set in a wood of oak trees and Mediterranean vegetation, have the pronounced typical architecture of period buildings: long and low with arches and white walls with wooden ceilings and beams. The furnishings are the rustic kind, typical of a region that is linked with the earth, with fireplaces in some of the rooms, giving them a welcoming family atmosphere. The four two-roomed apartments are equipped with a number of comforts. A stay here gives guests direct contact with nature and the historic beauty around. Guests may also enjoy the flavours of this region in the local dishes served by the restaurant of the *agriturismo* (farm accommodation).

Recommended in the area

Restaurant:
Il Piccolo Mondo, *Francavilla Fontana*

Local Specialities:
Ceramics from Grottaglie

Visit:
The procession, horse-race and medieval tournament during the first ten days of August at Oria; Manduria; Fonte Pliniano Grotto

Salsello

The coast offers the delights of life by the sea, and the hinterland is full of interesting destinations for art tours and historical relics of whole civilisations: these range from prehistory to the archaeological excavations of Magna Grecia, to Romanesque churches, and to the journeys of Emperor Federico II – always surrounded by the delights of natural beauty. For a place to pause and rest visitors can choose this modern hotel situated by the shore, with rooms that mostly overlook the sea. The bright and airy bedrooms are furnished with modern furniture. The hotel has large spaces for communal activities: reception hall, sitting room and restaurant. There is also a reserved beach, swimming pool and a garden with gazebo.

In an old medieval village by the sea amongst history, art and natural beauty

☎ 080 3955953
🖷 080 3955951
via V. Siciliani 31-33
70052 BISCEGLIE (Bari)
Ref map 11, C5
A14, Trani exit, then S.S. 16, turning for Bisceglie
52 rooms, 3 suites; **££**
Credit cards: AE VISA SI ⊕, bancomat

RECOMMENDED IN THE AREA

RESTAURANTS:
Torrente Amico, *Trani*;
Bufi *and* Borgo Antico, *Molfetta*

LOCAL SPECIALITIES:
Extra virgin olive oil; classified wines; pasta; diary products; local cakes and sweets; conserves

VISIT:
Cathedral; museum of civic archaeology housed in the former monastery of Santa Croce

$\mathcal{R}$elais Le Jardin

In a garden among flowering terraces

☎ 080 4966300 🖷 080 4865520
✉ lejardin@mail.media.it
contrada Scamardella 59
70013 CASTELLANA GROTTE (Bari)
Ref map 11, C6
A14, Goia del Colle exit, then S.S. 604 for Noci, next Putignano and finally Monopoli direction as far as Castellana Grotte
10 rooms; ££
Credit cards: ᴀᴇ ᴠɪsᴀ sɪ ⓓ, bancomat

$\mathcal{T}$his is a romantic and elegant little building in the Mediterranean style that stands out in open countryside. It is surrounded by a green garden adorned with terracotta vases of lovely flowering plants, and is in a strategic position a short distance from the Castellana grottoes and the sea, and near Alberobello. The hotel's bedrooms open onto terraces covered with flowers even in winter. They are light and comfortable and furnished tastefully in rustic fashion. The communal rooms are equally welcoming. The restaurant is in a conservatory with large windows during winter, and in summer serves meals in the garden under gazebos. The food is carefully prepared and presented. The proprietors have run the hotel since 1993, and their family looks after it.

RECOMMENDED IN THE AREA

RESTAURANTS:
Fontanina *and* Taverna degli Artisti-da Ernest e Rosa

VISIT:
Castellana grottoes

$\mathcal{V}$illa La Meridiana

In a 19th-century villa by the sea

☎ 0833 758242 🖷 0833 758246
✉ atcaroli@tin.it
lungomare Colombo 61
località Marina di Leuca
73030 CASTRIGNANO DEL CAPO (Lecce)
Ref map 11, E8
A14, Bari Sud exit, *superstrada* (dual carriageway) 16 and 379 towards Brindisi, the 613 towards Lecce, then the 16 Maglie turning, S.S. 275 as far as the turning for Castrignano del Capo
1 apartment; £££
Credit cards: ᴀᴇ ᴠɪsᴀ ⓓ, bancomat

$\mathcal{S}$teep and gentle slopes alternate on this beautiful coast, rocks give way to beaches of pebbles or fine sand, the sea is clear and the area is full of history. Many of the grottoes that open out along the coast can only be reached by boat; they were shelters for prehistoric man. Roman ruins are everywhere here. Lovely late 19th-century villas stand in succession along the shore and in one of these, a villa with slightly oriental curved architecture that faces the sea surrounded by a large garden, is a two-bedroomed apartment with double bathroom, sitting room and little kitchen. The apartment is furnished with original early 20th-century pieces and has wrought-iron beds with canopies. The beach in front of the house is reserved, and the garden offers shelter and cool. There are bicycles for hire.

RECOMMENDED IN THE AREA

RESTAURANT:
Re Sole, *Gagliano del Capo*

LOCAL SPECIALITIES:
Extra virgin olive oil; classified wines; home-made pasta

313

$\mathcal{M}$asseria Salamina

A 17th-century building constructed as a defence against Saracen pirates

☎ 080 4897307
🖷 080 4898582
località Pezze di Greco
72010 FASANO (Brindisi)
Ref map 11, D6
A14, Bari Nord exit, *superstrada* (dual carriageway) 16 towards Brindisi, Fasano exit
7 rooms, 8 apartments; **££**
Credit cards: 💳 💳, bancomat

RECOMMENDED IN THE AREA

RESTAURANT:
Coccodrillo

LOCAL SPECIALITIES:
To buy from the farm: extra virgin olive oil, jam, fried beans and cacioricotta *cheese*

$\mathcal{L}$ow sandy shores and rich fertile ground excited the greed of the Saracens, and the people defended themselves from invasion by shutting themselves inside fortified, self-sufficient buildings.

The farmstead originated in this way. The nucleus was constructed in the 17th century and in the following centuries changes were made, but these did not alter the appearance of the original. The building has crenellated battlements which in the lower part open into arches recalling the architecture of the shore on the other side of the Mediterranean.

It was also the headquarters of the Allies during the Second World War.

These days there are seven guest bedrooms and eight apartments with spacious comfortable rooms. A room with lovely proportions and dimensions houses a restaurant. All around is olive cultivation with big ancient trees that are up to 400 years old and, for the use of guests, a garden, *bocce* (bowls) pitch, children's playground, archery and bicycles.

$\mathcal{L}$e Sirenuse

A pleasant stay facing the sea

☎ 0833 202536 🖷 0833 202539
✉ atcaroli@tin.it
litoranea Gallipoli-Santa Maria di Leuca
73014 GALLIPOLI (Lecce)
Ref map 11, E8
A14 to the end, S.S. 7, after Taranto, S.S. 7, after Manduria turning for Avetrana, then S.S. 174 for Nardò and Gallipoli
120 rooms; **££**
Credit cards: 💳 💳 💳 💳, bancomat

RECOMMENDED IN THE AREA

RESTAURANT:
Marechino

LOCAL SPECIALITIES:
Craft work; nasse *wicker baskets; local fishing equipment and baskets*

VISIT:
Castle and cathedral

$\mathcal{G}$allipoli is outlined on the horizon with the old village stretching into the sea, a tongue of land linked to the mainland by a bridge. This large, characteristic hotel stands on the coast a few kilometres from the city. It is modern and functional and has big rooms with balconies and bright furniture. The bathrooms are neat and practical and all the showers have hydromassage. Communal areas are large, in several light rooms that have wicker and rush furniture. There are many recreational facilities: cycling, archery, table tennis, tennis, beach volleyball, swimming, gymnastics (with equipment for exercises in the pine wood), riding and walks. There are also a reserved beach and a baby-sitting service.

*I*l Vignaletto

In the heart of the valley of the trulli *dwellings*

☎ 080 4490354 🖷 080 4490387
✉ vignaletto@peg.it
via Mingo di Tata 1
74015 MARTINA FRANCA (Taranto)
Ref map 11, D6

A14, Bari Nord exit, *superstrada* (dual carriageway) 16 towards Brindisi, Fasano exit, S.S.172, Taranto direction as far as Martina Franca
7 rooms, 1 apartment; **££**
Credit cards: 🏧 🆂🅸

*T*here are panoramas of unforgettable charm that remain impressed on the memory. The valley of the conical stone *trulli* dwellings is one of these: a magical balance where nature and human endeavour have created a wonderful landscape.

If a place is magical then the heart always wants to return there. This old farmstead on the hillside is in the centre of the valley, surrounded by woodland, and has guest rooms and a well-furnished little apartment. Following tradition the buildings are white, and their whiteness is reflected in an open-air swimming pool which has been constructed within the farm complex. There are also bicycles,

RECOMMENDED IN THE AREA

RESTAURANTS:
La Rotonda *and Murgetta;*
Il Poeta contadino, *Alberobello*

VISIT:
Ducal palace and collegiate church of San Martino, Martina Franca; Cisternino with its ancient oriental-looking village

horse riding, table tennis or walks in the woods. Not to be forgotten is the sea, or rather the Adriatic Sea and Gulf of Taranto. These are only 25 kilometres away and just a short distance away there are also the city and villages full of artistic treasures and interesting gastronomic routes.

$\mathcal{D}$ell'Erba

In the green of a large park

☎ 080 4301055 📠 080 4301639
✉ hoteldellerba@italiainrete.net
via dei Cedri 1
**74015 MARTINA FRANCA
(Taranto)**
Ref map 11, D6

A14, Bari Nord exit, *superstrada* (dual
carriageway) 16 towards Brindisi,
Fasano exit, S.S.172, Taranto
direction as far as Martina Franca
49 rooms; **£/££**
Credit cards: 🅰🅴 🆅🅸🆂🅰 🆂🅸 ⓪, bancomat

$\mathcal{T}$he old town has an elegant appearance – a place of 18th-century architecture with white houses adorned with graceful details, compact and full of charming corners, secluded squares and noble palaces.

The hotel stands in a fairly central position and is surrounded by the green of a large park. It consists of an old part with lovely architecture and beautiful rooms to which has been added a more modern wing. Its elegant bedrooms are tastefully furnished and so enchanting that it was one of the finalists for

RECOMMENDED IN THE AREA

RESTAURANTS:
La Rotonda; Murgetta, *San Paolo*

Hotel of the Year 1997 award. Naturally, it is equipped with all modern comforts. The communal rooms are welcoming and there is a wide range of leisure facilities for guests; apart from the beautiful garden there is also an open-air swimming pool, sauna, solarium, gym, and a children's playroom.

Il Frantoio

**A fortified farmstead in an
ancient olive grove**

☎ and 📠 0831 330276
✉ ilfrantoio@pugliaonline.it
S.S. 16 al km 874
72017 OSTUNI (Brindisi)
Ref map 11, D7

A14, Bari Sud exit, S.S. 379 as far as Fasano
and then S. S. 16
8 rooms; **££/£££**
Credit cards not accepted

RECOMMENDED IN THE AREA

RESTAURANTS:
Osteria del Tempo; Fornello da Ricci,
Ceglie Messapico

$\mathcal{C}$onstructed between the 16th and 19th centuries, this is a beautiful fortified farmstead whose first buildings date from the early 1500s. Successive additions increased and completed the whole complex up to the 19th century. An ancient olive grove on a hillside surrounds the farmstead and the trunks of the olive trees are like sculptures in the landscape. The sea, with a private beach, is a few minutes away by car. The organic farm supplies the kitchen with wild herbs and flowers for dishes, some even from medieval-inspired recipes. The bedrooms are all charming, furnished tastefully with antiques and embellished with many details. There are drawing rooms and parlours, a library, a dolls' room, children's playroom, ever-open bar and a kitchen where guests may prepare themselves snacks at any time of the day.

Lo Spagnulo

Among expanses of olive trees in a 17th-century building

☎ 0831 350209
📠 0831 333756
contrada Spagnulo
72017 OSTUNI (Brindisi)
Ref map 11, D7
A14, Bari Sud exit, S.S. 379 as far as Fasano and then S.S. 16 to Ostuni
36 rooms, 36 apartments; **£/££**
Credit cards: AE VISA SI ⓄⒹ

You go through groves of olive trees which are large and strong with twisted trunks that have been sculpted into interesting shapes over the years. Such wealth had to be protected and the farmsteads here are buildings for defence, work and habitation at one and the same time. This beautiful building dates from the 17th century. It has been restructured to provide accommodation in bedrooms and little apartments. The furnishing is rustic and simple. The farm business provides the restaurant with natural products for its regional dishes. Leisure facilities include use of the nearby private beach, a riding school and tennis court. There are bicycles for lovely excursions in the vicinity.

RECOMMENDED IN THE AREA

RESTAURANTS:
Spessite; Cibus, *Ceglie Messapico;*
Gino, *Montevicoli*

Masseria Salinola

A delightful contrast between the blue of the sky and the green of the old plants

☎ 0831 330683
📠 0831 308330
✉ agriturismosalinola@tin.it
contrada Salinola
72017 OSTUNI (Brindisi)
Ref map 11, D7
A14, Bari Sud exit, *superstrada* (dual carriageway) 379 to Fasano, then S. S. 16 to Ostuni
3 rooms, 7 apartments; **££**
Credit cards not accepted

This square white building has kept the lovely proportions of the fortified farmstead it was in the 17th century. Over time arches, balustrades, pergolas and little balconies suited to an open-air, sociable life have been added to the architecture that was originally designed for defensive purposes. But the whitewashed walls of the characteristic and attractive building are a wonderful contrast with the blue of the sky and the green of the ancient olive and pine trees around it. The bedrooms and small apartments that have been made under the ancient vaulted ceilings are simple, very clean and furnished in a practical way. The dining room and communal rooms still have a big fireplace, wooden beams and stone arches.

RECOMMENDED IN THE AREA

RESTAURANTS:
Titanic *and* Vecchia Ostuni

VISIT:
Cathedral and museum of pre-classical civilisation in southern Murgia

$\mathcal{M}$asseria Santa Lucia

Refined comfort in an old building

☎ 0831 3560 📠 0831 304090
📧 info@masseriasantalucia.it
S.S. 379 al km 23500
località Costa Merlata
72017 OSTUNI (Brindisi)
Ref map 11, D7
A14, Bari Nord exit, *superstrada*
(dual carriageway) 16 and 379 towards
Brindisi, after about 90 km Costa
Merlata exit
93 rooms; **£££**
Credit cards: AE VISA SI ⑩, bancomat

*R*efurbishment has carefully preserved the character and original features of the enclosed, powerful architecture of this old fortified building, but has been free in introducing modern elements of refined comfort. While the building is enclosed, the welcome and service offered to guests, on the other hand, is open. The defensive structure that contains the communal rooms is now just a source of fascination and character. The bright and attractive bedrooms are furnished in elegant modern style. Each room has picture windows that open on to a patio or garden. A wide range of facilities offered includes a swimming pool, tennis courts, reserved beach and garden, five-a-side football, archery, table tennis and bicycles.

RECOMMENDED IN THE AREA

RESTAURANTS:
Porta Nova; G.H. Rosa Marina, *Marina di Ostuni*

LOCAL SPECIALITIES:
Dried figs; almonds; orecchiette *pasta; whistles from Ostuni; ceramics from Grottaglie*

$\mathcal{D}$egli Haethey

Where even the sea has a history

☎ 0836 801548 📠 0836 801576
📧 haethey@mail2.clio.it
via A. Sforza 33
73028 OTRANTO (Lecce)
Ref map 11, E8
A14, Bari Sud exit, *superstrada* (dual
carriageway) 16, 379 for Brindisi, then
superstrada 613 for Lecce, next continue on
superstrada 16 as far as Maglie and S.S. 16
as far as Otranto
21 rooms; **£/£££**
Credit cards: AE VISA SI ⑩, bancomat

*O*tranto is the most easterly town in Italy, and is linked to the Orient by history and legend. The old town is in a defensive position on the promontory within a lovely Aragonese castle encircled by walls which no longer serve for defence purposes but provide panoramic walks. The hotel stands in the new part and is a white modern building. The bedrooms are big and light, the pretty furniture is modern and functional. The communal rooms are bright and neat. The use of majolica and glass as materials and of blue and white as colours strengthens the impression of functional neatness. A well-equipped garden surrounds the open-air swimming pool and there are bicycles for guests to hire.

RECOMMENDED IN THE AREA

RESTAURANTS:
Masseria Gattamora, *Uggiano la Chiesa;*
Barbablu, *via Umberto 17, Lecce*

LOCAL SPECIALITIES:
Craft products: wrought iron, terracotta, papier mâché, lace and embroidery; extra virgin olive oil

*G*rotta Palazzese

A restaurant built in the mouth of a beautiful natural grotto formed by the sea

☎ 080 4240677 ☻ 080 4240767
via Narciso 59
70044 POLIGNANO A MARE (Bari)
Ref map 11, C6
A14, Bari Nord exit, *superstrada* (dual carriageway) 16, towards Brindisi, Polignano a Mare exit
19 rooms; **££**
Credit cards: 🅰🄴 🆅🅸🆂🅰 🆂🅸 ⓄⒹ, bancomat

RECOMMENDED IN THE AREA

RESTAURANT:
Castellinaria

LOCAL SPECIALITIES:
Apulian orecchiette *pasta made by hand;* mozzarella *cheeses;* tarallucci *(little almond cakes)*

VISIT:
Castellana grottoes

*T*his is a modern hotel in the historic centre of the town, standing sheer above the sea and with a breathtaking view. It is carefully furnished with antiques, which with modern paintings give the rooms a warm and welcoming atmosphere. The bedrooms are delightfully furnished in Mediterranean style with wrought-iron beds and antique writing desks. The bathrooms are small but neat with windows, showers and hair-dryers. In addition there are small suites separate from the hotel in old premises with very characteristic architecture, terracotta floors and stone walls. The attractive small communal rooms have good views. Breakfast is served in charming summer room on the terrace with a wonderful view of the cliff and the sea below. The summer restaurant is unique, for it has been made at the mouth of a large and very beautiful natural grotto formed by the sea. The hotel has no lift. There is a free garage for guests but it has only a few spaces.

Tenuta del Barco

In an old Ionian farmstead

☎ and 🖷 059 5333051
✉ tenuta@iname.com
Strada provinciale 123
contrada Porvica
74026 PULSANO (Taranto)
Ref map 11, E6
A14 to the end, S.S. 7, S.S. 7ter,
before San Girogio Jonico turning for
Pulsano
7 apartments; £/£££
Credit cards: AE VISA SI

These old buildings were designed for defence and hard work but today are delightful stopping places with gracious style and lots of character. The farmhouse is white with powerful architecture, yet at the same time calmly welcoming. The former storehouses and stables have been restructured to accommodate seven apartments. Inside whitewash emphasises the old vaults and thick walls. The furnishing is carefully chosen, bright and in good taste.

The courtyard is the heart of the farmstead and from here there is access to the restaurant which is furnished in rustically elegant style. The kitchen prepares typical Apulian dishes and uses ingredients from the vegetable garden and the local area. The sandy beaches of the Ionian Sea are a short distance away and can easily be reached on foot or bicycle. The farm has private access to the public beach and has bathing facilities with supervised parking.

RECOMMENDED IN THE AREA

RESTAURANT:
Monsieur Mimmo, *via Virgilio 101, Taranto*

LOCAL SPECIALITIES:
Ceramics from Grottaglie

Al Centro Storico

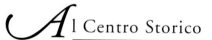

A small mansion that has been a shelter and an inn since the 18th century

☎ and 🖷 0884 707030
✉ cstorico@viesteonline.it
via Mafrolla 32
71019 VIESTE (Foggia)
Ref map 10, A4
A14, Poggio Imperiale exit, towards Rodi
Garganico, then the coast road as far as
Vieste
13 rooms; £/££
Credit cards: VISA SI

The history of this old building started with the adjacent church of San Pietro di Alcantara. In fact since the 18th century these premises have been used as a shelter and inn for the first travellers and merchants visiting this area. The small mansion then became the private residence of one of the most important families of Vieste and retains all the flavour of that period. Recent careful restoration work has emphasised the original features. There are antique furnishings and coloured marble floors in the communal rooms, and in the bedrooms facing Vieste's historic centre and the sea. Everything is stamped with delightful hospitality and has the patina of the past. Buffet breakfast is served on the terrace, and from here the little island of Santa Eufamia can be admired.

RECOMMENDED IN THE AREA

RESTAURANT:
Locanda Dragone

LOCAL SPECIALITIES:
Local and regional wines

VISIT:
Cathedral

Basilicata

Mountains divide Basilicata, a region which is less than one tenth level plain. The Metaponto plain faces the Gulf of Taranto and the Tyrrhenian Sea and, for a short distance, the Gulf of Policastro. The high parts of the region, mostly within the Apennino Lucano range, are concentrated in the west, with the highest peaks – Sirino and Pollino at over 2,000 metres – in the south.

Landscapes are varied, often rough, with grassy ridges, large beech woods and villages positioned high up like castles. There is skiing on Mount Sirino, 15 kilometres from the sea. Mount Pollino, on the border with Calabria, is at the centre of a vast and fairly inaccessible protected area of limestone plateaux of absorbent rock, gorges, oak and beech woods and high meadows. This is an unspoilt home to wolves, deer and otters. The *Vulture*, a magnificent extinct volcano, stands impressively to the north in the Melfi region, surrounded by green woods right up to the shores of its crater lakes.

In the west the landscape slopes down along the valley and the river loops towards the sandy Ionian coast. These very shores,

Castelmezzano, against the background of the so-called 'Lucan Dolomites'

colonised by the Greeks (at Metaponto, where Pythagoras taught, and at Eracleus) were then depopulated over the centuries due to malaria and invaders from the sea; they have now been reconquered by seaside tourism. The same has happened to the rugged stretch of the Tyrrhenian coast dominated by the panoramic village of Maratea, and dotted with Mediterranean vegetation and maritime pines, rocky cliffs, coves and hidden beaches.

The region has scattered artistic treasures: at Metaponto (Tavole Palatine, the famous ruins of a Doric temple), at Venosa (Trinità Abbey); at Acerenza (the cathedral); at Potenza (the archaeological museum); at Matera, the provincial capital (a Romanesque cathedral). Labyrinthine neolithic rock dwellings, *sassi*, can be visited, especially in the district of Matera. This remote, long-suffering urban landscape is now protected, and open to new forms of culture and social life.

Here visitors can experience perhaps the most authentically regional hospitality.

*R*icciardi Chiaromonte

*T*his hotel is to be found at around 800 metres above sea level on a natural terrace that dominates the whole Sinni Valley as far as the sea. We are in the heart of the Pollino National Park where wolves, otters, woodpeckers and wild boar live and *loricato* pine trees grow, where beech and spruce woods cover the mountains. This area of great natural beauty and little tourism has been inhabited since the Bronze Age.

The hotel building is modern and linear and is situated in the historic centre. Its rooms are furnished simply with a few refined touches and bathrooms have all been renovated recently. On the second floor there is a panoramic terrace. From this lovely sunny place for resting and meeting guests, there is access to the large, bright communal rooms inside the hotel. When weather permits, breakfast is served in the garden.

The members of the family who own the hotel give it a touch of rare charm with their kindness, courtesy and willingness to help.

Ref map 10-11, E4-5
A3, Lauria Nord exit, towards Latronico, then go on for Chiaromonte
36 rooms; £
Credit cards: SÌ

RECOMMENDED IN THE AREA

RESTAURANT:
Morel Due Palme, *Scanzano Jonico*

VISIT:
Bishop's Palace and contemporary Giura Palace; Sanseverino Castle and parish church of San Tommaso Apostolo

$\mathcal{M}$idi Hotel

A warm professional welcome near the ski lifts

☎ 0973 41188
📠 0973 41186
viale Colombo 76
85042 LAGONEGRO (Potenza)
Ref map 10, E4
A3, Lagonegro Sud exit
36 rooms; **£/££**
Credit cards: AE VISA SI ⓪

*T*his hotel is situated on the edge of the Pollino National Park and at the foot of the Sirono-Papa massif, at 2,008 metres, the highest peak of the Lucanian Apennines. It is near the ski station of Laudemio where skiing continues until late spring, and where in summer there is an expanse of territory to discover on walks and excursions. This modern hotel, built on a small scale from carefully chosen materials, opens out on the ground floor into a large bright hall. The bedrooms on three floors are furnished in warm-coloured wood. They are functional, comfortable and convenient. The bathrooms are well presented. Cooking is inspired by the specialities of Lucania, with a well-stocked wine store and there are rooms for meetings and banquets. In the large garden there is a children's playground, illuminated tennis court and *bocce* (bowls) pitch. There is a garage.

RECOMMENDED IN THE AREA

RESTAURANT:
Antica osteria Marconi, *viale Marconi 233/235, Potenza*

VISIT:
Piazza Grande, with Trinità parish church, Carrado Palace and the church of Madonna delle Grazie

---

I Sassi

In a group of early 18th-century buildings

☎ and 📠 0835 331009
via San Giovanni Vecchio 89
75100 MATERA
Ref map 11, D5
A14, Gioia del Colle exit, S.S. 171 as far as Altamura, then S.S. 99 to Matera
14 rooms, 1 suite; **£/££**
Credit cards: AE VISA SI ⓪, bancomat

*I*n a building dating from the early 1700s, this small hotel has the gracious form and warm gold-coloured stone of the area, with the typical appearance of the *sassi* rock dwellings that do not just lean against the rock but are part of it. Accommodation is in large attractive bedrooms, all facing the splendid and unique panorama of the *sassi*. These characteristic houses are built on the sheer rock face and the crowded accumulation of roofs and play of light and shadow provide a unique view which can be enjoyed from the little terrace of the hotel. The internal courtyards, breakfast room and communal room – all carved out of the rock – are permeated with an unusual charm.

RECOMMENDED IN THE AREA

RESTAURANTS:
Casino del Diavolo, *via La Martella 48, and* Da Mario, *via XX Settembre 14*

LOCAL SPECIALITIES:
Olives from Ferrandina; Aglianico del Vulture *wine*

VISIT:
Panoramic dei Sassi street

*D*el Campo

In the town of the sassi *rock dwellings*

📞 0835 388844
📠 0835 388757
✉ hdc@hsh.it
via Lucrezio
75100 MATERA
Ref map 11, D5
A14, Gioia del Colle exit. S.S. 171 as far as
Altamura, then S.S. 99 to Matera
16 rooms; **££/£££**
Credit cards: AE VISA SI OD, bancomat

$\mathcal{T}$ his modern-looking hotel was created out of an 18th-century noble residence owned by Senator Domenico Ridola, the founder of the interesting national museum bearing his name. It stands in the vicinity of the railway station, in tranquil surroundings but not far from the centre.

It has well-equipped modern bedrooms, all with air conditioning, modem points, satellite televisions, mini-bars and safes, and avant-garde design and furnishings. A special feature of the reception hall is the large bookcase that both decorates the room and divides it into different areas.

The restaurant serves local and Mediterranean food and is housed in two elegant little rooms facing the hotel's garden.

RECOMMENDED IN THE AREA

RESTAURANT:
Venusio, *Venusia*

LOCAL SPECIALITIES:
Caserrecio *bread baked in a wood-burning oven*

VISIT:
Duomo *(cathedral)*, Matera; park *of* chiese rupestri *(rock churches), towards Laterza*

$\mathcal{V}$illa Cheta Elite

In luxuriant, unspoilt countryside
☎ 0973 878134 🖷 0973 878135
via Timpone 24
località Acquafredda
85041 MARATEA (Potenza)
Ref map 10, F4
A3, Lagonegro Nord-Maratea, S.S. 585
towards Scalea, then turning for Sapri,
continue along the coast towards Maratea
as far as Acquafredda
20 rooms; ££
Credit cards: AE VISA SI ⑩, bancomat

$\mathcal{L}$ ooking on to a sheltered little inlet, this Art Nouveau style building is a few hundred metres from the most charming beaches of the Mediterranean. The villa was built at the beginning of the 20th century as a private home, and for years was a place for meeting and receiving guests and friends. In 1982 the family who now own it was inspired by that tradition of hospitality and transformed the villa into a hotel, preserving its elegant architecture and family atmosphere. Guests are first welcomed by the old rose-coloured façade that is decorated with white floral designs and surrounded by a Mediterranean garden. The rooms are furnished with period furniture that is both refined and attractive. The bedrooms look on to the garden and the lovely panoramic view, in a triumph of flowers, light and silence. The restaurant has embroidered tablecloths and carefully chosen details that show the attention given by the lady of the house. In summer, the restaurant serves meals on the terrace covered with flowers and overlooking the rocky coastline and the sea.

RECOMMENDED IN THE AREA

RESTAURANTS:
Taverna Rovita; Zà Mariuccia, *Fiumicello-Santa Venere*

VISIT:
The medieval village of Rivello

$\mathcal{D}$elle Colline

Opposite the castle and the cathedral

☎ and 🖷 0976 2284
via Belvedere
85054 MURO LUCANO (Potenza)
Ref map 10, D3
A3, Sicignano-Potenza exit, ring-road
for Potenza, Picerno exit, towards Picerno,
turning for Muro Lucano, S.S. 7 to Muro
Lucano
18 rooms; **£**
Credit cards: AE VISA SI ①, bancomat

RECOMMENDED IN THE AREA

RESTAURANT:
La Fattoria, *via Verderuolo Inferiore 13, Potenza*

LOCAL SPECIALITIES:
Cheeses and charcuterie

VISIT:
Castle, Muro Lugano

$\mathcal{T}$his hotel is in a modern building facing the village with a splendid view of the local brightly coloured houses and the castle and cathedral that are charmingly illuminated in the evening.

It is a small family-run hotel, with bedrooms that are simply furnished but bright and attractive. It has a busy restaurant, also open to non-residents, run by the owner who is a chef of international fame. Traditional dishes are served using local ingredients.

There is a tennis court in the garden and guests may hire bicycles for trips in the vicinity or for visiting interesting archaelogical sites nearby.

$\mathcal{G}$iubileo Hotel

The sign of relaxation and tranquillity

☎ 0971 479910
🖷 0971 479913
✉ hgiubile@tin.it
S.S. 92
località Rifreddo
85010 PIGNOLA (Potenza)
Ref map 10, D4
A3, Sicignano-Potenza exit, junction for
Potenza, Potenza exit, S.S. 92 towards
Laurenzana as far as Rifreddo
71 rooms; **£/££**
Credit cards: AE VISA SI ①, bancomat

RECOMMENDED IN THE AREA

RESTAURANTS:
Due Torri, *via Due Torri 6/8, and* Fuori le Mura,
via IV Novembre 34, Potenza

$\mathcal{A}$ short distance from Potenza, in a quiet and peaceful area surrounded by luxuriant trees and on the edge of the forest, stands this hotel: an angular white modern building with large rooms and comfortable bedrooms, offering good service. Apart from the bar and restaurant the hotel has a children's games room, a disco and a sauna.

There is green within the green, for a large garden surrounds the hotel and provides guest with many sporting facilities: an indoor swimming pool, tennis court, gym, basket-ball court and *bocce* (bowls) pitch. Peace, natural beauty, good service and sport all make for an agreeable stay and enjoyable holiday.

Villa Maria

*B*eautiful countryside and a large park surround the hotel with its sloping roofs inspired by architecture that is rustic but practical in the winters, that can be harsh and snowy. There are whitewashed walls, roof tiles, little shutters and big arched windows, as if to show that tradition is still present but that there is an eye to practicality, convenience and comfort. There are two apartments and big, light and simple bedrooms, with modern furniture. The communal rooms are large with some wooden decorations. In the park there is a swimming pool for adults and one for children, and a tennis court. The restaurant prepares good regional food using authentic local products.

The hotel also has a meeting room and a disco reserved for guests.

In the Monticchio lakes reserve

☎ 0972 731025 📠 0972 721355
località Laghi di Monticchio
85020 RIONERO IN VULTURE (Potenza)
Ref map 10, D3
A16, Candela exit, towards Potenza, turning for Rionero in Vulture, towards Laghi di Monticchio
31 rooms, 2 apartments; £
Credit cards: AE VISA SI OD

RECOMMENDED IN THE AREA

RESTAURANTS:
Vaddone, *Melfi;* Antica Osteria Marconi, *viale Marconi 233/235, Potenza*

VISIT:
Old centre of Atella; Monticchio lakes on the double crater of the old Vulture volcano

Miceneo

In the heart of Magna Grecia

☎ 0835 953200 🖷 0835 953044
S.P. per Montalbano, zona 167
**75020 SCANZANO JONICO
(Matera)**
Ref map 11, E5
 A14, Taranto Nord exit, S.S. 106dir.,
then S.s. 106 towards Crotone-Scanzano
Jonico
61 rooms; **£/££**
Credit cards: AE VISA SI DC, bancomat

*T*his hotel looks particularly modern with bright corners and jutting out structures, glass walls, portholes and futuristic lifts. The bedrooms are well furnished and attractive, with air conditioning, satellite televisions, safes and mini-bars. The bathrooms are practical. The communal rooms are large and spacious, with decorative features that are a modern interpretation of the traditional Magna Grecia style. Thus there are marble, majolica and glass, but also tapered pillars recalling the nearby temples of Metaponto. The *Limonaia* is the lovely citrus garden with two swimming pools (one for children) where gazebos are used for restaurant service during the summer. There is a shuttle bus service from the hotel to the beaches.

RECOMMENDED IN THE AREA

RESTAURANTS:
Callà 2, *Policoro;* Ai tre limoni, *Marina di Nova Siri*
VISIT:
*Archaeological site of Eraclea Minon;
Metaponto excavations*

Picchio Nero

Cuisine that is the fruit of never-forgotten tradition

☎ and 🖷 0973 93170/0973 93181

85030 TERRANOVA DI POLLINO (Potenza)

Ref map 10-11, E-F4-5

A3, Lauria Nord exit, S.S. 653 towards Valsinni, after 40 kms turning for Noepoli continue for San Costantino Albanese, turning for Terranova di Polino

23 rooms, 2 suite; **££**

Credit cards: A̲E̲ V̲I̲S̲A̲ S̲I̲ ◑

*T*erranova del Pollino is a terrace that faces a large and unspoilt panorama of natural beauty. The village is woven with steep little streets and characteristic houses, and along one of these streets is the hotel, a modern building inspired by traditional mountain architecture.

The owners give an attentive and kind welcome to guests here. The bedrooms are furnished with wooden furniture, the style is rustic and the rooms are delightfully secluded. The sitting rooms have furniture that harmoniously combines the traditional with modern functional; while the restaurant has all the warmth of a kitchen offering authentic local

RECOMMENDED IN THE AREA

RESTAURANT:
Luna Rossa

LOCAL SPECIALITIES:
Preserves in oil; herbs

dishes. Hotel management organises guided trips within the park, with its own cross-country vehicle and with the help of specialised staff. There is also a little garden for guests.

Calabria

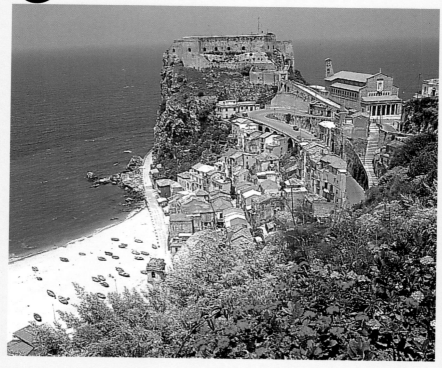

Calabria's sea and mountain have their own vivid character that is robust and dramatic. The Tyrrhenian and the Ionian seas are never more than 100 kilometres apart and there is only about 30 kilometres between the two gulfs of Sant' Eufemia and Squillace. Immense sandy beaches and rocky shores alternate along the coast. There are many crescent-shaped gulfs on the Ionian side, but long, straighter beaches and frequent indentations on the Tyrrhenian side. The transparent water invites sub-aqua sports.

On the hillsides, which are never far away, are ancient higgledy-piggledy villages and feudal castles. The mountainous area between the seas begins in the north with the majestic Pollino massif of dolomitic limestone, and carries on towards the Tyrrhenian sea with the Catena Costiera mountains. It widens in the east with the big wooded height of Sila and reaches south to the Serre chain of mountains, ending at last with the Aspromonte plateau. National parks protect Pollino, Sila and Aspromonte. The landscapes

Scilla, Homer's Scylla, slopes scenically towards the sea

are open, with large meadows and woods of beech, pine and spruce. At the bottom of the valleys the mostly dry riverbeds widen. Aspromonte is a land of waterfalls and ravines with steep terraces, vines, citrus orchards and fruit trees sloping towards the coast.

It is not surprising that tourism is growing in Calabria, with its temptations of both seaside holidays and inland nature trails. But the region also has historical interest. The era of Magna Graecia is documented in the archaeological museum of Reggio Calabria and symbolised in the bronze scuptures of Riace, but also in various other collections and excavation sites. The long Byzantine period comes to life in the domed churches of Cattolica di Stilo and Rosano and influences the cathedrals of Gerace and Tropea, amongst other places. This is a region of intense flavours and colours, in its food as well as its seas, woods, and exotic fragrances.

$\mathcal{B}$arbieri

Particularly fine food

☎ 0981 948072 📠 0981 948073
📧 barbieri@mail.telso.it
via San Nicola 30
87042 ALTOMONTE (Cosenza)
Ref map 12-13, C4-5
A3, Altomonte exit
24 rooms, 10 suites; **£/££**
Credit cards: AE VISA SI ①, bancomat

$\mathcal{A}$ltomonte is a pretty little town that, as its name suggests, stands high on a mountain 455 metres above sea level. Its cathedral and museum conserve important artistic treasures. From the windows of the hotel a lovely view of the cathedral can be enjoyed, and the bedrooms look on to wide horizons and lovely panoramas.

The bedrooms have simple and functional modern furnishings, and are equipped with air conditioning, televisions and mini-bars. The bathrooms are quite practical, with hair-dryers. The communal rooms are large, and one reception room can accommodate ceremonial meals and conferences.

RECOMMENDED IN THE AREA

RESTAURANT:
La Locanda di Alia, *Castrovillari*

LOCAL SPECIALITIES:
Local food and preserves in oil are sold in a shop run by the hotel's Barbieri family

The restaurant is among the best in the region and serves fine food using the best local ingredients. In the high season it is possible to have restaurant service in the garden. The hotel management organises guided art and nature tours in the vicinity.

Mediterraneo

This his hotel has been created out of the restructuring of a mid 19th-century noble palace, and is in the centre of Amantea, a short distance from the sea and from the middle of the old village that forms the historic heart of the interesting town. The restored exterior has kept the proportions and characteristic features of the old residence. The hotel's sitting rooms are lit by big windows opening on to a shady garden of luxuriant palms.

Large spaces and Mediterranean arches give character to the communal rooms. The bedrooms are well furnished and comfortable with air conditioning, mini-bars, modem points and satellite televisions. A beach is reserved for guests, with facilities for windsurfing and scuba diving, and there is a garden well equipped for outdoor pursuits. Bicycles can be hired.

In an old noble palace

☏ 0982 426364 🖷 0982 426247
✉ mediterraneo1@libero.it
via Dogana 64
87032 AMANTEA (Cosenza)
Ref map 12-13, D4-5
A3, Cosenza Nord exit, S.S. 107 for Paola, then S.S. 18 towards Vibo Valentia as far as Amantea
31 rooms; **£/££**
Credit cards: AE VISA SI ⑩, bancomat

RECOMMENDED IN THE AREA

RESTAURANTS:
Luna Rossa, *via Sicilia 94;* Marechiaro, *Gizzeria Lido;* Giocondo, *via Piave 53, Cosenza*

LOCAL SPECIALITIES:
Figs; preserves in oil; caviar from the south; peppered anchovies

La Locanda di Alia

This his hotel is at the gates of the town, in a quiet and peaceful position in a garden of olive trees, Mediterranean plants and herbs. The rooms are in rustic buildings linked by avenues of little brick walls and bordered by hedges of rosemary which lead to their separate private entrances. The bedrooms are tastefully furnished with carefully chosen details. They have a separate living area next to the sleeping area and are furnished with modern furniture. Bedroom windows look on to small brick courtyards or on to the garden. The bathrooms have baths with hydromassage. The restaurant, with bar, the reception hall and sitting room are in a separate small building and are elegant and secluded.

A temple of Calabrian cooking, surrounded by olive trees

☏ and 🖷 0981 46370
✉ alia@sirfin.it
via Setticelle
87012 CASTROVILLARI (Cosenza)
Ref map 13, B5
A3, Castrovillari-Frascineto exit, S.S. 105 towards Castrovillari
14 rooms, 3 suites; **££**
Credit cards: AE VISA SI ⑩

As for the cooking, there is only one piece of advice to follow: you need to taste everything to realise just how good it is. You will remember these flavours for a long time, and also the refined, friendly atmosphere that is personal, warm and never coldly formal.

RECOMMENDED IN THE AREA

RESTAURANT:
Barbieri, *Altomonte*

LOCAL SPECIALITIES:
The inn produces five kinds of its own rosolio *liqueur (traditionally drunk by women in the South)*

Grand Hotel San Michele

The charm of times past

☎ 0982 91012
📠 0982 91430
✉ sanmichele@antares.it
S.S. 18 Tirrena Inf. km 293+100
località Bosco 8/9
87022 CETRARO (Cosenza)
Ref map 12, C4
A3, Spezzano Terme exit, S.S, 283
towards San Marco Argentano,
go on for Guardia Piemontese as far
as the turning for Cetraro
65 rooms, 21 apartments; **££/£££**
Credit cards: AE VISA SI ⓪

Once a hunting lodge belonging to an Angevin baron stood where this hotel stands now. The last descendant of that dynasty was forced by gambling debts to emigrate to Argentina. He returned at the beginning of the 20th century, enriched by a profitable marriage, and decided to transform the old building into a luxury hotel, but he died before realising his dream. Years later, when the property was put up for sale, the buyer was the architect who had been chosen by the last baron to design the transformation. Nowadays, it is his daughter who runs the hotel.

The elegant white building contrasts with its green surroundings and is enhanced by the vivid colours of bougainvilleas. Inside there are spacious, well-furnished reception rooms, a plentiful library with 6,000 books, a bar that is always open and bright, charming rooms with stylish furniture, both practical and comfortable. Outside is a swimming pool with spring water, a little lake, tennis, a golf court, and a lift to the beach below that extends for two kilometres. All this is within a property that cultivates organic products which adds inspiration to the fine cooking of the restaurant. Finally there are some pretty apartments, the Casette del San Michele, that can use all the hotel's facilities.

RECOMMENDED IN THE AREA

RESTAURANT:
Il casello

VISIT:
Church of San Benedetto; beach and grottoes at Marina di Cetraro

La Mandria

In an area rich in archaeological sites

☎ and 🖷 0981 992576
contrada Sferracavallo 89
87072 FRANCAVILLA MARITTIMA (Cosenza)
Ref map 13, B5
A3, Castrovillari-Frascineto exit, S.S. 105 for Francavilla Marittima
8 rooms, 4 apartments; £
Credit cards not accepted

*I*n Pollino National Park, close to the famous Raganello and Timpone gorges, and in an archaeological area where the ruins of the temple of Athena were discovered, stands an old sheep pen and the former house of the herdsman. The buildings are low and typical of the region, and today have been restructured in the original rustic style into places for communal use.

RECOMMENDED IN THE AREA

RESTAURANTS:
Scanderbeg, *Frascineto;* La Trattoria del Sol, *Trebisacce*

LOCAL SPECIALITIES:
On sale from the farm: organic extra virgin olive oil, dried black olives, preserves in oil, charcuterie, sheep and goats' cheeses, bread baked in wood-burning ovens, olive liqueurs

The restaurant serves traditional food with a wide use of ingredients from the farm. A short distance away a modern building contains eight simply and practically furnished bedrooms on the first floor, and four little apartments on the ground floor. There are mountain bikes available for guests to explore the surrounding countryside and the 200 hectares of farmland used for the cultivation of olives.

A swimming pool has been created on a terrace in a lovely panoramic position with a view of the sea. On request, courses can be organised in cooking and crochet, and guided tours can also be arranged. In addition, the area offers the possibility for rafting.

A minimum stay of three nights for the bedrooms and a week for the apartments is required.

La Locanda del Parco

Lovely trips and long walks in majestic and almost wild scenery, in the heart of the Pollino National Park – in a very interesting spot for tourists but far from the usual crowded tourist routes. A fine modern building inspired by traditional mountain architecture welcomes guests. Accommodation is in attractive bedrooms with central heating. The wisdom of the farming way of life is reflected in the charming, characteristic restaurant heated by a large fireplace, and by the kitchen with its use of fresh farm products. The property organises cookery courses, animal observation and exploration of the neighbourhood. Guest may hire bicycles from the farm. The inn operates all year round and does not require a minimum length of stay.

RECOMMENDED IN THE AREA

RESTAURANT:
La Locanda di Alia, *Castrov*

VISIT:
The village with its medieva old buildings

Da Mommo

At the centre of the Gioia Tauro plain, Polistena is a very old town which conserves the artistic evidence of its long and difficult history. It is situated a short distance from the Tyrrhenian coast and at the foot of the first spurs of the Aspromonte massif. The building is in the centre of the little town, opposite the green public park. The hotel provides attentive, kind hospitality and has bedrooms furnished in the modern style that are simple and very clean. A small reception hall welcomes guests, and the restaurant in a large traditional room serves Mediterranean dishes. For enthusiasts of ecological tourism, the hotel management provides assistance and guides for trekking in the area.

RECOMMENDED IN THE AREA

RESTAURANTS:
La Fontanella, *Moschetta;* Kerkyra, *Bagnara Calabra*

LOCAL SPECIALITIES:
Pezzare *carpets woven from different coloured oddments*

VISIT:
Locri Epizefiri excavation site

Cozzo di Simari

The warm intimacy of an old family house

☎ and ℻ 0983 520896
✉ sere_flower@hotmail.com
via Cozzo di Simari 8
contrada Crocicchia
87068 ROSSANO
(Cosenza)
Ref map 13, C5

A3, Spezzano Albanese-Sibari, S.S. 534
towards the sea and S.S. 106 towards Crotone
as far as the turning for Rossano, go on for
Madonna delle Grazie and follow signs for the
agriturismo (farm accommodation)
12 rooms, 2 suites; **£/££**
Credit cards not accepted

*T*his is an old family house that is whitewashed
and has a roof of curved tiles. Around it are
other little buildings that together make up a tiny
village on the hillside in a panoramic position 15
minutes from the perfect blue sea on the horizon.
The bedrooms are large, very light and furnished with
period furniture. All but three have private
bathrooms. Surrounding the house are terraces
covered with flowers and lovely chestnut woods for
peaceful walks. The owner is a *Commandeur des
Cordon-Bleu* and personally oversees the cooking:
a large vegetable garden provides organic produce
for the kitchen. The hotel also organises cookery
courses (a minimum of six people is requested).

There are delightful spots in the garden for guests to
rest or read, as well as an open-air swimming pool,
small gym, sauna, table tennis, barbecues on the
beach and trips in the nearby Sila and Pollino parks.

RECOMMENDED IN THE AREA

RESTAURANTS:
Europa Lido Palace *and* Scigliano

LOCAL SPECIALITIES:
*For sale from the farm: wine, oil, jam, poultry,
rabbit, salami, sardines, sun-dried tomatoes and
preserves in oil*

VISIT:
*Cathedral and church of San Marco Evangelista,
Rossano; Corigliano Calabro village of medieval origin*

Contrada Guido

A thick pinewood separates the property from the private beach. There are pretty guest rooms with stylish furniture and modern practical bathrooms. The cooking of the *agriturismo* is inspired by local Calabrian and Mediterranean specialities and uses products that come directly from the farm. There is a grass football pitch on the farm and tennis, riding and golf in the immediate vicinity.

In an 18th-century village

☎ and 📠 0961 961495
contrada Guido
88050 SELLIA MARINA (Catanzaro)
Ref map 13, D6

A3, Lamezia Terme-Cantanzaro exit, *superstrada* (dual carriageway) 280 towards Catanzaro, after the town follow the signs for Catanzaro Marina, turning for Belladonna on the S.S. 19b, then S.S. 106 for Crotone as far as the turning for Sellia Marina
10 rooms; **£/££**
Credit cards not accepted

A small village arose here in the 18th century: a few houses and a tiny chapel, simple and secluded, harmonious in design and materials used, and practical for farming life. The building that houses the *agriturismo* (farm accommodation) was restructured a short while ago in the style of those old rural habitations, and it is large and set within a large shady garden in the middle of a farm facing the sea.

RECOMMENDED IN THE AREA

RESTAURANTS:
Osteria da Teresa, *Catanzaro;* Brace, *Catanzaro Marina*

VISIT:
Carriage Museum in the district of Stano, Catanzaro

Camigliatello

*T*his is a graceful modern building set deep in the countryside and facing a lovely panorama that slopes down towards the valley. It is surrounded by tall trees and immersed in quiet peace, a short distance from the centre of the village and three kilometres from the ski lifts.

The hotel has large bright bedrooms with the warmth of light-coloured wood and upholstery, and tasteful furniture. Many of the bedrooms open onto large balconies. The sitting rooms are arranged in different zones for conversation, games and meetings. Hence there are comfortable sofas, a little fireplace, a delightful bar area and a dining room with big windows overlooking the pinewood. The rooms are all very welcoming and well lit, and the staff are considerate and professional.

In the conifer forest of Sila Grande

☎ 0984 578496
🖷 0984 578628
via Federici
località Camigliatello Silano
**87052 SPEZZANO DELLA SILA
(Cosenza)**
Ref map 13, C5
A3, Cosenza Nord exit, then S.S. 107 towards Cosenza as far as Camigliatello Silano
29 rooms, 4 apartments; ££
Credit cards: Ⓐ Ⓥ Ⓢ ⑩, bancomat

RECOMMENDED IN THE AREA

RESTAURANT:
Edelweiss

VISIT:
Cecita Lake; reservoir at Mucone

I Basiliani

Elegantly refined architecture

☎ 0967 938000
S.S. 182 delle Serre al km 65,5
contrada San Basile
**88060 TORRE DI RUGGIERO
(Catanzaro)**
Ref map 13, E5
A3, Pizzo exit, S. S. 110 towards Serran San Bruno, then turn off on the S.S. 182 towards Soverato, then Torre di Ruggiero
6 rooms; ££
Credit cards not accepted

*T*he main house is constructed on the ruins of a 10th-century Greek Orthodox monastery and its main feature is an arched buttress in unplastered stone which is all that remains of the old building. Around the house is a large garden with ancient trees. The rooms are decorated with unique frescos after which the six bedrooms are named. The cooking is very good, faithful to traditional Mediterranean flavours, and uses organic products from the farm that extends over 35 hectares. Here there are woods, pastures and orchards 650 metres above sea level, and within this area there is a riding school for treks in the woods, as well as a swimming pool, *bocce* (bowls) pitch and mountain bikes.

RECOMMENDED IN THE AREA

RESTAURANT:
Palazzo, *Soverato*

LOCAL SPECIALITIES:
Dairy products, especially ricotta *and* caciocavalli *cheeses; briarwood pipes, Brognaturo; stone and wood crafts, Serran San Bruno*

Masseria Torre di Albidona

Close to the Pollino National Park in characteristic Mediterranean vegetation

☎ and 🖷 0981 507944
contrada Piana della Torre
87075 TREBISACCE (Cosenza)
Ref map 13, B5
A3, Castrovillari-Frascineto exit, then S.S. 105 and 92 towards the sea, next *superstrada* (dual carriageway) towards Taranto, Torre di Fergia exit, follow the signs for Trebisacce
10 apartments; **£/££**
Credit cards: ⓢ ⓪

*T*his farmstead stands out on a little plateau 100 metres above sea level and less than two kilometres from the sea. It is surrounded by cultivated fields and by the green of characteristic Mediterranean vegetation, and enjoys a very beautiful view over the Gulf of Sibari with its watch-tower standing out not far away. The old stone farm-workers' houses have been carefully restructured and transformed into independent apartments equipped with every modern comfort.

The apartments can accommodate from two to eight people and have fitted kitchens and private terraces. Breakfast and dinner must be ordered in advance, and are prepared with natural products from the farm and served around a big communal table. There is a restaurant serving local dishes, a swimming pool, tennis courts and a beach with equipment and private, shaded parking for cars. Only a short distance away is a riding school and a boathouse. Boat excursions and fishing parties can be arranged.

RECOMMENDED IN THE AREA

RESTAURANT:
La Locanda di Alia, *Castrovillari*

VISIT:
Pollino National Park

Sicily

Sicily is a formidable crossroads of culture, flavours and history. It is an intriguing place to visit: two centuries after visitors on the Grand Tour, tourists continue to be amazed by the complex layering of a still-evident past – Phoenician, Greek, Roman, Byzantine, Arab, Norman and Swabian. The Mediterranean scenery includes agave plants and cactus-type plants, maritime pines, olives and low vines which grow in sand, citrus, almond and pistachio, mulberry and carob trees.

Classical antiquities include ancient Mozia (Motya) and the Whitaker Museum, and Segesta's Greek temple among deserted hills with the theatre open to the mountains and the distant sea. Then there is the large archaeological park of Selinunte; the ancient site of Eraclea Minoa; Agrigento's temples and Hellenic Syracuse. There are the *latomie* stone caves on the plateau; Taormina with its Greek theatre between Mount Etna and the sea; Tindari; and the Roman mosaics at Piazza Armerina. There is the sickle shape of Trapani and above it the salt deposits of Erice; and the panoramic view on clear days from Enna

at the centre of the island. Finally there is the great brownish-purple cone of Etna with green patches of citrus groves and white snow at the top during winter and spring.

The cities and towns range from fascinating Palermo with its gold mosaics, red Arab domes and deep green parks, to baroque Catania, Ragusa and Noto, and to Cefalù and Monreale with their superb Norman cathedrals. Natural parks protect the mountain regions of Etna, Nebrodi and Madonie, areas of woods and high meadows. Nature is also protected in the Mediterranean Zingaro Reserve and in Ustica Marine Park. Other enchanting places are the islands of the Egadi, the far-off Pelagie, Pantelleria with its black lava and green vines, and the Aeolian islands, from Lipari to Vulcano, and from Stomboli to Salina. This last group forms a spectacular volcanic universe of fire that unites the sea, climate, wild scenery and archaeology. The contrasts in Sicilian culture are reflected in the variety of its food.

The Greek Theatre at Taormina

Villa Athena

At Agrigento, in the Valle dei Templi
(the valley of temples)

☎ 0922 596288 📠 0922 402180
via Panoramica dei Templi 33
92100 AGRIGENTO
Ref map 14, D3
A19, Imera exit, S.S. 640 as far as Agrigento
40 rooms; £££
Credit cards: AE VISA SI ◑

*T*here are magic places, places where natural beauty blends with history, tradition and architecture: a union which can be very moving.

The villa is in a wonderful setting in the *Valle dei Templi* (the valley of temples), 50 metres from the temple of Concordia. It is a small and gracious 18th-century building in pale colours and perfectly suited materials and is in keeping with the splendid scenery of the archeological site of the valley of temples and with the countryside around.

A garden full of plants and trees surrounds the hotel, helping to make it yet more tranquil, sheltered from tourists and passers-by. The communal rooms are tastefully furnished, with some painted decorations

and in the traditional Sicilian style. The bedrooms are comfortable and well lit. There is a wonderful terrace, with a panoramic view of the temples, where the spirit of the place really seems to be present. The swimming pool, in the greenery of the garden, fits in sympathetically with the surroundings.

RECOMMENDED IN THE AREA

RESTAURANTS:
Dei Templi, *via Panoramica dei Templi, and* Ruga Reali, *cortile Scribani 8*

VISIT:
Archaeological Museum; Valle dei Templi *and archaeological site*

La Magnolia

A relaxing holiday on the seafront

☎ 0942 716377
📠 0942 701815
via Lungomare 18/A
**98021 ALI TERME
(Messina)**
Ref map 15, C6-7
A18, Roccalumera exit, then S.S. 114
towards Messina as far as Ali Terme
22 rooms; £/££
Credit cards: AE VISA SI

*T*his hotel is in a modern building, situated on the seafront just across the road from the beach.

It is a small building with simple, neat bedrooms that have restrained modern furnishings. Most of the bedrooms have little balconies and enjoy a lovely view. The bathrooms are practical. The family management is very attentive and contributes to the atmosphere of tranquillity. There is also a solarium terrace for guests, as well as a private beach.

The restaurant serves Sicilian specialities based on fresh fish and seafood.

RECOMMENDED IN THE AREA

RESTAURANTS:
Savoja, *via XXVII Luglio 36/38, Messina;*
'A Zammàra, *Taormina*

LOCAL SPECIALITIES:
Limoncello *and* mandarinetto *liqueurs; Sicilian* cassata *ice cream;* granita *(crushed ice drink)*

VISIT:
Church of Triade at medieval village of Forza d'Agrò

$\mathcal{E}$limo

In a noble 17th-century house

☎ 0923 869377 📠 0923 869252
✉ elimoh@comeg.it
via Vittorio Emanuele 75
91016 ERICE
Ref map 14, D3
A29, then A29dir., towards Trapani, Trapani
exit, S.S. 187 towards San Marco, then
turning for Erice
21 rooms, 3 suites; **££/£££**
Credit cards: AE VISA SI OD

Restoration has preserved the charm of the communal areas, where there is an exotic Oriental atmosphere: the high ceilings still have the old beams interspaced with variously coloured tiles. The restaurant serves local dishes. The hotel belongs to the *Charme and Relax* chain, and also has a garage, car park and a pretty garden with a solarium.

*T*his little hotel has been created in a 17th-century house that stands in the historic centre of the lovely little town of Erice which is full of charm and seems like an eagle's nest enclosed in a circle of ancient walls.

The heart of the hotel, which has tastefully furnished modern bedrooms with elegant upholstery, is the lovely courtyard and the panoramic terrace where guests can rest and savour the beauty of the place.

RECOMMENDED IN THE AREA

RESTAURANTS:
Monte San Giuliano *and* Osteria di Veneria

VISIT:
Castles of Pepoli and Venere

$\mathcal{N}$ike Hotel

A white house set between the green of the garden and the blue of the sea

☎ 0942 51207 📠 0942 56315
✉ nike@cys.it
via Calcide Eubea 27
località Schisò
**98035 GIARDINI NAXOS
(Messina)**
Ref map 15, C6
A18, Gardini Naxos exit, S.S. 185 towards
Giardini Naxos as far as Schisò
51 rooms, 3 suites; **££**
Credit cards: AE VISA SI OD

where there is a landing-stage for boats. On this terrace there are tables and sunshades for guests to enjoy bar service and breakfast. The cooking is traditional Sicilian and there is family management. The use of the beach facilities is included in the price of accommodation.

*W*ith its Mediterranean architecture shaped with arches and terraces that give a view of the sea, the hotel is situated on a charming little bay with a view stretching as far as Taormina and Etna. Nearly all the bedrooms have little balconies, and they are furnished very simply. The reception hall is pretty and welcoming. The hotel has no lift.

The white hotel building stands out against the deep green of the surrounding garden that is full of palm trees and bougainvilleas and extends on to a terrace at ground level. This reaches the edge of the sea

RECOMMENDED IN THE AREA

RESTAURANTS:
Sea Sound, *Giardini Naxos;* A Massaria, *Trappitello*

LOCAL SPECIALITIES:
Wrought-iron work; crafts in ceramics and clay

Codavolpe

Rediscover a sense of the past in the countryside

☎ and 🖷 095 939802
✉ codavolpe@dns.omnia.it
strada 87 n. 35
località Trepunti
95010 GIARRE (Catania)
Ref map 15, C6
A13, Giarre exit, S.S. towards Giarre as far as the turning for Trepunti
6 apartments; £
Credit cards not accepted

*T*he old and gracious late 19th-century villa is in a defensive position on a hillside, on the slopes of Mount Etna, 200 metres above sea level. We are in the heart of eastern Sicily facing an extraordinary panorama that stretches from the coast to the surrounding valleys, as far as the snowline on Etna. Around the house is a garden that is in fact an expanse of citrus cultivation: these orchards, as well as the surrounding vegetable garden, ensure a supply of fresh, natural products. In front of the villa is a pergola, supported by characteristic pillars of grey stone, and there are flowers everywhere.

The communal rooms are very welcoming and blend rustic and modern styles in a tasteful mix. There are wooden tables and floors, unplastered stone and wrought iron. The apartments are furnished simply, in keeping with the rest of the rooms: here too the rustic style and pale sunny colours predominate.

RECOMMENDED IN THE AREA

RESTAURANTS:
La Giara, *Taormina;* La Siciliana, *viale Marco Polo 52/A, Catania*

Piano Torre Park Hotel

In the Madonie Park

☎ 0921 662671
🖷 0921 662672
contrada Torre Montaspro
90010 ISNELLO (Palermo)
Ref map 14, C4
A20, Gibilmanna exit, signs for Isnello, go on for Collesano, then turning for Petralia-Santa Lucia as far as Torre Montaspro
27 rooms; £/££
Credit cards: AE VISA SI ⓪

*P*reviously a castle, the building housing this hotel dates from the 18th century and was restored a short while ago, conserving the old architectural features and remaining in keeping with the unspoilt natural beauty that surrounds it. It is situated 850 metres above sea level, in the Madonie Park. This is a little world of peace and rest, but it also offers many opportunities for recreation and sport with numerous sports facilities, walks and excursions in the countryside. The internal courtyards and the gardens are large and well presented, with little ponds and flower-beds. The sitting rooms are modern and comfortable. The decorations are in the style of mountain houses, the furnishings are modern and the upholstery is vividly coloured. There are many possibilities for recreation and sport: cinema, disco, piano bar, swimming pool, tennis court, volleyball, basket ball, five-a-side football, *bocce* (bowls), mini golf, amphitheatre, and a football pitch. The restaurant serves food with ingredients from the Madonie area.

RECOMMENDED IN THE AREA

RESTAURANT:
Rifugio Orestano, *Piano Zucchi*

VISIT:
The church of Chiesa Madre, Isnello

*P*apuscia

In the black pearl of the Mediterranean

☎ and 🖷 0923 915463
contrada Sopra Portella 28
località Tracino
**91010 ISOLA DI PANTELLERIA
(ISLAND OF PANTELLERIA) (Trapani)**
Ref map 14, F1
Ferry from Trapani to Pantelleria,
then coast road as far as turning for Tracino
11 rooms; **£/££**
Credit cards not accepted

*T*his hotel is in an 18th-century *dammuso*, the characteristic Pantelleria building in rough stone with flattened curved roof tiles that is typical of Arabian-inspired island architecture. The area is a few hundred yards from the most beautiful coves in Patelleria, sheltered from crowds and confusion. The premises are arranged in three low constructions where the bedrooms have been created. These have light and bright furnishings of simple modern design. The little buildings enclose a lovely courtyard where guests may take breakfast or relax after sea-bathing. The rooms are furnished in a basic way, with all the walls painted white and so thick that they provide cool and rest from the strong colours and heat outside.

RECOMMENDED IN THE AREA

RESTAURANTS:
I Mulini *and* La Nicchia

LOCAL SPECIALITIES:
Ravioli *filled with minted* ricotta *cheese;* mustazzoli, pasticciotti *and* baci di ricotta *(little pastries);* vino passito *(raisin wine)*

VISIT:
Display of Panetelleria crafts in August

*G*iardino sul mare

On a cliff directly above the sea

☎ 090 9811004
🖷 090 9880150
📧 conti@netnet.it
via Maddalena 65, 98055 Lipari
**ISOLE EOLIE (AEOLIAN ISLANDS)
(Messina)**
Ref map 15, B6
Ferry from Messina or from Milasso
to Lipari
40 rooms; **££/£££**
Credit cards: AE VISA SI ⓪, bancomat

The airy sitting rooms seem like a continuation of the garden, with coloured floors, white rattan armchairs and sofas, and large french windows. The terrace is typically Aeolian, shaded by a pergola and ready for guests to take breakfast or simply to relax. The garden around is full of luxuriant Mediterranean vegetation and has a terrace, solarium and swimming pool.

From the hotel there is direct access to the sea.

*S*ituated on a steep rocky ridge overlooking the delightful bay of Lipari, this hotel is a few minutes from the characteristic little port of Marina Corta, the landing-stage for ferries and hydrofoils. It is in a modern white building with Mediterranean architecture. Nearly all the bedrooms have panoramic views and little private terraces, and they are bright and furnished simply with modern furniture in dark wood.

RECOMMENDED IN THE AREA

RESTAURANTS:
Filippino *and* E Pulera

LOCAL SPECIALITIES:
Capers; Pollara malmsey wine; conserves in oil

VISIT:
The castle

$\mathcal{A}$ugustus

In a garden of orange trees and flowers

☎ 090 9811232 ✆ 090 9812233
📧 villaaugustus@tin.it
vico Ausonia 16, 98055 Lipari
ISOLE EOLIE (AEOLIAN ISLANDS)
(Messina)
Ref map 15, B6
Ferry from Messina or Milasso
to Lipari 34 rooms; **£/££/£££**
Credit cards: VISA SI

$\mathcal{T}$his hotel is on a peaceful sunny road not far from the port and close to the sea, with its privacy protected by an enclosing wall covered with creepers. A big portal leads into a patio garden that looks almost Arabian and is restful, shaded and cool. A gazebo is used for bar service outside.

Facing the garden is the entrance to the villa with a little reception hall, sitting rooms and breakfast room, and a parlour that has a piano and some period furniture. Then short avenues and small courtyards lead, between orange trees and flower-beds, to the bedrooms. These are light and welcoming, of ideal size and simply furnished with modern light-wood furniture and ceiling fans. The bathrooms are neat. There is a solarium terrace for the use of guests.

RECOMMENDED IN THE AREA

RESTAURANT:
Filippino

VISIT:
Archaeological excavation area with finds from 14th century BC to the Roman times

$\mathcal{L}$a Piazza

Shady canopies and flower gardens on an Aeolian Island

☎ 090 983154 ✆ 090 983003
via San Pietro, 98050 Panarea
ISOLE EOLIE (AEOLIAN ISLANDS)
(Messina)
Ref map 15, A6
Ferry from Messina or Milasso to Lipari, then
ferry for Panarea
31 rooms, 2 suites, 2 apartments; **££/£££**
Credit cards: AE VISA SI

$\mathcal{I}$n a wonderful area of natural beauty, this white Mediterranean-style building stands in a defensive position on steep rocks above the sea. It is only a short distance from the landing-stage and the crowds, but there is peace and tranquillity here.

All the bedrooms have balconies or little private patios and nearly all enjoy beautiful panoramic views. The furniture is in the traditional Aeolian style; white-painted brickwork that forms part of the furnishing and coloured fabrics that contrast delightfully with the white walls. Nearly all the bathrooms have been renewed recently.

The areas outside are very lovely, with terraces, bar, saltwater swimming pool, shady canopies and flower gardens – all seemingly suspended between the sea and the sky. But inside too there are corners for conversation, the dining room and bar are beautiful, well-furnished and delightful places in which to spend time. From the hotel guests may go directly down to the sea where there is mooring for boats.

RECOMMENDED IN THE AREA

RESTAURANT:
Lisca Bianca

Locanda del Barbablù

Almost opposite the pink house where Roberto Rossellini and Ingrid Bergman stayed during the shooting of the film *Stromboli* (a plaque records this) is this very pretty inn, run with enthusiasm and good taste. Six charming bedrooms have been made on the top floor in what used to be a sailors' hostel, some of them facing the sea and the islet of Stombolicchio and some overlooking groves of orange trees and the volcano. All bedrooms have restored antique floors, period furniture, tasteful ornaments and details after which they are named.

The lady of the house is in charge of the kitchen. Here dishes are prepared with a skilful mix of delicate flavours of the Veneto region and the stronger ones of Sicily. Her husband, meanwhile, takes care of the guests in the dining room. During fine weather meals are served outside on the terrace beneath a pergola of bougainvilleas that flower nearly all year round. In winter, restaurant service is indoors, in the secluded and romantic corners of little rooms around the bar.

In an old patrician residence that was also a hostel for sailors

☏ 090 986118
🖷 090 986323
via Vittorio Emanuele 17-19
98059 Stromboli
ISOLE EOLIE (AEOLIAN ISLANDS) (Messina)
Ref map 15, A6
Ferry from Messina or Naples to Stromboli
6 rooms; ££/£££
Credit cards: AE VISA SI ⓄⒹ, bancomat

RECOMMENDED IN THE AREA

RESTAURANTS:
Zurro *and* Punta Lena

Tenuta Volpara

In old premises that have been restored, amid natural beauty and tradition

☏ 0923 984588
🖷 0923 984667
lungomare Mediterraneo 672
contrada Volpara
91025 MARSALA (Trapani)
Ref map 14, C1
A29, Salemi exit, S.S. 188 to Marsala
18 rooms; £/££
Credit cards: AE VISA SI, bancomat

This building stands in open countryside, in a panoramic position surrounded by the olive trees, palms and Mediterranean vegetation that flourish in the big garden. The centre of the hotel is antique in origin but there is a new part for parties, receptions and banquets. Accommodation is in large simple bedrooms furnished in modern style with bamboo furniture. Spacious rooms with an atmosphere of past times contain the restaurant. There are arches and beamed ceilings, and where the building is modern the architecture follows the traditional design. Breakfast consists of local products: *zabbina* (hot *ricotta* cheese), home-made tarts, and cheeses. There is a large veranda for meals outside, and a children's playground in the garden. The sea is a short distance away and there is a reserved beach for guests.

RECOMMENDED IN THE AREA

RESTAURANTS:
Delfino; La Torre, *Birgi Vecchia;* Baglio Oneto, *Trapani*

VISIT:
Tapestry Museum

Villa Favorita

An atmosphere of magical peace

☎ 0923 989100 📠 0923 980264
via Favorita 27
91025 MARSALA (Trapani)
Ref map 14, C1
A29, Salemi exit, S.S. 188 as far as Marsala
29 apartments; ££
Credit cards: AE VISA SI ⓄⒹ, bancomat

This old building, where wine was produced, was constructed at the beginning of the 19th century, its unusual architecture modelled on the traditional style of the southern Mediterranean. It immediately became a meeting place for Sicilian intellectuals. The original wine-producing factory was skilfully restored over a number of years and now belongs to the town of Marsarla. Some bungalows have been created in the large park. These are little buildings, a modern form of the ancient Arabian-inspired *dammuso*, with cool and welcoming rooms and attractive furnishings.

The villa, on the other hand, has reception rooms and small sitting rooms in the Art Nouveau style, meeting rooms with old vaulted ceilings, an elegant restaurant that also serves meals outside on the terrace and, during the summer, a *pizzeria*. In the green garden there is a tennis court, as well as a football pitch, children's playground and a swimming pool under the palm trees.

RECOMMENDED IN THE AREA

RESTAURANT:
Delfino

VISIT:
Museum dedicated to the traditional wine production of Marsala; Berbano quarter of Marsala; Island of Mozia

Baglio Conca d'oro

In a wonderful 18th-century building

☎ 091 6406286 📠 091 6108742
✉ hotelbaglio@libero.it
via Aquino 19, località Borgo Molara
90134 PALERMO
Ref map 14, C3
A19, Palermo exit, then *tangenziale* (by-pass) as far as the turning for Piano degli Albanesi, then signs for Molara
27 rooms; ££/£££
Credit cards: AE VISA SI ⓄⒹ

In an old building in the centre of an ancient little village near the gates of Palermo, this is a charming hotel, certainly among the best in Sicily. Refinement and good taste define the hotel; a love of discrete luxury creates a delightful atmosphere.

The courtyard at the heart of the house is a place for resting and for taking breakfast. The communal rooms are a succession of arches and ochre colours fusing into bright sunny shades. The hotel is furnished with period pieces, and has soft carpets and wooden ceilings.

The bedrooms are large and comfortable with fitted carpets, embroidered bedspreads and beautifully finished upholstery.

The sitting, dining and meeting rooms, piano bar and pub are nicely arranged within the antique, charming interior.

RECOMMENDED IN THE AREA

RESTAURANTS:
Le Absidi, *piazzale De Gasperi 19, and* Il Ristorantino

VISIT:
Duomo *(cathedral), Monreale*

Centrale Palace

In an antique and refined patrician residence of the 18th century

☎ 091 336666
📠 091 334881
✉ cphotel@tin.it
corso Vittorio Emanuele 327
90134 PALERMO
Ref map 14, C3
A20, then A19, Palermo exit, towards the historic centre
63 rooms; £££
Credit cards: AE VISA SI ⓪

RECOMMENDED IN THE AREA

RESTAURANT:
'A Cuccugna, *via Principe Granatelli 21/A*

VISIT:
Cathedral

*T*his hotel is central in name and in fact: it stands in the historic centre of the city in an 18th-century patrician palace that has been recently restructured, conserving the delightfully refined atmosphere of an old residence. The elegant reception rooms are embellished with antique furniture arranged in areas that are full of character, as conference rooms or as parlours for conversation. Particularly charming is the *Sala dei Tetti* (room of the roofs) that has an uninterrupted view of the spires, rooftops and bell towers of old Palermo.

The bedrooms are spacious and very well furnished, all equipped with adequate bathrooms, telephones, air conditioning, mini-bars and satellite television. Guests receive a welcome that is attentive to every detail of their wellbeing, whether they are staying on holiday or on business.

The hotel belongs to the *Best Western* chain.

Mediterraneo Palace

Refined and prestigious surroundings for a perfect stay

☎ 0932 621944
📠 0932 623799
via Roma 189
97100 RAGUSA
Ref map 15, E5
A18, Catania exit, continue on the *tangenziale* (by-pass), S.S. 114, turning for Lentini on the S.S. 194, then S.S. 514 as far as the turning for Ragusa
91 rooms, 2 suite; ££
Credit cards: AE VISA SI ⓪

*M*editerranean in its name and its architectural style, even if this is interpreted in a modern way on clean angular lines, this hotel stands in the centre of the town. A short while ago it was completely renovated. It has large comfortable rooms with modern furnishings. The bathrooms are well equipped, finished in marble, and some have hydromassage baths. The hotel has many meeting areas: reception hall, little sitting rooms, restaurant, banqueting room, breakfast rooms, and extremely attractive conference rooms that are especially suited to business meetings. These are all air conditioned for extra comfort.

RECOMMENDED IN THE AREA

RESTAURANTS:
La Pergola, *piazza Luigi Sturzo 6/7, and* Il Calesse, *contrada Magazzinazzi*

LOCAL SPECIALITIES:
Ragusano *cheese; honey; olives*

VISIT:
Cathedral

$\mathcal{E}$remo della Giubiliana

Ancient walls and a magical atmosphere

☎ and 🖷 **0932 669119**
S.P. per Marina di Ragusa al km 9
contrada Giubiliana
97100 RAGUSA
Ref map 15, E5
A18, Catania exit, *tangenziale* (by-pass), S.S.
114, turning for Lentini on the S.S. 194, then
S.S. 514 to the turning for Marina di Ragusa
9 rooms, 2 suites; **££/£££**
Credit cards: AE VISA SI ◍, bancomat

*T*his lovely inn has an old history: in the 1400s
it was a hermitage and religious house, used
also by the Knights of Malta, then in the 18th century
it became a fortified building, with defensive
structures and watch-tower, and was the property
of a noble Sicilian family. The present owners are
descendants of that family and have undertaken the
restructuring and transformation of the building into
a place of accommodation.

The sitting rooms have an irresistible charm; their
ancient walls create a magical atmosphere. But first
there is the reception hall that was created out of the
former chapel. The bedrooms are lovely and
tastefully decorated. The restaurant is open to non-
residents too.

There is a shuttle service to the beach, an airport
with a grass runway for trips to the islands of
Pantelleria and Lampedusa, archery, and a riding
school with a highly qualified instructor.

RECOMMENDED IN THE AREA

RESTAURANT:
Villa Fortugno, *Marina di Ragusa*

VISIT:
Donnafugata Castle

$\mathcal{V}$illa Paradiso dell'Etna

*A reference point for Sicilian culture
and hospitality*

☎ **095 7512409** 🖷 **095 7413861**
✉ **hotelvilla@paradisoetna.it**
via per Viagrande 37
95037 SAN GIOVANNI LA PUNTA
(Catania)
Ref map 15, D6
A18, Catania exit, S.S. towards
San Giovanni La Punta
34 rooms, 4 suites; **£££**
Credit cards: AE VISA SI ◍

*F*ounded in 1929, this hotel was for many years
a meeting place for artists and famous
people: 'the Paradiso dell' Etna is pure paradise for
the soul', wrote the Sicilian actor Angelo Musco.
During the Second World War it was chosen by
Rommel as the centre of German military operations,
then became a military hospital. Recently
refurbished, it looks like an elegant private villa set in
an oasis of peace on the slopes of Etna among palm
and citrus trees and flowering shrubs.

Restoration has conserved the building's original
features: the reception rooms with big windows and

Art Nouveau chandeliers, walls decorated with
trompe-l'oeil, stucco-work and original floors. The
bedrooms are large and furnished with old Sicilian
furniture from the early 20th century. The bathrooms
are sumptuous. The garden with swimming pool is
full of plants and trees which provide shady corners
at any hour of the day. The restaurant serves typical
Sicilian dishes and in summer meals are outside on
the terrace.

RECOMMENDED IN THE AREA

RESTAURANT:
Giardino di Bacco

$\mathcal{P}$omara

☎ 0933 978143 ☏ 0933 977090
via Vittorio Veneto 84
**95040 SAN MICHELE
DI GANZARIA (Catania)**
Ref map 15, D5
A19, towards Piazza Armerina, S.S. 192,
then 117 towards Gela, then turning for San
Michele di Ganzaria
39 rooms, 1 suite; **££**
Credit cards: AE VISA SI OD, bancomat

$\mathcal{T}$his is a recent building with modern architecture in a panoramic position. The hotel has bedrooms of a comfortable size that are well furnished: the furniture is modern and made of warm, cherry-coloured wood, and the atmosphere is functional and welcoming. The bathrooms are very practical. The sitting rooms are also furnished in modern style and are bright and attractive.

The hotel restaurant is well known in the area for its good food and is a short distance from the hotel. The Pomara family runs both hotel and restaurant with great attention and courteous, smiling service. There is a garden and also a car park.

RECOMMENDED IN THE AREA

RESTAURANTS:
San Giorgio, *Caltagirone;* Al Fogher, *Piazza Armerina*

VISIT:
*Archaeological site of Casale Roman villa,
Piazza Armerina*

$\mathcal{C}$apo San Vito

Unspoilt countryside and unpolluted sea

☎ 0923 972122 ☏ 0923 972559
via San Vito 1
**91010 SAN VITO LO CAPO
(Trapani)**
Ref map 14, C2
A29, Castellammare del Golfo exit,
S.S. 187, turning for Custonaci,
continue for Castelluzzo, then for
San Vito lo Capo
35 rooms; **££/£££**
Credit cards: AE VISA SI OD

$\mathcal{S}$ometimes the island itself is more beautiful than the surrounding sea: there are so many archaeological and artistic treasures inland that enjoying the coast and the sea can take second place. But here, at Capo San Vito, facing this natural beauty you forget everything. There is a beach stretching for kilometres where, as if drawn by an artist, sandy inlets and rocky coves alternate, bathed by a clear sea with colours that advertisements have led us to believe exist only in the tropics.

The hotel is a modern building by the sea, with a bright Mediterranean interior and a garden surrounding it. The bedrooms are simple and welcoming and face a wonderful panorama.

The hotel has a private beach and, for wandering around the area, there are bicycles for hire at reception.

RECOMMENDED IN THE AREA

RESTAURANTS:
Tha'am *and* Alfredo

VISIT:
Scurati Grottoes

Capo Scalambri

In the Sicilian baroque area

☎ 0932 239938 ☏ 0932 915600
via Cagliari 42, località Punta Secca
97010 SANTA CROCE CAMERINA (Ragusa)
Ref map, 14-15, E4-5
A18, Catania exit, *tangenziale* (by-pass), S.S. 114 turning for Lentini on the S.S. 194, then S.S. 514 as far as the turning for Marina di Ragusa, then coast road as far as Punta Secca
7 apartments; **£**
Credit cards not accepted

*P*unta Secca is at the foot of the Iblei mountains, and is a characteristic little outlying district of Santa Croce di Camerina, which is 500 metres from the *agriturismo* (farm accommodation). The farm buildings stand practically on the sea at Punta Secca. They are white, modern and small, and are surrounded by a green pine woods separating them from a very long, almost empty golden beach and the clear sea. Around the farm buildings is the estate with its glasshouses and citrus cultivation.

Accommodation is in small stone houses and apartments and in a few prefabricated bungalows. Leisure facilities for guests include: *bocce* (bowls), five-a-side football, playground and bird-watching.

RECOMMENDED IN THE AREA

RESTAURANT:
Alberto, *Marina di Ragusa*
VISIT:
Caucana Archaeological Park

Dolce Casa

A private residence for a peaceful, relaxing stay

☎ and ☏ 0931 721135
✉ giuregol@qsconsul.it
via Lido Sacramento 4
96100 SIRACUSA (SYRACUSE)
Ref map 15, E6
A18, Catania exit, *tangenziale* (by-pass), S.S. 114 as far as Siracusa (Syracuse)
6 rooms; **££**
Credit cards not accepted

*T*his villa has modern architecture and is situated only 10 minutes away from the centre of Syracuse; a free shuttle service guarantees connection with the city centre.

The bedrooms are furnished in romantic, English country style, diluted by the traditions of the Italian south. There are flowered wallpapers and upholstery, small tables covered with cloths, and mixed old and modern furniture. The whole effect is bright and welcoming. Spacious verandas with views over the pine wood can be used for open-air breakfast in the morning breeze. The sitting room is rustic with 'old America' style furniture, but the terracotta floors and white arches remind visitors that they are in the Mediterranean.

The whole house is surrounded by the green of a well-tended garden.

RECOMMENDED IN THE AREA

RESTAURANT:
Archimede, *via Gemmellaro*
VISIT:
Island of Ortigia

Grand Hotel

In an elegant Art Nouveau building by the sea

☎ 0931 464600
🖷 0931 464611
viale Mazzini 12
96100 SIRACUSA (SYRACUSE)
Ref map 15, E6

A18, Catania exit, on the *tangenziale* (by-pass), S.S. 114 as far as Siracusa (Syracuse)
58 rooms, 19 suites; **££/£££**
Credit cards: AE VISA SI ⓞ

This is a hotel full of history and tradition that has recently been renovated. It stands in the Ortigia, the historic centre of Syracuse, and faces the Porto Grande, a few metres from the sea and a lovely beach that can be reached by a paying boat service from the landing stage in front of the hotel.

The Art Nouveau building retains its large rooms decorated with stucco-work and pictures and with large windows. It is now very carefully furnished. The bedrooms are delightful, fully equipped and completed by bathrooms finished in marble.

The restaurant overlooking the Porto Grande and the Ortigia shore is charming, both as a room and because of the view.

In underground passages it is possible to see the ruins of the Spanish wall which came to light during recent restoration work.

RECOMMENDED IN THE AREA

RESTAURANTS:
Arlecchino, *via dei Tolomei 5*, Darsena-Da Iannuzzo, *riva Garibaldi 6, and* Da Camillo

VISIT:
Duomo *(cathedral)*

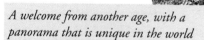

Villa Ducale

A welcome from another age, with a panorama that is unique in the world

☎ 0942 28153
🖷 0942 28710
✉ villaducale@tao.it
via Leonardo da Vinci 60
98039 TAORMINA (Messina)
Ref map 15, C6

A18, Taormina exit
15 rooms, 3 suites; **££/£££**
Credit cards: AE VISA SI ⓞ

This early 20th-century villa has recently been transformed into a hotel by a young couple who have managed to combine enthusiasm and good taste into the changes. The view of the sea and the coast is unequalled: the sea is below, Mount Etna in the background, and there are impressive sunsets and breakfasts in the cool morning breeze.

Inside the atmosphere is that of an elegantly welcoming house: furniture, upholstery, sofas,

books – all contribute to the delightful character of the place. Some of the bedrooms have period furniture, others are furnished in period style, and all of them are pretty, and have lovely views.

The garden and solarium provide further opportunities for relaxation and recreation.

RECOMMENDED IN THE AREA

RESTAURANTS:
Al Duomo *and* La Giara

VISIT:
Greek Theatre

352

$\mathcal{V}$illa Sirina

$\mathcal{P}$ ervading the air around this old villa is the scent of citrus fruit and oleanders. It stands at the foot of the main town, 500 metres above sea level. All the villa's bedrooms have balconies or terraces and are sunny and bright, simple yet well cared for, with 19th-century furnishings. The sitting rooms are spacious and their lovely antique furniture tells the history of the house. Light colours predominate, and there is a touch of originality in the paintings and in the vivid colours of ornaments made by craftsmen on the island.

The restaurant is rustic and brightly decorated, and serves traditional regional dishes. The garden/park is full of luxuriant Mediterranean vegetation and there is a swimming pool on the terrace. The hotel has a private beach for guests.

In an old villa at the foot of the town

☎ 0942 51776 📠 0942 51671
contrada Sirina
98039 TAORMINA (Messina)
Ref map 15, C6
A18, Taormina exit
15 rooms; **££/£££**
Credit cards: AE VISA SI ⓪, bancomat

RECOMMENDED IN THE AREA

RESTAURANTS:
Griglia *and* Da Lorenzo

VISIT:
Medieval village of Castelmola with ruins of 16th-century castle

---

$\mathcal{T}$onnara Trabia

In an area full of history and natural beauty

☎ 091 8147976
📠 091 8124810
✉ info@tonnara.com
largo Tonnara S.S. 113
90019 TRABIA (Palermo)
Ref map 14, C3
A19, Trabia exit, then S.S. 113 towards Trabia
31 rooms, 2 suites, 2 apartments; **££/£££**
Credit cards: AE VISA SI, bancomat

$\mathcal{A}$ t the entrance to Trabia, next to the castle of the Princes of Lanza and right on the sand and pebble beach, stands a 16th-century building. This used to be the old tuna fishery, but it has been renovated and restructured to form an attractive hotel. Modern features have been introduced into the ancient building: there are rough materials and varnished furniture – character and functionalism live side by side and enhance each other. The bedrooms are light, modern and bright and are furnished in a rustic style: all face the sea

RECOMMENDED IN THE AREA

RESTAURANTS:
Il Rais; Il Mulinazzo, *Mulinazzo*

LOCAL SPECIALITIES:
Almond-flavoured granite *(crushed-ice drinks);* cannoli *pastries and* cassate *(Sicilian ice-cream cake); decorated, highly-coloured ceramics from Santo Stefano di Camastra*

and their colours are inspired by it. Some of the sitting rooms have large windows overlooking the countryside; others have an atmosphere typical of old rooms that are enlivened with elegant furnishing and skilful lighting. There is a soft green lawn between the hotel and the private beach, and an open-air swimming pool with sunshades on the terrace.

353

$\mathcal{A}$telier
sul mare

With rooms designed by artists facing an enchanting little blue bay

☎ 0921 334295 ✆ 0921 334283 ✉ apresti@eniware.it

via Cesare Battisti 4
località Castel di Tusa
98070 TUSA (Messina)
Ref map 14, C4
A20, Furiano exit, continue on S. S. 113 as far as Castel di Tusa
40 rooms; **£/££**
Credit cards: AE VISA SI

*T*his hotel is unique with its rooms designed by major contemporary artists, and it stands by the sea in a very beautiful bay.

RECOMMENDED IN THE AREA

RESTAURANT:
Ostaria de Duomo

VISIT:
*The annual 'kilometre of canvas' exhibition in which
many painters work on a kilometre-long canvas
stretched out along the roads of the village;
Halaesa and Tindari archaeological sites, Norman
Cathedral and Mandralisca Museum, Cefalù*

The hotel has large comfortable bedrooms. Fourteen of these are an artist's work: an artist who has been asked to come and create a room has reconstructed the space and furnishing in an original way, making each room a real artistic invention. 'A living museum to enjoy, not a hotel with nicely displayed works, but a place where people can live in the museum, a museum on the scale of man, and with all its works on a human scale,' as Hidetashi Nagasawa said.

A short distance from the hotel, in the Nebrodi Nature Park, other contemporary works strewn over the slopes of the valley mark the landscape with imposing, sculptural forms. These start from the beach with works by Tano Festa and Consagra, and then go upwards, continuing along the area crossed by the River Tusa. There are works by Lanfredini, Dorazio and Graziano Marini culminating in a wall of ceramics made by 40 artists from all over Europe.

Inside the hotel a studio gives courses on ceramic art in close contact with the artists.

However, art is not the only thing on offer here: in the immediate vicinity there are tennis courts, riding centres, facilities for water skiing, windsurfing, subaqua fishing and boat trips. The hotel also has a private beach.

Baglio Santacroce

This is a 17th-century *baglio* where wine was produced in an old rural house. The stone building that is now a hotel has severe but attractive architecture and is situated on the slopes of Mount Erice. It stands on a little rise not far from the village and overlooks the Gulf of Comino with a wonderful view. It is an ideal place for peaceful holidays in a charming setting.

From the internal courtyard that still has a floor made of white local stone cut by hand, there is access to the reception rooms, all furnished in an elegantly rustic style with antique Sicilian furniture in precious wood, hand-woven carpets and many examples of Sicilian crafts. The bedrooms bear reminders of their rustic origin with terracotta floors and wooden beams, and are furnished with wrought-iron beds and olive wood chairs.

An old 17th-century building in a charming setting

☎ 0923 891111
📠 0923 891192
S.S. 187 al km 12,300
91019 VALDERICE (Trapani)
Ref map 14, C1-2
A29, Castellammare del Golfo exit,
S.S. 187 for Valderice
25 rooms; ££
Credit cards: ⒜ⓔ 🆅🆂🆁 🆂🅸 ⓓ, bancomat

A splendid garden surrounds the property and, hidden on a terrace, is a swimming pool for guests. The restaurant is a modern room and serves very good regional specialities.

RECOMMENDED IN THE AREA

RESTAURANTS:
Monte San Giuliano *and* Taverna di Re Aceste, *Erice;*
Peppe, *Trapani*

La Tonnara di Bonagia

An old seafaring village, with small buildings in humble but stylish architecture, this is an enchanted world with courtyards, watch-towers and a little chapel. Here, until the end of the 17th century, were the homes of the *tunnaroti*, the fishermen dedicated to catching tuna.

Nowadays it is an elegant hotel equipped with every comfort. The decorations are in local style, with rustic furniture and light colours. The bedrooms, some of

A 17th-century Sicilian tuna fishery

☎ 0923 431111 📠 0923 592177
piazza Tonnara, località Bonagia
91010 VALDERICE (Trapani)
Ref map 14, C1-2
A29, Castellammare del Golfo exit,
S.S. 187 for Valderice
44 rooms, 4 suites,
57 apartments; ££/£££
Credit cards: ⒜ⓔ 🆅🆂🆁 🆂🅸 ⓓ

which also have private gardens, look onto the splendid Cofano Bay and the little beaches that frame it, or else on to the harbour. There are also small apartments and a few suites.

Leisure facilities include a private beach, sea-fishing, a diving and marine archaeology centre, hire of boats and scuba equipment, tennis courts, five-a-side football, volleyball, and a children's playground.

RECOMMENDED IN THE AREA

RESTAURANTS:
Meeting, *Trapani;* Delfino, *Marsala*
LOCAL SPECIALITIES:
Oil; wine; ricotta *cheese;* bottarga *(tuna roe)*

Sardinia

When Sardinia is mentioned, the sea comes to mind: unforgettably clear water with deep gulfs, enchanting beaches and rocks sculpted by the sea and the wind.

This image is indeed true but it is not the whole picture: in reality the island's culture is more inland than coastal. The high ground consists of a succession of mountain ranges, terraces with harshly eroded granite rocks, sparse vegetation and sometimes simply bare rock.

Standing out in the north are the Limbara mountains, and in the west the Gennargentu massif at the centre of the Barbagie mountains. In the south-west, more modest heights stand beyond the Campidano plain linking the gulf of Oristano and Cagliari. The coast is more varied than that of any other Italian region, and a few parts (such as the *Costa Smeralda* – the Emerald Coast) are famous, whilst many others deserve to be equally well known. Chalky spurs, precipitous rocks, grottoes and strange cliffs alternate with bays and deep crescents of very white sand.

National parks protect the island of Asinara, the Maddalena archipelago, and the Gennargentu and Supramonte mountains.

Cala Gonone, in the vicinity of the Bue Marino grotto

Rare plants and animals have been preserved by the geography of the island, and the countryside ranges from pinewoods and Mediterranean vegetation to the humid coastal area of the south and west, and the rough, unspoilt landscape of the interior.

Sardinia's originality lies in its history, or rather its pre-history. The most evident traces are those of the *nuraghic* culture, seen in the celebrated megalithic monuments (of which there are at least 7,000) and bronzes in the archaeological museum at Cagliari. No less rare are the Phoenician-Punic archaeological finds in sites such as Nora, Tharros and Sulcis (Sant' Antioco).

The capital Cagliari is set amidst beaches and lagoons and has monuments from many different eras: Roman (the amphitheatre), Byzantine (San Saturno Basilica), Pisan (the cathedral and the town gates) and Catalan and Spanish (in various churches). Mixed with traces of Piedmont and Liguria, they well express the complexity of this place.

Traditional culture is as much alive in the food as it is in the Sardinian language.

Villa Las Tronas

I n the 1940s this villa was the residence of the Italian royal family during their holidays in Sardina, and it stands on a private promontory.

The exclusive atmosphere of an aristocratic buen retiro

☎ 079 981818 📠 079 981044
lungomare Valencia 1, 07041 ALGHERO (Sassari)
Ref map 16, C1
Superstrada (dual carriageway) 131, Alghero exit, then S.S. 291 as far as Alghero
28 rooms, 1 suite; **£££**
Credit cards: AE VISA SI ⓘ

The villa is a few steps from the centre of Alghero. Its park separates it from the traffic of the town and creates a real and exclusive oasis. The building faces a rocky coast: little jetties and terraces by the sea enable guests to take the sun, bathe and fish. There is a dock for the summer mooring of little boats.

The bedrooms are all different, both as rooms and in their furnishings (some antique); but all are equipped with air conditioning, telephones, satellite televisions, mini-bars and safes.

The parlours still have valuable antique furniture well arranged in particularly elegant, charming surroundings. From the dining rooms there is an enchanting view of the Gulf of Alghero and the Capo Caccia headland. Great care is taken over cooking and service.

Complimentary facilities for guests are bicycles, a gym, a salt-water swimming pool and fishing rods for hire.

RESTAURANTS:
Al Tuguri *and* Pavone

VISIT:
Historic centre of Alghero

$\mathcal{L}$e Dune

*An atmosphere beyond time,
among unpolluted sand dunes*

☏ 070 977130
🖷 070 977230
via Bau 1
località Piscina di Ingurtosu
09030 ARBUS (Cagliari)
Ref map 16, E2
S.S. 131 as far as Sanluri, S.S. 197 towards

*T*he landscape is majestic – almost a miniature desert – with high golden dunes that stretch out by the sea. The hotel is reached along a rough road through an oak wood, past abandoned mining constructions and the tracks of an old railway. The hotel is a piece of industrial archaeological reclamation and was once an old storehouse. The complex has been declared a national monument for its historical interest and artistic value. It is composed of three buildings linked by an internal courtyard and a small square area that opens out on to the sea shore. The courtyards are paved with 18th-century terracotta tiles and here some Punic and Roman ruins are preserved. The buildings, with their very characteristic architecture, contain sitting and meeting rooms that are delightfully welcoming places with 18th- and 19th-century furniture. The bedrooms are agreeable and simple, with bamboo furniture. Meals are served on the veranda and the terrace, and the food is simple and authentic. There is bar service on the beach, a children's playroom and an open-air bath with hydromassage.

RECOMMENDED IN THE AREA

RESTAURANT:
Rosy, *Sanluri*

VISIT:
Grotto of Su Mannau; temple of Antas

$\mathcal{L}$e Querce

RECOMMENDED IN THE AREA

RESTAURANTS:
Grazia Deledda *and* Casablanca, *Baia Sardinia*

VISIT:
The country church of Santa Maria, Arzachena

*H*aving left the bay of Sardinia with the sea at your back, you go up Mount Moro as far as a green hillock with myrtle and oak trees and set between pink granite rocks.

Here are the *querce* – or the old *stazzi* (shepherds' houses), that because they were so close to the sea were never used for agriculture but instead for hunting. They have been transformed into residences, each with its own garden and its own privacy. They are ideal places for enjoying the silence and watching the sunsets over the gulf, a few minutes from Porto Cervo. The apartments are furnished with care, as if for friends rather than guests, and the rooms are rustic in style with a harmonious balance of whiteness and earthy materials: the result is great elegance. The bathrooms are decorated with antique majolica tiles and are hand painted.

Here you can spend a relaxing holiday combined with the chance of dedicating yourself to your well-being and physical fitness. There is massage, aromatherapy, yoga, stretching exercises and postural relaxation, as well as other facilities.

A place to refresh the body and mind in converted stazzi *(old shepherds' houses)*

☎ and 🖷 **0789 99248**
✉ **lequerce@esweb.it**
via Vaddi di Iatta
località Baia Sardinia
07020 ARZACHENA (Sassari)
Ref map 16, A3-4
Superstrada (dual carriageway) 131d.c.n. as far as Olbia, continue on the S.S. 125 towards Palau as far as the turning for Porto Cervo, then turning for Baia Sardinia
5 apartments; **£/££**
Credit cards not accepted

Cà la Somara

*A*round are great open spaces and lonely horizons. In the tall grass full of flowers Sardinian donkeys graze peacefully: they are reared on the farm in order to protect them from a real possibility of extinction.

Waiting to be discovered by those who appreciate simple old-fashioned pleasures

☎ and 🖷 0789 98969

località Sarra Balestra, 07021 ARZACHENA (Sassari)

Ref map 16, B3-4

Superstrada (dual carriageway) 131 d.c.n. as far as Olbia, continue on the S.S. 125 towards Palau as far as the turning for San Pantaleo

9 rooms; **£/££**

Credit cards not accepted

The donkeys, which graze in the wild without burdens to carry, are the happy result of a project by the owners of this property. Situated a few kilometres from Porto Cervo and an equal distance from Arzachena, the lovely building that contains the *agriturismo* (farm accommodation) was originally stables, and years of patient, careful work were necessary to convert it into accommodation. The place can be reached on foot, with a lovely walk through fragrant juniper bushes and characteristic granite rocks. In such spots it is possible to enjoy the silence and the natural beauty of the countryside.

The nine bedrooms are strictly reserved for non-smokers; there is a bathroom for every two rooms, but all the bedrooms have wash basins. The delightful bedrooms are large and carefully presented, decorated in white and tastefully furnished. Some of them, making use of their large dimensions, are arranged on two levels. The furniture is rustic, Sardinian style, and in perfect accord with the place and the rooms.

Guests may use the communal kitchen to cook meals, or else may taste the vegetarian dishes of the *agriturismo*. There is also a big barbecue in the garden and a private car park.

Apart from rearing donkeys, the farm cultivates fruit and vegetables using organic methods and guests can use these in their cooking. Bicycles are available for guests to ride round the area and explore the nearby archaeological sites. Besides this, the *agriturismo* is headquarters of a centre that organises fitness and relaxation courses.

RECOMMENDED IN THE AREA

RESTAURANT:
Zattera, *Arzachena*

LOCAL SPECIALITIES:
Energetic walks with a guide from the Uomo-Natura-Energia association that has its headquarters at the agriturismo and conducts 'recharging' sessions of 15 minutes in places noted for their electro-magnetic properties

VISIT:
Tomb of the Giant of Capichera Lu Coddu Vecchiu, and the Li Muri burial site, towards Luogosanto

Capriccioli

Amidst Mediterranean vegetation, beside the sea of your dreams

☎ 0789 96004 📠 0789 96422
località Capriccioli
07021 ARZACHENA (Sassari)
Ref map 16, B3

Superstrada (dual carriageway) 131 d.c.n. as far as Olbia, continue on the S.S. 125 towards Palau as far as the turning for Golfo Aranci, then turning for Porto Cervo, then for Capriccioli
46 rooms; **£££**
Credit cards: AE VISA SI

Capriccioli is a dream of a place, a Mediterranean dream that has no reason to envy glossy tropical paradises. The coast alternates between granite rocks and bays of the finest white sand; you could say that the sea is the colour of jade, but no description would fully convey the beauty of this sea. The hotel is hidden in Mediterranean vegetation, mastic trees, juniper and myrtle; the wind wafts their fragrances. The beach is only a few steps away.

The bedrooms are white and pale blue, a colour that has always been used in the southern Mediterranean for its beneficial influence and the power to banish evil spirits. The furnishings are simple and the whole effect is bright and original.

The restaurant is in seafaring style with nets and boats for decoration and a veranda overlooking the sea. There are also quays, boat hire, water-skiing and scuba-diving. Near the hotel is a tennis court, and the Pevero golf course is 500 metres away.

RECOMMENDED IN THE AREA

RESTAURANTS:
Golf Club di Pevero, *Pevero;* Pescatore, *Porto Cervo*

$\mathcal{P}$aola

This hotel is situated on the small island of San Pietro, off south-western Sardinia. It consists of two buildings: a main building that contains 12 comfortable bedrooms with bathrooms, and an outbuilding in the private Mediterranean garden that houses another 12 bedrooms with lovely panoramic views over the sea and the surrounding countryside.

The pink-coloured buildings are small, low and pretty and blend with their natural surroundings. The furnishings are simple but with character; there is a lovely sitting room with rustic furniture arranged around a big fireplace, and with the friendly air of a family house.

The restaurant serves local dishes on a terrace with a panoramic view of the sea and of Carloforte port.

On a little island south-west of Sardinia

☎ 0781 850098
🖷 0781 850104
località Tacca Rossa
09014 CARLOFORTE (Cagliari)
Ref map 16, F1

Superstrada (dual carriageway) 130 as far as Iglesias, then S.S. 126 as far as Portoscuso, here the ferry for Carloforte, then S.P. towards La Pubta tothe turning for Tacca Rossa
24 rooms; **£/££**
Credit cards: AE VISA SI

RECOMMENDED IN THE AREA

RESTAURANTS:
Al Tonno di Corsa *and* Da Nicolò

LOCAL SPECIALITIES:
Couscous; dishes with tuna fish, fish roe and musciame *(salted, dried tuna); carpets, tapestries and hand-woven linen; craft baskets and terracotta dishes and pots*

$\mathcal{H}$ieracon

In an elegant Art Nouveau mansion

☎ 0781 854028 📠 0781 854893

corso Cavour 62

09014 CARLOFORTE (Cagliari)

Ref map 16, F1

Superstrada (dual carriageway) 131 as far as Iglesias, then S.S. 126 as far as Portoscuso, from here the ferry for Carloforte

16 rooms, 6 apartments; **£/££**

Credit cards: AE VISA SI ⓪, bancomat

*I*n the shade of palm trees in a large garden surrounding the little mansion, guests can enjoy the cool and relaxation at the end of long days by the sea whilst enjoying the family atmosphere of the hotel.

Apart from the large, light rooms furnished with antique furniture that retain the gracefully delicate style of Art Nouveau, there are attractive one- and two-roomed apartments.

The restaurant has an interesting menu with delicious combinations of local food, Arabic and Ligurian.

RECOMMENDED IN THE AREA

RESTAURANT:
Da Vittorio

LOCAL SPECIALITIES:
Tuna products – both fresh and dried: salted roe and musciami (salted, dried tuna)

$\mathcal{R}$iviera

Facing a beautiful emerald sea

☎ 079 470143

📠 079 471312

📧 hfofò@tin.it

via Lungomare Anglona 1

07031 CASTELSARDO (Sassari)

Ref map 16, B2

Superstrada (dual carriageway) 131 as far as Sassari, then S.S. 200 as far as Castelsardo

34 rooms; **£/££/£££**

Credit cards: AE VISA SI ⓪, bancomat

*O*n a point stretching out into the sea a hill rises up from the water. On top of this is a medieval look-out castle that gives its name to the old village clinging to the slope. Over time more modern houses have sprung up on the coast facing a transparent sea of the most beautiful colours, with rocks and beaches alternating along the shoreline.

The hotel is in this new part and is a modern building opposite the sea, only ten metres from the beach below. It has large, well-furnished bedrooms with modern furniture. Many have lovely terraces and all are bright and attractive. There are also other well-equipped terraces for communal use, and a restaurant that takes as much care over its mainly seafood and traditional dishes as it shows in its decoration. The welcoming sitting rooms are also designed for meetings and conferences. There is a beach reserved for the hotel's guests.

RECOMMENDED IN THE AREA

RESTAURANT:
Guardiola

VISIT:
Cathedral and the church of Santa Maria delle Grazie, Castelsardo

Oasi

Delightul contrast between green and blue

☎ 0784 93111
🖷 0784 93444
via Garcia Lorca 13
località Cala Gonone
08020 DORGALI (Nuoro)
Ref map 16, C4
Superstrada 131d.c.n., Nuoro exit, then
towards Dorgali, after Dorgali turning for
Cala Gonone
30 rooms, 5 apartments; **£/££**
Credit cards: VISA

The gulf that the hotel overlooks is one of the most beautiful in Sardinia. The hotel stands on a sheer cliff above the sea, in the midst of Mediterranean vegetation and surrounded by its own garden and a pinewood: so much green, in fact, that it creates a restful contrast with the pale blue of the sea.

The hotel has bedrooms in separate buildings, and all of them have balconies and simple modern furnishings. There are also five one-roomed apartments that can each accommodate two people. The sitting rooms are bright. There is attentive management and the Carlessi family takes good care of guests' wellbeing. In the vicinity it is possible to hire bicycles, there is a tennis court and

guests can go rock climbing. The surrounding area is full not only of natural beauty but also of interesting archaeological sites.

RECOMMENDED IN THE AREA

RESTAURANT:
Al Porto

LOCAL SPECIALITIES:
For sale from local co-operative, excellent olive oil

VISIT:
Bue Marino limestone grotto. Arvu nuraghe *(prehistoric Sardinian monument of almost conical shape)*

*I*l Querceto

*Moments to enjoy the sea and relax
in an unspoilt setting*

☎ 0784 96509
📠 0784 95254
via Lamarmora 4
08022 DORGALI (Nuoro)
Ref map 16, C4
Superstrada (dual carriageway) 131d.c.n.
Nuoro exit, then towards Dorgali
22 rooms; £/££
Credit cards: AE VISA SI ⓄⒹ

*T*he name of the hotel was not chosen by chance: this is a building set within a natural park of oak trees where peaceful green alternates with the colours of the sea. Cala Gonome Bay is only eight kilometres away. The hotel has large bright bedrooms that open on to a horizon of natural beauty and are equipped with satellite television; their simple furnishings are inspired by the rustic surroundings. The communal rooms have a welcoming family-style appearance; some contain sculptures by Pisano. The restaurant is run by the hotel owners and offers dishes with authentic regional flavours. Outside there is a tennis court, children's playground, a well-equipped patio and a large, well-tended garden with scented flowers and Mediterranean vegetation. The hotel organises guided tours in the Gennargentu and Blu parks, trips in motor vessels and nature treks on foot.

Recommended in the area

Restaurant:
Canne al vento, *viale Repubblica 66, Nuoro*

Visit:
Parish church of Santa Caterina and the Archaeological Museum, Dorgali

$\mathcal{M}$onteviore

RECOMMENDED IN THE AREA

RESTAURANTS:
Al Porto, *Cala Gonone;* Giovanni, *via IV Novembre 9, Nuoro*

LOCAL SPECIALITIES:
Cannonau *wine*

VISIT:
Cantina Sociale, *co-operative wine factory with museum*

In a magnificent green basin

☎ 0784 96293 📠 0784 96293
località Monteviore
08022 DORGALI (Nuoro)
Ref map 16, C4
Superstrada (dual carriageway) 131d.c.n.
Nuoro exit, then towards Dorgali
20 rooms; **£/££**
Credit cards: VISA SI ◍

*O*riginally an old farmhouse, this hotel has been well restructured and shines white with little pale blue windows, curved tiles on the roof and lots of flowers. It is situated in a magnificent green cultivated basin that is dominated by the imposing Supramonte massif in the Gennargentu Park. But staying here does not mean having to renounce the sea because the beaches of Cala Gonone and Cala Sisina are only a few kilometres away. The building has a panoramic terrace and shady patio. These are delightful places for breakfast and for spending time at sunset and during the evening.

The hotel has simple, bright bedrooms, some split-level, and there are also two bungalows suitable for families or groups of friends. The hotel management organises guided tours on foot or with cross-country vehicles in the Gennargentu Park. There is a riding school in the neighbourhood.

$\mathcal{S}$'Adde

A comfortable hotel amid harsh natural surroundings

☎ 0784 94412
📠 0784 94315
via Concordia 38
08022 DORGALI (Nuoro)
Ref map 16, C4
Superstrada (dual carriageway) 131d.c.n.
Nuoro exit, then towards Dorgali
28 rooms; **£/££**
Credit cards: AE VISA SI, bancomat

*T*his hotel, in a panoramic position, is in a modern building that has no particular architectural character but is special for its natural surroundings and for the love which the owners have for this area. Here the atmosphere is family-style and simple, close to the heart of those who enjoy exploring the natural world.

Guests are welcomed into a little reception hall with its wood decoration, and into sitting rooms and a dining room with a delightfully homely atmosphere. The bedrooms are airy and well kept, with large balconies and rustic furniture. Annexed to the hotel is a restaurant/*pizzeria*. Tours on foot or in cross-country vehicles are organised by the hotel to enable guests to explore the villages of *nuraghi* (ancient conical houses), the Dorgali area and the Gennargentu Park. These are places of stark natural beauty and charming white beaches washed by a beautiful sea.

RECOMMENDED IN THE AREA

RESTAURANTS:
Cikappa, *Oliena;* Ai monti del Gennargentu, *Orgosolo*

$\mathcal{M}$ argherita

*T*his pretty little hotel is well presented and welcoming and its family management is very attentive. It is in a modern building that was completely refurbished in 1992 and stands in the centre of the village but close to the sea – about 100 metres from the beach. The lovely reception hall also serves as a sitting room with a large veranda overlooking the greenery and a swimming pool with hydromassage and solarium. The bedrooms are comfortable and classically furnished, and either face the sea or the swimming pool. The bathrooms are practical and well equipped, with granite basin surrounds and large mirrors. The buffet breakfast is carefully prepared.

Facing the sea, close to the Costa Smeralda *(Emerald Coast)*

☎ 0789 46906 📠 0789 46851

📧 hotelmargherita@tiscalinet.it

via Libertà 91

07020 GOLFO ARANCI (Sassari)

Ref map 16, B4

Superstrada 131 d.c.n. as far as Olbia, continue towards Golfo Aranci

26 rooms, 2 suites; **££/£££**

Credit cards: AE VISA SI ⓪

RECOMMENDED IN THE AREA

RESTAURANTS:
Palumbalza, *golfo di Marinella;* Gallura, *Olbia*

I l Sillabario

A comfortable hotel in the old mining area

☎ 0781 33833

📠 0781 33790

S.S. 130 al km 47,400

09016 IGLESIAS (Cagliari)

Ref map 16, E2

S.S. 130 as far as Iglesias

12 rooms, 1 suite; **£/££**

Credit cards: AE VISA SI

*I*glesias, meaning church, takes its name from the many churches here. The name of this town also conjures up a place full of the mines that made it an important mineral centre, and there are interesting industrial archaeological remains here. The hotel is one of the most comfortable in the area and is a modern building ten minutes from the centre of town. The bedrooms have simple white modern furniture. The sitting rooms are very big and are at the heart of the hotel which is surrounded by a large garden. There are also an open-air swimming pool and a tennis court.

RECOMMENDED IN THE AREA

RESTAURANT:
La Ghinghetta, *Portoscuso*

LOCAL SPECIALITIES:
Sant' Antioco wines

VISIT:
Cathedral, church of San Francesco and sanctuary of Santa Maria delle Grazie, Iglesias

Nido d'Aquila

An agreeable, comfortable stay amidst green countryside and by the sea

☎ 0789 722130
🖶 0789 722159
✉ hotelnidodaquila@tiscalinet.it
località Nido d'Aquila
07024 LA MADDALENA (Sassari)
Ref map 16, A3

Superstrada 131 d.c.n. as far as Olbia, then S.S. 125 as far as Palau, ferry for La Maddalena
40 rooms, 6 apartments; **££/£££**
Credit cards: AE VISA SI ⓪, bancomat

*T*his is an eagle's nest (*nido d'aquila*) by the sea, not far from the port of Maddalena, in a lovely peaceful area of the island. The hotel is situated at the foot of a rocky coast that, rising steeply and dramatically, could be a lookout point or an eagle's nest. The building is small and white and surrounded by a green garden that contrasts restfully with the bright colours of the surrounding landscape.

The hotel stands just 20 metres from the water, a beautiful sea surrounding one of the most charming points on the island of Maddalena. It has a cool white, simply-furnished interior. The air-conditioned communal rooms are light and clean as are the bedrooms. These are provided with telephones, satellite televisions and mini-bars.

A veranda overlooks the garden and its protective shade offers shelter from the burning heat. In addition there are six one-roomed apartments fitted with kitchen areas and with private space outside. There is also a floating quay for small and medium-sized boats, as well as a baby sitting service.

RECOMMENDED IN THE AREA

RESTAURANT:
La Grotta

VISIT:
Central piazza Garibaldi and the nearby parish church, Maddalena

Rocce Sarde

*A delightful stay in the countryside
with the most attentive hotel service*

☎ 0789 65265 🅵 0789 65268
🅴 roccesarde@tiscalinet.it
località Milmessiu
frazione San Pantaleo
07026 OLBIA (Sassari)
Ref map 16, B3
Superstrada 131 d.c.n. as far as Olbia, then S.S.
125 as far as Palau, turning for San Pantaleo
80 rooms, 10 suites; **£/££**
Credit cards: ⒶⒺ 𝖵𝖨𝖲𝖠 𝖲𝖨 ⓄⒹ, bancomat

A midst granite rocks on a hillside , this hotel is in a white building surrounded by juniper trees and Mediterranean vegetation. It has a garden full of flowers and faces a panorama of the Gulf of Cugnana.

The bedrooms are cool and welcoming and furnished in original Sardinian style. Some have terraces; others face the lawn with a lovely veranda. The suites also have the convenience of large sitting rooms and independent entrances.

A minibus service transports guests to the Portisco beach; each morning a 15-metre motorboat takes hotel guests to discover the most beautiful beaches on the *Costa Smeralda* (Emerald Coast).

There is a snack-bar service by the enchanting swimming pool hidden amongst the rocks, as well as afternoon tea and the aperitifs before dinner.

RECOMMENDED IN THE AREA

RESTAURANTS:
Zattera, *Arzachena;* Gallura *and* Il Portico, *Olbia*
VISIT:
Church of San Simplicio, Olbi

There is also children's entertainment.

The restaurant offers Sardinian specialities and provides service outside; inside service is in an old restructured sheep pen. In addition there are two tennis courts, croquet, *bocce* (bowls), a small fitness room, and mountain bikes for hire.

Cikappa

The strong and definite flavours of interesting peasants' dishes

☎ 0784 288024/0784 288733
corso M.L. King 2/4
08025 OLIENA (Nuoro)
Ref map 16, C4
Superstrada (dual carriageway) 131 d.c.n., Nuoro exit, continue towards Orosei
7 rooms; **££/£££**
Credit cards: AE VISA SI ⓪, bancomat

Cikappa (CK) is the name of the hotel; the 'C' stands for Cenceddu and the 'K' for Killeddu, or the nicknames of the two proprietors, valiant upholders of tradition.

The premises are situated in the historic centre of Oliena, at the foot of Supramonte, an area of great natural beauty and a destination for those who love trekking. The hotel is an elegant small pink building with several arches adding interest to the façade.

The bedrooms are attractive and comfortable. Great care is taken by the restaurant in the preparation of homely food, with many varied dishes inspired by the season and by the most typical Sardinian cooking. During the autumn there is always plenty of game.

The *pizzeria* is famous for its pizzas prepared and

RECOMMENDED IN THE AREA

RESTAURANT:
Su Gologone, *Su Gologone*

VISIT:
Su Gologone on the riverbed of the Fatale brook; church of Nostra Signore della Solitudine overlooking the Isporosile and Marreri valleys; church of Madonna di Valverde

cooked in a wood oven by Cenceddu. Killeddu, meanwhile, is in charge of the bar. For their guests Cenceddu and Killeddu organise weekends with trips in the charming Lanittu valley or other parts of Supramonte. On their return guests are offered tasting sessions of local specialities.

Cala Ginepro

A thick pinewood and a white sandy beach

☎ 0784 91047 📠 0784 91222
località Cala Ginepro
08028 OROSEI (Nuoro)
Ref map 16, C4
Superstrada (dual carriageway) 131 d.c.n.,
Nuoro exit, continue towards Orosei
136 rooms, 10 suites; **££/£££**
Credit cards: AE VISA SI ⓪, bancomat

*T*he hotel stands 200 metres above sea level, within a natural bay on the edge of a thick pinewood separating it from a beach of the finest white sand that is indented with inlets and cliffs. It is a recently built complex of two buildings surrounded by gardens. It has different grades of bedrooms as well as some two-roomed apartments that can accommodate between two and four people. All have balconies with a view of the garden or the swimming pool and are attractive and comfortable.

The bathrooms are good and well presented with big mirrors. There are different restaurants offering various choices: à la carte or local specialities, or else pizza. Then again there is an ice-cream parlour, snack bar, disco and piano bar. There is a swimming pool with hydromassage pool. A membership card may be

RECOMMENDED IN THE AREA

RESTAURANT:
Al Porto, *Cala Gonone*

VISIT:
Orosei with the four churches of San Giacomo Maggiore, Santa Croce, del Rosario and delle Anime

bought on arrival (and is essential between 1 June and 30 September) which gives access to the beach. Here there are sun loungers and sunshades, windsurfing, paddleboats, sailing, beach volleyball, volleyball, archery, basketball and group courses in swimming, gymnastics and aerobics as well as a mini-club for children. During the summer a minimum stay of a week is requested.

$\mathcal{P}$alau

A very professional establishment

☎ 0789 708468
🖷 0789 709817
✉ info@palauhotel.it
via Baragge, località Monte Zebio
07020 PALAU (Sassari)
Ref map 16, A3
Superstrada (dual carriageway) 131 d.c.n. as far as Olbia, then S.S. 125 as far as Palau
83 rooms, 12 suites; **£/£££**
Credit cards: ᴀᴇ 🆅🅸🆂🅰 🆂🅸 ⓄⒹ, bancomat

O ther islands of the archipelago stretching as far as Corsica surround the islands of Caprera and Maddalena. This is the view from the small, modern hotel that stands in the upper part of Palau. The long low building has at its centre a pool and a courtyard, which provide a meeting place. On the ground floor the rooms open directly onto this area which is surrounded by greenery and flowers. The bedrooms are on the upper floor. These are carefully furnished with sunny-coloured upholstery and windows that look out on to the great expanse of pale blue sea. The bar, sitting rooms, reception hall and dining room are painted and decorated with floral designs. They are illuminated by suffused lighting and have secluded corners for conversation.

RECOMMENDED IN THE AREA

RESTAURANTS:
Gritta, Franco and Zio Nicola

$\mathcal{L}$a Ghinghetta

Special cooking with a seafood menu for real connoisseurs

☎ 0781 508143
🖷 0781 508144
via Cavour 26
località Sa Caletta
09010 PORTOSCUSO (Cagliari)
Ref map 16, E-F1
Superstrada 130 as far as Iglesias, then S.S. 126 as far as Portoscuso
8 rooms; **££**
Credit cards: ᴀᴇ 🆅🅸🆂🅰 🆂🅸 ⓄⒹ, bancomat

RECOMMENDED IN THE AREA

RESTAURANTS:
Vittorio, *Carloforte on the island of San Pietro*

A former sailor's house in an old village facing the sea opposite the island of San Pietro, and a short distance from the tuna fishery and the Spanish tower. This hotel is surrounded by the splendid colours of the sea and by beaches in this corner of Sardinia and the Sulcis archipelago. The comfortable bedrooms are all delightfully furnished in seafaring style and equipped with every comfort, with good bathrooms. A few paces through the green vegetation take you to a charming little bay.

Adding to the natural beauty and charm of the hotel is the refinement of the restaurant where the Vacca family demonstrate an astonishing passion for cooking and care for their guests. The cuisine can truly be considered a beacon of modern gastronomy. The use of tuna fish is famous and perfected in unusual dishes. *Ghinghetta* in local dialect means beacon – and La Ghinghetta really is a comforting light for the quality of its accommodation and delicious food.

$\mathcal{N}$ora Club

*I*t is called a club, but it seems like a little village. The small white houses back onto one another, their roofs covered with curved and flat tiles. Many little terraces create unexpected spaces.

The architecture is typical of villages in the southern Mediterranean. The buildings are grouped around a big garden where short terracotta paths create a contrast with the English-style lawn. In the centre a large noble olive tree lends character and gives a traditional appearance to the grounds.

The interior is spacious, light and varied with arches, brightened with ceramic panels hand-painted in floral designs, and furnished with lovely hand-made Sardinian furniture in carved wood.

There is a beautiful swimming pool in the garden and this is surrounded by shrubs and flowerbeds and shaded by palms. There is bar service here. The hotel is 800 metres from the sea and a short distance from Pula. There are bicycles for hotel guests to use along the paths in the neighbourhood.

Refined surroundings in an area full of ancient history

☎ 070 924422
📠 070 9209129
viale Nora
09010 PULA (Cagliari)
Ref map 16, F2-3
Superstrada 131 as far as Cagliari, S.S. 195 as far as Pula, then signs for Nora
25 rooms; **££/£££**
Credit cards not accepted

RECOMMENDED IN THE AREA

RESTAURANTS:
Grotta; Su Gunventeddu, *Nora*

VISIT:
Excavations of the ancient city of Nora

$\mathcal{M}$oderno

☎ 0781 83105
✆ 0781 840252
✉ albergomoderno@yahoo.it
via Nazionale 82
09017 SANT'ANTIOCO (Cagliari)
Ref map 16, F1
Superstrada 130 as far as Iglesias, then S.S.
126 as far as Sant' Antioco
10 rooms; **£/££**
Credit cards: AE VISA SI ⓓ

RECOMMENDED IN THE AREA

RESTAURANT:
La Laguna

LOCAL SPECIALITIES:
Tuna fish products, such as bottarga *(fish roe) and*
musciame *(salted, dried tuna)*

VISIT:
Parish church of Sant'Antioco

*T*his is a small hotel with only ten bedrooms but it has existed since 1955 when Mario and Giovanna Pinna decided to welcome tourists to the island. Nowadays their children Serena and Achille run the hotel, and with the second generation the initiative has been transformed into experience that soon will become tradition.

The hotel has been recently renewed and its bright bedrooms are furnished with great simplicity in pale colours and with elegant little details.

Its restaurant is open only in the summer season from June to September when it serves delicious seafood in a comfortable terrace/garden outside. The family management is willing and attentive.

$\mathcal{L}$e Zagare

A residence set deep in a luxuriant citrus plantation

☎ 070 791581 ✆ 070 791582
località Campus
09049 VILLASIMIUS (Cagliari)
Ref map 16, F3
Superstrada 131 as far as Cagliari, then coast road as far as Villasimius
42 rooms, 2 suites, 42 apartments;
££/£££
Credit cards: AE VISA SI ⓓ

RECOMMENDED IN THE AREA

RESTAURANTS:
Moro *and* Il Giardino

*T*he colours of the luxuriant citrus plantation surrounding this pleasing modern building are reflected in the architecture of the hotel: vivid yellow and orange brighten the plasterwork, while inside the large rooms are adorned with charming wooden furniture, oil paintings of sunny landscapes, little fireplaces in stone and terracotta amphoras.

The atmosphere is delightfully relaxing in the bright, attractive communal rooms with their strongly Mediterranean appearance. The light, spacious bedrooms are carefully furnished with elegant simplicity and are all located around the central building. In addition, there are different sized apartments, all with kitchen areas, within the establishment itself. Guests may pass their time between the very beautiful seaside at Villasimius, the hotel's little courtyard, the bar and swimming pool. Breakfast and other meals provided by the hotel are delicious.

*I*ndex
of towns